The Dutch Republic and American Independence

The Dutch Republic and American Independence

by Jan Willem Schulte Nordholt

Translated by Herbert H. Rowen

The University of North Carolina Press
Chapel Hill & London

The publication of this work was made possible in part through a grant from the National Endowment for the Humanities, a federal agency whose mission is to award grants to support education, scholarship, media programming, libraries, and museums, in order to bring the results of cultural activities to a broad, general public.

Translation of Voorbeeld in de Verte:
De invloed van de Amerikaanse
revolutie in Nederland

© 1979 Uitgeverij In den Toren (Baarn, Netherlands)

© 1982 The University of North Carolina Press

Manufactured in the United States of America

Library of Congress Cataloging in Publication Data

Schulte Nordholt, J. W., 1920–
The Dutch Republic and American independence.

Translation of: Voorbeeld in de verte.
Bibliography: p.
Includes index.
1. United States—History—Revolution, 1775–
1783—Dutch participation. 2. United States—
Foreign relations—Revolution, 1775–1783. 3. United
States—History—Revolution, 1775–1783—Influence.
I. Title.
E269.D88S3813   973.3'46   82-2563
ISBN 0-8078-1530-6   AACR2

Contents

List of Illustrations

Preface

1976 was only the beginning, the first of many bicentennials to follow! The life of the historian is apt to be determined by nothing but commemorations. We now have had, since 1976, the bicentennials of Saratoga, the French Alliance, Yorktown, and some more which I perhaps have overlooked. And now, in 1982, the Dutch are entitled to their own special bicentennial. On 19 April 1782, John Adams was allowed to offer his credentials to the Dutch States General, and this implied the official recognition of the United States by the United Provinces, as the Netherlands were called at that time. On 8 October of the same year a treaty of amity and commerce was concluded between the two nations. And so we can look back on two hundred years of uninterrupted friendship between these two democracies. A good reason to celebrate, for sure.

But what exactly do we celebrate? What happened in 1782, and why? What was the impact of the American Revolution on Holland? What was it that drew these two nations together? That is what this book is about. It deals with the origins of our mutual sympathies. It is an elaboration in more than three hundred pages of a paper of about twenty pages which I wrote in 1975. In that year the Library of Congress dedicated one of its annual bicentennial symposiums on the impact of the American Revolution abroad, and I had the honor to represent the Dutch aspect of that problem (*The Impact of the American Revolution Abroad*, Library of Congress, Washington, 1976, pp. 41–63). Since then the subject has captivated me. The result is this book.

I have often wondered which is more difficult: to condense such an extensive subject to just twenty pages or to stretch it to fill a book? I am not certain. I can best illustrate my problem with an intriguing passage from Laurence Sterne's famous *Life and Opinions of Tristram Shandy*, a book which, by the way, was well known to all the persons who appear in this book, for hardly another novel (if we may call it that) was so popular. Sterne writes:

Could a historiographer drive on his history, as a muleteer drives
on his mule—straight forward;—for instance, from Rome all the
way to Loreto, without ever once turning his head aside either to the
right hand or to the left,—he might venture to foretell you to an
hour when he should get to his journey's end;—but the thing is,
morally speaking, impossible: For, if he is a man of the least spirit he
will have fifty deviations from a straight line to make with this or
that party as he goes along, which he can no ways avoid. He will
have views and prospects to himself perpetually soliciting his eye,
which he can no more help standing still to look at than he can fly;
he will moreover have various
    Accounts to reconcile:
    Anecdotes to pick up:
    Inscriptions to make out:
    Stories to weave in:
    Traditions to sift:
    Personages to call upon:
    Panegyrics to paste up at this door:
    Pasquinades at that:—All which both the man and his mule are
quite exempt from. To sum up all; there are archives at every stage
to be looked into, and rolls, records, documents, and endless
genealogies, which justice ever and anon calls him back to stay the
reading of:—In short there is no end of it.

It is in this spirit that I have written my book and that I hope my
readers will enjoy and criticize it. For there is no end of history. To put in
a short quotation of another classical author: "All things are full of labor,
man cannot utter it, the eye is not satisfied with seeing nor the ear filled
with hearing." And I can only hope that my readers will take some satisfaction from my labor, as a kind of contribution to the celebration of our
two common centuries.

The most important and attractive task of a writer is to express his
gratitude to so many scholars and institutions, so great a cloud of witnesses. I am deeply obliged to the following persons, many of them
good friends: Dr. Cornelius H. E. de Wit, the best connoisseur of late-
eighteenth-century Dutch history, for his help and advice; Sister Mary
Briant Foley of Mount Mary College, who was so kind to send me a
copy of her excellent dissertation on John Adams in the Netherlands;
Dr. Lyman H. Butterfield, former director of the Adams Papers at the
Massachusetts Historical Society, and his staff, for their willingness to

help me and their permission to quote so frequently from the letters of John Adams; Dr. Whitfield J. Bell, director of the Library of the American Philosophical Society, who supported my endeavors not only with several photographs of manuscripts but also with a whole set of the Calendar of the Benjamin Franklin Papers; Mrs. Claude-Anne Lopez of the Franklin Papers, who shares my enthusiasm for poor Mr. Dumas and forgives me for studying Adams instead of Franklin, I hope; Professor Henry F. Jackson of Utica, New York, biographer of Francis Adrian Van der Kemp, who with so much hospitality received me and showed me around in the world of the Holland Land Company; Freule A. L. Baroness Van Aerssen Beyeren van Voshol, who, ninety-six years old, showed such a lively interest in the activities of her ancestor Charles Guillaume Frédéric Dumas and who gave me the permission to publish here for the first time his portrait, the original of which is in her possession; Mr. A. N. Baron de Vos van Steenwijk, who kindly lent me the precious manuscript of the diary that his ancestor Carel de Vos van Steenwijk kept of his travels to the United States in 1783; Reverend J. J. Kalma of Leeuwarden, who furnished me with so much material on the relations between Friesland and America; Dr. Jan Wim Buisman, who, as my research assistant, did so much to help lay the foundations of this book; Dr. Jacob Osinga, student and friend, whose strong convictions on the French-American alliance often convinced me.

I also want to express my gratitude to the following institutions and their staffs; they all proved to me their friendly efficiency: the Oneida Historical Society, Utica, New York; the American Philosophical Society, Philadelphia, and the Historical Society of Pennsylvania in the same city; the Manuscript Division of the Library of Congress, Washington, D.C.; the William L. Clements Library, Ann Arbor; the New York Historical Society, New York; the Algemeen Rijksarchief, The Hague; the university libraries at Leiden and Amsterdam; the municipal archives at Amsterdam and Utrecht; and the Friese Bibliotheek (Frisian Library) and municipal archives, Leeuwarden.

A special word of thanks is certainly due to the Van den Berch van Heemstede Foundation, which through its generous support helped to make possible the American publication of this book. Its original financial backers in the Netherlands, the Nederlandse Organisatie voor Zuiver Wetenschappelijk Onderzoek (The Dutch Organization for Scholarly Research) and Royal Dutch-Shell, should also not be forgotten in this enumeration of benefactors.

Finally I am happy that I have the opportunity here to express my warmest gratitude (without his knowing that I planned to do it) to the man who, spontaneously and without any prospect of reward, took upon himself the great task of translating my book, my good friend Herbert H. Rowen, professor of European history at Rutgers University. What more could an author wish than to have his work rendered into a worldwide language by the man who is more able than anybody else to do the job? In the first place, as a good scholar (there is hardly anybody outside of Holland who knows more of Dutch history), he knows the technical problems involved. In the second place, as the reader will notice, he has a fine ear for the momentum and gradations of the language. Last of all, he did the work with the enthusiasm and sympathy of a volunteer. Is there anybody who still believes, as is so often said in Europe, that American friendships are only superficial and momentary? I suppose that it is on friendships like Herb's that the strength of the Dutch-American relation is really built.

The Dutch Republic and American Independence

I modestly blush for my nation when I consider the sangfroid, the non-chalance, with which they have received the magnifical testimonies of the esteem, confidence and affection of the Dutch towards the United States, and the low estimation in which we have held the importance of their connections with us. Their separation from England, union with France and Spain and their treaty with us was the event which ultimately turned the scale of the American Revolutionary war and produced the peace of 1783. But the truth is that neither France nor England nor the friends of France or England in America would even acknowledge it to be of any weight and consequently it has fallen into total oblivion. But in some future day it may be thought of more importance.

John Adams to Francis Adrian Van der Kemp, 3 January 1823

Prologue

A N we imagine a more harmonious reality than that presented to us by Dutch painters of the eighteenth century
in their vivid paintings? It seems a world washed clean,
where everything is sparkling and bright; white clouds
sail by over the wide landscape that swarms with plump
cattle, or they are mirrored in the canals of the cities, where everything
breathes neatness and industry. In a word, it is a world that has long
basked in pleasant peace, from which all pain and passion have been
banned, a bourgeois world in the best sense of the term.

Art historian Anthony Staring has suggested that this Dutch harmony,
this calm and purity, was the result of great changes in the political life of
the Republic.[1] The country was no longer what it had been in the seventeenth century, a great power with the passions, bravado, and international involvement that came with being a great power. It was a country
that had made its fortune and was living on its investments (indeed,
making investments was its greatest concern); it lived with what was
within reach, not beyond the horizon, and with aims that could be fixed
and counted. It is probable, as another art historian has written, that the
mantle of the Baroque was a bit too heavy for Dutch shoulders, and that
this attitude of acceptance of reality brought with it not only loss but a
gain in a wise return to what was their own self. "In its satisfaction with
the world as it is, Dutch art showed a preference for order, neatness and
regularity; it lacked burning passion, the exaltation of a fiery faith, and
the extremes of doubt."[2]

The painters' intention, so it was said, was only to reproduce the visible reality. "There is no land," asserted the German painter Wilhelm Tischbein in 1772, "that you can learn to know better through paintings without being there than Holland. Painters there paint everything exactly as it looks."[3]

Of course this is only half true. Nowhere and at no time, not even in intimate and idyllic Holland, has the world been as harmonious as it seems to be in the friendly pictures of the brothers La Fargue, Isaac Ouwater, Jan ten Compe, and all their kind. What we do not see is the dirt, the smell, the noise, the ceaseless commotion, the poverty of no small part of the population.

Foreign travelers visiting the Netherlands voiced a chorus of delight in Dutch cleanliness; it had to be seen to be believed, and was almost painful in its attention to detail.[4] But they also saw the other side of the medal. Rather, they heard and smelled it. Reporting on his trip to Holland, a professor at the University of Jena gave praise to the canals for their usefulness, "except, alas, that there rises out of these canals a mixture of noxious vapors that make the air thick and unhealthy."[5]

Holland, a land of waters, surprised and astonished most visitors. What they admired is exactly what we still see in the paintings: the neatness and the clarity of a land where nothing was left to chance and everything was dependent upon the diligent inventiveness of the inhabitants themselves, a land that was their own creation. But what annoyed them is just what we cannot see in a museum: the smells and sounds, the cold, and the unhealthy vapors. John Adams, one of the two principal characters in this book, is himself an excellent example of the foreigner's ambivalence toward Holland. When, in 1780, he had been in Amsterdam for just three weeks, he wrote enthusiastically to his wife: "I am very pleased with Holland. It is a singular Country. It is like no other. It is all the Effect of Industry and the Work of Art. The Frugality, Industry, Cleanliness, etc. here, deserve the Imitation of my Countrymen." But in the long run his rapture ran down. About a year later, when he fell seriously ill, he wondered if he would ever get better "among the pestilential Vapours from these stagnant Waters."[6]

One of the most delightful descriptions of the country in this period comes from another American, Elkanah Watson, who during a fine spring in 1784 traveled through Holland, usually by the distinctively Dutch means of passenger transportation, the canalboat. His comments breathe something of the same clarity that we see in the paintings. He is delighted with the "neatness which dazzles our eyes on all sides"; he finds the cities splendid with their broad streets and their wide canals planted with trees on both sides. "The verdure of the trees reflecting strongly upon large windows which are kept bright and free from dust, add infinitely to their lustre and magnificence." He admires the universal orderliness, the regularity that is unique even in civilized Europe. How much greater is the impression this country must make upon an American "who has been accustomed from his infancy to a country of nature, laid out upon a large and copious scale: This on the contrary is a country of art, as it were wrested from the sea." Holland is "a perfect garden," "an enchanted fairy land," but after awhile it becomes monotonous, for all the towns and all the houses are the same. And this American too suffers from the dampness and the bad-smelling waters: "The stench of the canal was intolerable."

There is the same ambivalence toward the people as toward the land. At first sight everything is attractive: in an orderly country live decent, hard-working, God-fearing people. But someone who has longer and closer business with the inhabitants, someone who needs something from them, finds the praise dying on his lips. Again there is no better witness than John Adams, so ready to think in extremes. How exuberant is his initial praise for the Dutch: "Their Industry and Economy ought to be the Examples to the World. They have less Ambition, I mean that of conquest and military glory, than their Neighbours, but I don't perceive that they have more Avarice. And they carry Learning and Arts I think to greater Extent." And how bitter is his judgment a few months later when he doesn't get the loans he sought. Then he ascribes to these same Dutchmen nothing but avarice, and he deprecates in them "a general Littleness arising from the incessant Contemplation of Stivers and Doits, which pervades the whole People."[7]

Stinginess was, next to cleanliness, the most common stereotype for the inhabitants of the Low Countries. They were true materialists. James Harris, the English ambassador at The Hague after 1784, put it nicely: "Dutch hearts lie to the leeward of their stomachs," and Benjamin Franklin was even more pithy: "Some writer, I forgot who, says that Holland is no longer a *nation*, but a great shop." The image endured. Half a century later, Balzac used it in his novel *La Cousine Bette*: "Our age is that of the triumph of trade, industry, of the bourgeois wisdom which created Holland."[8]

Alas, things were not going particularly well in trade and industry for Holland in the late eighteenth century. The wealth that had been earned by energetic ancestors was taken too much for granted. As the Dutch historian Herman T. Colenbrander writes: "The national passion remained to earn money, but there was no longer the necessity which in earlier days drove profit-seeking Dutchmen over the whole world. They did not have to go abroad any more to gain gold, it could be found at home, the heritage from the fathers, and they wanted only to increase it further by piling interest upon interest. Once the freight carriers of Europe, they had become its money-lenders." He adds the remark of Diderot: "The Republic's ambition is not to get bigger but richer."

Sir Joseph Yorke, the English ambassador until 1780, was also of the opinion that the Dutch were possessed by "Cupidity." "They are all literally Merchants or Money-getters at present."[9]

The picture of a serene, prosperous Holland, gazing in self-satisfaction upon its reflection in the canals of town and countryside, is in fact rather deceptive, as Dutchmen themselves know full well. Dutch boys at school learn to think less well of their country in the eighteenth century. That time is called in denigration "the Periwig Age," a period of decline after the glorious Golden Age of the seventeenth century. But the notion of decline is a difficult one, for it is a matter of comparisons. Is it really fair to measure the eighteenth century by the seventeenth? Is Colenbrander perhaps too one-sided in his relentless accusations against the Dutch burghers of the eighteenth century as "prosperous, self-satisfied, and drowsy" men whose civilization had become "phlegmatic or grotesque"? Pieter Geyl reacted vigorously to these charges, pointing to the new forces in the nation that were present in the very Patriot movement that Colenbrander maligned.[10] This is a theme to which we shall return many times.

There were indeed signs of fresh new life in the Republic. We need only think of the great interest in science and art and the foundation of numerous learned and literary societies, many of which are still in existence. It was, after all, the age of philosophers and scientists like Hemsterhuis and Van Marum, the age of a fascinating intellectual life that sought to wrest itself free from the arid tradition of orthodox Dutch Calvinism in church and society, that sought for new paths even within the Reformed Church, so happily displayed in the publication of the new verse translation of the Psalms in 1773. It is not right to present the Netherlands as an island of intellectual stagnancy over which blew no winds of change. Much was translated and much read, Locke and Hume, Montesquieu and Moses Mendelssohn. Pope's magnificent *Essay on Man* found several different translators, and Voltaire's works were in great demand. Yet, despite all this activity and intellectual discussion—as in the emotional debate over Marmontel's *Bélisaire*, with the salvation of the souls of Socrates and other Enlightened "heroes" at stake—something was missing. There was, it seems, an absence of an elusive but essential driving force, the shared élan that had marked the Dutch in the seventeenth century and made them great.

In one respect this decline was relative: the neighboring countries were able to catch up after having fallen behind in the seventeenth century as a result of civil wars and divisions. But it was also absolute. While considerable prosperity remained, the signs of deterioration were visible everywhere, in trade and industry and in the increasing unemployment and mendicancy, as Geyl himself has set forth clearly. Other historians have amplified his assertions. They have pointed out that the economic decline was inevitable because Holland was losing its traditional function as the staple market of Europe. No longer was the world's economy dependent on a central market; better methods of communication and stronger competition were among the chief causes of the deterioration of the Dutch economy.[11]

Whatever the actual situation of the economy, there was in any event an awareness at the time, difficult to measure now but certainly demonstrable, that Holland was not quite as flourishing as it looked, that it actually was in great danger of losing its position of power and even its very existence. The Dutch historian Ernst H. Kossmann has summarized the situation with great succinctness.

> It was realized by broad sections of the population that the system no longer worked adequately. In foreign policy, particularly, the impotence of the Republic was repeatedly demonstrated. The Republic, once an arbiter in matters of war and peace, was seen to be degenerating into a passive object of other countries' craving for power. This awareness of decline, it is true, was accompanied by the smugness with which the Dutch treasured their ancestors' achievements, exalting what they possessed and what others were still passionately seeking: liberty, tolerance, civil order. . . . Yet in this society, so given to futile self-complacency and ostentatious prosperity, an uncomfortable feeling accumulated that the country had lost its place, belied its past, and was gambling away its future.

Many foreign writers bear witness to this sense of decline. The German philosopher Herder, on his famous journey from Riga to Nantes in 1769, commented philosophically on this situation as he passed the Dutch dunes.

Holland is on the point of sinking. . . . This decline is scarcely to be avoided any longer: the shape of Europe is now such as to require it; but Holland is sinking of its own weight. Its ships make unprofitable voyages, the prices of [East India] stock are falling, the Republic counts for less in the balance of Europe. . . . There will come a time, probably in my own lifetime, when Holland will be nothing more than a dead warehouse, which is emptying out its goods and is unable to replace them, and thus disappears like a *Galanteriebude* which cannot be replaced.

Harris was more moralistic about the causes; he maintained that Holland lacked a unifying "public spirit," in a passage so impressive that I want to quote it in full here.

Thus *virtue*, the main spring of a commonwealth, no longer subsisted among the Dutch; the public was poor; the great riches of individuals destroyed the equality necessary to a free state; their avarice, still greater than their wealth, extinguished public spirit, its necessary principle; their trade was decreasing, their manufacturing diminished; their navigation on the decline; their public finances in ruin, and their fisheries expiring; and their navy, their barrier, their military strength, their foreign settlements, their great commercial companies, their government, their administration, their consequences, their whole republic, were in the last state of degradation, debase and decay.

From the other side the American John Adams was no less bitter in his judgment: "This country is indeed in an melancholy situation; sunk in ease, devoted to the pursuit of gain, . . . incumbered with a complicated and perplexed constitution, divided among themselves in interest and sentiment, they seem afraid of everything."[12] Such opinions had become virtually a commonplace. It is hard to find a foreign observer who does not reveal his shocked surprise when he writes about the decline of the Dutch. The long slow slide of the Republic from the ranks of the great powers must have made a deep impression.

In an age when pietist and philosophical demands for simplicity came together, it was easy to identify the causes: the Dutch nation had grown too rich, too sumptuous in its tastes, too fond of its comfort; it had fallen into the perilous grip of Luxuria. The very ability of the state to survive was thought to be in question. A good example of such ideas again comes to us from our American tourist of 1784. Watson's praise of bright Holland turns eventually into a tirade against the disintegration of Dutch society,

> a great degeneracy from their virtuous ancestors, who procured them their independence, and left the government established upon the broad basis of justice, industry, enterprise, and frugality. Those who pretend to pry deep into futurity, predict their total annihilation as an independent power. It is at least evident that their vast and rich possessions in the Eastindies will eventually produce the same effect upon Holland, as the gold mines of Southamerica have upon Spain—I mean national debility, corruption, loss of manufactures, and consequently poverty.

We can find plenty of examples of the same ideas in the Republic itself. But probably no one put them more pithily than the desperate man at the helm of the state, the stadholder William V, Prince of Orange. He compared his country with "a paralytic who claimed he could walk, lame as he was."[13] His little opponent in hiding, Charles Dumas, who, with Adams, is the principal character of this book, was in agreement with the Prince on this point at least. Holland was "a sick state," or, changing the metaphor, "a poor vessel without rudder and sails, to float as it pleases the winds and waters to toss it, and the Current of foreign Events to drag it."[14]

It was not relative but absolute decline—the deterioration of the economy, the painful difference between poor and rich, the savage party conflicts, the lack of a sense of national unity—that in the end brought about the downfall of the Dutch Republic. It was not the Prussian invaders in 1787 or the French invaders in 1795 but its own failings that doomed it to disappear. Decades later the Dutch statesman-historian Jan Rudolph Thorbecke wrote that the French "expelled the ghost of a Republic that had already died of its own impotence."

The United Netherlands became a warning example of decline and fall down to our own times. There is a nice illustration of this in an anecdote about President Truman, who was an amateur historian. Journalist Drew Pearson went to visit him in 1959, after his retirement. Truman seemed happy to see him, played for him on both his pianos, and showed him his library. Pearson writes with deference: "He really knows his history. As I was about to leave, Truman made a little speech about the grave crisis faced by the United States and the question of whether we would go the way of the Roman Empire, the Greek cities, and the Dutch Republic. I didn't like to express my ignorance but I asked him what happened to the Dutch Republic. He replied: 'They got too complacent, too fat, and too prosperous. We are in grave danger of being the same way.' "[15]

· II ·

The "bourgeois wisdom" of which Balzac spoke may be small, even small minded, but was it not also the foundation of one of the universally praised virtues of the Netherlands, its spirit of freedom? If there was, besides neatness and frugality, any trait that distinguished the Dutch, it was their long-esteemed sense of independence, their republican temper. The Dutch themselves took pride in it; it was a kind of article of faith to them that true freedom, as they liked to call it, ruled in their country, with everyone his own master and a fundamental equality among all people. They were, they believed, really the happiest people in the world, and one of their poets, Simon Stijl, bragged in rhyme:

> Where else in all the world are farmers rich as here,
> Sailors so beloved, so utterly without fear,
> And all do their merchants respect and honor give,
> And servants like masters a happy life do live![16]

Such enthusiasm which can be partly attributed to the rhetoric of the age rings a bit hollow; yet there is also in it an element of conviction. Men were ready to believe such words, and they were not completely without truth. Compared to most neighboring countries, the Republic did not come off badly. In their travel accounts foreigners often expressed surprise at the general prosperity that they saw there as compared to elsewhere. Abigail Adams was struck by the "spirit of liberty" that she met all about. "They appear to be a well-fed, well-clothed, contented, happy people."[17]

The Dutchman's freedom was a widespread and fondly held myth. Voltaire repeated it in his *Vers à Monsieur Van Haren*.

> Our spirit conforms to the place where we are born,
> In Rome one is a slave, in London a citizen,
> The grandeur of the Dutch is to live without a master.

Mirabeau consoled the Dutch after the Prussian invasion that, after all, they were "the most ancient of free peoples." And a French envoy sent to the Batavian Republic in 1795 was warned in his instructions that the Dutch had always considered themselves to be the only free people on earth and therefore had a certain pride (*fierté*). They were phlegmatic but sensitive, and although their affections "do not soar and shine, they are therefore all the deeper and more lasting."[18]

What this widely acclaimed freedom amounted to in reality is a difficult question to answer. In the constitutional structure of the Dutch Republic, which was derived from the Union of Utrecht of 1579, "True Freedom" meant (to adapt Lincoln's words) government not by the people but for the people. Authority rested in the States—provincial and national assemblies that corresponded to the British Parliament or the American state legislatures, but that had policymaking as well as lawmaking powers. They represented the people, but the people had no say in them. The problem of representation was a central problem of the time and one that aroused and divided the public.

The popular revolt against an oligarchy of officeholders came principally out of the desire of the citizenry to have a voice in government. The strongest demands for participation came from the middle class, whose sense of insecurity had been awakened by the economic crisis. A loose party began to form, consisting of merchants, manufacturers, intellectuals, and dissenters from the established Dutch Reformed church. Deeply disturbed by the difficult situation, the decay of the economy, the petrified system of government, the deplorable general state of affairs, this group began to take the name of Patriots. They refused to be satisfied with representation without participation, which was essentially the same sop that the English vainly offered to the Americans—"virtual representation."

A second problem involving liberty was the federal relation between the provinces. The complicated system gave less and less satisfaction; the power to make decisions was more and more crippled by the antagonism between the seven provinces and, within each province, between the divided interested parties, the town councils, the nobles, and all the rest. It was more than despairing foreign observers could figure out. Yet the system found its defenders. Although reformers pressed for overhaul of the complex system, most of them honored the basic structure to some extent. The classic example in the period that interests us is the great work on the Union of Utrecht by Pieter Paulus, a brilliant young lawyer. He wanted changes, but only within the inherited framework. In the dedication to burgomaster Joachim Rendorp of Amsterdam he stated his purpose: "To explain and bring into the brilliant light of day the only Fundamental Law of my country, however much it has fallen into darkness in the cloudy perspective of past centuries: a Fundamental Law that

I cannot contemplate except with affection, and that I never read without feeling overpowering admiration for the shining wisdom and prudence of its Framers."

In his third volume, Paulus asserted that the Dutch Union served as the shining example for the American Articles of Confederation, which had just been published. He cited the complete text of the articles, even praised them, but came to the conclusion that the Union of Utrecht should be ranked far above the American imitation.[19] Did he himself really believe this? Or, budding reformer that he was, did he know that reality was not as pretty as he pretended it to be? However beautiful the system might seem, it was actually nothing but a reflection of the individualistic, personalistic society of a country that was hardly a nation, a people torn apart by short-sighted selfishness. Gijsbert Karel van Hogendorp, a young and promising nobleman (he was later, in 1813, to become the founder of the Kingdom of the Netherlands), saw it distinctly: "The Republic goes to its ruin because no one thinks of all but everyone cares only for himself and his own family." The fascinating diaries of the aging courtier Gijsbert Jan van Hardenbroek are filled with the same observation: "No member of government thinks of anything but his own interest." The Prince of Orange himself saw clearly what the consequences would be: "If there is no unity, the Republic will go to the dogs, to pot."[20]

"True Freedom obeys the laws" it was written in the books of the Republic. But in its old age, "True Freedom" became mostly confusion, selfishness, and impotence. The foreign envoy who wanted to make his way through this maze faced a difficult task. John Adams repeated his complaint in numerous letters: Where in heaven's name does sovereignty rest in this state? Who bears responsibility? How are things decided? "The constitution of government is so complicated and whimsical a thing, and the temper and character of the nation so peculiar, that this is considered everywhere as the most difficult Embassy in Europe."[21] Only after he had analyzed the system in all its multifariousness was he able to solve the problem of how to get inside it and influence it.

Next came partisanship. Various historians have pointed out that we should not speak of parties, clear cut and organized in the modern meaning of the word. Rather, there were cabals and factions here and there in opposition to each other. Yet it would be wrong to stay with such a bits-and-pieces picture. There really were affinities and conflicts of interest, and tensions were strengthened by concealed emotions. To stick with the term, we may say that there were, in the main, three distinct parties— Orangists, Aristocrats, and Democrats. Among them all kinds of com-

binations were possible. Sometimes it seemed that the democratically
minded burghers would act together with Orange against the regent
oligarchy, to which the name of Aristocrats was given ("regents," in
Dutch usage, were members of the ruling government bodies). Then
Orange took the side of those who ran the government (the unrest of
1748 had been marked by such a reversal of alliances). A hazy enthusiasm
for the new freedom of the Americans for a while bound together the
regents and the burghers against Orange under the name of Patriots, but
the radicalization of the Revolution drove the regents back into the arms
of the Prince. An American observer in Paris, Thomas Jefferson, described the situation with precision: The Aristocrats, he wrote, held the
balance and finally threw their weight on the conservative side. And John
Adams might well call out in despair, "All parties are enveloped in clouds
and darkness," but he slowly came to understand how things were going
and on which side he would find the most support for his American
ideals.[22] That put him into opposition with the Orangists. He more and
more began to understand the anomaly of the stadholdership in the
Republic, but he also grasped how important an institution it continued
to be.

As a matter of fact he was, from the beginning, fascinated by the institution itself, studied all kinds of sources about it, and wrote long letters
about its historical background. As a conservative, he could appreciate
the advantages of a strong executive, and his ideas in favor of *imperium
mixtum* (the Aristotelian equilibrium of monarchy, aristocracy, and democracy) enabled him to understand the prince as the *tribunus plebis*, the
tribune of the people, the "little man's God" (*der keerlen God*, as the
Dutch would say). But as it happened, this particular Prince, William V,
was not at all a defender of the common man but a timorous conservative, a partisan of the status quo, and, moreover, by tradition and family
connections a staunch friend of Great Britain. A weak and uncertain
man, he was not able to give the much-needed leadership in this time of
crisis. John Adams compared him with his illustrious predecessors: "If
however the present P[rince] of Or[ange] had the Genius and the Enter-
prise of the 1st or 3rd William or of Frederick Henry this nation would
now display as great Virtues and Resources as ever."[23]

He was certainly not alone in this judgment. William V has had a bad
name among his contemporaries and among later historians. It was not
his odd constitutional position that played him false, for there was still a
broad mass who loved him because his name was Orange. He might have
been, as was wittily said in his own day, no more than the moon that

takes its luster from the sun of the States General, but the common people found in him their own hero. His personal weakness, however, his eternal hesitancy, his inability to make a decision by himself, often drove to despair those who knew him better and had to work with him. While still a young man, he was already known as a waverer, both at home and abroad. The instructions given to the French ambassador, Baron de Breteuil, in 1768, warned, "The young prince has neither talents nor the virtues of his birth and his state." Years later, James Harris, the English ambassador who did everything he could to rescue the stadholdership, was bewildered by the "insensibility of the Stadtholder." "It is impossible to see without being hurt, even to dejection, the want of energy and vigour of mind in the Prince of Orange. . . . Such a man can never win any game; and unless a sleeping potion is administered to him, total ruin must follow."[24]

Yet there is something in the poor man that strikes and fascinates us. Pascal's words fit him: He might have been a miserable man, but he knew his misery. We probably learn to know him best in Van Hardenbroek's *Memoirs*: his childishness, especially in a clumsy love affair with Lady Van Lynden, his quickness to take fright at any bad news, his helpless floundering between impossible positions. But we also see how well he could define a problem and analyze a situation, how broad his interests were and how philosophical his judgment. The great gentlemen, princes, dukes, and the like, William brooded, are like other men; they can err. But to admit one's errors does a great lord honor. William well understood his own weakness. Van Hardenbroek heard that the Prince "had described himself to a confidant, saying that he felt how he needed to be ruled." He felt that he was a prisoner of his own condition, and sometimes he was driven to despair: "I really do not know where things are going, I wish I were dead and that my father had never become a Stadholder. . . . I feel I am not up to the job, I wish I were dead, I can't and I won't hold on a year longer. . . . My head reels."[25]

A pathetic little man, but a kind-hearted and loyal one, he was indignant when the domineering English ambassador proposed to him that in the event of war he should leave the country with his whole family and go to England. He was also a good scholar, knew his history, and wrote and spoke Latin well. Perhaps his greatest problem was that he married a wife who was far his superior in firmness and willpower; she was a princess of Prussia, Wilhelmina, a niece of Frederick the Great. William was jealous, as Harris observed, not "of her virtue, but of her sense and power." He would, he said, rather not go to Paradise if she would have to show him the way. But she remained loyal to him. When it was suggested that she should separate her fate from the Prince's, she was appalled. I know his faults, she told Harris, but "these feelings I conceal in my own breast. . . . I am bound to share his fate, let it be what it may."[26]

William V was no William I or III, and among his advisers there was no Oldenbarnevelt or De Witt, no statesman of caliber. Pieter van Bleiswijk, the grand pensionary (the leading official of the province of Holland who was a kind of prime minister in the Republic), was a clever and skillful man, but he was a weather vane, turning with the political winds. No one knew exactly what to think of him. He did not get on well with the other principal adviser of the Prince, Duke Louis of Brunswick-Wolfenbüttel, and the irresolute stadholder himself continued perpetually to vacillate between these two poles. The "fat duke" was no less difficult a figure to make out. He was attacked from many sides because of his decisive influence behind the scenes. It is again Van Hardenbroek who informs us about the strong resistance that the duke aroused even in the circles of government, long before the opposition made him a special target of hate and derision.[27]

Things were not going well in the United Provinces, and the internal decay and loss of power naturally had its effect on the position of the Republic in the international system. There was much keeping up of appearances, but the country could no longer play its old role in Europe. The old relationships had lost their force. It had been a tradition in Dutch foreign policy since the late seventeenth century to be allied with England. The treaties that were concluded then were officially still in force a hundred years later, but they blocked Dutch freedom of action. Actually, there were two treaties. The first, the peace treaty of Westminster of 1674, had the important clause that either party was permitted to carry to countries with which the other party was at war any goods whatever except for specific war supplies, like powder and shot. Naval stores were expressly excluded from contraband. That treaty was followed by the defensive alliance of 1678, which was always renewed. It obligated the Dutch to support England with an army of six thousand men and a fleet of twenty ships if it was attacked. The former treaty was much to the liking of Dutch merchants, and they remained stubbornly attached to it, but they had no difficulty forgetting about the latter treaty. The British, on the contrary, were less and less willing to tolerate Dutch contraband trade, and suffered it only so long as they had some confidence in Dutch fidelity to the alliance. Yorke spoke more than once in his letters of the "infernal" treaty of 1674, "one of the plagues of my life."

In the long run the Dutch became too unimportant to be treated with respect. That happened, as we shall see, in the years of the American Revolution.[28]

But the Dutch were bound to England in another way, by their enormous holdings in the English public debt. British bonds were highly valued in Holland, and it was only to be expected that the weight of these "golden chains" should be a political factor of great importance. Confidence in British securities played a large role in the long hesitation of Dutch bankers to lend money to the American rebels. It is true that genuine commitment to the English alliances, although sealed by intermarriage in the royal and princely houses, was declining steadily. In every war in which the Dutch remained neutral, first in 1756 and again in 1778, they could not help but become victims of English measures of inspection of ship cargoes, and the weaker the Dutch became, the more arbitrary was their treatment at English hands. Resentment against such friends grew steadily, especially among the merchants, and it made them all the readier to look for new sources of wealth.

As early as 1776, the year of the American Declaration of Independence, a young American diplomat, William Carmichael, could write home that the Dutch "have the greatest inclination to serve us and at the same time themselves, for no people see their interests clearer, but their fears that we shall be subdued, the confident assertions of the friends of England confirming these apprehensions, the prodigious sums they have in English funds . . . all conspire to prevent direct speculation." However much these merchants are insulted and humiliated, his letter continued, they do not care to break with England. The States General may keep the ports open to all belligerents, but it forbids the export of war materials. If England lost some battles, the American chances in Holland would be better, "for this country may be called the treasury of Europe."[29]

The Dutch no doubt had a sharp eye for their interests, but they did not have their former energy. The "treasury of Europe" was administered with fear and suspicion. Neutrality was hence the highest wisdom. But it was no simple matter to gather in the riches of the world without being hurt by the world. An old dilemma of Dutch foreign policy was involved. Theoretically, the best policy of a republic was to have peace with all nations and to keep strictly neutral in all conflicts. That was the attitude in foreign affairs which had been proclaimed in the seventeenth century by most of the political theorists of True Freedom. But as the Dutch Republic became a great power in the middle of that century, it had become more and more difficult to stay aloof from the surrounding world. Jan de Witt, as well as his enemy William III, had to adhere to a policy of involvement. Not neutrality but participation in the European balance of power was, as they understood it, the best guarantee for Dutch independence and commerce. But in the eighteenth century the Republic, steadily in decline, started again to seek its salvation in neutrality. During the Seven Years' War, as has been pointed out by historian J. W. Smit, "the Republic withdrew completely from European affairs. Owing to the decline of Dutch importance and to the existence of a European balance of power, a situation had finally been created in which the diplomatic dogma of True Liberty seemed to function."

It is interesting to note that this dilemma of Dutch policy has in some ways been an example, or at least a prelude, to American attitudes of later days. Not only is it quite probable that John Adams considered Dutch examples of treaties (especially the Treaty of Utrecht of 1713) when he drafted his model treaty in 1776 but in general it might be said that the American Republic was confronted with the same dilemma of neutrality and involvement, purity and power, as its Dutch counterpart had been two centuries earlier, a dilemma that stemmed from the same moral and commercial ideas and interests.[30]

However that may be, maintaining their neutrality and meeting their obligations at the same time had been a difficult task for the Dutch during the Seven Years' War, and it proved impossible when the American conflict spread to Europe. When the "shot heard around the world" rang out on 19 April 1775 in Concord, the sound at first seemed barely to reach calm Holland.

But the storm that rose did not leave the Dutch untouched. The peaceful Dutch mirror was stirred. Not only Dutch prosperity but, in the end, the constitution and indeed the very existence of the country were at stake. That is the theme of this book—that, and how the American Revolution elicited the radical changes that convulsed the Netherlands in the decade of the 1780s. Or as an appalled Dutch spectator of the time, the historian Adriaan Kluit, put it, how "the evil of American Freedom" was the origin and beginning of "all the subsequent disasters, sufferings and losses that befell the Republic."[31]

· CHAPTER 1 ·

A Nobleman Takes the Lead

If he (Van der Capellen)
comes in these circumstances,
there will be quite a fuss.
WILLIAM V

OR all its immense strength, the British Empire was not able to bring the American rebels swiftly to their senses. The thirteen colonies proved to be tougher and more tenacious than had been expected, and the number of troops needed to continue the war soon began to increase steadily. In the days of standing armies and regiments of mercenaries, this meant that the government in London had to look around for new sources of manpower, and their eyes turned automatically to the European mainland. In the first place there were the numerous German principalities, whose rulers were only too ready to peddle off their subjects to pay for their private pleasures. But the British also remembered that they had possible sources in Holland. Thus it was that in 1775 the Republic was first involved in the American conflict.

There was no point in the English government's calling upon the treaty of 1678, for the obligation in it to send a support force of six thousand men applied only to the case of war between England and another country, and this was only an uprising within the British Empire. But ever since the Dutch War of Independence (1568–1648) a brigade consisting of Scots officers and originally Scots soldiers had been stationed in the Republic. The brigade, which had won much renown, had been sent to Britain several times, in 1715 and 1745, to protect the Protestant succession against Jacobite risings; now, however, it sat in garrison duty in cities in the Austrian Netherlands held by the Dutch as a "barrier" against France, and it was no longer what it had been. Mercenary soldiers from every country served in its ranks. It had gradually fallen below its authorized numbers, and according to the well-informed Prussian envoy, Friedrich Wilhelm von Thulemeyer, it now had no more than eighteen hundred men.[1]

But every little bit helps. Early in October 1775 the Dutch government received a request from the English to make temporary use of the Scots Brigade again. The Prince of Orange was asked in an accompanying letter to support this request. It sounded most reasonable: George III, it said, had exhausted all peaceful means to persuade his American subjects to cease their rebellion, and now he had to use force to bring them back to obedience. He looked to the Netherlands because of the long friendship between the two countries. He did not wish to ask too much lest he embarrass the Dutch, but sought only to borrow the Scots. He gave several arguments in support of his request: The officers had taken an oath of loyalty to His Britannic Majesty. This was an opportunity to bring the brigade back up to full strength. And the Republic was under obligation to England, since it had refused during the Seven Years' War to provide the six thousand men required by the treaty of alliance.[2]

The stadholder naturally asked his advisers what he should do. The *griffier* (secretary) of the States General, the old, experienced, and very pro-English Hendrik Fagel, of course recommended acceptance: the friendship of the king of England was worth more to Holland than the whole Scots Brigade. The grand pensionary, Pieter van Bleiswijk, was less enthusiastic, but still in favor, and he even thought he could give the assurance that the States of Holland would give its approval. But the duke of Brunswick put his foot down in opposition. As a soldier, he found it obvious that to give up a whole brigade, no matter how understrength it was, would be too great a weakening of Dutch defensive forces. He understood how sensitive a matter this was. There had long been deep divisions in the Republic over the problems of defense. The maritime provinces (Holland, Zeeland, and Friesland) could not spare a penny for the "augmentation," as the proposal to strengthen the army was called. The land provinces (Utrecht, Gelderland, Overijssel, and Groningen) played tit-for-tat and would do nothing for the navy. The disastrous result was that Dutch strength grew steadily less on land and at sea. The duke explained his objections in a long report: eventual replacement of the Scots by some of George III's Hanoverian troops, an idea that the Prince of Orange was playing with, would only produce new problems. Dutch neutrality would be in peril, while they would not get sincere English friendship in its place. And would the maritime provinces really agree to make good the reduction in land force?

At this point the whole affair became hopelessly stuck. The Prince still attempted to achieve a solution by providing certain stipulations; the city of Amsterdam let it be known that it would agree only to an outright sale of the brigade, which drew an indignant protest from Brunswick to the Prince; the States General wished to give its approval only if it cost "no money whatsoever for the state"; powerful opposition arose in several of the provincial States. The result was the imposition of such impossible conditions that the British preferred to let the whole thing go. For one thing, what use would the brigade be under the emphatic stipulation, added at Amsterdam's insistence, that it could be used only in Europe? Besides, it would have to be paid for in full. This much is certain: the relations between Great Britain and the Republic were painfully damaged by the affair. Sir Joseph Yorke, who was anything but easygoing and was fully familiar with Dutch weaknesses, having been resident in the country since 1751, made a vain plea to the Prince based on their long friendship, "with none of the haughty ways to which His Excellency was sometimes given," as William reported to the grand pensionary. His failure infuriated him, and Thulemeyer, whose dispatches are such an excellent source for the history of this period, reported that he was "in a very bad mood."[3]

Yorke was no friend of the Netherlands, and he had few personal friends in the country. Dutchmen who had to have business with him described him as a "high-and-mighty Character," "proud and quick-tempered," and they complained about his "scorn for the Republic." We shall see many examples of this. But his attitude is not hard to understand, especially in this affair of the Scots Brigade. He could see why Brunswick had taken a stand against him, for they had always gotten on badly, and the duke had even proposed to the Prince that London be asked to recall its ambassador.[4] But in this affair Yorke met much broader resistance with a distinctly anti-English aspect. It became more evident than ever to him that Britain had many enemies in the country. The noisiest of these was a nobleman who suddenly came to the fore with little influence upon matters of state but with a gift for winning the ears of the multitude.

· II ·

Joan Derk van der Capellen tot den Pol was and continues to be one of the most controversial figures in Dutch history. In our age, with its infatuation with every kind of radicalism, he has been rediscovered as a forerunner of revolution. A new edition has been brought out of his famous pamphlet *To the People of the Netherlands*, and in their introduction the editors described him as a radical; a prophet of the revolt of the people; a

man of the type of Mirabeau, Saint-Simon, Bakunin, and other heralds of
a new era, down to Ho Chi Minh; a true "red baron." But a comparison
carried too far destroys itself, for it tells us little of the man in his own
time. Another modern historian, who has studied the late eighteenth century with care and in depth, has come to an opposite conclusion. He is
willing to admit two tendencies in Van der Capellen's soul, the aristocratic and the bourgeois, but he sees him as still primarily "a regent of the
radical wing of the Old [i.e., conservative] Patriots," emphatically "no
adherent of democracy or one who wanted to clear the way for it"; "he
stood with both feet in the tradition of ancient law in Europe."[5]

He was a nobleman to the core. When he was refused the place that he
claimed as noble member in the States of his native Gelderland, he purchased an estate in neighboring Overijssel, from which he took his title,
Baron tot den Pol. He was admitted to the States of Overijssel and started
to play a conspicuous role. He was no radical in the revolutionary sense
of the word, no Mirabeau, and certainly no Bakunin. If he became a
"tribune of the bourgeoisie," it does not at all mean that he wanted a real
revolution. On the contrary, it was his very sense of citizenhood that
made him averse to popular influence, and the American historian Robert R. Palmer, in his *Age of the Democratic Revolution*, characterizes Van
der Capellen as someone who struggled against the excesses of the Dutch
political system without any intellectual basis in the Enlightened philosophy of his time.[6]

Palmer here goes too far. The difficulty is that all judgments on Van der
Capellen have been very strongly shaped by two factors: one is the Dutch
tradition of the nineteenth century which equated Orangism and nationalism and hence condemned the Patriots of the previous century who opposed the Prince of Orange; the other is the very complicated character
of the man himself. Historians of a century ago berated him as "a true
aristocrat, all vanity," "a Lafayette with an even lighter head," "a hard-
working but vain peddler of ideas . . . without the slightest talent as a
statesman or any real knowledge of the world, . . . no creator but a fol-
lower, in all a mind of the second rank." But others defended him, nota-
bly Willem Hendrik de Beaufort, the editor of his correspondence, who
saw him not as a revolutionary before his time but as a forerunner of modern Dutch democracy, "the knight who awakened this sleeping beauty
with his magic wand of courage and eloquence." In the realm of ideas,
Van der Capellen belongs in the camp of those English moderate radicals
characterized so well by Caroline Robbins as "Commonwealthmen," and
he had contact with some of them, especially Richard Price. There is in

fact an element of abstract principle in his activity, a yearning for justice, a love for mankind in the typical eighteenth-century way, and this makes him a path breaker.[7]

His political ideas may not have been very progressive and were certainly rather contradictory, but there was nonetheless in his character a streak of radicalism, a readiness to fight for deep convictions. In the only biography of Van der Capellen, a work by M. de Jong which appeared in 1922, this ambivalence between political perceptions and inner feelings is well brought out. According to De Jong, there was in Van der Capellen a dualism that set tradition against renewal, history against ethics, which was caused by the deeper contradictions between his conservative instinct and his radical temperament. This psychological explanation rings true, especially when it is amplified by reference to his probably unhappy youth, about which, however, we do not know much more than that he did not get on very well with his father. Be that as it may, the tensions in Van der Capellen are very obvious and are not to be explained only by the anomaly in his position as both regent and popular leader.[8]

It seems to me that Van der Capellen cannot be understood by his rational ideas only. What is remarkable in him is his restlessness, his passion, his doubts, his rage against everything around him, his unfairness even to his friends, his often extreme language. A good example is his reaction to the news that the democratic party had been defeated in Geneva. In his fury he expressed the wish that the atmosphere over the city be poisoned, so that it "would be inhabited only by screech-owls and bats, providing other still free Commonwealths with a horrible warning." Such inclination to violence is sometimes found in idealists, and it is no wonder that opponents, such as Adriaan Kluit, a well-known conservative professor of history at Leiden University, sharply rebuked him for this use of "gruesome language that would raise the hair of the most savage barbarians." Those who met him were impressed by his fierceness, even an admirer like Pieter Paulus, who described him as "a man on whose countenance candor and uncompromising honor can be read." The judgments of contemporaries are at least as contradictory as those of historians, and this in itself tells something about him. In any case he was able to arouse the most violent emotions. After his death the poet Jacobus Bellamy pictured, in the typical style of the times, a triumphal entry of Van der Capellen into heaven, where Jesus, "the leader of the hosts of freedom," placed upon his head a liberty crown. An opponent, on the other hand, expressed the hope that the quiet burial vault would spit out "the stinking body of this most villainous of rogues," who "deserves no resting place." This is exactly what happened, for when the Prussians entered the country in 1787, foes of the dead nobleman blew up the beautiful sepulchre that had been erected by his admirers.[9]

A reasonable judgment would be that while Van der Capellen may indeed be called a conservative who set great store by the past, who was proud of his title of nobility and was afraid of "too much reforming," by temperament he was what we would now call an "angry young man," passionate, hot-headed, quick to speak whatever he felt, always fighting those "insufferable Periwigs," the regents. "*Almost* our entire nation consists of fools and knaves, but *all* the regents." He was thin skinned and oversensitive, which can probably be explained psychologically; but it must be said that he was sincerely concerned for the weak, the less-advantaged, the oppressed. While still a young man he had wrestled with the problem of evil in the world. In a letter to his friend Meinhard Tydeman he confessed in a moving way the temptations that he had felt. I am an orthodox Calvinist, he wrote. "I am, thanks to God's goodness, wholly devoted to St. Paul's teachings in his letter to the Romans, . . . but nonetheless the *origo mali* remains for me an insuperable obstacle; it poisons all my religious thinking and keeps me in truth far from God. . . . I know that there are signs of God's goodness everywhere, I know what Christ did and suffered; but then the old question besets me: why is there so much evil in the world? If the angels had not sinned, then Christ would not have had to die, then thousands upon thousands would not have had to suffer eternal misery, and all would have served God."

If we do not want to reduce men to nothing more than their psychological and social circumstances, which does no justice to their human dignity, should we not say that our Overijssel Patriot drew life from just this spiritual perturbation? How unfair, then, is the comparison that his foes, with William V in the lead, so willingly and maliciously made between him and the English radical John Wilkes! Both admittedly were battlers against the established order, but how humane and noble a man Van der Capellen is by comparison with the dissolute Englishman. How pure his impulses are and therefore how tragic his shortcomings! He may often have acted halfheartedly, but his defense of the Overijssel peasantry and the black slaves in America was sincere. The common people understood his genuine unselfishness, and he became highly popular among them.[10]

It is possible to follow closely in his writings why Van der Capellen was attracted by the American struggle for freedom and why he was the first in the Netherlands to come out openly for the American cause. Even as a young man he looked more to England than to France, and he mastered English (along with the obligatory French) so well that he could write letters in that language. He enjoyed reading the English writers, the "Commonwealthmen" or "real Whigs," as well as Locke, and it was their influence that determined his ideas. No more than he were most of them radical democrats, but their mixture of empiricism and faith in the goodness of man, their strivings on behalf of the majority, spoke directly to his heart. He could not easily go along with their deism, even when he grew older (however much he disliked the Dutch preachers, a *genus irritabile,* as he called them). But he readily adopted their belief in the "omnipotence of the People," no matter how much they might differ in their various conceptions of what it actually meant. Nor did he himself define it precisely. Sometimes he backed away from its radical consequences, warning "that we should not understand by the *People* the *riffraff* or a handful of malcontents and agitators, but the respectable, honorable, and venerable part of the Nation; the proprietors, the shareholders of the great society." But at other times he seemed more radical, even using the old language of the English Levellers (although he wrongly attributed it to a member of the House of Lords) when he wrote to Pieter Paulus that some men imagined "that they were created with boots and spurs and the rest of the human race with saddles on their backs," words that Thomas Jefferson, like him an aristocratic leader of the people, was so fond of.[11]

Van der Capellen established closer contact with one of the English reformers, the many-sided Dissenting clergyman Dr. Richard Price, who was well known as a philosopher, mathematician, and statistician, friend of Benjamin Franklin, and fervent defender of the American cause in England. In February 1776, Price published a little book under the title *Observations on the Nature of Civil Liberty and Justice and the Policy of the War with America.* It became an instant success, and it was not long before Van der Capellen had a copy in his hands. He quickly and enthusiastically prepared a translation, so that the *Observations* appeared in Dutch in the same year. Soon the contact became more direct through the exchange of letters.

But Van der Capellen's commitment to the Americans dates from even before he read and translated Price's booklet. It began with the issue of the Scots Brigade. When the States of Overijssel met on 14–16 December 1775 at Kampen to discuss the English request for its use, the nobleman from Zwolle made a speech that reads like a clarion call. It was soon published, in defiance of custom and even of ordinary good manners, as Van der Capellen's opponents declared. What it actually proved was that there was a great hunger for news, and perhaps also a latent anti-English feeling. The kernel of Van der Capellen's argument against release of the brigade was that it would be a violation of Dutch neutrality. But it would also be an act of injustice, he asserted, for the Americans were fighting for a righteous cause. It would be disgraceful if Dutch troops fought against them: "This is considered repulsive by the Undersigned, who judges the Americans to merit everyone's respect and admires them as brave men who defend in a steady, manly, and God-fearing way the Rights that they have received not from the *Legislative Power in England*, but from God himself." The right to liberty is an inalienable right. How close Van der Capellen was in this speech to the ideas formulated half a year later by Thomas Jefferson in the Declaration of Independence.

Van der Capellen's bold speech in the States of Overijssel brought down on his neck the rage of the stadholder and led to his eventual expulsion from that body. But the affair caused such a furor that it also became known beyond the Atlantic and brought him into contact with several important leaders of the American Revolution, including Jonathan Trumbull, governor of Connecticut, and William Livingston, a member of an illustrious New York family of Dutch origin, who was governor of New Jersey. They became interested in the enthusiastic Dutchman through the intermediary of a merchant who had emigrated from Holland to America, Gosuinus Erkelens. They wrote to Van der Capellen to pay him their compliments and naturally to publicize their revolution. Livingston, who was a born propagandist and had made a name for himself in New York with his newspaper, *The Independent Reflector*, in which he urged every kind of reform, informed his correspondent in Zwolle that he himself was of three-quarters Dutch stock, but that what mattered were not such accidental origins but love for all mankind. Van der Capellen jumped at the chance to make contact with Americans. Curiously, he boasted of his noble parentage, but added that he placed the praise of the Americans above it. Full of zeal, he proposed to compose a pamphlet on the heroic deeds of the nations that had defended their liberty, from the Thebans down to the Dutch and finally the Americans.

The correspondence, which plays up the glories of the Americans, was soon published, with the result that Van der Capellen became even more celebrated, or, to some, notorious. A member of the States of Overijssel, according to Van der Capellen's own account, told him publicly "that he would not allow me to be readmitted as long as he had eyes in his head, because I had engaged in forbidden correspondence with the Americans." Other adversaries collected all the facts they could find to use against the fiery Patriot. There is a file in the archives of Fagel, the secretary of the States General, labeled "Correspondence of Mr. Van der Capellen with the Americans."[12]

By some, Van der Capellen was accused of looking to his personal interests in his relations with his American friends. In the very first letter he received from Erkelens it was suggested that Congress should send an envoy to Holland "under your good offices (and protection, as far as possible)." The thought that Van der Capellen himself would be the best man for the post must have come up very soon, in all likelihood among the Americans and certainly with Van der Capellen himself. He put out feelers quite early, very cautiously and secretly. He sought his goal through the intermediary of the Amsterdam banker Jean de Neufville, who had many ties with the Americans. "It would be best," he wrote to De Neufville, "not to mention my name in your American dispatches; even, if it can be avoided (but you can judge this best yourself) not to give any sign of personal ties with me. I do not see the Republic as yet disposed to receive any acknowledged minister. But this does not defeat my plan, because I will be satisfied with the promise of our Court, of Amsterdam and of America that at the proper time I will be recognized and preferred. The earlier we prepare for this, the better: before someone else is picked out in America." He realized quite well, he added, that he would probably not be to the court's liking, but they also might like to get rid of him. But he armed himself at the same time against disappointment. A month later he pretended that he would rather end his days "at his fireside, far from all bustle." He was indifferent to whatever would happen now, he averred, but in any event they would "have to seek me out." "I have experienced the delights of a life without office and the bitterness of a public position, and will not go about gaping like a newcomer. I am already in my thirty-eighth year and thus past the first ferments of passion." But he did not really want to give up his dream, and he continued to busy himself with it. It is certain that the man who brought Trumbull's and Livingston's letters to Holland, the officer Jacob Gerard Dircks, discussed it with the baron. Van der Capellen felt the current was running too strongly and finally instructed Dircks to say nothing about his appointment as minister when he returned to America. Dircks promised to be silent, but he kept the door open; "he couldn't very well prevent Congress from doing something on its own."

But, in reality, Congress had no such plans in mind. For that matter, it was quite well understood in Holland that Van der Capellen, who was persona non grata with the powers that be in The Hague, was certainly not the most suitable person to plead the American cause. The American secret agent in The Hague, Dumas—of whom we shall hear much more —spoke to the powerful pensionary of Amsterdam, Van Berckel, about the situation, and was warned by him that Van der Capellen had too little influence to count. Dumas passed the warning on to Benjamin Franklin in Paris and to the American authorities in Philadelphia. He added that the Overijssel nobleman had told him that he indeed had entertained the idea of becoming the American envoy, but that he was giving it up because he saw how well Dumas was serving Congress. With a touch of sourness, Van der Capellen had declared, "Now he would give it up and not envy me a coach and horses. I gave him to understand that I had never been concerned with horses, but only with men and their needs, and therefore would not interfere if he should apply for his horses to America." This acidulous exchange was characteristic of the situation.

It must have been a blow for Van der Capellen that he did not get the post, but he was trying to make the best of it. In the fall he received a letter from another traveling American, Stephen Sayre. Sayre was both an agent of Congress and a man of business; like so many others, he was very good at serving his country's interests simultaneously with his own. He had come from Paris to Amsterdam looking for a ship to buy. He wrote that Dumas, "that little insignificant shoemaker" (obviously a term of abuse, for Dumas had nothing to do with shoes), had influenced Franklin (he had gone to Paris on a visit in the fall of 1779) and was the cause of all the difficulties. Franklin had asked Sayre whether Van der Capellen had not solicited the post of "Minister to the States General." "I conceive," Sayre added in his letter to the baron, "the idea must have been suggested by the shoemaker. My reply was, whoever supposed that, must be totally ignorant of your character, that if you had done it, you had no other motive than the sincere wish to serve America." Van der Capellen replied promptly. He warmly thanked Sayre for having defended the purity of his character to Franklin against such slander. It was quite unlikely, he added, that he would have sought a post from Congress when he had refused to take any personal benefit whatever from his connections in his own country.

The whole thing was a concoction, he said, "of a wretch who, having thought up a plan to raise himself, has taken alarm at the sight of all those whom he considers to be obstacles in reaching his goal." Dumas was jealous, that was all, and certainly not as disinterested as Van der Capellen, who had already spoken up for America back in December 1775. He had only written to Trumbull and Livingston that they should send an American to the Netherlands, and when Dircks had told him that Trumbull had him in mind for the post, he had firmly refused. He had informed Dircks that he was not suitable for it, for his health was not good enough. So our hero acted as though it had all been nothing, but inside he must have felt otherwise: "A worn-out ailing old man like me [he was thirty-eight while writing this!] is of no use to them. Besides, my friend, think of Dumas. Let us not take such strong revenge for a silly compliment. Recommend him to Congress. He has a wife and family, he has been truly zealous in the service of America, and he deserves payment." Thus ended a dream of dubious prospect. But it was not ended completely, for it came back in different form a few years later. In 1782, after the States General had recognized the United States, the name of his second cousin, Van der Capellen van de Marsch, was mentioned for the post of Dutch envoy to the American Congress. This was again a disappointment to Baron tot den Pol. "Why am I not being considered? I have a good deal more relation to America than my cousin, who has never corresponded with that country, not supported the rebels with *word* and *deed* as I did—with 26,000 guilders."[13]

It is true that Van der Capellen was thin-skinned and vain to boot; yet he vouched by his actions what he preached so fervently. In 1779 he placed ten thousand guilders of his own funds in an American loan (which, however, was a general failure), and in 1782 he was good for another sixteen thousand guilders. His love was noisy but unselfish, except for his desire to be recognized. He was driven not by self-interest in a material sense but by the ambition of honor. He wanted his friends in the New World to know that "it is my highest ambition to be known and loved in America, and that is what gives me real solace and strength to hold up under the humiliations I have suffered for years." He would have done anything for America, and if his wife and child had not held him back, he would have gone there to shed his blood for the cause of freedom.[14]

His love was unselfish but not uncritical. This shows best in his attack upon slavery. In the Netherlands he had protested furiously against the edict of the States General of 23 May 1776 determining that blacks brought from the colonies to the Netherlands did not thereby acquire their freedom; instead they were to be shipped back. He had reacted with general indignation: "The ownership of men (an invention, alas, that dishonors mankind!) has been re-introduced and made legal in this free country by High Authority." He pleaded with humane feeling for the principle of equality: "Created by the same mighty Hand; born of the same blood; endowed with the same capabilities of soul and body; driven by the same desires; pressed by the same needs; subject to the same weaknesses, the same death, and the same future judgment, and crawling in the same dust before the face of the Great Creator of Heaven and Earth, all men are equal to each other."

No wonder, then, that a man with such feelings was struck with bafflement when his beloved Americans were so intolerant as not to abolish slavery. He wrote to Price about it, but, idealist that he was, he also expressed his conviction that the Americans would free their blacks as soon as they had won their struggle. If they did not, they would be denying the very principles they professed. A nation that treated human beings as beasts did not deserve to be free.[15]

In general his faith in America remained unshakable. He was one of the small number of Dutchmen who dreamed of a better world in the West. He took no part in the land speculation that was the rage among Dutch businessmen. He did dream of eventually going to America, but was prevented by his ill health. To his friend Adriaan Valck, who did emigrate, he wrote: "Do not consider it chimerical that I will come to visit you sometime in your new Fatherland." America meant for him, as for so many others, escaping the burdens of the past and, even more, escaping from oneself, from all the painful disquiet he knew in himself. "My sickness lies mainly in the soul. As soon as there is a little less need of me here, I'll come over."[16]

CHAPTER 2

Neutral on Land and at Sea

Let them fight, I'll sack the chink.
ENGLISH CARICATURE

HE Scots Brigade calmly continued to while away the time in the garrisons of the moldering Barrier towns of the Southern Netherlands. But, to use a military metaphor, the king of England had other arrows for his bow. As a half-German and elector of Hanover, George III had close relations with the princes and princelings in the great but decaying Holy Roman Empire. Therefore he started to recruit Germans for his army, amid the derision of the Enlightened philosophers. The method in itself was not very strange in a time when armies were made up only of mercenaries and professional soldiers; what was unusual was that the transactions filled the princes' treasuries, not the pockets of the poor devils who were pressed into service. Some were not pressed, but tempted in by fine promises. In the little towns of Germany placards were posted under the name of "George III, by the Grace of God, King of Great Britain, France, Ireland and the great Empire of America," promising good pay, new uniforms every year, safe passage, and care for stragglers and disabled soldiers. New England, they claimed, had the same climate as Germany, and many persons had won prosperity there. Finally, the placards informed their readers that "the principal assembly point is Dordrecht beyond Nijmegen." At Dordrecht each soldier would receive ten to thirty guilders.

Despite its asserted neutrality, the Dutch Republic did not prevent the passage of these troops from Germany to England. Quite the contrary, the Dutch government cooperated fully, telling the English that they need expect no difficulties, and it had its own troops stand guard during the embarkation to prevent desertion. The duke of Brunswick informed the Prince that formally the English ought to request the permission of the Dutch government for the German mercenaries' passage, but that it would be better not to irritate Yorke any further, particularly after the difficulties over the Scots Brigade. The whole affair ran off rather quietly, even though it made the Americans bitter.

Dumas kept the American commissioners at Paris informed in vivid detail. He reported the number of ships and men ("1200 pigs from Ansbach") and told them that at the gates of Ansbach (the town that he came from and where he may well still have had relations) the text of Psalm 44 had been nailed up—"You have sold your people for a pittance"—and he gave an account of the visit of the margrave of Ansbach, who was hooted in The Hague as "seller of souls." Dumas maintained that the number of desertions was considerable.

He also sent newspapers and pamphlets to Paris. One of these was the celebrated *Notice for the Hessians* (*Avis aux Hessois*), which, as Dumas reported, was written by a Frenchman who had run off with a married woman and was living with her under a false name in Amsterdam. At the request of the French ambassador, the philandering pamphleteer was arrested along with his "Helen," and he was sent back to his own country. In Dumas's letters the Frenchman remained nameless; we know him, however, as Mirabeau, still a wild youth but one with a future before him. From another side we hear more about the excitement set off by his pamphlet: Benjamin Sowden, the English preacher at Rotterdam, assured Franklin that it had had "a surprising run in this country." He asserted that it had been printed not, as it claimed, in Cleves but in The Hague.[1]

To remain neutral became more and more impossible, but the States General did its best. It permitted the Hessians to pass, but prevented a second English attempt to recruit troops from the ranks of the States General's own army. What happened was that the contract between the Netherlands and the prince of Waldeck for his two regiments ran out. The English government sought to take them over, but on the demand of Amsterdam, again on the alert about the "augmentation" problem, the contract with Waldeck was renewed for ten years. It was a second disappointment for the Britons.

· II ·

It was really a sorry tale, all this Dutch prudence, dexterity, sedateness, at its best enlivened by the wrath of a baron from Overijssel, which was colorful but of little effect. Where is the Dutch Lafayette, Pulaski, or Von Steuben? Was that the best the Dutch could contribute? A few years ago a candidate for such a hero's role was put forward in a splendidly documented article by H. Hardenberg with the exciting title "Colonel Dircks, a Forerunner of Lafayette." He describes his warrior in detail: Jacob Gerard Dircks, born in Deventer in Overijssel, raised in the Dutch colony of Surinam, an officer in the lifeguard of the count of Steinfurt, in Westphalia, and in 1776 a volunteer in the new army of the rebels in America under the name of Diriks (following the Dutch pronunciation). He fought at Trenton (and he probably is in Leutze's famous painting of Washington crossing the Delaware!), but he did not become a Lafayette. He has left the impression of a quarrelsome little man, or perhaps one whose wife drove him to complain endlessly and to come up constantly with new plans. In 1779 he was sent on a semiofficial mission to Holland, and we have met him with Van der Capellen, but he did not succeed that time either and finally ran into a bitter quarrel with the baron. He continued then on his wanderings, going to America, coming back to Holland, joining the Patriots just in time to share in their defeat by the Prussians, after which he was caught up in the exiles' squabbles. In 1795 he returned to Holland, now the Batavian Republic, with the French, and died quietly ten years later. He was no Lafayette, to be sure, and hardly a forerunner. Hardenberg described him as a bird of bad luck, but one who, in his best moments, knew the ideal of a freer mankind in a better world. That may be true, but overall we get more the impression of an adventurer, uncertain of himself and with little self-control. He has been almost forgotten, and not unjustly.[2]

· III ·

Dutch neutrality was in greatest peril not on land but at sea, for that was where Holland's essential interests lay. The cities of Holland, most of all Amsterdam, were willing enough to concern themselves with such problems as the expansion of the army, but these were small matters compared to what happened at sea. Who really cared whether a pack of German farm boys were dragged through the Netherlands on the way to battlefields in America?

Now that the Republic was no longer a great power, war in Europe meant for the Dutch, on the one hand, a fearful clinging to neutrality and, on the other, a glittering gamble, a magnificent chance to get rich quick. Dutch foreign policy had to be conducted within this context of conflicting interests. Officially, there was every display of honest neutrality; secretly, all possible smuggling was permitted.

Every opportunity for smugglers was provided by the American rebellion. For Dutch trade the situation was both a threat and an opportunity, each almost without precedent. This is reflected in the first complaints and letters that came from the Dutch West India Company. Its governing board asked the States General whether England could not be "induced" to lift the blockade of American ports, at least for the products of the Dutch colonies in the Caribbean, molasses especially. The position of the Dutch possessions would become very trying without trade with New England, and even famine was possible.

The government correctly expected little to come of such a request to the British. The stadholder, who was so pro-English, even wrote Fagel that if he were the king of England, he would never grant it, and the *griffier* wholly agreed with him. There was nothing done officially, but all the more was done in secrecy. As early as 1774, in the month of August, more than eight months before the rebellion actually started, Yorke called attention to a shipment of gunpowder going to America from the Amsterdam firm of Crommelin, which had close family ties with the Americans. In October, Yorke again complained that a ship from Rhode Island was lying in Amsterdam harbor and he asked that an eye be kept on it. Thulemeyer, the Prussian envoy, informed his king that Yorke's information was correct. Actually, three American ships lay at Amsterdam, and they had taken on "a considerable quantity of gunpowder, cannonballs, and firearms." The city fathers in Amsterdam have done nothing about the English complaints, he continued, for the inhabitants of Boston were after all not the enemies of England. But an English sloop, he wrote in a later dispatch, had chased a ship from Boston, the cutter *Wells*, almost into Amsterdam harbor.

Reporting the incident to London, Yorke told of the excitement caused in the Amsterdam Exchange by the defiance of the English man-of-war. The merchants of Holland began to fear that the British government intended to shut down the whole trade of St. Eustatius, the little Dutch Caribbean island that was the center of their shipping to and from North America, and they complained to the States of their own province and to the States General. Fagel went to see Yorke about the matter, but the *griffier* was so pro-English that he did not present the complaint but only discussed the best reply to give. Yorke suggested to the government in London that it be a bit more cautious and that it would be better to check secretly on Dutch smuggling and not to send ships so close to Amsterdam.

We learn from the reports of the British authorities in America how extensive this clandestine trade was and how threatening it seemed to the

English. The aged but still alert lieutenant governor of the colony of New York, Cadwallader Colden, wrote to the secretary for the colonies, Dartmouth, on 2 November 1774: "The contraband trade carried on between this place and Holland is, my lord, an object that I must behold with great concern. It prevails to an enormous degree, must destroy the morals of the people, create the most inveterate enemies to government, nourish the spirit of mobbing, and abolish all fair trade." Action must be taken against the smugglers, he continued, but it would not be easy, because the American coast was very convenient for them. "The vessels from Holland or St. Eustatia do not come into this port but anchor at some distance in the numerous bays and creeks that our coast and rivers furnish, from whence the contraband goods are sent up in small boats."

No wonder, then, that the English government angrily decided to take sharper action against the Dutch Republic even before the American rebellion began. Yorke received instructions to demand that the States General place an embargo upon all materials of war. He presented his request in February 1775 and got what he wanted, for the embargo was proclaimed on 20 March and extended for a year on 18 August. The natural result was a rapid expansion of smuggling: whole cargoes of what was ostensibly tea, coffee, flour, sugar, and rice were sent to America by way of St. Eustatius, the smuggling center in the Caribbean Sea. Profits were large: a pound of gunpowder cost eight and a half stivers in Holland and forty-six in St. Eustatius. The smuggling proceeded on such a large scale, reported Thulemeyer, that the gunpowder mills could not meet the demand, although they were working without interruption in all the provinces. Deliveries to France fell two months behind. A few months later, Thulemeyer declared, there were no fewer than seven American ships in Amsterdam harbor.

It is remarkable how powerless the British Empire was in the face of this virtually public violation of all the promises, old and new. But that was just the British problem: their relations with the Dutch Republic were based on a strongly traditional friendship and were so sensitive that strong action did not seem possible.

A Dutch friend advised Yorke to take a simple way out: The English government should buy up the gunpowder mills and their entire production (no less than 150,000 pounds a month) and use it for themselves. It could be done for the moderate sum of sixty-five thousand pounds. But there was no interest in the proposal at Whitehall, which no doubt thought it unpractical. Protests were sent, and for a time that was all.

The English ambassador was full of reproaches for the States General.

Munitions were being put aboard ships in Dutch harbors so publicly that it seemed that an embargo had never been promulgated. He insisted that Their High Mightinesses make sure their orders were obeyed. To friends he complained that he could get nothing done. What did English power matter, he wondered, when Dutch merchants could go about their business so tranquilly? "All our boasted Empire of the Sea is of no Consequence, we may seize the shells, but our neighbours will get the Oysters." It was true. The smugglers exchanged their powder for vast quantities of valuable products—tobacco, rice, indigo. On one single day in March 1777, it was learned in London, four ships from St. Eustatius put in at Amsterdam carrying cargoes with two hundred hogsheads of tobacco, six hundred to seven hundred barrels of rice, and a big quantity of indigo, all coming from America.

Too little of this is recounted in the familiar American textbooks. They tell at length the story of the renowned business firm run by the French playwright Beaumarchais under the name of Rodrigue Hortalez and Co., which began activity only in May 1776. By that time the Dutch had been busy for more than a year and a half delivering powder and shot to the rebels. Yorke's conclusion that the Dutch Republic was the Americans' source of supply and that they would have had to abandon their insurrection if they had not been aided by Dutch greed cannot be disputed. Thulemeyer was of the same opinion, and it is supported by modern scholars like J. Franklin Jameson and Richard Van Alstyne.

Dutch gunpowder traveled by all kinds of routes, including French and Spanish ports, and this had led some historians to set too high the French share in the delivery of these supplies. But in 1776, Yorke had already sent three reports that Nantes and Bordeaux were the ports from which Dutch milled gunpowder was exported directly to America. And the British consul in the Spanish city of La Coruña informed Lord Weymouth that Dutch ships brought the powder in barrels to Bilbao and Santander, where it was transferred to American ships. The most important suppliers of munitions to the American insurgents were the Dutch, not the French, who get far more frequent mention. The Republic, as Yorke wrote a friend, was "the common sewer of Europe thro' which all the filth circulates." Some of the shipments to the Americans went directly from France and Spain, but the roundabout route through the Caribbean was more important. An English official in Boston reported the situation from across the Atlantic: "What surprised me exceedingly was the trade they carried on. At most of the ports east of Boston . . . there were daily arrivals from the West-Indies but most from St. Eustatia, every one of which brings more or less of gunpowder."[3]

Which brings us to the little island in the Caribbean Sea, already mentioned several times, that was named after the patron saint of the hunt, Saint Eustatius. It was a tiny bit of land, no more than twelve square miles, but still one of the most famed places of the eighteenth-century world. Hunting was practiced, but only in a metaphorical sense, and the prey was the big profits to be had from smuggling to the American rebels. Long before the war the Dutch island, spared the mercantilist constraints of its English and French neighbors, had become a trading center. The growth of its commerce may be seen in some comparative figures: in 1744 the number of ship arrivals was 1,233 and departures 1,249; in 1759–60 it was 1,852 and 2,081; and in 1777, 2,315 and 2,460. The little patch of land, some of it uninhabitable because of a volcano more than eighteen hundred feet high and the rest not very fertile, had a population in 1774 of 2,223, of whom 1,491 were slaves. At least these are the official figures; the number of slaves was probably larger.

Hundreds of people packed together on so small an area could only mean trouble, and in the annals of the island, all neatly drawn up and sent to the governors of the West India Company in Amsterdam, we can read our fill of their squabbles and childishness. It was worst with matters of government. In 1775 the governor, Jan de Windt, died, and there were four or five others ready to fill his place. Each gave convincing proof in long letters to the "Nineteen," the board of directors of the West India Company, that he, and he alone, was the best candidate for the post. It went finally to Johannes de Graaff, who had been secretary of the island administration for no less than twenty-four years. He gives the impression of being a skillful and energetic man of affairs, one who was able to combine the interests of the West India Company and his own in outstanding fashion—but this of course, was the usual thing at the time.

According to his enemies, and they were many, De Graaff and his wife were a pair of vulgarians, "all beneath the common standard," who together had become wealthy by "all the arts that avarice can suggest, or fraud practice, or authority employ, or industry exercise . . . , bribery, extortion, smuggling, speculation." This was the judgment of an Englishman who was far away. A Dutchman on the scene, secretary Alexander le Jeune—and what was *he*, a man who could not tolerate the slightest injustice, or just an ill-mannered quarrel-seeker?—sent report after report to the company administrators in Amsterdam filled with serious imputations as well as low gossip, especially about De Graaff's wife: "Sir, if you saw her, you would be amazed, she really looks like an old whore. And she is stingy as Sin. She served us food that was three days old. And where do you think her tablecloths came from? From Osnabrück! Have you ever seen Decent People use them? Let alone common folk like them."[4]

Even if we disregard all the mudslinging, the question still remains how De Graaff, who was no more than an officeholder, was able to become so enormously rich. For the fact is that he managed during the years that he governed the island to pile up a truly huge fortune, which his descendants would squander at an even faster rate. But he also succeeded in making a place for himself in history; his portrait—a swarthy, intelligent, wary, and self-assured face—still hangs in the state capitol in Concord, New Hampshire. The Americans are still grateful to him. We must now turn our attention to the question of how far that gratitude is deserved.

Even before De Graaff took over the helm—he was sworn in as governor on 5 September 1776—the island's smuggling trade with the rebellious Americans was in full swing. St. Eustatius was the ideal meeting place for ships coming to the West Indies from the Netherlands, sometimes by way of Africa, and for American merchantmen. The route was safer than the direct crossing and the weather more favorable, and it had become familiar to sailors after many years of use. The Americans came to St. Eustatius to pick up molasses, sugar, slaves, and all kinds of European products, and they brought timber, foodstuffs, tobacco, indigo, and horses. Of the 1,852 ships that cleared into St. Eustatius in 1759–60, 103 came from the thirteen colonies, and no less than 40 from busy Salem alone. The number came to 120 out of 2,315 in 1770, with about 100 out of 2,400 on the outgoing journey. These are not overwhelming figures, but we must keep in mind that most shipping was engaged in local trade to nearby islands.

In any case the trade with the Americans became a thorn in the side of the English as early as 1774, when the breakaway of their colonies already threatened, and they gradually intensified their measures to restrain it. On 3 January 1776 the temporary governor, Abraham Heyliger, complained to the company administrators in Amsterdam about the brutality of the English, "the numerous Irregularities . . . which in my opinion are so flagrant that they must be considered as a total violation of the laws of All civilized nations." Incidents followed closely one after another. English ships chased American vessels right into the island's harbor, in the conviction that necessity gave them rights. King George personally gave the order for strong action. On 11 January 1776 he wrote the First Lord of the Admiralty, the Earl of Sandwich, that more warships had to be fitted out, "for every intelligence confirms that principally St. Eustatius, but also other islands, are to furnish the Americans with gunpowder this winter."[5]

Not long afterward, in May, the British ship *Seaford* attempted to seize an American ship, the *Mifflin* out of Philadelphia, just off the shore of St. Eustatius, but the commander of Fort Orange, Abraham Ravené, was able to prevent it. Heyliger at once sent a protest to the *Seaford*'s captain, and this led to an acrimonious exchange of letters with the English admiral, James Young. To Young's accusations that the "very pernicious traffic carried on between his Brittanic majesty's rebellious subjects from North-America and the inhabitants of St. Eustatia for gunpowder and warlike stores has been so general and done in so public a manner as to be no secret to any person in the West Indies islands," Heyliger replied that these were just vague accusations, slander, and imagination, and the issue was really punishment of a British captain who had violated the neutrality of Dutch waters.

Discussion in such broad terms led nowhere. But vague accusations were swiftly followed by the naming of names. In The Hague, Yorke complained that the merchant Isaac van Dam had delivered gunpowder to William Goodrich of Virginia. He put the water-blurred proof of the transaction on the table, with its indication of how the smuggling was conducted. Goodrich had gone in September 1775 from St. Eustatius to the French island of Martinique, but when he could not obtain what he wanted at once, he left funds for buying gunpowder that would be delivered to him by Isaac van Dam. "Shortly afterwards, when the aforementioned William Goodrich was still on this Island, eighty barrels of gunpowder arrived here which the aforementioned William Goodrich conveyed with him to North America, along with 30 barrels of gunpowder which this same Goodrich had bought here, three blunderbusses and seventy pounds of musket bullets; all of which was clearly ammunition of war, as is known to him, the witness [Johan Blair, Van Dam's bookkeeper]." More gunpowder soon arrived from Martinique, which was sold by Van Dam to one Knox from St. Thomas, "but with what purpose he, the witness, does not know."

Thus a culprit, Van Dam, had been found, but one, alas, who had died not long before. His widow testified that her husband had never violated the embargo on munitions, and the bookkeeper amplified his statement with testimony that Van Dam had had no interest in this traffic, "but had acted as a friend of the aforementioned Goodrich." Their declarations put the matter to rest, but only for a while, for another incident was in the making.

In November 1776 the English brigantine *May* was taken by the American bark *Baltimore Hero*, and furious English complaints followed that the American privateer had been fitted out on the Dutch island, and had furthermore attacked the English vessel just off the coast without any action on De Graaff's part to halt it. St. Eustatius was a pirates' nest. The governor willy-nilly could not avoid undertaking an official investigation and examined the captain of the American ship, Thomas Waters, who showed him his official papers. He had a commission from the ruling council in the province of Maryland, called The Council of Safety, signed by John Hancock, president. He stood upon his rights under the rules of war, but swore that he had had no business with anyone on St. Eustatius. His ship had cleared into the port on 11 November and sailed out on 20 November without any cargo being taken off or on. In all, it was a rather curious bit of testimony.

There was a witness for the prosecution, a certain George Scott, who said he knew that Abraham van Bibber, a big merchant on the island, was involved in the business and had even offered a portion of the captured ship's cargo for sale to a relative. But this relative, William Aull, vigorously denied it, and De Graaff concluded that Scott had spoken "very loosely, imprudently and with prejudice." He should hold his tongue, the report continued.

De Graaff brought a whole series of witnesses. He wanted to know from them whether anyone had a share in the *Baltimore Hero* or any other American vessel, if it was true that Abraham van Bibber had blank commissions from the Congress of North America, and whether Van Bibber had promised shares in the prize to anyone. All the questions were answered in the negative, including those put to Van Bibber himself: "Had he ever signed any blank Commissions of the Congress of North America, or seen any such signed by anyone else on this Island? Says, that he neither signed nor saw any and was assured that the North American Congress had never issued such Blank Commissions." Out of respect for the council of St. Eustatius "and to clear His Own Character," he was willing to swear to this, although an oath was not really needed. It all sounded fine—much too fine, in fact.

As we know from Van Bibber's correspondence with the Americans, which has been preserved, he was up to his ears in the arms traffic, and

De Graaff knew it. In that same month, Van Bibber wrote to the Council of Safety of Maryland that the Dutch understood quite well that the enforcement of the laws (that is, the embargo) would mean the ruin of their trade. He was on good terms with the governor, who had made promises to him that gave him great satisfaction, "and puts much in our powers. I was not so happy some time ago, and had every bad consequence to apprehend on our new Governor's taking the Command, but we are as well fixed with him now as we were with the former."[6]

As long as it worked, the assiduous inhabitants of the island hid behind a smokescreen of words, formulas, and false oaths. Secretary Fagel wrote to the Dutch envoy at London, Count Jan Walraad van Welderen, that the best way to curb the smugglers would be now and again to "burn the wings" of those who were caught, but the merchants seemed too wily.[7] The enemy could not catch them in the act. But at the same time that Fagel was writing, something so blatant and so challenging happened that every English official, high and low, was brought to his feet. On 16 November 1776 the American ship *Andrew Doria* (named after the sixteenth-century Genoese admiral, famous for his fight for his city's freedom) appeared in the harbor of St. Eustatius, flying the rebels' flag of thirteen stripes at its masthead, and it was greeted by Fort Orange with the official salute usually given to ships of friendly nations. The haughty captain of the *Seaford*, John Colpoys, announced that after such an insult to his king he would never give the salute on coming into St. Eustatius. Admiral Young angrily insinuated that De Graaff's conduct was more than an arbitrary act of the governor himself; he had to conclude, he told the governor, that "you have received Instructions from Europe and are guided thereby." The commander of the adjacent English islands, Craister Greathead, protested in a rage: It was scandalous that the Dutch supported the treason and piracy of the rebels by recognizing a flag "hitherto unknown in the catalogue of national ensigns." He demanded "exemplary Attonement."

De Graaff replied with a flow of words. He knew nothing "of any attonement I have to make," for he was completely impartial; it was his honest hope that the struggle between England and her American colonies would come to a happy end "to the satisfaction of both." Such a pious wish was too incredible, and the English did not take it at face value. De Graaff assembled another full batch of witnesses. Nothing untoward had taken place, he claimed. Warships of friendly countries were greeted with a salute of the same number of shots as they gave and merchantmen with two less, and he had numerous witnesses to attest to the

Andrew Doria's having been greeted as a merchantman, "hence not in a public but in a private character." He swore before the eyes of the administrators of the company "and also before the eyes of an all-knowing God" that it had never been his intention to take sides or to do any insult to the flag of "His Majesty of Great Britain." As for smuggling, he added, it was of course possible that some greedy persons broke the law, and it was not always possible to prevent their misconduct. But he strictly enforced the ordinances of Their High Mightinesses the States General, and he had even appointed a special inspector to search ships.

The English were not persuaded. They had their own witnesses. The principal one was a seventeen-year-old youth from Barbados, John Trottman. A student at Princeton, "in a school held there by the Rev. Dr. John Witherspoon," he had been kidnapped with a friend and shanghaied (a common practice of the time) aboard the *Andrew Doria*. He declared that, so far as he recalled, thirteen shots had been fired in salute and Fort Orange had replied with eleven. The American ship, he said, came to the island to buy clothing and other necessities.

This was meager proof, according to De Graaff, "Singular testimony of *one witness*, testimony given *without the slightest basis of knowledge*, resting on the witness's guess or belief." The English allegation that the Dutch were the "avowed collaborators" of the Americans was "an insult of the most ungracious and shameful kind." For that matter, how could he, De Graaff, know that the flag flown by the ship was the American flag? The English would have to show that it was already known in November 1776 that Congress's ships "flew a flag with thirteen *Stripes*, and that the undersigned at that time already had knowledge of it." And when it came to insults, the English repeatedly addressed him as *Mijnheer* De Graaff, "knowing full well that in the English language this was a common way of mocking and deriding the Dutch Nation."

But De Graaff's arguments were to no avail. English indignation carried the matter to the very highest level. The government in London drew up an acrimonious memoir demanding disavowal of the salute and De Graaff's recall. It closed with a threat of other measures if no satisfaction were given. Ambassador Yorke acquitted himself of the task of presenting this memoir with more than his usual acerbity, and he was no less insolent in his speech than his government in its note. The agitation within the leading circles at The Hague on that day of 21 February 1777 was no less either. "The fulminating style of this piece, coupled with their threats of little less than the worst, have aroused a very great sensation here," the grand pensionary Van Bleiswijk wrote to Van Welderen. The duke of

Brunswick was furious, calling the memoir "the most insolent and improper piece that I have ever seen sent from one sovereign to another." It displayed "a sovereign scorn" for the Republic, and such intimidation should not be accepted. Proof would have to be put on the table first. In general there was agreement with the duke. Indignation rose high, and demands were made for manly firmness, as Brunswick called it. But for the moment, it was easier to say than to be. The pensionary of Dordrecht, G. Boschaert, wrote sensibly to his cousin Van Bleiswijk: "The language of the Memoir is surely not easy to swallow, but *vana sine viribus ira* [wrath without power is in vain], and so we'll be compelled to come down a peg or two."

Now that the country was in trouble, its ears tweaked by the mighty neighbor like a mischievous street urchin, there was realization of how much was lacking. To gain time was probably best, "while in the meantime we arm at sea as much as possible and prepare to resist a first blow," as Van Bleiswijk wrote.[8] But the insolent tone of the English declaration was actually an advantage, for it gave the Dutch government a chance to take cover behind its indignation. In its reply the States General complained vigorously about the insinuations and the "threatening tone of the memoir, at such far variance with what is required between sovereign and independent powers." It was decided to send for the governor of St. Eustatius, but only to examine him and give him a chance to defend himself. This was an excellent way out of a ticklish position, and for the time being the English government had to be satisfied with it.

So did De Graaff, who was making difficulties. He felt quite safe in his smugglers' nest, but feared a trap in the mother country. It is still amusing to read how he tried to wriggle out of having to make this "fatiguing Voyage in an advanced Season of the Year." He would not survive a winter in Holland, for he was "of a very weak constitution and had never enjoyed full health after an attack of the pox a Year ago. Furthermore, the Petitioner has a natural fear and aversion for the sea. And is subject to sea sickness to an amazing degree," so that for the whole voyage he would not be able to hold his head up to eat and drink. But this jeremiad did not succeed, and back home he had to go. But not quickly, for he did not arrive in Holland until July 1778. The investigation was placed in the hands of the West India Company—in itself a highly significant decision—and two of its administrators, J. B. Bicker and P. Warind, placed the accusations before De Graaff. There were three: the smuggling traffic, the taking of the English ship by the American privateer, and the salute to the American flag.

De Graaff went to work and produced a defense, the so-called *Deduction*, which ran to no less than 202 pages, plus more than 700 pages of appendixes as supporting evidence. It was mostly the same material that he had already sent. He knew nothing of any smuggling, he said, the ship seizure had taken place at some distance from the coast, and the salute was customary for all merchant ships and did not imply any recognition. The West India Company's administrators were convinced of his "innocent and proper conduct," and the government agreed. De Graaff was found completely innocent, and he was allowed to return to his island.[9]

There has been a long debate about whether the salute given on 16 November 1776 was in fact the first given to the American flag. In fact, an American schooner had been saluted by a Danish ship a few weeks earlier. But in this case it was a privateer that was involved, a ship armed with letters of marque from the American Congress. A greeting was given to its flag, though not the Stars and Stripes, for it did not exist at that time. Nor was it the Great Union Flag, with thirteen stripes and in the upper right corner the Union Jack, as is maintained by Hartog. All descriptions agree that it was a flag with just the thirteen stripes, red and white, and this corresponds with other data. Such a flag was in fact flown by American ships at the beginning of the Revolution. It was a new flag, although we do not have to believe that De Graaff did not know where it came from. In the years that followed there was much ado about the salute, and in 1939 President Roosevelt came to the island's harbor and offered a commemorative plaque that was unveiled later the same year. For the Americans as well as for the Eustatians, this first greeting, whatever its real worth, has had lasting importance. "American and Statian, both praise for it our Lord," gives the island's official anthem.[10]

In any case, with De Graaff's return everything again ran smoothly for a while. Smuggling went on indefatigably, and the English did their best to set limits on it. They halted the Dutch ships, confiscated forbidden wares, such as gunpowder, and sent off protests now and again. But the traffic did not cease. The Dutch authorities took action when the smuggling became too flagrant, but it was repression in moderation.

In the spring of 1777 (De Graaff had not yet left for Holland) strong proofs of Van Bibber's activity came into English hands when the captain of an American privateer, one George Rall, gave away the show by admitting that "the congress agent at St. Eustatia [Van Bibber] put several men on board his Schooner from other American vessels then lying in St. Eustatia-Road, and sent him out to sea, after a sloop belonging to the Island of Antigua loaden with cotton that had just left St. Eustatia, and says this matter was done publicly and in no wise hindered or forbid by the Government of St. Eustatia." Within three hours Rall was able to take the sloop.

The true situation on the island was undoubtedly depicted in this testimony, but its revelation made the situation untenable. De Graaff had to establish an inquiry. Van Bibber was summoned, but admitted nothing: he had warned Rall to be careful, had not given him any men, and had told him to take his prizes to Martinique. This was not at all clear proof, but De Graaff could not avoid putting the merchant under arrest. It was not very strict detention, for Van Bibber soon escaped and vanished.

Slowly but surely the smuggling through St. Eustatius grew into a *casus belli*: It became impossible for the British government to tolerate any longer this immense flow of supplies to the American rebels. Public opinion, if we may believe the English political cartoons of these years, turned steadily against the Dutch. The Dutchman was shown in many of these pictures as greedy, boorish, and untrustworthy. To make money was his sole aim, and to do so he calmly broke every treaty. It was better to have Holland as an enemy than to continue to suffer such neutrality.

Finally, if we may anticipate the progress of our tale, the chance came. At the end of 1780 England declared war upon the Republic. Even before then, Yorke had suggested to his government an attack upon St. Eustatius. Orders for the attack went out promptly on 20 December to Admiral George Rodney, the commander of the English fleet, a man of audacious character, who declared: "My one aim has always been and ever shall be to act offensively." He received his orders in the roadstead of Barbados on 27 January 1781. Six days later he appeared before St. Eustatius. "The Surprise and Astonishment of the Governor and Inhabitants of St. Eustatius is scarce to be conceived," the admiral reported with satisfaction. His superiority was so great that no resistance was offered. The booty was colossal. A convoy of twenty-three ships that had just sailed for Holland was overhauled, and the English let the Dutch flag flutter for some time, so that a good number of unsuspecting ships were also snapped up.

And so this smugglers' den, this "asylum for men guilty of every crime and a receptacle for the outrages of every nation," as Rodney called it, was swept away. The English acted with a harsh hand. There were widespread seizures and confiscations and such violence that Rodney found himself in great difficulties as a result. For there were still a good number of English merchants on the island, and they were not long in demanding compensation for their losses. They spoiled the sea hero's life, and for years he had to defend himself; he did not relent in his own accusation that these English merchants were nothing but cowardly traitors to their fatherland who had forfeited the protection of their own government. They had to be held up as examples to posterity, "so that people who betray their country for money run the chance of failing as they deserve if Providence so wills it and the just revenge of their country reaches them."[11]

The shock of St. Eustatius's fall was also intense in the Netherlands. John Adams gave a report of the reaction in a letter to Livingston, the American minister of foreign affairs: "You can have no idea, Sir, no man, who was not upon the spot, can have any idea, of the gloom and terror that was spread by this event." In England there was jubilation over the great victory and the sweet vengeance. It is true that the joy was not long lasting, for on the return voyage much of the booty was captured by a French fleet, and the island too was retaken by a French squadron in November 1781. It was probably also true, as Jameson has commented, very much to the point, that the presence of Rodney's fleet at St. Eustatius enabled the French fleet under De Grasse to sail into Virginia, where it helped bring about Cornwallis's capitulation at Yorktown. But the island's prosperity was shattered, and it would never be restored.

The role of St. Eustatius was at an end, but it had been a great role, decisive for the American Revolution. That, at least, was Rodney's own conclusion when he wrote to the lords of the Admiralty at Greenwich four days after its fall: "I hope this island will never be returned to the Dutch; it has been more detrimental to England than all the forces of her enemies, and alone has contributed to the continuance of the American war."[12]

CHAPTER 3

Dumas

Americanus sum nec quidquam
Americani a me alienum puto
DUMAS

RUDITE friends whom I told that I was working on Dumas asked, "*Père ou fils?*" and I was tempted to reply irreverently, "*Saint Esprit.*" For the man whom I was studying—let me state my conclusion at the very beginning—is the rare example of a pure "enthusiast." Utterly enraptured by America, he set to work for the cause of America; for more than twenty years he was indomitable, grudging nothing, steadfast in his faith even when he fell into the worst difficulties, even when he got small thanks for his efforts. He has never received the honor that is his due, either during his lifetime or in the pages of history. Samuel F. Bemis, in his *Diplomacy of the American Revolution*, observes that the United States owes to Charles Dumas "a debt of gratitude never adequately recognized." There is one outdated French book about him and one American article, whose author is not familiar with the sources, and that is about all.

The problem is twofold: on the one hand, the sources are quite abundant; on the other, we do not know much about Dumas himself. In the National Archives in The Hague we have his great letterbook, eleven hundred pages full of draft letters to all his French and, even more, American connections: Franklin, Jefferson, Adams, and so forth. (Many of these letters are reprinted in the various editions of the diplomatic correspondence of the American revolutionaries by Jared Sparks and Francis Wharton). They give us a very good picture of the activities of our hero, but not enough for us to know much about the man himself. He was all ardor and wore his heart on his sleeve, but he tells us little about his own background, and it is difficult to find out more about him.

We have to understand him through his letters, and we happily also can look at a portrait, a typical late-eighteenth-century pastel, which tells us quite a lot about him. Perhaps that is only my biased impression. After having read hundreds and hundreds of his letters, it was for me like a shock of recognition to see his face in the portrait, only recently rediscovered, that is in the possession of one of his descendants. He was as I expected him to be. He has big eyes and a willful mouth in a fine, alert face; we observe a nervous self-consciousness and a certain melancholy dignity. A scholar and a dreamer more than a man of action.

What we know of his background and early life comes down to this: Charles Guillaume Frédéric Dumas was born on 15 February 1721 in the little town of Kloster Heilbron in the German principality of Ansbach, where his French parents had come as émigrés. He spent many years in Switzerland and probably came to the Netherlands about 1750. There he chose the life of an ordinary scholar of the eighteenth century who had to earn his keep by his pen. He did translations right and left. After his marriage to a widow in The Hague, Maria Loder née Garnier, he was compelled to take the post of governor of a pair of wealthy youths in 1763. His wife had two sons from her first marriage and two daughters with Dumas: Anna Jacoba, born in 1766, and Elisabeth Wilhelmina, who was born in 1768 and died in 1770. The father poured all of his wild dreams upon his surviving daughter, and the down-to-earth mother must have looked on with worry, for Dumas was a prize fool who easily lost his grip on reality.[1]

Books were his life, and there is no question that he possessed at least an average knowledge of antiquity and whatever else an educated man was supposed to know. His books are filled with citations from the classics, and he took up the challenge of translating Pliny into French. He made a deep impression upon John Adams, who had a true Puritan's respect for learning. In a letter to the historian Mercy Warren, Adams described Dumas as "so much a man of letters, that he was one of the most accomplished classical scholars that I have been acquainted with and [he] had taken as general a survey of ancient and modern science as most of the professors of the universities of Europe and America."[2]

He was almost fifty years of age when he became an enthusiast for America and all things American, perhaps the first such in the Netherlands. This is what brought him into contact with Benjamin Franklin. He probably met him in 1766 when Franklin came to Holland, and he certainly wrote him a letter (unfortunately now lost) asking for his opinion about a plan to emigrate to Florida. We do not know where he got this wild idea, but Franklin (in a letter that has been preserved) strongly advised against it, and suggested that if he was not satisfied with his situation in Holland he should go to New York, New Jersey, or Pennsylvania, where many German and Dutch people lived. The correspondence (in French) with the American philosopher, who was the agent of Pennsylvania and other American colonies in London during these years, continued. There is another letter in which Dumas, in 1771, reported that he had two young patrician sons in his home in Amsterdam and that he was engaged in translating into French a long book in English by Adam Anderson about the history of commerce.

A later letter to Franklin, undated but probably of 1774, accompanied a large shipment of books, including several by "my intimate friend" the philosopher Franciscus Hemsterhuis. He also confessed to his faith in the future of America; he told one and all that the valiant Americans would be victorious and would create "a system of nations" that would be "as brilliant as ancient Greece or modern Europe." It is fascinating to see Dumas's early enthusiasm for the American cause, which came several years before the Revolution actually broke out. It was certainly fed by the contact with Franklin, who also sent him newspapers, as appears from one letter. Dumas was an avid reader, a dreamer full of yearning, and a hard worker. Among the books that he translated there is at least one American work, a report of the expedition of Colonel Bouquet against the Indians along the Ohio River, and he sent Franklin a copy of the translation. He must therefore have obtained some knowledge, however vague, of the New World. In 1775 he sent his American friend another book, an edition which he had prepared of Emerich de Vattel's celebrated book on the law of nations. Dumas admired Vattel's emphasis on the rights of neutral countries, which agreed so well with his own ideas of the role that the Dutch Republic could play in an eventual conflict between France and England in spite of its ancient treaties with the British. In his introduction he again expressed his great admiration for the Americans, "brave colonials" who raised against oppression the voice of true freedom. And in another long accompanying letter he proclaimed that all honest hearts in Europe beat for the American cause. "The general shout is that your cause is that of nature and the human race."[3]

About a month later another long letter followed, again with several copies of Vattel and a few other books. He would send two others later, one about the spreading of oil on water, which he had translated into French, the other about the events in America since 1763, a provisional little work and not from his hand but which he had recommended for publication. When the war was over—he had just received news that it had begun!—a Tacitus would certainly arise to place its true value upon this notable piece of history.

In Dumas's letters we can follow how his enthusiasm grew word by word until he no longer quite knew what he was saying. Take this passage, a splendid example of America-love and even more of America-romanticism. What a spectacle, he wrote, "a fine field for a great genius! Vice at grips with virtue! The twilight of a total revolution in the world! Seven or eight new States called by Providence to retrace for us the great ages of Ancient Greece! Eternal monuments of Admiration and gratitude to be erected to the noble defenders of Liberty and the fatherland who have been devoured by the parricide sword, for whom the splendid Epitaph of the Spartans slain at Thermopylae is so fitting: *Passer-by, go announce to Lacedemonia that we died in obedience to her Laws.*" Can we imagine a finer mingling of romanticism and classicism, of posturing and enthusiasm? Such great enthusiasm could not long remain without striking a responsive chord.

Having returned to his homeland in 1774 to become one of the most important men in Congress, Franklin was named at the end of November 1775 as one of the members of the newly formed Committee of Secret Correspondence, the first body with the task of maintaining the rebels' contacts abroad. He now remembered his enthusiastic correspondent in Holland, and he wrote him a detailed letter in reply, first thanking him for the books he had sent and then coming out with a question of importance: Congress had instructed him to ask Dumas to become the American agent in the Dutch Republic. The Hague continued to be a center of diplomacy, he wrote, and Dumas should put out feelers to the envoys of the different courts as to their ideas about an eventual alliance with America. To establish his credibility, Dumas should make use of this letter from Franklin as a letter of credence, but very prudently, so that the English ambassador would not notice anything. Franklin went on to boast about the true unity of the colonies against England and finally wrote an urgent request for arms and ammunition and, not to be forgotten, several good engineers who understood siegecraft, fortifications, and the like. Expenses would be met, and meanwhile a check for one hundred pounds was enclosed. Finally, he told Dumas that he should establish contact with Arthur Lee, the American agent in England, and that it would be best to send his letters to Congress by way of Robert and Cornelius Stevenson, merchants on St. Eustatius.[4]

And so it came about! The reader must picture the situation for himself: Dumas, a simple pen pusher and schoolmaster, with a heart much too large and a head much too hot for his paltry position, is suddenly invited to be the representative of his dream, the dream of mankind. His reply was all jubilation and awe: "I am deeply impressed by the honor fallen to me. . . . I shall die in bliss now that I may devote the rest of my life to such a glorious and just cause. I therefore accept with joy the task given to me, and I promise to dedicate myself to it with cordial good will and indefatigable zeal!"

He began his duties with youthful impetuosity. One of the first things he did was to work out a secret code with numbers that corresponded to a particular passage in his edition of Vattel. Secrecy was one of the first necessities. The question is whether Dumas really had the capacity to play a secret role. Everything about him was on the surface, passionately straightforward. As he himself wrote, he argued with one and all in the coffeehouses. He was much too conspicuous to stay in concealment for long. In September 1776, four months after Dumas had accepted the role of agent, Yorke knew about it and informed London.[5]

Dumas was not really up to diminishing his own role by remaining in effective secrecy. On the one hand, he burned with longing to play a great part in the service of the America he admired; on the other, he sometimes took fright at himself, a man too small for his own ambition. We find this duality in the few descriptions that we have of him. Sometimes he is portrayed as a "busy-body," a noisy fool; at other times he is shown as a fearful fellow anxiously looking up to his betters, Franklin principally, but no less the French ambassador.

These two sides constantly reappear in him. We have already seen that Sayre called him a wretched little shoemaker in his letter to Van der Capellen. Yorke described him as "the agent and gobetween" for the French ambassador and the Amsterdammers. In his history of the late events in Holland, published in 1788, Harris does not mention Dumas by name, but gives a description of him when he enumerates the French agents from the highly placed gentlemen "down to the editor of the Leyden Gazette [Johan Luzac, whom we are still to meet] and that wretch so well known at The Hague by the appellation of Don Quixote and so remarkable for his noisy contests in coffeehouses with those whom he thought were attached to the British interest, particularly with Pinto, the Jew pensioner of England." This picture of Dumas in action is unfriendly, to be sure, but it is probably true; it closely corresponds to the almost equally harsh description in the memoirs of John Paul Jones: "This gentleman [Dumas] is a most amusing specimen of the diplomatist in the small way, busy and bustling about nothing, shrouding every trifle in mystery; one who writes about 'the great man' and hints darkly at 'the certain friend in high station', and intimates dark meanings through which every body could see in any way save simply and directly." Others were annoyed by his fearfulness; Silas Deane, the first American agent in Paris, found him much too timid, and Arthur Lee, in his characteristically merciless way, dispatches him as "entirely his [Franklin's] creature and an old woman."

But there were milder voices as well. Van der Capellen, who was a bit jealous of him, nonetheless wrote of him as "the old, loyal servant Mr. Dumas." John Adams, who so admired him as a scholar, was impressed by Dumas's tireless dedication as soon as he arrived in Holland, and he continued to value him as an excellent servant of the United States. Jefferson, who was involved with him a few years later, was satisfied too. And even Vergennes, the mighty French minister, in the end entered the lists for him and argued for better pay for a man "known advantageously to General Washington and Mr. Franklin." His foes agreed; by their statement too Dumas was the friend of the Founding Fathers.[6]

· II ·

What did he himself say? When a man gives so much of himself in his letters, we must not listen only to others. In the hundreds of letters that he wrote, we may learn to know him at least as well. Although he seldom talked about his past and put on an air of mystery, he was still fully present in his correspondence, in his almost fanatical convictions, his swift surges of emotion, and his paranoid proclivity to martyrdom. He knew what he wanted and was ready to do anything to get it, but he felt himself under constant threat and sometimes felt totally defeated.

We have, I think, a fascinating example in Dumas of the eighteenth-century man living on the boundary between the Enlightenment and Romanticism. He believed in humanity and in its progress, but far away in the New World. America was his ideal; it was also an alibi for the dream that he could not make come true at home and could not give up. It was in America that he truly lived; it was his reality, however literary, even his religion. Here in The Hague, he wrote to Franklin and Deane, there is a little church of five members (he meant his family) which is distinguished not by its orthodoxy but by its feelings, its simplicity, and its innocence. It prays each day for the salvation of America. He was the precursor, he wrote in a number of letters, the John the Baptist in the wilderness who prepared the way. His messiah was the deeply venerated Benjamin Franklin. When he heard that Franklin was coming to Europe, he prayed that he would have a safe passage with a paraphrase of the second stanza of

Horace's ode on Virgil's sea voyage to Greece: "*Sic te ventorum regat pa-ter*: May the Father of Winds, confining all but the Zephyr, guide thee so, O ship, which owest to us Franklin entrusted to thee—guide thee so that thou shalt bring him safe to the shores of France, I pray to thee, and pre-serve the half of my own soul!" At the vaguest mention of the possibility that the great man himself might come to Holland, he described himself and his wife as Philemon and Baucis who want to entertain the gods. "When you come here," he wrote Franklin about a year later, "a nation of republicans will welcome you with shouts of joy. I know it, I weep as I write this." And a bit later he wrote: "I yearn for you as the Jews for the Messiah."

His ideas of America were one great idyll expressed in classical forms. To Congress he wrote that he called them what Cineas had called the Ro-man Senate, "an assembly of Kings." He exhorted his friend William Car-michael, who visited him at The Hague: Take me with you to Jersey or New York, to drive out the enemy, and then we will go to your estate in Maryland "with crowns of oak leaves to dance with the nymphs of the district around the huge tree that twelve men cannot put their arms around." He would later write to Carmichael again that he yearned for the delivery of America "like a pregnant woman"! He repeatedly asserted that he was an American. Finally, he found full-bodied expression for his feeling in the masterly aphorism of Terence, slightly adapted: *Ameri-canus sum, nec quidquam Americani a me alienum puto* (I am an Ameri-can, and nothing American can be foreign to me).[7]

Dumas was a true mythologist, but that does not mean that he knew nothing whatever about the reality of America. Although his notions were vague, he tried to keep learning. He eagerly read Thomas Paine's *Common Sense*, a copy of which Carmichael had brought with him. As appears from a letter to the French ambassador, he was well informed about American motives and about their theory that under the principle of *imperium mixtum*, on which the British Constitution was founded, Parliament had no right to manage their affairs. For his part he was will-ing to contribute to the Americans' education, proposing to send his friends three copies of the French *Encyclopédie*, for when Mars yielded the field, America would devote itself to art and science. But his knowl-edge of America was not authentic; it remained at best constitutional in-terpretation and idyllic glorification.

Yet Dumas had been the official agent of the Committee of Secret Cor-respondence, the representative of the new nation, since December 1775. He could not live by dreams alone. Practical action was required. The first step taken by our brand-new diplomat was a wholly practical one. He realized that he could not remain on his own but needed support. He gives his sensible reasons at the beginning of his letterbook: "Common sense told me that it was only France of all the Powers to which I should and could successfully make this opening." So he went to pay his respects at the French embassy. At that time—April 1776, just after Dumas had received his appointment—the embassy was under the direction of a chargé d'affaires, Abbé Desnoyers. Without too much embarrassment, but, on the contrary, conscious of representing the future, Dumas asked for an appointment. He wished to leave a letter for Vergennes on a subject of the highest importance, "that would change the face of Europe." Desnoyers was willing, providing that the letter was unsealed; he could not send it otherwise. When he saw his visitor hesitate, he spoke to him in a priestly tone: "Confide in me, my child. . . . I am a Priest and will receive what you tell me under the seal of confession." There followed a delightful and, for Dumas, characteristic exchange, for Dumas felt compelled to reply that he never went to confession. What was his religion then? asked the amazed priest. "I replied, 'My own'. 'But which is your own?' 'It is no one else's!' 'Are you a Jew?' 'I am honest.' 'A Quaker?' 'I belong to no sect.' 'What are you then?' 'A Christian.'"[8] Can there be a better example of eighteenth-century prejudice and broadmindedness? This was the beginning of Dumas's relations with the French embassy.

The consequences of this contact were to be greater than Dumas could anticipate. Practical as his step might have been, his connections with the French were of advantage to them as well as to the Americans. From the very beginning the French diplomats did their best to involve him in their own political plans, and it took quite some time before he realized that he was caught in a trap. The French ambassador who came to The Hague in the fall of 1776 became more his master than his colleague, and this false position would exact its price. But what could the poor dreamer attempt with an honest-to-goodness French duke? The full name of the new representative of Louis XVI was Paul-François de Quélen de Stuer de Caussade, duke of La Vauguyon. He was a young man without experience in diplomacy, but soon displayed his gift for it. It was not long before he established total domination over Dumas, who for his part allowed himself to be overwhelmed by this great lord's amiability toward him, and did not dare to make any move without him.

That was Dumas's problem. On the one hand, there was his belief in his mission, in the cause of humanity; on the other, he was, as we have said, too little a man for the great game in which he found himself. On the one side, he wished to remain out of the public eye; on the other, he wanted to play a great role. He was proud and fearful at the same time. He wanted everyone to pay attention to him and that caused him both to put on airs and to quake in his boots. He was at the playhouse in The Hague, as were the Prince and the Princess, he wrote Franklin, and they observed him closely. He got the feeling that the Orangists had it in for him especially, and he found an unforgettable image for his ambivalent situation: Among the birds that taunted him, he said, he felt like an owl in daylight. It was not only his imagination that made him speak in this way. When his activities became known, he found himself in real diffi- culties. In the summer of 1777 he was dismissed from his post as tutor, after being subjected to every kind of petty nagging. Sensitive as he was, he described the last months in the home of his pupils as a hell "governed by a fury," for it was their mother, recently widowed, who turned him out, disregarding, he claimed, the promises made by her husband. It meant a loss of five thousand guilders. He felt that there was a conspiracy, a "cabal," directed against him, and he wondered whether the stadholder was behind it.[9]

He described all these troubles at full length in his letters to his Ameri- can friends. It was for their cause that he suffered, and they had to help him. This brings us again to a melancholy aspect of his restless existence. He was put to use by the American government, but badly paid. Plead as he might in long entreaties, he did not receive even a small regular sal- ary until 1785. Before then he was dependent on occasional payments, which made his position almost hopeless, for he was a simple man with little to fall back on. His sacrifices demanded much, sometimes far too much, of his nervous constitution, and, alas, of his wife as well. His pleas went over the ocean with regularity. He was America's first diplomat, he pointed out; he had received a thousand guilders in 1777 through the banking firm of Grand in Paris. He could just make ends meet; *monsieur* Grand was surprised that he could get by with so little. Why, he asked, didn't they give him a regular appointment and a fixed salary? And so it went, year after year. In 1780 and 1781 he was at his neediest, and almost every one of his letters is full of his problems. But the reply that came back was always the same, that there was no money.[10]

The desperate Dumas tried to find a solution by swearing allegiance to the country that he served: "Charles William Frederick Dumas personally appeared before us and took the oath of Allegiance to the United States of America upon the holy Evangelists of Almighty God," reads the declaration signed by "John Adams, Minister Plenipotentiary from the United States, James Searle, Member of Congress for the Commonwealth of Pennsylvania, Amsterdam 16 Dec. 1780." Dumas believed he had really become an American. It was a fine gesture, on which Franklin sent him congratulations, but one that was in vain, for it did not make him legally a citizen of the United States. Just when need became greatest in those difficult years, however, rescue was near.[11] In the beginning of 1782, Dumas was able to take up residence in the American embassy in The Hague. His position was unclear, taking in everything from a chargé d'affaires to a concierge. But we shall have more to say about this later.

During all these years, Dumas was truly the dedicated servant of America. He was active in many fields. Some of the things he did strike us as fantastic; others would prove of great utility. He maintained good relations with the press and passed on news of every kind from America to important newspapers like the *Gazette de Leyde* and the *Courier du Bas-Rhin*. He formed big plans for trading in American products like tobacco and rice; he gave tips about English ships to American privateers; he drew up a complete plan for establishing relations between Prussia and the United States by opening up a trade route through Emden; he helped with the translation of pamphlets and became involved in a fierce debate with the extremely pro-English merchant Isaac de Pinto, who was said to be in the pay of the English government. He passed on a jest about himself, "a pleasantry" of a young man, that to silence Dumas one would have to pay him a pension, just as De Pinto was paid to get him to write.[12]

Does he have no right to recognition and gratitude, much more than he ever received? As he himself wrote in a very characteristic comparison: "At table the lion should give the mouse his share."[13]

CHAPTER 4

The Secret Treaty

Amsterdam maintained it made an
agreement in eventum.

G. J. VAN HARDENBROEK

O sooner had Dumas entered the service of the Americans as their agent than he realized that their historically appointed ally was France. He put several pertinent questions to the French chargé d'affaires: Would France mediate? And if that failed, would she come to America's support? Two weeks later he was able to report a reply. King Louis XVI could not intercede, because England would not accept it. Nor could France give help, at least not by joining in the fight. But she recognized the Americans as belligerents with the same right to protection and freedom as everyone else. Dumas persisted. He described the French position as that of a lion, secure to the east and north behind her "chain of fortresses from Basel to Dunkirk" and "showing her teeth," but vulnerable on her flank. There an alliance with America would create a good counterbalance to England.[1]

The French did not need Dumas's fervid recommendations to become interested in the American question. In the great game of political chess in which the revolution across the Atlantic was the first move, the positions of the powers, including the Dutch Republic, were redefined. In it, Dumas was no more than a pawn, but one important enough to keep under control. The new French ambassador, the duke of La Vauguyon, arrived in The Hague at the end of 1776 with a "diplomatic mentor" at his side, the chargé d'affaires, de Bérenger, who had served at quite a few embassies.

La Vauguyon would play a very important role in the Netherlands, so much so that Yorke once bitterly called him the country's true stadholder. From the beginning the French ambassador kept Dumas under strict control. He received him very soon, "most graciously," as Dumas wrote, but bluntly admonished him at the same time that his position was that of a "private person" with a special interest in America. The ambassador requested that he keep him posted about everything he heard from his American contacts, but added that he, La Vauguyon, was naturally not involved in the negotiations between France and America. Those would take place between Benjamin Franklin, when he was sent over, and the foreign minister, Vergennes. La Vauguyon finally asked Dumas to be "more circumspect." Our worthy admitted that he had written "more familiarly" to the ambassador's predecessor, who, at the agent's own request, purged from his dispatches to the French court whatever Dumas said that "went too far" because of his zeal. Dumas's effusions were indeed not quite the thing to go into diplomatic dispatches.[2]

Naturally, he was not able to stop writing, pleading, and insisting. Only a month later, in a long letter to La Vauguyon, he laid out how great would be the advantages for France in recognizing America. And he told his American friends in Paris, Deane and Carmichael, how he had ceaselessly plied the French ambassador (for whom he used the pseudonym of the Great Factor) with his news reports and his pleading. He harped on the danger of a reconciliation between England and the colonies. The Americans, who were very experienced in using this line of argument, especially Silas Deane, provided him with materials. A picture was conjured up for him by Deane of how England, having become friendly with Russia and reconciled with America, would be like a Colossus standing over the globe with one foot in the East and the other in the West, and the poor nations of Europe would then, to use Shakespeare's words, "creep about between its legs to find dishonorable graves." The English came forward with the opposite argument that if America became independent, it would become much too strong and would be a threat to European colonies elsewhere. What a specimen of false arguments! exclaimed the indignant Dumas.[3]

La Vauguyon was not much impressed by Dumas's arguments, but he did not neglect him as a result. The ambassador had his own plans for the American agent, particularly in order to stimulate contacts with the municipal authorities in Amsterdam. The merchants of the city followed the American struggle with close attention; they put great hopes on the new opportunities for trade with an independent America and hence feared lest it be reconciled with England.

In the summer of 1777 the French ambassador instructed Dumas to come to Amsterdam and present himself at the hotel Het Wapen van Amsterdam. Dumas was all joy: Despite the quibbling of his pupils' parents, he hurried one Saturday noon to Amsterdam, where he was received the following morning by La Vauguyon. The ambassador informed him in deep confidence that an alliance between England, Russia, and the Republic was being contrived—the English ambassador had already drawn up the draft of a treaty—and then sent him with this report to the city's pensionary, Engelbert François van Berckel. Dumas, as it happened, had traveled by canalboat shortly before in the company of the mighty man's wife, and this constituted an introduction of a sort. Van Berckel, whom Colenbrander characterizes as "a lawyer by character, doctrinaire, combative and high-handed," an "intriguer with an arrogant manner," proved to be all affability to the simple Dumas. When Dumas appealed to him for the friendship of Amsterdam for America and especially for its opposition to the treaty rumored to be in the making, the pensionary promised to do so, as Dumas wrote Franklin, "with an abundance of words worthy of a Batavian of yore." For the time being caution was necessary, Van Berckel told him, but still he was glad that there was an American agent in the country. It was a pleasant conversation that ended with a dinner and friendly toasts to Amsterdam, America, and other causes.[4]

Late in the year came the report of the great American victory at Saratoga. If we can believe Dumas, who gave the news to the newspapers, there was overwhelming enthusiasm. It was the talk of the day in all the coffeehouses, the *Haarlemse Courant* put out an extra edition, and Luzac in Leiden was unhappy that he had not been the first to publish the news. Van Berckel, with whom Dumas had become steadily more intimate, told him that the time had come for Holland to take advantage of the situation and to seek America's friendship. Dumas felt himself growing in his role, and his meetings with the Amsterdam pensionary became more frequent. He began to believe that he could get Holland to shift its position. But it was necessary to be patient, he wrote: the Dutch were like peat, slow to catch fire but long burning. He suggested to the American commissioners in Paris that they pay numerous compliments to Van Berckel, who was susceptible to flattery.[5]

About the turn of the year the Republic buzzed with rumors. A treaty between France and America was in the offing, with war between England and France the likely result. De Bérenger was angry because these rumors got into the newspapers, but Dumas calmed him down: to put out denials would only make the matter worse. Opinion in the Netherlands was meanwhile becoming steadily more favorable, Dumas maintained in his letters. There was talk even of loans and investments. Van Berckel was completely on America's side and had assured him that the grand pensionary too had come around and that even the stadholder was wavering.[6]

Then the news came of the French-American treaty of 6 February 1778, Franklin's crowning achievement. Actually there were two treaties: one of commerce and friendship, which followed almost word for word the model proposed by Congress in 1776, and a second of "contingent and defensive alliance." It was contingent because the French government not only recognized American independence but both parties were bound not to conclude any separate peace in the event of England's declaring war or before England acknowledged American independence. It was undoubtedly a major success, but not as great as many thought at the time in their enthusiasm and as later historians have often made it appear. Vergennes was not as generous as he looked, for he had only French and not American interests in mind. A guarantee of the independence of the United States remained vague as long as it was not clear what the boundaries of the new nation were. The French desire to bring Spain into the war against England meant that there was not much support in Paris for setting the western boundary of the new union at the Mississippi. Spain had held the mouth of the mighty river and a part of its basin since 1763. There were also other possibilities for future friction, and Vergennes continued to be extremely cautious.

At any rate, neither France nor England—which was officially informed of the treaties in March—felt at all eager to appear the aggressor. If France began the war, England would be in a position to call upon the Republic under the old treaties, which would put the delivery of masts and other material for the French fleet by the Dutch in total jeopardy. The French-American rapprochement, however, did not lead to an immediate French-English collision—that was still months away.

Dumas, though, was not one to look closely at the dark side of events. He saw the great light on the horizon; he was beside himself with joy; he saw the dawning of mankind's fraternity. De Bérenger (La Vauguyon was at the moment in Paris) had shaken his hand warmly and said they were brothers now. Dumas in his report added words of thanks and praise to the great architect of the universe. The Frenchman also told him a charming anecdote. A few days before he had been at a reception at the home of the English ambassador, who haughtily said to him, "You are raping my daughter!" De Bérenger had replied, "She is emancipated, Frenchmen do only what the ladies like." Yorke went on grumbling, "You are not satisfied to kidnap my daughter, you are making a wh—— of her by prostituting her to the whole world."[7]

France gave the Netherlands official notice of the treaty on 12 March. Thought had been given in Paris to seeking support of other powers before taking the big step, and The Hague too had been sounded out in December. But on further consideration the French government decided that it would be better to keep the Republic neutral in view of her position as the supplier of timber and other ships' needs. It is possible to see in this shift of French foreign policy an explanation of the subsequent strange behavior of La Vauguyon. It seems equally plausible, however, to seek behind it a difference of opinion between La Vauguyon and his master, Minister Vergennes. Be that as it may, French policy in the spring of 1778 gives an impression of clumsiness, of which Dumas became the victim.

At first he lived as though on wings. At the end of March, La Vauguyon returned to Holland, and Dumas had an interview with him at once. Events had come to a head, he thought. Now he could take the part of "Saint John the Baptist" and prepare the way. The Republic, he wrote to the American envoys in Paris, was wavering. It could go in any direction. Everyone was hungry for the American trade, but the old treaties with England got in the way. As soon as they succeeded in a rapprochement, Franklin had to come to the Netherlands to "strike the great blow." La Vauguyon urged him on, advised him to press Franklin and his fellow envoys to present an official proposal to Their High Mightinesses the States General for a treaty on the French model. At the same time, in order to keep the affair warm, a memorandum by Arthur Lee was placed in the Dutch newspapers through Dumas's intervention. In it the idea was drummed into the Dutch that they, as merchants par excellence, had a greater interest in American freedom than anyone else. It would put an end to the hated Navigation Act, and it would achieve at last what even the great abilities of Jan de Witt had not been able to bring about, *Mare Liberum*, the Free Sea.[8]

But it all came to nothing. To be sure, the Amsterdam merchants warmed to such arguments, and they were excited by the French example. "It would not surprise me," wrote the pensionary of Dordrecht to the grand pensionary Van Bleiswijk, "if Amsterdam now also pressed for following France's example," and he warned of the need for caution. But the grand pensionary was already half won for the proposal, as Dumas had just been informed by Van Berckel.

Dumas himself was in great excitement. Finally the time had come, and he could take the first big step. In the middle of April the letter arrived from the Americans in Paris informing him of the treaty and promising to transmit its text without delay. They also urged the Dutch government to make an alliance with the United States. Guided by La Vauguyon and in close contact with Van Berckel, Dumas expected everything to work out when the request was presented. He believed he had assurances that Van Bleiswijk would not keep it to himself but would have to turn it over to the members of the States. He would drop hints that Amsterdam was in the know about everything. If he could not take the place by storm, he wrote excitedly, he would still compel it to capitulate.[9]

But the whole situation changed all at once a few days later. La Vauguyon suddenly did an about-face. He summoned the stunned Dumas and showed him a letter from Vergennes informing the ambassador that to submit the American demarche would be moving too fast. It is hard to say whether the French government was afraid that Dutch neutrality would be imperiled or if Vergennes had still other motives, but in any event poor Dumas fell into great perplexity. He argued that it was all wrong and that he himself would lose all credibility after what had been agreed upon, especially with the Amsterdammers. La Vauguyon assured him that he would tell Van Berckel that Dumas had nothing to do with it, that he himself was at fault. But it was soon apparent nonetheless that Dumas's position with the Amsterdam magistrates was badly damaged. Nor could La Vauguyon take back everything that had happened, and his excuse to Vergennes was that Dumas had pressed for the demarche. Dumas now had to present the proposal on his own, as a private person. La Vauguyon stipulated that France was not involved in any way; the king was indeed favorable to a rapprochement between Holland and the United States, but most of all he wanted calm in the Republic. The entire proposal therefore became, as Thulemeyer wrote home, "a private matter put forward by a man who has been sojourning for some time at The Hague in the hope of being admitted and accredited some day on the part of the United States."

Dumas kept up his courage. He went to Van Bleiswijk, showed him the letter, and told him that Amsterdam was already informed. The grand pensionary was curt, but the next day Dumas heard from Van Berckel, who had sounded out the reaction of the authorities in The Hague, that Van Bleiswijk had been delighted with the document and would distribute it to the towns of Holland not officially but secretly, in order to avoid English chicanery. Dumas asked if he had also given it to the Prince and the duke of Brunswick, but Van Berckel did not know and had not wanted to ask.

The position of the Dutch government was, as always, ambivalent and it would remain such for a long time. On the one side, there was the pressure of the covetous Amsterdam merchants, who indulged in the most unrealistic dreams about trade with the New World; on the other, the fear of the English ally felt by the government in The Hague.[10] The grand pensionary, who acted as a kind of foreign minister, consulted the Prince of Orange, who at once balked and would not give any consideration to the idea. He told the duke of Brunswick, "with much passion," that it was Van Bleiswijk's belief "that the State ought to recognize the Americans as an independent State and that very sharp arguments on this point took place between His Highness and the Grand Pensionary." The Prince became so worked up that he declared he would lay down the stadholdership and quit the country together with his entire family rather than accept anything of the kind.

Brunswick could scarcely get William to calm down. When he attempted to defend Van Bleiswijk, the Prince gave him to understand "that he suspected him too of being for the Americans and favoring the French party." At last William's wrath cooled down, and he permitted himself to be persuaded to approve secret distribution of the American proposal. He thereupon fell into difficulties with the English ambassador, who learned soon enough what was going on and reproached him for not speaking of it first to the English ally. William defended himself, saying that it was a secret document of state that he was not obliged to show to anyone whomever. But Yorke would have none of that, for a letter by "three wretches" (the American envoys in Paris, Franklin, Lee, and Adams), rebels against their king, could not be a state secret.[11]

Sometimes there seems to be a certain similarity, amid all the differences, between the Prince and Dumas, although each would have shuddered at the comparison. Both had a talent for giving themselves away too hastily, for taking positions that got them into trouble; both were really unfit for the game of politics. But be that as it may, nothing came of the proposed treaty, not only because the stadholder was opposed to it but also because, as the grand pensionary said correctly, the Republic was not yet ready for it. It seems improbable that the other provinces would have followed Holland or even Holland Amsterdam in a policy of such grave political consequences for the country's relations with England. Van Bleiswijk was caught between two fires, as Van Berckel made clear to Dumas. The grand pensionary was for America only because he was even more afraid of Amsterdam than of the Prince's court, and what he himself wanted was uncertain. In any case, Van Bleiswijk could for the time being take cover behind the fact that the treaty had not been received with the letter. That gave La Vauguyon the chance to put on the brakes even harder. When the text of the treaty arrived, he did permit Dumas to take it to the grand pensionary, but he had to bring it back at once and not leave it in Van Bleiswijk's hands. Poor Dumas could not do anything but obey, and the second meeting between him and Van Bleiswijk became a farce. "You can at least leave it with me, can't you?" asked the grand pensionary. But the agent had to stand absolutely firm, and Van Bleiswijk did not insist. He glanced at the document and quickly concluded it was a quite ordinary treaty of amity and commerce. He inquired whether there were any secret clauses, but Dumas had to admit that he did not know. A few civilities followed, Van Bleiswijk spoke of his respect for Franklin and his sympathy for the Americans, and then his visitor departed.[12]

Nothing more happened. The spring of 1778, which had begun so full of hope, passed without anything being achieved. In the meantime the rumors grew that the British peace mission to the rebels would succeed. Uneasiness and uncertainty resulted, especially in Amsterdam, where there was concern lest England recognize American independence in exchange for an exclusive right of trade. The city fathers trembled at the thought. Burgomaster Egbert de Vrij Temminck let the Prince know clearly how worried they were by the possibility that the English would recognize American independence and regain exclusive trade with the Americans. Dutch trade would take a hard blow. The Amsterdam burgomaster did not understand what independence without free trade meant.[13]

· II ·

Amsterdam is not the Netherlands, as London is not England and New York is not America. This aphorism is true today, but it was even more true in the days of the Republic. The interests of town and countryside did not coincide, and much strife resulted. It is Amsterdam's glory and honor, writes the city's foremost historian, that as a rule she has had to help herself. There was a great to-do about this honor and glory in the years that interest us. Then, as earlier in their history, the Amsterdammers, finding that they could not get their own way at the national level, decided to act on their own.[14]

There was great disappointment at the failure to obtain an American treaty. It became worse when Dumas sent the magistrates a copy of the French treaty, so that they could read with their own eyes the chance they had missed. Amsterdam's pensionary, Van Berckel, probably the most powerful man among the magistrates, did not let things go unchallenged. That was not his way, both friend and foe were sure. We may quote one of the latter, the stadholder. The Prince told Van Hardenbroek that Van Berckel "was a scoundrel who was in league with the French ambassador and assuredly engaged in correspondence to thwart what was happening. The Amsterdammers, when one spoke to them separately, each admitted that he, Van Berckel, was too hot-tempered, that no one dared to contradict him, and that he drove through everything that he wanted according to his own feelings. He was a high-handed man and he, the Prince, had always seen and experienced that high-handed men got their way." [15]

This happened this time too, we could say, but with the difference that the pensionary did not act high-handedly but arranged everything behind the scenes. The one-sided portrait that the Prince gives of Van Berckel is not fair to him; he championed the interests of his city and her trade, and that was his job. He was driven by a dream and a fear about America that, in hindsight, we must at the least characterize as exaggerated, and he made some mistakes. But could he follow any other policy than that which he did, a policy that was Amsterdam's to the bone?

Be that as it may, he went his own way. He succeeded in establishing a secret contact with an American agent in Germany, William Lee. A brother of the Arthur Lee accredited as an agent in Paris and, like him, a restless and self-willed man, William had been appointed "commercial agent" in Vienna and Berlin in 1777 and soon thereafter also "commissioner." But he was not able to achieve anything in Germany and hence used even more fully his opportunity to score a small success in the Netherlands. If we are to believe Dumas, Van Berckel had not yet noticed that this was a different Lee than the one in Paris and took advantage of the "accidental" contact with him to reach further agreements. By accident, as it was claimed, an Amsterdam merchant, Jean de Neufville, made the acquaintance of Lee in Frankfurt. De Neufville was another odd personage, a banker with a reputation less than the best who dreamed of becoming the financial commissioner of the United States in the Dutch Republic. After their first meeting in Frankfurt, De Neufville and Lee had another meeting at Aachen at which they came to a more definitive agreement and drew up the draft of a treaty.

This secret document is probably the most irregular treaty in the whole history of the Netherlands. It was concluded by two men, neither of whom had the right to do so, in the name of two parties, one of which was a state only coming into being and still with virtually no international recognition, the other a city without juridical status among the nations. The major excuse that was always given afterwards was that nothing but a preliminary accord was ever involved, which only anticipated the time when America would really become independent. Its formal title was "A Preparatory Plan of a Treaty of Commerce of the Seven Provinces of Holland and the Thirteen United States of North America, to be Put on the Table of their High Mightinesses in the event that England should recognize them as Free Nations"! It was only a draft, that is all, but still worked out in almost every detail after the model of the French-American treaty of February, with all the clauses and provisions usual in such a document.[16]

It is also a strange fact that Dumas was not informed from the very beginning. Van Berckel may have wished to keep him out because, after what had happened that spring, he still felt that Dumas carried too little weight, or that he was too much under the control of the French ambassador. After the draft treaty was concluded, Van Berckel did inform Dumas of what had been done, and Dumas blamed this disparagement on William Lee, who he thought wished to undermine his position. He was very upset because a promise had been made to him that all American relations in Holland would go through his hands.[17] Nonetheless, the motives of Amsterdam in this queer bit of history are easy enough to explain. The merchant lords who governed the city were deathly afraid that they would miss out on the trade with America from which they promised themselves such mountains of gold. This was how Van Berckel defended his action; he understood clearly that Their High Mightinesses could not do anything and therefore there remained "no other means, as he thought, to restrain Congress from making engagements disadvantageous to this State and to prepare for surprises by the English, than by providing Congress with an authentic proof of the sentiments of the Burgomasters of the City of Amsterdam." It was necessary to be ready for the eventuality of the independence of the United States.[18]

But it was just this emphasis upon eventuality, this use of the phrase "in the event that," which naturally did not sit at all well with the American agents in Paris. Franklin was scandalized, but Dumas laid out for him how things really were in the Netherlands. He himself kept on the go, and he was not too downcast by the strange treatment he had experienced. In October he paid another visit to the grand pensionary Van Bleiswijk with a printed copy of the French-American treaty and an accompanying letter from Franklin with a quite open threat. If the "Grand Pensionary" again failed to respond, "we shall naturally conclude that there is no disposition in their h.h.M.M. [High Mightinesses] to have any connexion *with the United States of Am.*; and, I believe, we shall give them no farther trouble." But that would be a pity, for "our Virgin State is a jolly one, and though at present not very rich, will in time be a great fortune to any suitor; and where she has a favourable disposition it seems to me to be well worth cultivating." Van Bleiswijk "read this missive attentively" and thanked him in friendly fashion, Dumas added.

The grand pensionary was indeed friendly but uncommitted. He sent the French-American treaty with the accompanying letter of the commissioners to the towns of Holland. The text of these documents was inserted in the Secret Resolutions of the States of Holland together with an explanatory note by Van Bleiswijk

> that on the last July 27 a copy of the aforementioned treaty was tendered to him, the grand pensionary, by a certain correspondent of the [American] gentlemen in this country: but with the added request to keep it under seal and provisionally not to use it. . . . That since the aforementioned missive and the information about the treaty had not been answered by him, the grand pensionary, it then had happened that the correspondent of the [American] gentlemen a few days ago, on the 22d of this month [October] had presented himself for the second time at his house, and had informed him, the grand pensionary, while offering him a printed copy of the aforementioned treaty, that since the treaty now had been printed in France, the reason of his earlier request [to keep it under seal] no longer existed.
>
> That at this opportunity it had become clear to him, the grand pensionary, that the aforementioned gentlemen were expecting an answer from him, and that they would deduce from his maintaining silence that there was no disposition in this state to have any connection with the United States of America.[19]

Once again nothing happened. The Americans' repeated request put the rulers of Holland in great perplexity. The Prince at once recommended that no reply be made before the States of Holland and its Secret Committee had been heard, but he himself saw what the dilemma was: "We cannot yet know which turn the affairs of America will take. It is probable but not yet certain that a portion of the colonies will become free and independent, but assuming that it turns out otherwise and that England again receives sovereignty over these same North American colonies, what would be the effect if they ever put their hands there on a copy of your missive to Mr. Franklin?" But, on the other hand, if the Americans become free, would it be good not to reply "and thereby to run the risk that they will wish to form no liaisons with the state?" But, since commercial interests know no gratitude, William reasoned, that would not be so bad. When it will be to the Americans' advantage to trade with us, they will surely do so, and when it will be to their advantage to destroy Dutch commerce "and to raise up their own on its ruins," they would do that too.

This letter to the grand pensionary is a fine example of how the stadholder's ability to see both sides of a question so very well made him indecisive. William also wrote to the Dutch ambassador in London that the Netherlands should not allow itself to be drawn in by Franklin's "insinuation," although there was a risk that, "against my expectations and the hopes of all right thinking men, America will become some day completely free and independent." Therefore nothing happened, for the other members of the government were hardly any more hopeful. Dutch national policy had fallen into the grip of a dilemma, and for the time being no one dared to make a decision. All that was done, in the time-tested fashion of administrators, was to push the question off into the future in the vague hope that somehow a solution would show up that they themselves had been unable to find. A "person of weight" brought a message to Dumas, and he asked him to forward to Franklin the message that *as yet* no reply could be made because of compelling secret reasons. Thus the effort was made to cover all sides.[20]

For a while the Dutch kept out of harm's way. For a year or even more it was possible to avoid commitment to either side. In this period of suspended decisions and fearful neutrality the industrious Dumas was able to put all his energy into promoting what he considered as his own great plan—the conclusion of a treaty between the Dutch Republic and the United States of America. If he could not achieve its actual conclusion, at least he would get such a treaty ready by preparing a precise and definitive text, so far as possible. He worked steadily at it, in constant consultations with the Americans in Paris and the Amsterdammers. The French treaty naturally served as a model to be adapted to Dutch circumstances. The Amsterdammers certainly also had at their disposal the draft treaty concocted at Aachen. But for the moment the rapprochement between the United States and the Dutch Republic that Dumas so fervently sighed for had reached an impasse. The poor American agent accomplished nothing, no matter how stubbornly he struggled on. In the spring of 1780, after consultation with Franklin, he sent Congress a definitive text of a draft treaty in triplicate with a request for comments and improvements. It was not his humble urgings, however, but the total change in the international situation in that year which brought the affair finally into rapid movement. By a quirk of events, the American treaty was an important catalyst, as it became the alibi needed by the British government in order to declare war upon the Netherlands. How that happened, how the secret became public, and why it had such large consequences are matters that we shall examine more closely in a later chapter.

CHAPTER 5

Here Comes Paul Jones!

Een geboren Amerikaan
Gansch geen Engelsch ventje. *
DUTCH FOLK SONG

URING the long war that broke out between France and England, the Dutch attempted to remain neutral with a scrupulosity that only well-understood self-interest could cause. Although King Louis XVI recognized the American rebels as early as February 1778 and concluded a treaty with them, it did not become a *casus belli* until the summer. Neither of the two parties wished to be branded an aggressor, and only a naval fight off Ushant set off war.

The Dutch Republic hoped to remain neutral in this conflict, as it had been able to do during the Seven Years' War, but it would require the utmost tact. Although England did not immediately demand Dutch assistance, as she was entitled to do under the treaty of 1678 if attacked, Dutch trade on the high seas was the subject of broils from the beginning.

France counted upon being supplied by Dutch merchant shipping, particularly with naval supplies, and England of course had to try to prevent it. But old treaties were involved, and the question of what was contraband arose again, as well as what the Dutch might and might not protect with her fleet. In the Netherlands a bitter quarrel arose over the question of convoys, setting the commercial towns, led by Amsterdam, against the Prince of Orange and his party. It became entwined with the interminable conflict over the expansion of the army or the navy, and England and France meddled in it in various ways. The quarrel lasted from the fall of 1778 until the end of 1780. It was finally decided to break the old agreements with England and to introduce unlimited convoying for Dutch shipping, including cargoes of contraband. The conflict over rearmament dominated Dutch politics for many years, but it has been fully described elsewhere and in any case it falls outside the specific scope of this book.

---

* A born American / Not at all an English bloke.

We need merely keep in mind that it is the essential background for everything that happened later.[1]

The key point is that the American revolt led to a European war which the Dutch could not keep out of, no matter how much they would have liked to. Usually they became involved in wars because they wanted to profit by the conflict, but in the case of John Paul Jones they were caught off balance and became entangled against their will in an affair that painfully revealed their perilous situation and put the Dutch dilemma in the sharpest light. It was thought at the time that the real reason why the renowned American privateer captain came to the Netherlands was to fan the flames of the party struggle, to win souls for the American cause, and to intensify polarization, as we would now call the division of minds.

John Paul Jones, the American pirate, patriot, and naval captain, arrived early in October at the Texel roadstead at the head of the Zuider Zee. A week before, on 25 September 1779, he had fought his greatest battle. After having sailed his squadron all around Scotland and England, he met two English warships and their convoy off the coast of Yorkshire, near Flamborough Head, and became locked in a heroic battle—heroic in truth, for the battle was so furious that Jones lost his flagship, the *Bonhomme Richard*, but gained the victory anyway, taking the English ship *Serapis* by boarding. He then set course with all his ships, now five in number, to Holland. It was a full week before he arrived, for his badly damaged vessels had a hard crossing of the North Sea.

Jones was a hero, a figure out of a romantic epic. From afar he was a legend; from closer up, he was a nuisance—egoistical, foolhardy, and unpredictable. John Adams, who met him in Paris, called him "the most ambitious and intriguing Officer in the American Navy" and gave a warning: "Excentricities [*sic*] and Irregularities are to be expected from him— they are in his character they are visible in his Eyes." Was it his irregularity, a wild whim, that made him decide to set his course for the Texel? Or was he driven by wind and currents, as he himself claimed at the time? We now know that it was neither, and that Jones was ordered to sail to Holland, but did so unwillingly. Indeed, he sulked as long as he was held at Texel by circumstances, but there was nothing he could do about it. "Speaking with him further, I was strengthened in my belief that before he fell in he had had correspondence here about it and that the sojourn of Mr. du Ma [Dumas!] here for some time was the cause of it," reported Vice-Admiral Pieter Hendrik Reynst to the Prince after he had negotiated with the American.[2]

Reynst had hit the target. Dumas was informed well before Jones's arrival at Texel. On 2 September he had already received instructions from the French naval official L. R. de Chaumont, who was responsible for fitting out Jones's expeditionary force, to go to Texel to give assistance to the American squadron and, if need be, to call in the help of De Neufville. On 20 September he informed the Americans in Paris that he would leave for Texel the following day to give instructions to Jones. He was two weeks too early therefore. While Dumas was gripped by excitement and joy, the rest of the country remained peacefully ignorant of what was about to happen. It was only on 4 October that the little fleet, made suddenly famous by its victory, arrived in Dutch waters. Now there was the devil to pay! What, really, could be done with a privateer ship of a power that had not been recognized and which had entered Dutch neutral waters with the prizes it had taken? Voices suspicious about the whole affair were heard. The Prince of Orange was among the mistrustful. He wrote to Van Bleiswijk expressing his belief that "a secret treaty has been made between Amsterdam and the Americans," so that Jones had come to Texel "to put the Republic under the necessity of taking various steps that could be considered as a kind of recognition of their independence, and this had been agreed upon by the Amsterdammers and the duke of La Vauguyon."[3]

Was this surmise wide of the mark? Such notions may well have contributed to the decisions taken in Paris, in which the French authorities, including De Chaumont, and the American envoys shared. But what was decisive was that the French government wanted Jones to take under his escort a convoy of French ships returning from the Baltic Sea. He was not himself enthusiastic about taking on this task, and he had to be warmed to it by being given a different motive. The hope was dangled before him, by Franklin among others, that when in Holland he would have put into his hands the splendid ship that had been built for the Americans in Amsterdam in 1777. It had been earlier promised to him, and the promise was repeated just before he departed, however impossible it was in fact in view of the certain refusal of the Dutch government to permit such a violation of neutrality. The promise was nothing more than bait to catch the sailor with.

However that may be, the American's presence put the Dutch authorities in a position of awkward perplexity. As was to be expected Yorke went at once to the grand pensionary to demand loudly that the seized ships and their captured crews be released. Really, he added, Jones himself should also be turned over to him as a criminal. But the States of Holland, and after it the States General, was not very favorable to his demand. True neutrality, the two assemblies replied, compelled them not to become involved in the question whether Jones had taken his prizes lawfully or unlawfully. All they could do was urge the admiralty of Amsterdam to compel Jones to sail as soon as possible, to make sure that he received no ammunition, and to help him only with the repair of his ships. They based this decision upon a resolution of Their High Mightinesses of 1756 permitting foreign warships and privateers to enter Dutch waters to seek shelter, but forbidding them to unload cargo and requiring that they show their commissions.

This was not enough for Yorke. In a second memoir he pressed for more, basing his argument upon the old treaties. The stadholder was very favorable to meeting the English demands. "It is my judgment that a refusal of that court's request and recognition of the independence of America have precisely the same results," and therefore would mean war. But all that Yorke obtained was a decision by the States General in a subsequent resolution to press Jones to leave immediately. If need be, force would be used to compel him. Such vigorous measures went much too far for the merchants of Amsterdam and other towns, who still had dreams of winning America as a trading partner, and they protested against any use of force. In fact none was used. For the moment, Jones stayed where he was. He had to repair his ships and take on supplies, with the help of De Neufville, who had garnered the contract for himself. Then, when ready, he would have to wait for the right moment and a favorable wind in order to sail out through the Marsdiep channel without being caught by the English ships lying in wait outside.

Jones had problems of his own besides. In the first place, there was the difficult question of the wounded. The only point on which he and Yorke were in agreement was that they had to be brought ashore as quickly as possible and given good care. But they differed about those wounded who were the American's prisoners. Jones wanted them to be kept under close guard, and Yorke obviously did not. Jones had in mind exchanging them for American prisoners of war in England, who he believed were receiving harsh treatment. But to permit English prisoners to be guarded by American soldiers on neutral Dutch soil was something that caused many a Dutch headache. Jones finally got his way at the end of October, when he reported to one of his officers that he now had permission to land a number of wounded prisoners on Texel and "to guard them by our American soldiers in the fort of that island, with the drawbridges hauled up or let down at our discretion." Providing for these unfortunates—for we can scarcely imagine nowadays how the poor fellows must have suffered—was a problem all by itself. Jones discussed it in Amsterdam with Pensionary Van Berckel and met Yorke there in person. "He was most civil," Jones relates, and in the matter of the care of the wounded they were able to work together for the moment. The romanticism of heroic battle softened men's hearts, and a few days later Yorke wrote to the doctor on duty that the supplies he was sending—medicine, blankets, and food—of course had to be shared honorably with the American wounded, "because we all know that Old England can never tell the difference between friends and foes among brave men wounded in battle, even if some of them may, per adventure, be rebels."

Jones himself quoted these lines with a certain pride, but he preferred not having to depend upon the Englishman's charity. Dutch help was soon organized for his men, and "the lovely Holland dames and daughters of the Helder," the Dutch naval harbor nearby, swarmed each day over the decks of the *Serapis* and the *Pallas* before the wounded were brought ashore, and they brought dainties and showed kindness which Jones called "a tribute that came from the hearts of the people, and therefore far overlaid in effect all statecraft and all diplomacy for or against us!" This showed, Jones willingly believed, that the Dutch people were sympathetic to the American cause. Resentment against England also played a part, he understood.[4]

Another problem that nagged at Jones was desertion among his own men. In one October day no fewer than twenty-five men took to their heels. They were quickly discovered and fired upon; fifteen had to come back, five drowned, and five got all the way to Amsterdam, where, thanks to the zeal of De Neufville and the cooperation of the bailiff, they were caught at eight o'clock just as they were trying to go out through the Utrecht gate. Jones, badly shaken, demanded a special oath of loyalty from his crews. They swore on 22 October "by solemn oath upon the Holy Evangelists in the presence of the Creator of the Universe and by his sacred name which had made us free and which finally will judge us, that as subjects of the free and independent Republic of America we renounce all ideas of submission to any other Government."[5]

In all these affairs, Dumas acted as a mediator and a messenger. He made the journey to Den Helder several times; he settled matters with De Neufville; and he received the American hero at his own home in The Hague. That must have been a moment of glory in his life, and it was a touch of tender romance for his thirteen-year-old daughter, Anna Jacoba. A year and a half earlier the good-natured father had written to his friend Carmichael that in five or six years he could send a couple of American lads, for his daughter preferred them to lords and princes. Now a true hero came into her home, a man of thirty-two years in a magnificent uniform. The proud father orchestrated the meeting. While Jones was still on Texel, Dumas sent him "a Virgin song, of a true Virgin (my little girl) on a heroe of our Virgin State. I can assure nobody has helped her. Your idea only has rised a poetical vein in her; and they are the first verses she ever attempted in any language." He had found them in her "little pocket-book" and had trouble getting them away from her. But she gave them to her father on his promise that the naval hero would surely answer "on the same strain; when once at leisure Pray do it by a short oration ode for the sake of kindling the poetical spark in such a young bosom."

Unfortunately, I have not been able to discover Anna Jacoba's virgin song anywhere. Jones's reply is well-known, for he was an effective promoter of himself. But he did not simply throw together a little piece of verse; he worked up an entire ode after he had gone out to sea again, and he sent it to her. It began:

> Were I, Paul Jones, dear maid, "the king of sea"
>   I find such merit in thy virgin song,
> A coral crown with bays I'd give to thee,
>   A car which on the waves should smoothly glide along,
> The nereids all about thy side should wait,
> And gladly sing in triumph of thy state
>   "Vivat, vivat, the happy virgin muse!
>   Of liberty the friend, who tyrant power pursues!"

And so on with more of the like. Anna Jacoba, we may be sure, found it all marvelous.[6]

Jones was the great hero in many places besides Dumas's home. He was received with enthusiasm everywhere, especially in Amsterdam. There are many descriptions of his reception. One cross Englishman wrote home: "This desperado parades the streets, and appears upon Change [the Amsterdam *Beurs*, or Exchange] with all the effrontery of a man of the first condition. . . . The Dutch look upon him to be a brave officer, and therefore bestowed many fulsome compliments during his stay here." The Dutch banker, George Grand, piqued because the delivery of supplies to Jones had been awarded not to him but to his competitor, De Neufville, wrote to Franklin that the privateer captain had aroused "the greatest sensation," but that De Neufville had made himself Jones's master and showed him off everywhere as though he were a curiosity. In a letter to Paris an elated Dumas reported: "The appearance of the Comod.re at

Amst. has been exceedingly agreeable to the people of that City. We have almost been smothered at the Exchange and in the streets, by an innumerable multitude, overjoy'd and mad to see the vanguisher of the English. They applauded him, bowed down to his feets [*sic*] and would have kissed them." Spontaneous ovations broke out at the theater. We have an additional testimony of a different kind for the theater visit, for one of those present was the artist Simon Fokke. He drew a portrait of Jones which he distributed in an etching, "Paul Jones, sketched in the Amsterdam Theater, October 9, 1779" (see Figure 7). Honor was also paid to Jones in a political print, one of the fascinating naive caricatures then so popular. In this print, entitled "Wages after Work," we see in the foreground the "English Dog," which is getting a beating from its foes, and "in the distance the Arrogant Queen of the Sea is seen being whipped by J. Paul Jones."[7]

The visit of Jones to the Dutch Republic has been preserved for us not only in pictures but also in word and song. His brave exploits spoke vividly to the imagination of his time. Besides the numerous English and American ballads devoted to him, there is a Dutch children's verse, as anonymous as caricatures of the period, and as naive as it is delightful:

> Here comes John Paul Jones,
> About him ev'ry Dutchman raves!
> His ship went down 'neath the waves,
> An English ship he boards and owns,
> If we had him here,
> If they had him there,
> There is still no end to all his pluck,
> He's ready again to try his luck.*

There is a variant in lines 3 and 4 of the second stanza: "A born American, / No English chap at all! [Een geboren Amerikaan, / Gans geen Engels ventje!]." And in the third stanza: "He does such heroic deeds, / His little friend to please [Het doet zovele heldendaan, / Tot welstand van

---

* Hier komt Pauwel Jonas aan
  't is zo'n aardig ventje!
  Zijn schip is na de grond gegaan
  op een Engels entje.
  Hadden wij hem hier,
  hadden zij hem daar,
  Hij wist het te proberen,
  Fortuin kan anders keren.

zijn vrindje!]." The ditty must have come from a Patriot's pen, for his "little friend" is the Dutch Republic, which showed in it her lasting gratitude. (Jones, we must note, was born in Scotland, not America.)

Van der Capellen tot den Pol contributed his share to the celebration of Jones's visit. It was a fine opportunity, he saw, to make propaganda for the American cause. He wrote to the hero asking for a complete report of the battle off Flamborough Head, and promptly received in return a letter full of high-flown phrases, but with useful enclosures including a copy of a letter from Jones to Franklin which gave a full account of the battle. Yes, indeed, Jones wrote, he was born "in Britain, but I do not inherit the degenerate spirit of that fallen nation, which I at once lament and despise." He was fighting for freedom, and America had been the land of his choice since he was thirteen years old. In a following letter, the Overijssel baron asked for more information, among other things whether Jones had a commission from France in addition to that from Congress. The sailor proudly replied that he had never been in any service except that of the United States of America.[8]

This happened to be just the question under discussion in the Dutch Republic. The States General had decided not to meet Yorke's requests, but exerted every kind of pressure upon Jones to be gone as quickly as possible. There had to be an end soon to the awkward situation in which the Dutch found themselves. Jones had submitted his commission from Congress, dated 10 October 1776, and he was asked, according to the rules of neutrality, to take his ships out to sea with the first good wind. But he was fully aware that Dutch sympathies made the use of force against him impossible, however much it was favored by the stadholder. He had much still to do, for his ships had been badly damaged and the supplies sent by De Neufville were inadequate. He complained to the French ambassador that he had had to wait two weeks for fresh water and that the bread he had received from Amsterdam was spoiled and made his men sick. Repairs required a good deal of time, and the materials were bad. This report by Jones throws a significant light upon the activities of the enthusiastic banker De Neufville. It is quite odd that Franklin, who had no fondness for the banker, nonetheless approved his receiving the contract. It turned out to have been done at Dumas's urging. When we read how De Neufville thanked Franklin in his letters with such effusive enthusiasm and promised to do his very best, it becomes all the stranger that so much went wrong, but we cannot doubt the truth of Jones's complaints and can only conclude that De Neufville, who was careless and irresponsible, let things get out of hand.[9]

Fig. 1. *Charles Guillaume Frédéric Dumas.* Pastel by Isaac Schmidt,
probably painted in 1783, when Schmidt also made a portrait of the
young John Quincy Adams, who was at that time staying with Dumas.
(This portrait is published here for the first time by graceful permission of
Mrs. A. L. Baroness Van Aerssen Beyeren van Voshol, Naarden.)

Fig. 2. *The Stadholder William V and his wife, Princess Wilhelmina,*
during a reception by the burgomasters of Amsterdam in 1768.
Detail of an engraving by Reinier Vinkeles.
(Collection of the author.)

Fig. 3. *Pieter van Bleiswijk, grand pensionary of the States of Holland.*
Engraving by Reinier Vinkeles.
(Collection of the author.)

Fig. 4. *Joan Derk van der Capellen tot den Pol.*
Engraving by T. de Roode.
(Collection of the author.)

Fig. 5. *Sir Joseph Yorke, British ambassador at The Hague.* This portrait by an unknown artist has an English publisher mentioned, but the charming Dutch winter scene at the bottom points to a Dutch artist. 1780.
(Collection of the author.)

Fig. 6. *Johan Luzac.* Engraving by Lucas Portman after a drawing by A. Delfos.
(Collection of the author.)

Fig. 7. *John Paul Jones, sketched in the theater at Amsterdam, 9 October 1779.*
Engraving by Simon Fokke.
(Collection of the author.)

Fig. 8. *Francis Adrian Van der Kemp.* Painting by an unknown artist, 1787.
(By permission of the New York Historical Society, New York.)

La Vauguyon had a way, a simple way, out of the problems. All that had to be done was to put the whole squadron under the French flag and provide it with French papers, and then they would be beyond the reach of the Dutch authorities. But there were implications that the American could not accept so easily. It would mean that the prizes would become French property, that the prisoners of war whom Jones wanted to exchange for American prisoners would be exchanged for French prisoners, and, worse yet, that his ships would be taken from him, especially the *Serapis*, the flagship that he had won with such boldness. Nonetheless, Jones went halfway with the French in their game. La Vauguyon had Dumas tell him to say that he possessed a French commission along with an American, and for a time he did so. "I asked the aforementioned Paul Jones," a Dutch captain reported to the admiralty, "whether he was also provided with a French commission, which he said he had mislaid or lost when his ship sank, but would nonetheless search for among his papers; but later told me he had not been able to find it." [10]

With this lie and many delays, Jones was able to stretch out his stay, but not without deep discontent. And as happens in such situations, he finally refused to go along with the degrading game. The affair came to a head in mid-November. On the one side, the French went into action. La Vauguyon received from Paris the orders that he desired; the prize ships must be placed under the French flag. Jones therefore would have to quit the *Serapis* and go over to the only ship in the squadron that had originally been American, the *Alliance*. It was a bitter pill for him to swallow, but there was no alternative. In the second place, the Dutch policy turned harsher. On 19 November the States General adopted a resolution which, while not conceding the English demands, ordered the admiralty of Amsterdam to put renewed pressure upon Jones.

. Now, however, the French played their trump card. When Reynst sent one of his officers, Captain Van Overmeer, to the *Serapis* to call upon Jones for the last time to leave, he found not the American but a French captain, Cottineau de Corgelin, and a French flag. The next day, Reynst came to see for himself, and the Frenchman calmly explained that the squadron had always been French and had been fitted out in France, and that it had never been under Jones's command. "When the Vice-Admiral expressed his astonishment that it had flown two different flags, using first one and then the other, he replied that he had received permission from Mr. Franklin to fly the North American flag too." There was nothing to be done; no one, not even the perplexed stadholder, wanted to take up arms against France. William easily saw through the maneuver, perceiving that the order of the French king was dated 8 November, but was acted upon only on 23 November. But what could he do? He was power-less and speechless. The Jones affair, he had written earlier to Van Welde-ren, "causes me real distress," and now the change of flags had left him "utterly perplexed, . . . indeed, so much so that he said virtually nothing the whole day."[11]

The American naval hero was no more happy over the course of events than the speechless stadholder. Jones took exceeding offense at his super-vision by the French, which drove him, he said, to the "breaking point." When the French ambassador sent the French agent in Amsterdam to him with a commission as a privateer captain, he turned it down brusquely. He did not want to tell any more tales about mislaid commissions, and he would not run up the French flag on the *Alliance*. To Franklin he ex-plained what a spiritual trial he had been through. Could it be his inten-tion, he asked Franklin, "that the commission of America should be over-laid by the dirty piece of parchment which I have this day rejected! They have played upon my good nature too long already, but the spell is at last dissolved. They would play me off with assurances of the personal and particular esteem of the king, to induce me to do what would render me contemptible even in the eyes of my own servants. Accustomed to speak untruths themselves, they would also have me give, under my hand, that I am a liar and a scoundrel!"[12] Jones persevered in this attitude to the end. No matter what summons he was given, he would not hoist the French flag. At Christmas, two and a half months after he had come in, the wind began to blow from the east, driving the English ships on watch away from the coast and giving him, and the French ships with him, the chance to sail out. The tedious play came to an end on December 27.

All in all it had been a bizarre adventure. All parties involved came out of it half satisfied. Yorke wrote to his government that things had really worked out well. The Americans' intention had been to force the Dutch to make "some kind of avowal" of their independence, but in the end it had been the Court of Versailles that had found itself compelled to hide the affair under a French mask. The better part of the Dutch—by which he no doubt meant the English party—was indignant that their country had been treated with such contempt. Jones, on the contrary, wrote that his arrival had spoiled Dutch-English relations beyond repair. The Prince of Orange voiced a pious hope that England would quickly gain a glorious victory and that everything would return to what it had been before "the American troubles began." Dumas, finally, was not dissatisfied. He had played a central role in the whole affair, a humble role to be sure but a not unimportant one. To Franklin he wrote that he had encouraged Jones in his refusal to hoist the French flag. That was his duty, he said, and he had stood behind him, although he drew down upon his head the displeasure of one and all. He amplified what he meant in a later letter: False friends were disappointed in him now because he was not as compliant as they thought.[13]

· II ·

Among these false friends, Dumas counted first none other than the duke of La Vauguyon, the ambassador of His Most Christian Majesty! The Jones affair, as we may call it, brought the first estrangement between the Frenchman and Dumas, until then his most humble servant.

At the same time that La Vauguyon had been trying to oblige Jones to raise the French flag, Dumas was stiffening the captain in his recalcitrant American attitude. It seems to me that there was more behind this than only a difference of political opinions. Dumas wanted to play a role in history and felt that he represented the new age, the new mankind. Why then, he must have wondered, did he have to make the bows in a hierarchical relation? Why did he have to play the pawn in the game of politics? For once he would show who he was, who this haughty Frenchman was dealing with.

Yet he was still just Dumas, just a little man, quite learned but not at all versed in the ways of the world. He attacked with clumsy secrecy and indirection, and he met disaster. The conflict with the duke is one of the great dramas in Dumas's career. It shows him in all his ambition and all his lack of power and stamina. The clash took shape as he began to resent more and more the bullying of the great nobleman. He did not go as often to the "Great Factor," he wrote Franklin, because he wished to teach La Vauguyon not to boss him around anymore.

The wise American diplomat in Paris, however, observed the difficulties with concern. He warned Dumas to set aside his differences of opinion with the ambassador, whatever their cause. He admonished him for being much too suspicious. Did Dumas really believe that a certain person was selling weapons to the Americans at a great profit? The truth was that they had bought nothing from him. Franklin was alluding, I think, to the insinuations against the banker Grand, which apparently had been whispered in Dumas's ear by De Neufville. The previous summer, when Dumas had been in Paris, Franklin had attempted to persuade him of the reliability of the Grand brothers—according to the venomous Arthur Lee, this was because Franklin and Deane were financially interested in Grand's ventures.[14]

Once back in Holland, Dumas came again under the influence of De Neufville, who also strongly desired to look after the American needs. Franklin's words of wisdom were forgotten; his advice was thrown to the winds. It was about this time that Dumas committed his great mistake. He wrote a letter to the first of his American friends, William Carmichael, who was in Madrid with John Jay to look after American interests. Dumas spewed out to his old friend all his spite against the ambassador. But, disastrous error, the letter reached the wrong person! It was in fact no error but a piece of outright improper conduct. Franklin, to whom Dumas had sent the letter to be forwarded to Carmichael, wrote to tell what had happened. He had given the letter to F. Grand, "our banker here," who was to send it on to Spain, because he himself did not know Carmichael's address. The next day Grand had come to him, embarrassed and distraught. George Grand, his brother who took care of Dutch business, had seen the letter lying on his desk and said, "Why, that is Dumas's handwriting!" and had opened it and read it. George Grand had been enraged by Dumas's ingratitude and had taken the letter with him to Holland. He had already departed, and there was nothing that could be done anymore.[15]

The brothers Grand thus took their revenge upon poor Dumas for going over to De Neufville. We unfortunately do not know exactly what Dumas wrote to Carmichael, but we can figure it out. Dumas had written a letter to John Paul Jones that was certainly of the same tenor; in it, Dumas reported that he would convey his greetings to La Vauguyon, but that he had to warn Jones about the ambassador, for La Vauguyon deceived him when he thought convenient. There is more, too, in the brief account that Dumas included in his report of the incident to the president of Congress. He set forth what Franklin had written him, how George Grand, "without any respect to his Excellency Franklin," had stolen the letter and taken it to La Vauguyon, "of whom I had imprudently put down, that I thought him not a friend to Am[erica]; which I fear he will never forget." The source of all this fuss, he added, was Grand's jealousy of De Neufville for getting the contract to supply the squadron at Texel.[16]

The fuss was in any case so deafening for poor Dumas that he almost collapsed. There is in his letterbook a draft letter, black with deletions and scratched-out words, and with spots (tears of the overwrought writer?); it is undated but probably from the beginning of April. In it he wallows in his remorse before the great lord. He begins by telling him that his wife has fallen ill in her misery. He begs forgiveness: "I am your friend, Monsieur Duke. . . . I was wrong to have thought and written as I did about Your Excellency although I had a heavy heart at the moment." How often he had committed mistakes in his letters, he added, but now it could not be corrected. "I have been deprived of the ability to recall and destroy the Letter which has caused me the greatest vexation of my life, the sand on which I wrote has been metamorphosed into marble." And he ended: "May Your Excellency (soon) generously forget the brief instant when I incurred his displeasure for the thousand times when it was my joy to please him, and may he permit me to renew my duties and my services to him. He will be satisfied with me." [17]

Dumas knew no further repose so long as he received no forgiveness. At the same time he reproached himself for seeking it. He was whipped to and fro like a reed in the wind. One letter after another streamed from his pen. He saw the frightful scene again in his imagination: "I must have lost my nerve seeing this Letter in your hands." But the duke wrapped himself in proud silence. Finally Dumas spilled out his heart to Franklin, repeating again what he had written to Carmichael (and what was so frightfully bad in that?), how he had lost his nerve and then had written "my cowardly letter" to La Vauguyon. What in Heaven's name could he do now?

Franklin answered with a chilly reprimand that the quarrel between Dumas and the ambassador was "inconvenient." "Permit me to tell you frankly what I formerly hinted to you, that I apprehend you suffer yourself too easily to be let into personal prejudices by interested people, who would engross all our confidence to themselves. . . . There does not appear to me the least possibility in your supposition that the [ambassador] is an enemy to America."

Dumas was put in the wrong, and he confessed that he was also guilty with regard to Franklin. The wrangle hung on for a long time, and although Dumas was able to report during the summer that the duke had received him again, he was never fully taken back into his favor. That fall he wrote to Franklin that he had learned much from these events. He no longer came to a judgment so quickly, and he claimed that he had paid too dearly, almost with his own life and probably his wife's as well, for writing with too much naivete. [18]

Dumas had been put in the wrong. But was he wrong? Must we not say when we look back at what happened that he was really right in his conclusions about La Vauguyon, however imprudent he was to put them into written words? In the affair of the draft treaty, as well as in the question of John Paul Jones, what had the duke done but put French interests ahead of the American, if not on his own, then on instructions from Vergennes? And what could Dumas expect from Franklin, whom he trusted and worshiped so greatly, but whose policy toward France was circumspect and conciliatory in the extreme? Franklin represented a tendency in the unsettled foreign policy of the new nation that is best characterized as Francophile. It was by following such a line that Franklin had succeeded in getting France as an ally. But was he not too trustful, too unsuspicious with regard to Vergennes's intentions? And was it not Dumas's tragedy that he got caught in the same track of overdependence on France, which had to lead to a break sooner or later? The interests of France and the United States might run parallel, but they certainly did not coincide. The man who, in contrast to Franklin, saw this discrepancy ever more clearly and who wanted nothing to do with a Francophile policy, John Adams, was on his way in order to bring about a change. He was on the way to Holland to give a new impulsion to the work of poor, bewildered Dumas.

· CHAPTER 6 ·

John Adams on the Way to Holland

He is gone to Holland to try, as he told me,
whether something might not be done to
render us less dependent on France.
BENJAMIN FRANKLIN

ow does one tackle writing about John Adams, this most remarkable and exceptional Founding Father? Once he was almost forgotten but in recent years he has been held in high esteem. The facts are at hand in the biographies: his birth into a simple Puritan family living on the outskirts of Boston, a long life (1735–1826), a rapid career as a lawyer, a radical during the Revolution and even before. But he also demonstrated a sense of fairness: he defended the English soldiers on trial for their part in the "Boston Massacre" of 1770. A member of the Continental Congress in 1774 and of its committee that drew up the Declaration of Independence in 1776, he was sent to France in 1778 as one of the American commissioners and returned there in 1779. Back home in the meantime, he was the author of the constitution of Massachusetts. His activity never halted.

In 1780 he came to Holland and two years later was recognized as the American minister, the first envoy of the United States to the Netherlands. In 1783 he joined Franklin and John Jay in Paris to conclude peace with England, going there as the first American ambassador. He returned to his homeland in 1788 to become the first vice president, serving under Washington for eight years and then following him as a second president (1797–1801). He then withdrew into private life. He died in 1826 at the age of ninety-one.

His wife, Abigail, was at his side for almost all of these years. In a biography of John Adams, Abigail needs special attention, for his marriage was a remarkable one. His wife was an exceptional woman, with a personality of her own and feminist tendencies; she was his equal in every respect. She died in 1818, three days after their fifty-fourth wedding anniversary. He lived on without her for another eight years.

During all these years of consuming activity, writing hundreds, nay thousands, of letters, drawing up accounts, signing bonds, drafting treaties, composing pamphlets, he found time for a profound study of political institutions. The result of these investigations was a number of works of political theory; among them is the great *Defence of the Constitutions of the United States of America*, in which he displays the learning he had accumulated endlessly with characteristic passion. For he was a driven scholar. From his writings we learn to know him as a man driven by unbridled forces. I have read his writings, most of all his letters, with admiration, and I think sometimes of storm clouds piling up swiftly and wildly on the horizon and then spreading out until they cover the whole of the sky.

As I write this, I realize how romantic a picture it is, as though we were looking at paintings by Cozens or Constable. Yet Adams was a man of the eighteenth century, a man of Reason. Or are we thinking too schematically? When we say "a man of the eighteenth century," we see before us a person who sees his God in the stars, who puts his hopes in a harmony that will reconcile all things, who gives his faith to humanity and progress. But if such a century ever existed, John Adams did not quite fit into it. He did share the ordinary religious and philosophical conceptions of the Enlightenment, but had a different temperament. He was fiercer and more restless. He would like to have believed in the Progress of Humanity, but he was too steeped in the Puritan past not to have a deeper insight into the evil of the human heart. When he came to look back upon the eighteenth century, his judgment was ambivalent. He was willing to admit that a new beginning for mankind might be found in that age: "The eighteenth-century, notwithstanding all its errors and vices, has been, of all that are past, the most honorable to human nature," as he wrote to Jefferson. But he could also explode in anger when he saw in how much chaos and misery the century ended: "I am willing you should call this the Age of Frivolity as you do; and would not object if you had named it the Age of Folly, Vice, Frenzy, Fury, Brutality, Daemons, Buonaparte, Tom Paine, or the Age of the burning Brand from the bottomless Pitt; or any thing than the Age of Reason."[1]

We truly learn to know John Adams in this passage, the Adams who wrote prose as though it were a rapids in a river or an avalanche in the mountains. We can discuss the greatness of the Founding Fathers; we can admire Washington for his Olympian calm, Franklin for his bonhomie and his wisdom, Jefferson for his universality. But if we wish to recognize a living man close up, one who lives and is always present in his writing, we must turn to Adams.

How do we write about him, then? Do we praise his perspicacity, his passionate loyalty to his country, his stubbornness? Do we look at his dark side, his almost morbid concern with himself, his pompous pedantry, his inner insecurity? He is a witness testifying uninterruptedly to the division within himself; he is simultaneously self-assured and conscious of guilt. In a recent character study he has been described as the "Yankee [who] tended to express his anxieties not by suffering guilt like his forebears but through conflict with others." This is said to be the explanation of his lifelong "contentiousness." Admirable as I find the book from which I quote, I wonder whether we can really make such a division. The sense of inadequacy was strong in Adams precisely because of the freedom he received from his parents as well as from his time and his country. The conflict did not merely break out to the surface, as the author I have cited suggests, it continued to rage inside him. In his earliest diary entries he confesses: "Oh! that I could wear out of my mind every mean and base affection, conquer my natural Pride and Self Conceit, expect no more difference [*sic*] from my fellows than I deserve, acquire that meekness, and humility, which are the sure marks and Characters of a great and generous Soul."[2]

When he was very old he wrote to his friend Van der Kemp—with whom he kept up a very fascinating correspondence—that freedom and guilt belonged to each other, indissolubly: "The origin of Mal moral is Liberty, the self determinating Power of free Agents endowed with Reason and Conscience, and consequently accountable for their conduct." This is the experience of life that he had acquired painfully and that continued to gnaw at him. He had achieved so much and so little. He was so great and so petty. He was so proud that he wrote to Van der Kemp that it was really he and no one else who first got Burke to think about the French Revolution. And when someone said to Burke that Washington was "the greatest man in the world," he said, "I thought so too, till I knew John Adams." Very shortly thereafter Adams wrote of Franklin, whose French policy he could never forgive: "He was a successful Swindler of other Mens Laurells and so was Washington." Yes, Adams could be very petty even into his old age. But he was also able to see his own pettiness.

In his best moments he could draw a portrait of himself that in its characteristic self-accusation was certainly too black, but that is nonetheless a masterpiece. Take the entry in his diary during his first sojourn in France, in which he describes himself as he looks in the mirror. He certainly does not flatter himself about his good looks. He finds himself a sorry little figure of a man, flabby in appearance and in character. The special events of his time, he meditates, have pushed him far up in the world and brought him a little fame. But he is what he is, so that he can write: "Yet some great Events, some cutting Expressions, some mean Hypocrisies, have at Times thrown this Assemblage of Sloth, Sleep and littleness into Rage a little like a Lion." That is John Adams to a tee, the Puritan before the mirror, the little man in his authentic greatness.[3]

To cite one further, sublime passage: "It is fashionable to call me 'The Venerable'. It makes me think of the venerable Bede." Call Washington "venerable," or Jefferson, he continues, but not him. "I have worn it too long. It is become threadbare upon me. Do not however, I pray you, call me the 'Godlike Adams', the 'sainted Adams', 'our saviour Adams', our 'redeemer Adams', 'our Saviour on Earth and own advocate in Heaven', 'the Father of his Country', 'the Founder of the American Republic', 'the Founder of the American Empire', etc., etc., etc. These Ascriptions belong to no Man. no! nor to any twenty Men; nor to any hundred Men, nor to any thousand Men."[4] In a passage like this we can discover what Adams revealed by the very act of concealing it. He had to share his fame, and so did the others! Yet this self-same egotist could express in a most impressive way an attitude toward life that probably belonged to his time, but certainly was from himself. On his human insignificance he wrote: "I damn Nobody, I am an Atom of Intellect, with Millions of Solar Systems over my head, under my feet, on my right and on my left, before me and behind me; and my adoration of the Intelligence that contrived and the Power that rules the stupendous Fabric is too profound to believe them capable of any thing unjust, mean or cruel." Is this the eighteenth-century Adams? It is, truly, but one who forms the connection between the poet of Psalm 139 and Emerson and is, moreover, as great a stylist as either.[5]

It is tempting to give many more quotations from Adams. His style is livelier and more honest than what we find in the ordinary prose of his contemporaries. He is able to blow life, at least in his letters, into even his political ideas, which now call for our attention. It would carry us too far to treat them at length, and besides that has already been done by several historians.[6] I will try only to illuminate a few aspects of his political thought, drawing upon the never-published yet fascinating correspondence between Adams and his old Dutch friend François Adriaan van der Kemp (Francis Adrian Van der Kemp in America), whom we shall meet more fully later in these pages. The only difficulty seems to be that Adams is so exuberant in his letters that the words and the man are apparently running amuck. But I do not believe that this is so, for I find that we get to know him best precisely in his letters, even as a political thinker, for it is in these that he reveals their human background, which is his own.

In his political thinking, as in other things, Adams was a man full of tensions and passions. But he was fully aware of it, and it made him strive more than ever for a sane balance. His view of man was the foundation for all his plans and constitutional structures. Thanks to his personal tensions, he had a sharp eye for human folly down through the ages, and as a result he turned away from the current fashionable progressivism. Often he exploded against the "stupidity" of mankind, the vanities of the world, the bloodthirstiness of history, and we can hear the echoes of centuries of Puritanism. But he was never truly one-sided, and he maintained a ground tone of hope. Or rather he diagnosed his own tension, and he heard, he experienced, the dissonances of existence.

He did cherish a hope that a better future was possible in America— possible at least for a while. For Adams could never have made his own Jefferson's famed words that in the New World the biblical adage that there is nothing new under the sun had been proved wrong. He believed indeed that his country, freed of oppression by hierarchies of all kinds— ecclesiastical, aristocratic, and military—was better off, but he also saw that to be human is to have bounds. When Van der Kemp wrote to him of the eventual downfall of Europe, he replied:

> Now you come to a Subject that setts me all on fire. "God knows what threatens poor Europe". Here I have a great mind to let my Imagination look into boundless regions of Possibility, Probability, supposition and Conjecture. What do you think of the Possibility that America was once civilized and free: all Democratics [*sic*], then Aristocracies, then Monarchies, then Empires and at last so intolerably governed as to exterminate one another leaving only a few Democrats, nearly like Savages. How many years would it take to moulder away all their cities, obliterate all the Records and Institutions and leave only a few savage hunters? I believe a thousand years would do it. But we may allow two or three thousand if we will.[7]

Adams was no optimist. But he strove to keep in the middle; he did not want to run aground in total pessimism. He would have none of Jefferson's perfectibility, but still saw in man an element of goodness, of "benevolence." It is fascinating to see how he derived this belief in the limited possibilities of man primarily from literary sources. Like so many of his contemporaries, he was thoroughly familiar with Pope, especially his *Essay on Man*. "We must confess humanity and mortality, my friend, acquiesce and resign to our fate, 'wait the great teacher Death and God adore'." He found Swift too bitter: "He had none of the milk of human kindness in his nature." Sterne however, Sterne the bizarre, gave him confidence in man. "Can any man read Sterne's Tristram Shandy and still doubt whether there is simple benevolence in Human Nature?" That is why he rejected Calvin's doctrine of the "total Depravity of Human Nature."

The essential peril always threatening man was that he would become too powerful. Adams incessantly warned his friend that everyone who gets too much power must be mistrusted. It taints him. Man is a being in whom goodness and egoism do battle. A good form of government must hold them in balance. "Balance of power" is not only a prescription for the relations among states; it is also an absolute requirement for all human relations. It is best guaranteed—and here Adams remained in a true eighteenth-century tradition—by an *imperium mixtum*, the concept of a trinity of powers—monarchy, aristocracy and democracy—each of which would if left to itself, develop into tyranny, oligarchy, and anarchy, respectively. "Without a Ballance all is Despotism, throughout all Ages and Nations, either of one Military Conqueror, or of ten, twenty or a hundred petty tirants."[8]

Complete equality must be rejected, for men are simply not equal. The multitude must be protected against the elite. "If we do not preserve and strengthen our Ballance we shall soon have a Feudal System of Bankers and Landjobbers," he wrote prophetically. But contrariwise, it is equally necessary to protect the elite against too much equality. He exclaimed in an outburst of bitter sarcasm: "Van der Kemp! it will not do, in this World, for a man to have more sense more learning or more Virtue than his Neighbour. I know not, whether it is quite safe, to have as much, as the generality." He gave as an example the dismissal of Van der Kemp's preceptor, Van der Marck, in Groningen. And the most honest vote ever held was held in Corinth (if he remembered correctly) on the proposition "Resolved that all men of Superior Virtue be banished from this Commonwealth. We want no such men here. Let them go and carry their

Virtues elsewhere." Adams appended his own commentary: "What simplicity! What naiveté! What Liberty! What Equality! What Fraternity! What Patriotism!"[9]

We see here Adams from tip to toe, with all the fury of his sarcasm and indignation. This short portly man (for that was how he looked—"his Rotundity," he was called in mockery; "Mr Round Face" was John Paul Jones's nickname for him) was, despite his conviviality and kindheartedness, all passion, all impulsiveness. He was a man who stood on his rights, fought for his convictions, and was utterly committed to his work. We would not expect to find in such a man a diplomat, one who must conceal his thoughts in his words, one who lives by discussion and discretion.[10] And yet one of the most important roles he had in his life was as a diplomat, though not one who played by the rules. He came to Europe, and finally to Holland, to seek recognition and money for the revolutionary government that he served.

· II ·

Rebels who seek recognition put themselves in an ambiguous position. They pursue a dream, but they want to and have to give it the dimensions of everyday security. They want to give an example to the nations, but they are dependent for their existence upon these nations. They want at the same time to escape history and to enter it.

The American revolutionaries furnish an excellent example of this dilemma. When, after a year of struggle, they decided to proclaim their independence, they were at once confronted with the question of what to do about foreign nations and what relations to establish with them (in 1776, we must remember, "foreign" meant European, for the rest of the world was either colonies—Latin America, India, Indonesia—hermetically sealed—China and Japan—or, for the most part, undiscovered—Africa).

Two tendencies developed among the members of Congress. On the one side was a group of idealists, radicals whose enthusiasm knew no bounds. They were simultaneously isolationists and internationalists. They wanted to have nothing to do with the European power blocs, with "balance of power" and the clash of interests (and in this they accepted the ideas of the European Enlightenment), but at the same time they believed that they were engaged in a battle for all mankind. Their republican faith in virtue and simplicity, at once Puritan and Romantic, envisioned a free world without barriers, without alliances, without spheres of influence. They put their stamp deep on American history: their greatest heir was Woodrow Wilson.

When, in the sad here-and-now, it became necessary to make alliances at least for a time, as happened in 1778 with France, they voted their assent, but hesitatingly and with deep mistrust of the new friend. They were soon warning against French ulterior motives, secret purposes, and intrigues. They represented, in brief, a presumed American purity as against European corruption, the New World against the Old, a contrast that would become a stereotype in trans-Atlantic relations and which Henry James would depict with the hand of a master in his great novels.

On the other side were the prudent, moderate men, the men of business. They hesitated a long time before they decided for independence and were too much realists to believe in a new beginning. They understood that their new state was a part of a complex world and that they could not do without help from outside. They looked after their country's interests and their own interests at the same time, and saw no conflict between them. They were easily persuaded to put on harness to pull the French wagon, with the French envoy in the driver's box.

A multitude of cabals, factions, and connections were involved in the struggle between the two groups, and this simple division became in reality a labyrinth of enmities and intrigues. It was of course never true that anything like a virtuous America facing a depraved Europe ever existed. That is a story that we need not tell in these pages. For us only the part that Adams played in this muddle of calculations and passions is important. At first he belonged to the radical party, but in his own way. One of the first advocates of independence, he was wholly incorruptible and suspicious of other interests, especially those of France. As chairman of one of the committees established for this purpose, he was a major participant in the first formulation of the objectives of American foreign policy.

Two such committees were established in June 1776, when the first resolution on independence had been introduced but not yet adopted. One was the Committee on Secret Correspondence, with responsibility for foreign affairs, that is, for seeking assistance from the foes of England. The other was the Committee for Drafting the Model Treaty, which had the same task, but on a more theoretical level. This was a shaky foundation on which to build a method for the conduct of foreign affairs. No one had experience; there was a fumbling, unsure, and busy search for new ways.

Adams, who was certainly one of the sharpest legal minds in the assembly, took upon himself the task of drafting a model treaty. It was an idealistic text, strongly influenced by the ideas of Paine, the spokesman of the radicals. (Think of the hatred with which Adams would later speak of Paine!) Its point of departure was the dream that America would remain pure, untainted by the evil world. Adams had already set down on paper an outline of his ideas about an eventual treaty, in the first instance with France: "No political connection. Submit to none of her authority, receive no governors or officers from her. 2. No military connection. Receive no troops from her. 3. Only a commercial connection; that is to make a treaty to receive her ships into our ports; let her engage to receive our ships into her ports; furnish us with arms, cannon, salpeter [sic], powder, duck steel." His stress is upon remaining completely free, making no promises. When the realists observed that neither France nor any other foreign power would want to come to the Americans' aid on the basis of such conditions, the radicals replied with a laugh that France would have to be grateful for the commercial advantages for a long time! The model treaty emphasized that America must remain free even in making friends, that trade relations did not imply any political commitment. It also made very much of the rights of neutrals in wartime; only very specific goods—and, we mark, naval stores are not among these—could be considered contraband. Moreover, the principle of "free ships, free goods" was emphatically affirmed.[11]

Reality would naturally reshape such ideals as necessity dictated. When a treaty was finally concluded with France, it was in fact modeled upon Adams's ideal pattern, but with the force of its outstanding principle lost by the inclusion of a defensive alliance. America could not at the same time become independent and remain pure. She was drawn into international power politics despite herself.

In the meantime the United States slowly developed, by fits and bounds, an organization for the conduct of its foreign relations. The appointment in 1776 of the first agents sent abroad was a curious arrangement: Three agents were named at the same time. Benjamin Franklin, Silas Deane, and Thomas Jefferson (who declined and was replaced by Arthur Lee), and all went to France, where Deane was already present. In the spring of 1777 a Committee of Foreign Affairs was set up; Paine was its secretary, an indication that the radical influence was still strong. Not until 1780 was a Department of Foreign Affairs formed separate from Congress; it had its own secretary, the very moderate New Yorker Robert R. Livingston. Diplomacy was something from which the Americans continued to shrink for a long time. An idealist like Jefferson described it as late as 1804 as "the pest of the peace of the world, as the workshop in which nearly all the wars of Europe are manufactured." This idea became another stubborn tradition in American history, and Wilson had his roots in it too.[12]

Adams gradually changed his mind. It has been said that in these years he turned from idealism to realism, but was it really so? He only became strongly anti-French after he arrived in France, in indignation over the way in which Vergennes, the French foreign minister, put French interests ahead of American. It is true that in Europe he learned what power means and that power alone is the decisive argument in all politics, and that an "equilibrium, a balance of power," is necessary also in international relations. But he returned home with the firm conviction that America must stay out of European quarrels. He became a true isolationist. He was in agreement for once with the preacher, he wrote to Van der Kemp one Sunday morning, "in thanksgiving to God for creating the Atlantic Ocean between America and Europe." The sole aim of the American government from 1789, he wrote in 1811, had been "to spout cold Water upon their own Habitation, built, if not of Hay and Stubble, with wooden Timbers, boards, Clapboards and Shingles, to prevent its being scortched by the Flames from Europe." Europe, he wrote in another letter, was like a volcanic landscape; the Americans should keep themselves far away, "separate from all their wars and politics."[13]

· III ·

Adams became a diplomat despite himself. When his country called him in the fall of 1777, he hesitated for scarcely a moment. He sailed in February 1778 with an appointment to join Franklin and Lee as a "commissioner." His first sojourn lasted for well over a year, and it confronted the novice envoy with two problems with which he would never come to terms. One was France itself, a country that he admired and loathed as he came to know it better: "The Delights of France are innumerable. The Politeness, the Elegance, the Softness, the Delicacy, is extreme. In short, stern and hauty Republican as I am, I cannot help loving these People." France was everything he desired and feared, and French policy was the same: polite, elegant, subtle, and—as he found out—utterly untrustworthy.

The second problem he met was Franklin, or rather the whole chaotic situation in which he found the American mission in Paris. It was torn by disputes (Franklin and Deane, who was now recalled, against Lee); undermined by British bribery (it is probable that both Deane and Carmichael let themselves be bought); and riddled with espionage (its secretary, Edward Bancroft, was a British spy). Franklin himself was the great and much-admired philosopher about whom fluttered the cooing French women. He was the man who conquered France by his simplicity, but who from the first was distrusted by Adams. He did not like Franklin's involvement in all manner of speculation, primarily in western lands, and he thought Franklin's whole behavior false, a stage setting, a pretense. "The Life of Dr. Franklin was a scene of continual dissipation," the stern Puritan wrote later. Above all, Franklin was tied much too tightly to the French apron strings!

Adams attempted to clean the Augean stables. Putting the mission's papers in order, he discovered new iniquities and felt furious and powerless at the same time. It was at this time that he wrote the passage that I quoted a few pages earlier about how weak and small he felt, but how sudden events, scandals (a word he struck out), and, most of all, hypocrisy could make a lion of him. He was happy when he could return home in the summer of 1779 after a period of waiting that seemed endless. His joy did not last long, however, for in the fall of the same year he was again entrusted with a diplomatic task, "to negotiate peace and commercial treaties with Great Britain."

It is not possible here to discuss all the complications and fluctuations of Congress, all its various maneuvers, as it sought a middle way between a pro-French and a radical policy. Vergennes himself had pressed for the sending of a special plenipotentiary for the eventual peace negotiations, but he had hoped that the appointment would go to Franklin. France would then be able to keep an eye on what was stirring among the Americans. But the pro-French party in Congress was outvoted, and the radicals from Virginia and New England were able to push through the choice of Adams, very much against the desires of the French minister. This meant that from the very beginning Adams's mission had little chance of success. The whole concept was grossly premature, and French obstruction made the affair totally hopeless for the time being.

Adams set off on his journey with courage aplenty. The instructions of his government, which expressed its confidence in his "integrity, prudence and ability," were holy law to him. In his reminiscences, written thirty years later, he described his heroic role with self-satisfaction. He had not been held back by all the difficulties, the dangerous sea-crossing "among storms and British men of war," a new separation from his family. "I considered the voice of my country as the command of Heaven:

and held it my duty to resign all personal considerations, and as Luther said upon another occasion, I determined to go through, though there were as many devils in the way, as there were tiles on the houses of London."[14] He arrived in France after a long and adventurous journey by way of Spain, and he was game for a fight.

And a fight came, as it had to. There was a clash with Vergennes almost at once, and, most frustrating for Adams, Franklin seemed to him to stand wholly on the French side. Vergennes and Franklin together complained to Congress that Adams was not suited for his task and did nothing but create problems. Fundamentally, there appeared to be a deep division of principle between the two American negotiators. Franklin believed in a cautious, wait-and-see policy. "A Virgin state," he had written in 1777 to Adams's partisan Arthur Lee, "should preserve its virgin character, and not go about suitoring for alliances, but wait with decent dignity for the application of others." Adams, on the contrary, maintained that it was the immediate task of the representatives of the new nation to knock boldly at every door, to press for treaties, loans, and recognition. Diplomats of the old stamp, he wrote, would probably consider us as "a sort of militia and hold us . . . in some degree of contempt; but wise men know that militia sometimes gain victories over regular troops even by departing from the rules." With these words, Adams provided historians with a new term, for his undiplomatic impetuosity is now called "militia diplomacy."[15]

In France his assault shattered against the wall of Old Regime forms and interests. Embittered by scheming and frazzled by obligatory ceremonies, Adams saw the spring of 1780 bring forth nothing worthwhile. In this situation Holland was an escape, a chance to begin over again. For quite some time the Americans had been turning an occasional eye upon the Low Countries. We have seen how Dumas had labored in vain in Franklin's name for a treaty. There was the lure of Dutch trade and the indispensability of Dutch money.

On his return from his first European journey, Adams had given a detailed report on American opportunities and possibilities in the Old World, and the Dutch Republic took an important place in these. The similarity in customs, religion, and, from one point of view, their systems of government, the resemblance in their origins, and, most of all, the coincidence of their commercial interests had to bring the two nations together. But Holland was still too dependent on England, and patience was necessary. In the meantime Congress had to consider the advisability of sending an envoy. Dutch merchants could be tempted with the advantages that trade with the New World would offer them. There followed a sharp but already obvious judgment: "It is scarcely necessary to observe to congress that Holland has lost her influence in Europe to such a degree, that there is little other regard for her remaining, but that of a prodigal heir for a rich usurer, who lends him money at a high interest. The State which is poor and in debt has no political stability. Their army is very small, and their navy is less." The wealth of private persons therefore made the country an easy prey for "some necessitous, avaricious and formidable neighbor." [16] We see that even before Adams came to the Netherlands, his judgment upon it was clear and prophetic.

Congress decided to risk a few steps. On 18 October 1779 it gave Adams a tentative assignment to seek a loan in the Dutch Republic, but three days later it transferred that authority to another deputy, Henry Laurens of South Carolina. This rich merchant was named to go to The Hague as a special agent to attempt to obtain money and recognition. Although he accepted the assignment, Laurens did not begin his journey at once. It was the summer of 1780 before he went aboard ship. In the meantime it had become ever more apparent to the Americans in Paris, especially Adams, that there was a chance of striking a successful blow in Holland. The ties of the Republic with England seemed on the point of breaking, thanks to Dutch insistence upon their right of unlimited convoy of their merchant fleets. Was it not necessary to strike while the iron was hot? If only Laurens were already there, Adams wrote in despair. Unable to get anything going in Paris, he decided to go himself to scout out the situation in the Low Countries. At the beginning of July he went to pay his respects to Vergennes, from whom he had to get a passport, and told him he planned to go to Amsterdam and establish connections there. At first the minister attempted to prevent his journey, but he let him go when it appeared that for a time nothing would come of other negotiations, especially those between England and Spain. There was time now to go to Holland to have a look at things. At the end of July the American rode out of the gates of Paris in his coach, and he arrived in Amsterdam early in August.

What he could not know at that moment was that Congress had voted on 20 June to put back into his hands temporary authority to conclude a loan agreement with the Dutch bankers; for the time being, he would fill in for Laurens, who had not yet departed. He had gone on his own initiative, and he did not have the slightest anticipation that his stay in the Republic would last for years. Franklin wrote to Congress that Adams had gone to Holland "to try, as he told me, whether something might not be done to render us less dependent on France." And he added that it was true that he thought Adams ill-advised in his anti-French policy, but that he "at the same time means our Welfare and Interest as much as I, or any man, can do." Franklin had a more capacious heart than Adams. In his recollections, Adams confirmed what Franklin had written: He went to Holland "to see if something might not be done there, to render my country somewhat less dependent on France, both for political consideration, for loans of money and supplies for our army." [17]

There was one more reason why Adams went to Holland. The country might have lost its former power, but The Hague was still a center of political activities and information, particularly in diplomatic matters. As the young American who became Adams's friend, medical student Benjamin Waterhouse, would write years later, The Hague was "the eye and heart of the continental politics." "The Hague is the vantage ground, to use an expressive phrase of Lord Bacon, whence you can see all around. Place one foot of a compass in the middle of Holland and extend the other leg 50 miles and strike a circle, and you would include more learning and more information, and more riches than any other spot on the globe of the same extent." Adams himself believed in this "vantage point" from the start: "There is not in Europe a better station to collect intelligence from France, Spain, England, Germany, and all the northern parts, nor a better situation from whence to circulate intelligence through all parts of Europe, than this." [18] He set to work with furious zeal.

· CHAPTER 7 ·

John Adams Arrives in Holland

I am very pleased with Holland.
It is a Singular Country.
It is like no other.
It is all the Effect of Industry and the Work of Art.
JOHN ADAMS

ATHERS in the eighteenth century probably wanted their children to grow up faster than we do in our day; in any event, they exposed them sooner to the instructive dangers of life. When John Adams had to begin the great journey across the Atlantic for the second time in the fall of 1779 and had to say good-bye to his family, he solved the painful dilemma of whether or not to take them with him by leaving his wife at home with the two daughters but taking both sons along. They were still quite young lads—John Quincy was thirteen years of age and Charles was ten—but who knew how much they would benefit by such a "grand tour" in the Old World? We shall attempt to answer that question more specifically when we discuss their experiences in Dutch schools. The boys must have already been toughened by life, for they went through the whole journey across the ocean, through Spain, over the Pyrenees in the dead of winter, and then to France. Now they were going to another country, another strange world.

On 21 July the father recorded in his diary: "Setting off on a Journey with my two Sons to Amsterdam." They traveled by way of Compiègne and Valenciennes to Brussels, where they stayed the night. "This Road is through the finest Country I have any where seen," Adams set down in his diary, with his usual predilection for superlatives. What he, as a true man of the countryside, found so fine was the profusion of crops growing in the fields and the immense numbers of livestock. As good tourists, they visited the cathedral in Brussels (it was Sunday), but the enlightened American reacted with extravagant annoyance at the piety of the people,

who kneeled in crowds to adore a painting showing a Jew smashing the host. "This insufferable Piece of pious Villany shocked me beyond measure." Responding to his profound need to be fair, however, he added: "Perhaps I was rash and unreasonable, and that it is as much Virtue and Wisdom in them to adore, as in me to detest and despise."[1]

A few days later the company arrived in Rotterdam, where they were invited to dine by a merchant named Dubbeldemuts (Adams reduced this odd name, which in Dutch means "double cap," to Dubbelmets). They viewed the statue of Erasmus, the exchange, and the churches. It was Sunday again and, as good Puritans, they went to church. It was the English church, of course, and they were edified, except when the preacher prayed "for a certain king that he might have health and long life and that his enemies might not prevail against him." That was too much for Adams, and he gave a silent prayer of his own that the king—George III—"might be brought to consideration and repentance and to do justice to his enemies and to all the world."[2]

The countryside all around gave every delight to our rustic diarist— the cattle, grassy meadows, the striking combination of houses, trees, ships, and canals, the cleanliness of everything. On Monday morning they traveled by canalboat through this land of milk and honey to Delft, and at noon on to The Hague. There they were presented by Dumas to the French ambassador; the zealous agent also introduced them to various of his Patriot friends, among them the Leiden newspaper editor Wybo Fijnje. From Leiden they traveled, still by canalboat, to Amsterdam, their destination for the time being. There Adams made contact with a number of Americans. One of them was an adventurer from South Carolina, Alexander Gillon, who was a Dutchman by birth. He had just succeeded in buying a ship in Amsterdam, which he had named after his own state and which he hoped would soon carry him to America. He obviously had good connections in the city. With Burgomaster Hendrik Hooft he saw to it that Adams found decent lodgings in the boardinghouse of one Widow Schorn on the Oude Zijds Achterburgwal near Hoogstraat. It was at once said that Mr. Adams was staying "in too obscure lodgings," but he remained in them until April 1781.

The people with whom Adams made contact all came from the circles of the Patriots: Burgomaster Hooft himself, the old, vain, and highly popular civic father; banker Jean de Neufville, whom we already know; Jan Gabriël Tegelaar, a businessman full of enthusiasm for the Patriot cause and a friend of Van der Capellen; Pensionary Van Berckel, whom we have also met; bankers Nicolaas and Jacob van Staphorst; and still others, all with strong interests in American trade. Probably some of them also had motives of principle.

Adams had a major problem communicating with them. Language was a large barrier: "Business enough was devolved upon me, and that of a nature very difficult to execute among capitalists, brokers, and Hebrews, many of whom could speak or understand as little of the French or English languages as I could of the Dutch," he later recalled. The difficulties with languages gave him trouble, but he found solace in the thought of the eventual triumph of the English language. He had heard it said in Amsterdam, but he had once made the same prophecy to Franklin, and now he described the future at length in a dispatch to the president of Congress. In the last century, he said, Latin was the universal language of Europe. Its place had been taken by French for the present, but in the next century English would be victorious because America would become a populous and important country.[3] Gillon, who lived near Adams on Achterburgwal, was a great help in all his difficulties because he had been born in Rotterdam and had not forgotten his mother tongue.

In those first days of exploration and orientation, Adams did not have to complain about loneliness, for he was surrounded by cordiality. De Neufville invited him for a Sunday outing to his country place near Haarlem; Van Staphorst asked him to dine on Monday. On Wednesday he was at the home of Hendrik Bicker, who gave him advice on how to go about getting a loan; the next Sunday he was at the Crommelins. And so it kept on and on. He strove to become informed about the city and the country by purchasing a map, guide books, and other books, including a copy of Hugo Grotius's *De Jure Belli ac Pacis*. He found a school, the Latin school on the Singel, for his boys. He began to settle in, especially when he received the letter from Congress appointing him as Laurens's replacement, which arrived in the middle of September. He wrote to John Thaxter, a cousin of his wife Abigail, who had come with him from America to be his secretary but had remained behind in Paris, that he should come at once, bringing his books, letters, accounts, and the rest. The wine that he could not take he was to hide as safely as possible in a cellar. And he reported to Abigail that he would stay in Amsterdam, although the air was not as good there as in Paris.[4]

In the romanticized memory of his old age, the first days became a time of severe trial. Speaking about two young Americans, Edward Everett and George Ticknor, who got letters of introduction from his friend Van der Kemp for a European trip, he exclaimed: "Oh! that I had been so introduced when I entered Holland a forlorn Pilgrim in 1780, without a single Line of Introduction to any body. What a Knight Errant I have been."[5]

· II ·

Our knight errant was already comparatively well informed about the country when he came to Holland, insofar as that was possible out of books, and certainly better informed than the average American. Looking for examples by which to justify their insurgency, the American rebels referred fairly often to the Dutch revolt against Spain. But they knew almost nothing about it. The only book that was at all widely known was the work of the famed English envoy in The Hague during the administration of Jan de Witt, the *Observations upon the United Provinces of the Netherlands* by Sir William Temple. It was first published in 1672 and was repeatedly reprinted.[6]

The interest of Adams soon went beyond Temple's work. In 1777 he wrote to Abigail from Philadelphia that he had long been looking for a good book on the Dutch revolt. He had found Temple "elegant and entertaining, but very brief and general." He had looked into the *Annales* of Grotius and had read it in part, "but it is in Latin," and because he had borrowed it, he had not been able to finish it. Now he had found what he sought, the book of Cardinal Bentivoglio, *Delle Guerre di Fiandra*, in the English translation by the earl of Monmouth published in London in 1654. Although the author was, as Adams thought, "a Spaniard and a Tory" (two of the most frightful things anyone could be), one could learn from his book where the American rebellion was headed. "It is very similar to the American Quarrel in the Rise and Progress, and will be so in the Conclusion," Adams stated. A few days later he tried to rouse the enthusiasm of John Quincy, who had just turned ten years of age, for his discovery by giving complete summaries of all the twenty-four portraits depicted in the book and by calling special attention to the descriptions of three sieges—those of Haarlem, Leiden, and Antwerp. "You will wonder, my dear son, at my writing to you at your tender age, such dry Things as these: but if you keep this Letter you will in some future Period, thank your Father for writing it."[7]

These American travelers—Adams and those with him—had, in any case, a very prejudiced picture of the Dutch Republic—prejudiced *in favor.* Holland, as they invariably called it, was very much out of the ordinary. Thaxter, sounding like a school teacher, admonished young John Quincy that he had a great deal of studying to do, for Holland was not like other countries, but was "another Leaf of the great Volume of Nature." As soon as he arrived in Holland, Adams began to sing the praises of the country in his usual exuberant style. His plaudits when he wrote to Abigail were at first greatly exaggerated: "I have been here three weeks, and have spent my time very agreeably here. I am very much pleased with Holland. It is a singular Country. It is like no other. It is all the Effect of Industry, and the Work of Art. The Frugality, Industry, Cleanliness etc. here, deserve the Imitation of my Countrymen. The Fruit of these Virtues has been immense Wealth and great Prosperity. They are not Ambitious, and therefore happy. They are very sociable, however, in their peculiar Fashion."

Some ten days later he added: "The Country where I am is the greatest Curiosity in the World. This Nation is not known anywhere, not even by its Neighbours. . . . I doubt much whether there is any Nation of Europe more estimable than the Dutch, in Proportion. Their industry and Oeconomy ought to be Examples to the World. They have less Ambition, I mean that of Conquest and military Glory, than their Neighbours, but I don't perceive that they have Avarice. And they carry Learning and Arts I think to greater Extent. The collections of Curiosities public and private are innumerable."[8]

But gradually he began to see the dark side more clearly. The lovely canals stank; the industrious Dutch were absolutely intent upon their own advantages; they lived somber lives and seldom turned their eyes up to the sky. Their ideal was to make money. Wishfully, Thaxter wrote to Abigail that he would gladly leave this capital of Mammon: "I never was so thoroughly tired of any Spot of Creation as this Atom stolen from the Dominion of Nature." We hear in these words the classic contempt for the watery country in accordance with the English tradition, and we recall Andrew Marvell's poem *The Character of Holland*, of a hundred years before. The word that Adams soon began to use for the Dutch and their country was "littleness," and he meant not only the small extent of their land but ever more the spirit of a people whose attention was fixed only on pence and farthings.[9]

His disappointment grew, Adams discovered, as he went more deeply into the history of Holland's heroic past. He experienced this past as he walked through the streets, "scaenes once frequented by the great Princes of Orange, by Brederode, Barnevelt, Grotius, de Witts, Erasmus, Boerhave, Van Trump, De Ruyter and a thousand others." The country was still the same, but "it is too rich and loves Money too well." If only the stadholder were a man of the caliber of William the Silent or William III, or of Frederick Henry! Perhaps the problem lay deeper, and the whole office of stadholder was an anomaly. Adams repeatedly turned his attention to the complicated Dutch political system and the strong tensions at work within it. The stadholders, he believed, had taken too much power for themselves. "At critical, dangerous times, tragical scenes have been exhibited, and Barnevelt's head was struck off at one time, Grotius escaped by a sort of miracle, and the De Witts were torn in pieces, it is scarcely too bold to say by the open or secret commands or connivance of stadtholders." The stadholdership was indeed intended, he was willing to grant, "to protect the common people or democracy against the regencies or aristocracy." This fitted into the triple division in which he believed. But the stadholders had taken too much power for themselves.[10]

But, on the other hand, they were not sovereigns. It took quite some time for Adams to get a good grasp of the extraordinarily complicated Dutch political system. Where, in Heaven's name, was sovereignty located in this chaos of interests, influences, connections, and factions, in this motley, many-headed polity? Adams tried to explain it all in a letter to the president of Congress, an explanation undoubtedly intended for himself too: "The sovereignty resides in the States-general; but who are the States-general? Not their High Mightynesses who assemble at the Hague to deliberate; these are only deputies of the States-general. The States-general are the regencies of the cities and the bodies of nobles in the several Provinces. The burgomasters of Amsterdam, therefore, who are called the regency, are one integral branch of the sovereignty of the seven United Provinces, and the most material branch of all, because the city of Amsterdam is one quarter of the whole republic, at least in taxes." In later letters he went even deeper into Dutch politics, describing the structure of government in the towns, the cumbrousness of decision-making procedures, the antagonisms among the various parties, and he drew the conclusion, not wholly without self-satisfaction, that his diplomatic post in a country where the "constitution of government is so complicated and whimsical a thing, and the temper and character of the nation so peculiar" was the most difficult in the whole of Europe.[11]

He tried to size up not only the system but also the men with whom he did business, and he gave interesting portrayals of the Dutch leaders, although as usual he was given to exaggeration. Van Bleiswijk, for instance, was "a great scholar, linguist, natural philosopher, mathematician, and even physician, has great experience in public affairs, and is able and

adroit enough in the conduct of them." But he also understood very well
the weakness of the grand pensionary: "Not having a temper bold and
firm enough, or perhaps loving his ease too much or not having much
ambition or patriotism, or zeal, or health enough, to assume a great and
decided conduct, he is fallen in his reputation." He was being accused of
"duplicity," Adams reported, and he was bypassed in all sorts of matters.
Fagel, the secretary of the States General, was a man of the old stamp,
opposed to all ties with the Americans, but "a venerable man of seventy"
and always polite.

Adams found his best contacts among the Patriots, and it is not hard to
understand why. He praised their qualities extravagantly. He was glad to
have a friend in Cornelis de Gijselaar, the pensionary of Dordrecht, because of his "abilities and integrity, his industry, his great and growing
popularity, and his influence in the assembly of the states of Holland."
Van Berckel was "an excellent character of solid judgment, sound learning, great experience, delicate honor, untainted virtue, and steady firmness." Adriaan van Zeebergh, the pensionary of Haarlem, "is another excellent character," as honest and patriotic. Van der Capellen tot den Pol
excelled all the others in zeal and activity; his situation was so sensitive,
however, that Adams was cautious in what he wrote about him.[12]

In a word, the American observer kept his eyes and ears open and did
whatever he could to find his way in the mad maze of Dutch politics. It is
not very strange that he displayed partisanship, for he had to hope for a
breaking-off of the old Dutch ties with England, and besides the Patriots
were those who received him with open arms. He noted with much pleasure every sign of anti-English feeling, but he was sensible enough not to
build his hopes too high. The longer he stayed in the Netherlands, the
more clearly he understood how difficult it was to bring anything to completion there. His praise for this singular country became more and more
muted, his criticism steadily sharper, as we shall see often in the pages
that follow. But in the end his judgment would turn out to be favorable.
He retained good memories of the Netherlands in his later life, and he
forgot the disappointments. This can be heard constantly in his later letters. "I accord with every Eulogium on the Dutch nation. The Greeks
themselves excelled them in nothing but Taste."[13] What a delightful
exaggeration!

· CHAPTER 8 ·

Three Friends

But your endeavour to do good will not be in vain.
Neither your letters nor mine will be lost.
JOHN ADAMS
to Van der Kemp

E Dutch have become accustomed these days to having one or another rebel or representative from an improbable nation somewhere in Africa appear in our country in order to find support for what for him is the holy cause of its freedom. He does not easily obtain a hearing in The Hague, where the departments of government are, or at least were, the soul of caution. Still he has his opportunities: the journalists are ready for him; he appears in pictures and interviews in the newspapers, and often on television. He finds the response he has been looking for not in The Hague, the city of government, but in Amsterdam, among the news-gatherers, the restless, and the dissatisfied.

That is exactly what happened with John Adams. When he came to The Hague to seek support for his nation's cause, he found the doors closed, at least for the time being, but in Amsterdam he found them open. There he found the sympathizers for whom he yearned, people who were eager to learn more about the American rebellion. Their enthusiasm flowed easily to the new nation and to the dream of liberty which it proclaimed, but they knew very little about it. There were indeed people there who were curious about the war and knew something about the rise of the United States, he wrote home in September, but they were very few. Even in Amsterdam, where there existed the most attention for American affairs and the most favor toward the Americans, there were only a small number who did not view the American resistance as "a desultory rage of a few enthusiasts, without order, discipline, law, or government." And there was scarcely anyone who really had some knowledge of America and its growing population and trade.[1]

We have already seen how the Amsterdammers, Burgomaster Hooft, Pensionary Van Berckel, the bankers Van Staphorst, De Neufville, and others, gave Adams a cordial welcome. Commercial interests and honest curiosity ran together in their attitude, and Adams, who was very much aware of it, gladly met their desire for information. He used every opportunity offered him. He found the best occasion one evening when he was asked to dinner "at the house of a great capitalist," and many guests were present in order to meet him. One of them was a lawyer, Hendrik Calkoen, "the giant of the law in Amsterdam," according to Adams's customarily enthusiastic judgment. Calkoen wanted to know everything, overwhelming the American with "many ingenious questions." It was therefore decided to have the questions and the answers put in writing, and it was duly done. Calkoen was full of enthusiasm; he was completely persuaded; he trumpeted his new convictions everywhere; "and by that means, just sentiments of American Affairs began to spread, and prevail over the continual misrepresentations of English and Stadtholderian gazettes, pamphlets, and newspapers." It is truly remarkable that this catechism of America in twenty-six questions and answers was not published in the Netherlands. A first, private, English edition was published in London years later, in 1786, and it was not until 1789 that a New York publisher risked republishing these *Twenty-six letters upon Interesting Subjects respecting the Revolution of America, written in Holland in the Year MDCCLXXX by his Excellency John Adams.*[2]

These twenty-six letters were indeed only a small part of the flood of information that Adams poured upon his Dutch listeners. Other materials of every sort—letters from America, articles, and sermons—found their way to the printing presses and into books and newspapers. Several publications were more voluminous. One was a translation of a work that Adams had published back in 1775 in defense of the American cause under the name *Novanglus*, and which now appeared in Dutch under the title *History of the Difference between Great-Britain and America since its origin in the year 1754 until the present time.* Even more important was a complete edition of all the constitutions of the thirteen American states, together with other materials, entitled *Collection of the Constitutions of the United Independent States of America, along with the Act of Independence, the Articles of Confederation, and treaties between his Most Christian Majesty and the United American States.*[3] Anyone who wanted could now be truly well informed about the revolution in America.

One of those with whom Adams quickly made contact as a matter of course was Joan Derk van der Capellen. He had received a message of cordial welcome fron Van der Capellen, who was at his country home at

Appeltern, as well as the information that a relation had twenty thousand guilders he wanted to invest in the American cause. Adams replied gratefully that he had long desired to make the acquaintance of the baron, whose "virtuous attachment to the rights of mankind and to the cause of America, as founded in clearest principles, has been long known and admired in America." He asked him for advice and support, but Van der Capellen reacted a bit skittishly to the request. Yes, indeed, he was devoted to the Americans heart and soul, but his personal situation was too vulnerable and he had too many enemies for him to be able to throw himself into the turmoil of battle. That would mean "falling wantonly into the ambushes that my enemies are always setting for me." He was willing to give advice, but could not do anything more. He wrote again that he saw the situation as black, both in Holland, where a major crisis was at hand, and in America, where the English successes in the South and the decline in the value of money made the future precarious. Adams tried to wave these prophecies away, saying that they were tales invented by the English, but the baron kept at his point: if America did not become financially reliable, no capitalist would lend it money. "Do not expect anyone to do it on principle. Such generosity would go beyond the limits of most men's goodness."

Adams responded with a storm of arguments. The losses in the South were limited; America was rich enough in land, people, and products to be able to pay all debts when they came due; and even without loans it would continue the struggle and it would win.[4]

Years later, Adams recalled this dogged debate: "Capellen de Pol was a noble man by nature. A frank, manly, generous soul. Whenever I have met spirits I have always felt them." But the baron let himself be confused by the tales concocted by the Anglomaniacs and sometimes was close to despair. "Upon these occasions I made very light of his fears, contradicted the facts he had heard and denied the inferences he drew," and they therefore often had a "spirited argument," but without putting any damper on their friendship. Time had proved Adams to be in the right, he recalled, and Van der Capellen had gladly admitted he had not been.

But Van der Capellen wanted more than that. He would have most liked to have seen the whole Dutch nation possessed by his own enthusiasm and drawn up in a phalanx behind the Americans. He assured Adams that four-fifths of the Dutch favored the Americans (but we ask ourselves whether he himself really believed it to be true). In the moments of despair that Adams remembered, the baron felt no pride in his compatriots. "I am ashamed to be Dutch," he wrote Adams, and he bitterly regretted that, out of warm love for both peoples, he had tried to keep Adams from gaining a too unfavorable picture of the Dutch people. It would have been better, he said, to have remembered the reply of Statilius to Brutus: *"Sapientis non esse propter malos et stultos in periculum et turbas se dare* [The wise man does not put himself in peril for the sake of fools and knaves]." But this tendency, so characteristic of Van der Capellen, to flee reality when it came to the worst won no respect from the Puritan John Adams. Was Statilius's reply to Brutus really correct? he asked. "Is it not the duty of a wise man sometimes to expose himself to dangers, even for the good of Fools and Knaves?" He preferred, he wrote, to think of another adage, namely that a city was worth saving for the sake of ten just men, or even five or two.[5]

· II ·

Thanks to his good contacts, Adams met an ever-increasing number of Dutchmen. In one of his very first letters, Van der Capellen referred him to "my intimate friend Van der Kemp. . . . He is very learned, very straightforward, and intrepid far beyond what one would expect of a Mennonite minister."[6]

The Mennonite preacher in Leiden, François Adriaan van der Kemp, became one of Adams's most important friends in the Netherlands, and he remained his friend for forty years in America. He came from a well-known family of orthodox Calvinists (his cousin Johannes Theodorus van der Kemp was a celebrated missionary in South Africa), but even as a young man he went his own way. He finally became a Mennonite not because he had had such tendencies from the first but because it was where a long road of doubting and groping led him. That road began in Kampen in 1752. We read in his meticulous hand in the *Geslacht-Boek* (family book) of the Van der Kemps: "On May 4 between half-past twelve and one o'clock I, François Adriaen van der Kemp was born, and baptized on May 17 by Rev. Ramboulet, in the French church at Campen." And he continues: "1763 Sept. 13, became a Cadet in the Regiment of the Prince of Hostein [*sic*] Gottorp in Captain Muntz's Company, obtained my release 13 Oct. 1765." In his neat hand he continues to name the regiments in which he received his training as a youth. But he did not become an officer, although he retained a certain taste for soldiering all his life. He left military service for good in 1769 and went the next year to study at the University of Groningen. There, as always receptive for the new, he came under the influence of the Enlightened professor Frederik Adolf van der Marck, "who, pursued by the hatred of the churchmen, and discharged in violation of all forms of law, carried me along in his downfall."

Thus, inspired by a rousing teacher, Van der Kemp began his break with the faith of his fathers. He must have caused much disappointment to the "Pastor-Loving People infatuated with the name of Van der Kemp," as a later writer declared in his defense. He took another road: "He was born under a more favorable star, and he had received much too refined a judgment from Nature to remain a wretched Catechism-child." He became increasingly convinced of the "irrationality and meanness of the Religion of my Fathers," and so he broke away from the national church.

Van der Kemp himself told the whole story later in his autobiography. Having been deeply influenced by Van der Marck's theories about natural law and tolerance, he was no longer suited for orthodox Reformed theological training, and when he was warned to abjure his heresies, he did exactly the opposite. He disregarded the threat that his living allowance would cease, sold his fine library, placed himself on a diet of bread, butter, cheese, and a little wine, and plunged into the study of political science. But to what purpose even he did not know. He asked for advice all about, especially from his Remonstrant acquaintances, he considered an offer to go to the colonies, and finally he landed up among the Mennonites, "persuaded by their far-reaching tolerance." Being unable to do anything by halves, he permitted himself to be rebaptized, studied for several years at the Mennonite seminary in Amsterdam, and at last became a preacher, first at Huizen for a short time, and then from 1777 at Leiden.[7]

Van der Kemp may have been attracted by the Mennonites' tolerance, but it was an attraction between opposite poles. For he himself was not tolerant, and his conversion did not make him so, although his first apologist, whom we have already quoted, wrote that he "belongs to the Mennonites of the Lamb, who are all, in contrast of those of the Sun, without bile or bitterness, and do not hate, traduce or slander any erring sects, not even Calvinists." There was in Van der Kemp a core of radicalism, of abstract passion. He was enthusiastic, like so many young people, for ideals of liberty and equality, but he went beyond them to the extreme, and with vehement intensity. One example of this is the diet that he followed in his student years, but other examples followed later. As a pastor, he quickly came into conflict with his consistory over a number of questions. In the end politics would estrange him completely from his flock.

Van der Kemp was what we would call today a political preacher. In the pulpit and in his writings he concerned himself, with passion and partisanship, with everything that went on about him. Indeed, he went beyond words to action when he joined a Patriotic "free corps," or volunteer militia company. After the church service was finished, he put on his uniform and went to drill—something his Mennonite host had to get accustomed to.

He involved himself in every political problem of his time. He came to the defense of Van der Capellen when he was expelled from the States of Overijssel and supported him in his attack upon the corvée in Drente; he published pamphlets on the question of unrestricted convoy; he commented on the major study of the Union of Utrecht by Pieter Paulus; he vigorously fought extension of military jurisdiction.

In his published studies he went to work conscientiously, preferring to print the documents themselves, although provided, of course, with fiery introductions. Sometimes prose was not enough for him, and he broke forth in lyric song addressed to the Batavians. These appeared anonymously, but it was generally accepted that their author was Van der Kemp—even when it was not true. In 1780, *Lyric Song* was published, dedicated to seven Frisian Patriots who had protested against the restrictions on the convoys. Because it included a savage attack upon the government, Van der Kemp was brought to trial. He had neither written nor published the piece, but he did not tell the court this, in order to cover the real author, his friend Pieter Vreede. It was an act of heroism, and he was very pleased with it. He did not have to pay the price, however, for when the lengthy trial came to an end, on 23 January 1782, he was acquitted because lese-majesty had not been proved.

The Americans' struggle soon drew his attention. To him it smelled of the same conflict between oppression and liberty which he thought he met everywhere, in which he saw the former as the Past and the latter as the Future. The historian Murk de Jong has called him the *famulus*, the servant, of Van der Capellen, but that is not fair to him. He was more: He constituted a complement to the Overijssel baron, encouraged him, and helped him through his fears. He helped distribute Van der Capellen's pamphlet *To the People of the Netherlands*, and it was no accident that for a long time he was taken for its author.

Van der Capellen had great admiration for him: "Van der K. is as generous as he is capricious. His composure and intrepidity deserve admiration, his patriotism respect." And he spoke for him to all his friends when Van der Kemp tried to quit his pulpit. For the time being it was to no avail. Burgomaster Hooft replied to one such query: "With regard to friend Van der Kemp, the question of what office would be proper for him in case one came open here, these are not always at my disposition, and besides I have colleagues who would not be quite favorable to someone who had left the public church."[8] What could one do for a preacher who had deserted the public church?

What he did was to go on publishing. For the American cause it was very necessary work. At Adams's instigation, Van der Kemp put out in 1781 a documentary work on the New World, *Collection of Pieces relating to the Thirteen United States of North America*.[9] In it the letters of Trumbull and Livingston to Van der Capellen, which had already been published separately, were reprinted, along with all kinds of reports and commentaries on the "cruelty and savagery" of the English, the Articles of Confederation, and other materials, such as a speech of John Hancock and a sermon of a well-known Massachusetts preacher, Samuel Cooper. In his introduction, Van der Kemp opened all the stops. The Americans were an example for the whole world; their struggle filled "every bosom with a craving for freedom." Everything invidious said against the New World—that it was divided, weak, threatened by tyranny—was all slander. America went before the world, before the Netherlands, with which it had so much in common, on the path of virtue, freedom, and patriotism.

Our gallant author was proud of his contributions to the American cause, but he did fear that they would bring hatred upon him. He admitted his apprehension to Adams in an English still redolent of Dutch: "Perhaps shall the publication of the collection of American papers with a preface containing a Paralel between America and the United Provinces with several strictures in honour of the first against the last—render my ennemies an occasion to prosecute me at new." There was an obvious escape: "But America will be my asylum." It was a dream that Van der Kemp had in common with many others; Van der Capellen too played with the idea. The Leiden preacher, however, was the only member of this circle of friends who in the end made it come true; he was driven to it by his foes after their triumph in 1787. It did not reach that point for quite some time, but when he wrote that he had brought many enemies upon his head with his tempestuous writings, Van der Kemp was telling the truth.[10]

He was called an "unworthy servant of the altar," a "sedition-monger, and therefore a useless fellow in the State," "Evangelical Mountebank, a fanatical Preacher, the apostle or the soldier of a hateful clique," and much more like this. The grand pensionary told Van Hardenbroek that when he met Van der Kemp, "he had never seen as sinister a physiognomy" as his; the diarist added the pointed remark that Van Bleiswijk "gave little thought to his own visage, which quite often looks as sinister as anyone's, no matter who." A man like Van der Kemp, the historian-jurist Adriaan Kluit wrote years later, is "held by some in this country to be a *Martyr of Protestantism*. . . . What unfortunate times a Country experiences when it not merely nurtures such Preachers in its bosom, but then hears them publicly commended and extolled, and then sees them *encouraged* as well." [11] In a satirical print that found wide distribution, we see Van der Kemp in the pulpit, half in his robes, half in uniform, preaching out of Priestley (the English radical writer), with the soldiers of his "free corps" behind him (see Figure 9).

Thanks to Van der Kemp's irresistible urge to publish, we are well informed about what he actually said in the pulpit that aroused such a furious reaction. The most notorious sermon was one published as *The conduct of Israel and Rehoboam as a mirror of prince and people—Sermon on 1 Kings XII: 3b–20a*, in which the preacher propounded to his listeners "a sketch of an arbitrary hereditary government and the duties of the people before and after their subjection to it." That spoke for itself, but he set his words within a framework of grim Psalms of imprecation of obvious application, such as Psalm 52—"Why do you boast of evil, / Foolhardy Tyrant?"—and much more in the same vein from Camphuysen's rhymed version of the Psalms in use among the Mennonites. * There were voices raised at the time in favor of expunging the Psalms of imprecation on the occasion of the new Reformed rhyming of the Psalms "because these are not fitting upon the lips of Christians who profess an Evangel that breathes naught but peace." But Van der Kemp was not so irenic a spirit; there was no peace in the land, and he would not preach that there was. That was possible only in the New World. "America, my brethren, has confirmed in our own days the example of Israel, and taught other Peoples how to curb the insolence of Princes and how they can and must defend the rights of the Peoples." [12] In this way he scourged the reality of Holland with the dream of America.

In another sermon he lauded the land beyond the ocean even more extravagantly and gave it as an example for his own country. "In America the Sun of Salvation has risen, which will shine its rays upon us provided we so desire: Only America can revive our Trade and our Shipping: Amer-

---

* The first verse of Psalm 52 is literally translated from Camphuysen's Dutch text: *Waartoe U dus beroemd in 't kwade / Vermeetle Dwingeland?* The King James version reads, "Why boastest thou thyself in mischief, O mighty man?" with no obvious political meaning [Translator's note].

ica can make our Workshops prosper again, and restore our Leiden to its former luster. America provides us again, if we ourselves dare not look upon it, a striking proof of *how Righteousness exalteth a nation: but sin is a reproach to any people.* America can teach us how to resist the degeneration of National Character, how to check the corruption of morals, how to prevent bribery, how to choke off the seeds of tyranny and restore moribund Liberty to health." This summons to conversion of souls and investment of funds culminated in these words: "America has been ordained by the Supreme Being to be the Netherlands' last preacher of repentance. America is ordained to heal the flaws of the Dutch People provided they will follow in her footsteps and are ready to be converted and to live." [13]

· III ·

On entering the St. Peter's Church in Leiden through the southern portal, a visitor immediately sees on the right side (on the left stands the celebrated monument to Boerhaave) a severe, typically classicistic obelisk in black marble. It sets off sharply a sculpture in white stone, a portrait of a man in an oval relief, surrounded by a wreath of oak leaves and the other usual symbols of mourning and immortality, smoking torches inverted, a snake biting its own tail, and the like. On the socle we read: *To our friend Professor Johan Luzac. He was the terror of the oppressors, the solace of the oppressed.* Depicted is a short, high-shouldered man, whose grim features do have something frightening about them. The sculptor was able to capture his subject's undaunted quality. When we compare this portrait in stone with the fine one done in chalk on paper by A. Delfos, which has also been preserved, we can assume that the sculptor has given us a good likeness. Indeed, it is almost certain that he worked from the drawing. [14]

It was probably this quality of undauntedness and great steadfastness, to which all who knew him gave testimony, that drew from John Adams greater admiration for him than for any other of his Dutch friends. Years later, Adams described him as "a large portion of the Salt of the Earth, and if it were not for a few such Lotts, it seems to me the whole Sodom must soon be burned up." [15] (This passage, in which we may note a delightful associative mutation of metaphors, is typical of Adams's lively style.)

Johan, or Jean, Luzac was of French Huguenot descent. His grandfather had fled from Bergerac, in southern France, to Franeker in Friesland, from where his family had spread over the Netherlands. One grandson was the well-known journalist Elie Luzac, an intelligent conservative; another was our Johan, who joined the progressive camp, probably drawn in by members of his family: his grandmother was a De la Lande, his mother a Valckenaer (her cousin was the famed professor of Greek at Leiden University, Lodewijk Caspar Valckenaer, the father of the diplomat), and her sister was married to the Delft Patriot Wybo Fijnje. In his diary, Adams recorded the Luzac family relationships. The entry of 10 October 1782 describes the growth of the Patriot party in Leiden and then goes on: "Mr. John Luzac is now he says universally beloved. A Change of System, had made a Change of Circumstances. Mr. Elie Luzac was the most respected, and had the most Influence but his Anglomanie had brought him into Contempt. Elie Luzac's Father and Johns Father were Brothers. Elies Father is dead. He is called at Leyden een Agt en Veertiger. [These] Nicknames of Agt en Veertiger and Twee en Agtiger, Eight and Fortyer and Two and Eightyer, are adopted as Party Distinctions instead of Whig and Tory, Anglomane and Republican etc." [16]

Young Johan Luzac had been an unusual child, who came to very early maturity, enrolling as a student at Leiden at the age of fourteen and receiving his law degree at seventeen. He entered legal practice at The Hague, having turned down a lectureship in Greek at Groningen and a professorship in law at Leiden; in 1772 he returned to Leiden to join his uncle Etienne in editing the famed French-language newspaper of Leiden, officially entitled *Nouvelles Extraordinaires de Divers Endroits* but known throughout Europe simply as the *Gazette de Leyde*. In 1775 his uncle retired, and Johan assumed the full editorship. After that he was named a professor of Greek in Leiden University in 1785, succeeding his uncle Valckenaer, and he also received an appointment to teach Dutch history. He took up his chair with an oration very characteristic of his ideas, "De Eruditione, altrice virtutis civilis, praesertim in civitate libera" (On erudition as the educator in civic virtue, especially in a free society).

For Luzac, in contrast to his friend Van der Kemp, was definitely no radical. Liberty had to grow cautiously, in partnership with wisdom. The state should be led by wise men, not by notables; that was his progressive principle. Like so many others, he wanted to believe that the Platonic ideal of the Republic was being in large part fulfilled in America. From the start of the rebellion in America, it received a good deal of space in the columns of his newspaper. He had the enthusiastic assistance of Dumas, who felt, however, that he presented the news a bit too coolly and objectively. Dumas did praise Luzac's newspaper to Franklin as the most widely read and impartial in Europe, but he also complained that Luzac sometimes refused to print reports that he did not consider reliable. The ties between Luzac and Dumas remained close, however, even when Luzac took his news of America from other sources, for example, from an English officer in New York, as he told Dumas.[17]

It was Dumas who brought Adams and Luzac together, to their great mutual satisfaction, for what one very much wanted to give away—good information about America—the other very much wanted to receive. Already by the fall of 1780 there had developed a busy exchange between them. Adams sent Luzac all kinds of material, especially on intellectual developments in America, as proof that a new civilization was really arising there. "It is perhaps the first Instance of such Tranquillity of Mind in the midst of a civil war," he wrote in a letter accompanying a copy of the proceedings of the Philosophical Society in Philadelphia. Shortly thereafter it was followed by a copy of the constitution of Massachusetts and the statement: "To tell you the truth, as I had some share in the Formation of this Constitution, I am ambitious of seeing it translated by the Editor of the Leyden Gazette which without a Compliment I esteem the best both in Point of Style and Method in Europe."[18]

Luzac read such contributions with more than just a journalist's eye, recognizing in Adams's ideas much of his own moderate reformism. The "gazetteers" of this country, Adams wrote enthusiastically to Livingston, are more than mere printers; they are learned men with great influence. Through them he could influence public opinion in opposition to the stadholder's court and the government. It was in this way, he added, that he came naturally into contact with the Luzac family in Leiden, whose newspaper had meant so much for the American cause "and who are excellent people."[19]

The court knew what was up. Adams's enthusiasm for his new friend was equaled by the stadholder's annoyance with him. William V wrote to Fagel: "I am not surprised that Mr. Van Thulemeyer complains about Luzac, the gazetteer, who has been guilty of partiality for a long time, especially during the unfortunate troubles in America."[20] William V would still have a chance to unburden himself of his princely displeasure with the Leiden editor, but Luzac was no man to be scared by anyone. This was displayed in the proud words with which he reacted to a complaint against him presented by Sir Joseph Yorke. The English ambassador had sharply attacked Luzac in an extended protest to the States General: "His Sheet is filled with indecencies and calumnies against England." According to Yorke, the *Gazette de Leyde* had reprinted a memoir from the Russian government to the government of England in a distorted version, and he demanded that Luzac be punished.

Luzac did not take the accusation lying down. He set forth in a long letter precisely why the charge of falsification was untrue, and he also advanced the principle of freedom of the press: a newspaperman had the duty of "paying homage to truth in a proper fashion, no matter who may be displeased thereby." Had his uncle Etienne not been proved right in his predictions about America? he asked. When he had written in 1775 about the rise of a mighty republic in the New World, "this had been called *nonsense* at the time and attributed to a *partisanship* worthy of punishment. Now he asks with confidence whose ideas have been proved *false* or true *by time?*" Luzac knew how to defend himself and was not afraid to make enemies. That would be the proud tragedy of his later life, as we shall see.

The cooperation between Adams and Luzac started in very promising fashion, but ran into trouble on the same point of controversy that had caused the alienation between Dumas and Luzac. For the Leiden gazetteer would have nothing to do with any propaganda; what he wanted were documents, not rumors. When, in an editorial in his paper, Luzac also advocated a compromise peace in which Britain would retain New Hampshire and Georgia, Adams began to provide another paper, the *Gazette d'Amsterdam*, with his news items, and he even started a new propaganda organ.

Yet both men continued to hold each other in high esteem. Later, Luzac would dedicate his famous oration on Socrates to his American friend, and Adams would never forget, as he wrote to Van der Kemp in 1808, "the Evenings I spent with our Friend Luzac, with his Father and Unkle, one of four score and the other near it. These venerable Sages entertained me with the controversies in your country."[21]

· IV ·

The conflicts within the country, about which the old gentlemen of the Luzac family could chat so entertainingly, were in every way favorable to Adams's work for the simple reason that they multiplied the possibilities of publication. How busy the printing presses became as partisanship intensified! Books, newspapers, pamphlets, and prints flooded the country. Adams put the opportunities that came to him to masterly use, but he also created some on his own, once he knew his way about in the complicated society of the Dutch. Seldom had a foreigner looked about him so effectively, reading, talking, asking, and arguing on every side. No sooner had he arrived in the Netherlands, he tells us in his recollections, than he began to search out good books on the history of the country, and one book that came into his hands seized his attention. Its title was *Tableau de l'histoire générale des Provinces-Unies* (An account of the general history of the United Provinces). When he picked it up, it had reached six volumes; its author, one Antoine Marie Cérisier, was still at work at it, and eventually it would number ten volumes in all. He resided, Adams was told, in Utrecht. Adams was, as always, ready to take the initiative; confirming the information, he immediately took the canalboat to Utrecht and looked up the writer. Cérisier made a strong impression upon him. "I found him a well-bred man, a fine classical scholar, of an easy, civil and familiar address, so sociable and communicative, that in two or three days, we were as much at home with each other, as if we had been brought up together." [22]

The meeting was so successful that Cérisier moved to Amsterdam as soon as he could manage, attempting in not quite proper fashion to get out of his obligation to complete his history of the Netherlands. If we may trust Adams's memory—he was writing his account almost thirty years later—it was Cérisier who proposed that he publish a newspaper to give backing to the American cause, but it is not inconceivable that it was Adams himself to whom the idea first came, or who at least urged it upon Cérisier. Thus began the publication of a periodical devoted in large part to propaganda on behalf of the Americans, with many contributions by Adams himself. The paper, intended for the upper classes, was written in French and carried the name of *Le Politique Hollandais* (The Dutch politician). According to Adams, it was a big success, and was read and discussed everywhere.

And, of course, disputed. The few facts that we possess about Cérisier, who turned up in such sudden fashion, come to us in part from lampoons directed against him. A contemptuous sketch was given of him in the pamphlet *De Naakte Waarheid* (The naked truth): "When he slid down into our country, he had no cloak to cover his body. He was accompanied by a Savoyard and a couple of marmots; they both arrived from their respective homelands, sharing *taliter qualiter* the costs of the journey. He got his chance with a Bookseller in Utrecht, for whom he wrote from morning to night for his board, bed and a shilling of pocket-money." The story continues that he got into a furious quarrel with Bartholomé Wild, the bookseller, over the completion of his history and even had the whip put to him, and then escaped to Amsterdam to throw himself into the arms of a mistress. This is a more unfavorable version of what happened than Adams's; it is likely that Adams missed some of the facts, but also that the "naked truth" was not limited to the bare facts.[23]

Cérisier did not come from Savoy, although this was trumpeted about in word and song, as, for example, in the feeble jokes of a newspaper named *Lanterne Magique* or *Toverlantaern* ("Magic lantern"), which made fun of the Patriots in a kind of gibberish Dutch.[24] Cérisier was born in Châtillon-les-Dombes, to the north of Lyon, in 1749 and had come to the Netherlands while still quite young. There he lived by his pen in the service of publishers and book dealers. A literary hack who had an easy way with words, he worked in Utrecht, Amsterdam, and Leiden on his history of the Netherlands, on various newspapers, and on political publications such as the much-admired *Grondwettige Herstelling* (Constitutional restoration). In 1785 he spent a short time with Johan Luzac, who needed help in putting out his newspaper after he became a professor at the university; this collaboration soon ended in a bitter quarrel when Luzac, angered by Cérisier's slovenliness and indiscretion, fired him out of hand. Even before the French Revolution, Cérisier went back to his homeland, playing a minor political role but surviving the Terror and the Napoleonic era to die a loyal adherent of the Bourbons in 1828.[25]

He was only a fidgety and troublesome professional zealot with a nimble mind and a love of meddling, a foreigner who soaked himself "pedantically" (as Pieter Paulus complained) in Dutch affairs—but it was just this that made him of great service to Adams. And Adams was grateful to him with his usual excessiveness, writing to Livingston: "How shall I mention another gentleman, whose name, perhaps, Congress has never heard, but, who, in my opinion, has done more decided and essential service to the American cause and reputation within these last eighteen months than any other man in Europe?" Furthermore, Cérisier was "beyond all contradictions one of the greatest historians and political characters in Europe"; he possessed the noblest principles; his writings were superb, *monumentum aere perennius*; "his pen has erected a monument to the American cause more glorious and more durable than brass or marble"; he was read by everyone. But there was a sting in the tail (and how revealing this comment!)—Cérisier had one fault, his "too zealous friendship for me, which has led him to flatter me with expressions which will do him no honor."[26]

· CHAPTER 9 ·

The Great Debate

Such a Nation of Idolaters at the Shrine of Mammon
never existed, I believe, before.
JOHN ADAMS

HE danger in the approach we have been taking to our subject is that we see everything too much through one particular pair of glasses. Everything in Dutch society comes to look as though it were determined by what was happening in America, and this is a serious exaggeration. The question is whether there really was that much interest in the far-off revolution, and if there was, what were the reasons for it and what were the effects upon Dutch society.

The first problem that confronts us is the difficulty of quantifying the intensity of human excitement. The only Dutch historian who has written a book on this subject, F. W. van Wijk, attempted to measure Dutch interest in America by finding out how many pamphlets were put out devoted to the American Revolution. There were, according to his count, 97 such pamphlets, as against 364 on other subjects; he thought this a small number, but we can with equal right call it a very large number, more than 20 percent of the total. Other data can also be counted: the number of political prints, for instance, or the space devoted to the question in newspapers. It is quite possible to estimate such figures, but not to come up with exact numbers. Everyone is talking about America, wrote Nassau la Leck, a nobleman who speculated about the American Revolution at great length, and we have seen Dumas's description of the excitement in the coffeehouses after General Burgoyne's capitulation to the Americans at Saratoga. But their accounts were hardly without bias.[1]

Dumas, Van der Capellen, and other advocates of the American cause were ready with claims that a large majority of the Dutch people were favorable to the Americans, at least four-fifths of them, according to the repeated assertion of the nobleman from Zwolle. But they were probably talking to themselves as much as to others, and they doubted the truth of their own assertions. This explains Dumas's favorite image of the Dutch as being like peat, slow to catch fire but long burning once it caught, as well as Van der Capellen's outbursts against their general indifference, which made him ashamed to be a Dutchman. They counted up those who were for America: religious dissenters, especially Roman Catholics, according to Van der Capellen; the cities, according to Dumas; the Dutch Whigs; the youth. The echoes of their overwrought uncertainties are to be found in Adams's letters: at times he complains about Dutch ignorance of the facts; at others he is ready to take Van der Capellen's contention as truth.[2]

Dropping any attempt to measure in exact quantities, we can still say that the American Revolution probably had a large influence in the Dutch Republic. We have numerous witnesses who tell us so, from both left and right, if I may use this metaphor for political choices in the eighteenth century. We have, on the one hand, a moderate Patriot like C. L. Vitringa, who asserted that the States (anti-Orangist) party "had come to the understanding and the conviction that the spirit of the times required granting more influence upon the government to the people, thanks to the political concepts that the philosophers of this period had set in motion and that had been further developed to no small extent by the North American spirit of freedom." We have, too, a French literary hack like the book dealer Joseph Mandrillon, who ascribed the "source of the first ferment among the Inhabitants" of the Netherlands to "the excellent works published in England upon the subject of the American war." According to Mandrillon, Richard Price especially was "read with incredible eagerness . . . by every rank of Citizens." Finally, Adriaan Loosjes, the author of the supplementary volumes to Jan Wagenaar's history, treats the American uprising as a central fact for Dutch history and quotes repeatedly from books about America by Raynal, Price, Adams, and others.[3]

The same observation, although with contrary feelings, comes to us from the other, conservative, side. Laurens Pieter van de Spiegel, the last grand pensionary of Holland, who was jailed in 1795 after the overthrow of the old Republic, testified bitterly: "The Union of North America that emerged was a pure democracy that turned the heads of many, as if there were no freedom outside this Constitution." And Adriaan Kluit, as we have already seen, placed upon "the American Freedom-malady" the blame for all "the subsequent disasters, misfortunes and losses that befell the Republic." He cited Mandrillon's remark about Price's popularity and added sarcastically: "A precious testimony, certainly, to the splendid results that such writings as those of Price, Priestley, Paine and Rousseau have had in Europe and may possibly continue to have, unless All-

Governing Providence prevents it! . . . The American plans for Freedom were exalted to the skies, and together with them the Colonists."[4]

Foreign observers came to the same conclusion. In the numerous books about the Dutch troubles that appeared in England after the debacle of 1787, this judgment is repeated again and again. "The domestic calm which the United Provinces were able to enjoy was broken by the war between Great Britain and its rebellious colonies in America." Even James Harris, the English ambassador who replaced Yorke in 1784, saw matters no differently: After the American uprising began, when doubts arose about the authority of the stadholder, "an extraordinary alteration took place in the minds of a great part of the people of Holland." Indeed, all authority came under attack when the English colonists in America succeeded in their rebellion.[5]

Harris attempted to explain the real source of this strange "vertigo of resistance to the powers legally established." He showed understanding of the republican sympathies of the Dutch for the Americans, which were fed by the memories of their own similar situation as rebels two centuries before. But his analysis went deeper: he pointed to the relative decline of the Dutch as a result of the rise of new powers like Russia and Prussia and the prosperity of England. In his judgment, envy of the old maritime rival had to have played an important role in Dutch interest in the American Revolution. Idealism, strengthened by a desire for revenge and by self-interest, drove the Dutch. Loosjes pursued an analogous argument. "Considered from the side of Natural Law and Humanity, it was certainly reasonable to offer a helping hand to Three Million Fellow-Creatures against an Empire which in her ambitions trampled the most sacred Rights of Mankind. . . . But who does not know how little these usually meant in the scale of Politics when no other factors shifted the balance to the side of Justice?" Colenbrander came to the same conclusion a century later: "Enthusiasm and self-interest alike tended toward support for the Americans."[6]

· II ·

Besides the published materials in newspapers and books, a fair number of private writings have been preserved that point to a broad enthusiasm for the American cause. They are to be found primarily in the papers of Benjamin Franklin in the library of the American Philosophical Society in Philadelphia, for it was to him that most zealots turned first. He was clearly the personification of the revolt, and he was close, within reach in Paris after 1776, as the representative of everything that a generation on the verge of Romanticism was beginning to dream of—liberty, simplicity, truth.

The letters of Dutchmen to Franklin have already been put before modern readers by H. Hardenberg in a fine article, but it is worthwhile, nonetheless, to give full thanks to this historian and also to the long-forgotten correspondents themselves by returning to their letters in the context of this work.[7] In some of these letters the spirit of the later eighteenth century speaks distinctly, sometimes almost pathetically. They also tell us much about how public opinion was influenced in the Netherlands.

This is particularly true in the letters of several newspaper editors and writers like the Rotterdammer Reinier Arrenberg, who is better known for his bibliography of eighteenth-century books, and the Utrechter Claude Isaac Peuch. Arrenberg wrote to Franklin in his official capacity as second secretary of the Batavian Society in Rotterdam. His formal purpose was to send the American the society's transactions, but in reality, as he admitted, he wanted to receive, in his post of "Gazetteer of this city," news from America that would counterbalance the "false reports" spread by the English. He was ready to pay for the material. Franklin replied at once, sending Arrenberg a propaganda piece about English atrocities in America, which the Rotterdammer passed to Luzac to publish in his French-language newspaper. Through his friendship with the preacher of the Presbyterian church in Rotterdam, Benjamin Sowden, who was also in contact with Franklin, Arrenberg was in a position to obtain other materials from America, too, which he published assiduously. After the victory at Saratoga and the conclusion of the French-American alliance, Arrenberg wrote again to Franklin to give his congratulations and to ask for more information.[8]

There seems to have existed a jealous competition between the Dutch newspapers for American news. Describing himself as the "subject of a free state and an admirer of the American freedom struggle," Peuch, the editor of the *Gazette d'Utrecht*, also wrote to Franklin for news. He had noted, he said, that two of his professional colleagues already maintained relations with very well informed Americans; he did not know who these latter were, but in all fairness he too should be given information. He was not pursuing self-interest; as a writer for the public, he admitted, he had "neither Religion nor Fatherland," and as a free man, he did not wish the freedom of his fellow men to be exposed any longer "to the whims of ministers, whose selfish purposes seldom had as their aim the happiness of the peoples whose government had been entrusted to them by their Sovereign." Whether such strong language helped we do not know, for there is no answer from Franklin in his papers, and a later letter from Peuch has been lost.[9]

A different purpose was on the mind of Elias de Baussay. He wrote Franklin that he had been active in Amsterdam as an agent for the elector of Trier. Did Franklin need a secret agent in the Netherlands? he asked, offering himself for the job. Obviously he did not know of Dumas's existence. In a later letter he gave an overall view of the situation in the Republic. He told of Yorke's second attempt to obtain troops by an offer to the prince of Waldeck, which failed because the States General refused its consent. Amsterdam, De Baussay told Franklin, was the bulwark of pro-American feeling, and the city vigorously sought the strengthening of the navy, having submitted four petitions already to that end.[10] Franklin received far too many letters of this kind for him to be able to reply to all of them.

To these letters we may add the requests of young officers who yearned to enter the American service, but who had little notion of what they could expect. These volunteers seldom actually departed, for all the fire that their letters breathed. A priceless example of such an enthusiast was Wildricus Wildrik, the medical officer of a Dutch regiment stationed in the Barrier town of Namur. He wrote in very clumsy French to the admired American, offering to go to serve in an American hospital. Were the Americans not fighting for "heavenly freedom, the most pleasant gift in this world?" He wished to devote himself to their cause and was even ready to leave behind his beloved wife and their only son, who was eight years old. But naturally he would have to receive travel expenses and an allowance for his family. Would Franklin please excuse his mistakes "in the French language" (*dans l'engage Françoise*); he came from Overijssel, spoke Dutch, and could understand German. After this confession, he turned to pompous Latin: "*Interim Deus ter optimus maximus, cui suspiria mea omni de corde mitto, adesse velit tuis vestrorumque consiliis justis,* etc." (In the meanwhile may the thrice-highest God, to whom I send supplications from my heart, support you and the just deliberations of your people, etc.). "*Utinam aliquid boni, commodi, justi contribuere possem*" (If only I could contribute some thing good, useful and just to your cause). And, finally, "*vir doctissime, doctissime Domine*" (most learned Sir), please keep all this secret, "*sub rosa.*"

Another letter from him a few months later began right off in Latin (which I spare the reader). As long as the Americans, unjustly called rebels, had been fighting for their golden freedom, he said, so long had they been constantly in his thoughts. He kept dreaming about them. One night he awoke ten times in his excitement. His wife now called him *"meum Americanum"* (my American) and his little son said, *"Pater meus est amicus Americanorum"* (My father is a friend of the Americans). He did not know how it had come about; no one had tried to talk him into it. It had happened spontaneously; what the heart feels, the mouth speaks. He asked modestly if he could be Franklin's friend, and then he continued in French: *"Pardonnez moi, vir humanissime! cette arrogance, cette extravagance, cette sottisme, je suis comme d'être ravi en extase, quando pensito de Americanis"* (Pardon me, most humane Sir! this arrogance, this extravagance, this foolishness, I am in ecstasies, when I think about the Americans). But translation loses the savor of Wildrik's version of French, with its mixture of Latin and Italian! He was in the grip of the American fever, he wrote, and there was no cure. Could he join the Americans? He was willing to come to Paris; it was only a few days away from Namur. He could not go on this way. When in church he did not listen to the preacher; in company he lost the thread of conversation; he went to bed and arose by American time![11]

This was all to no avail, for Franklin did not answer. The Dutch doctor's feelings must have seemed to him excessive in the extreme. Besides, as we have seen, many letters arrived with such offers, although few in such extravagant language. One Baron Van Wijnbergen (a Dutch baron!) offered his services; he had been ready to fight for the king of Prussia, but had not been accepted, and anyway he preferred to fight for a republic. One Lucas Butot, from the little Dutch town of Bodegraven, had invented a new way of making bullets and pleaded for a moment's consideration. A member of the town council of the little Zeeland port of Zierikzee, Pieter van Noemer, poured out his heart in sixteen pages of Latin prose: he had been scandalously passed over in his province and wanted now to go to America. The list goes on. As in Adullam's cave, "every one that was in distress, and every one that was in debt, and every one that was discontented" (1 Sam. 22:2) turned his face to the West, but without much result. In most cases the fever passed quickly, even for our overwrought Wildrik. He rid himself of his obsession, or so it appears from the publication, in 1781, of his book *An Enquiry into Whether the Causes of Smallpox, Measles, Flux, bloody Flux and Other Diseases, but Especially Scabies, must be ascribed to Insects.*[12]

· III ·

There are questions we must ask before we go on with our story. What did the Dutch really know about America? Did they have any understanding of real life in the New World? If not, did they at least have a certain picture, a mythically colored vision, to put in the place of the reality? "This country has . . . little knowledge of the numbers, wealth and resources of the United States," John Adams wrote to the president of Congress, and he was probably right in his observation. In any case before 1775 almost nothing was known of American conditions, even though the Dutch had maintained a colony there during the previous century, the Dutch language was still in current use in the Hudson Valley, and all sorts of printed materials, chiefly of religious character but also some of a political nature in support of the brewing revolution, had appeared in Dutch.[13]

The curiosity about America that suddenly exploded during the seventies, as is apparent from the flood of books and pamphlets of those years, began with translations of works by French authors on this subject. A typical eighteenth-century abstract philosophical debate had developed in France about the significance of the New World. The great naturalist Buffon claimed that the natural conditions in America, the "combination of elements and other physical causes," stood in the way of a healthy development of flora, fauna, and even the human race. Even full-grown persons from other climates who settled there lost their powers; they had to "shrink and diminish under a niggardly sky and an unprolific land."

This scientific nonsense was eagerly spread far and wide by various "philosophers." One of them was the strange Abbé Corneille de Pauw, a Dutchman by origin, who for a long time enjoyed the favor of Frederick the Great and afterward settled in the western German town of Xanten, where he published a variety of *Recherches philosophiques* (Philosophical investigations) about the Egyptians, the Chinese, the Greeks, and, in 1768, the Americans. Another was the equally credulous Abbé Raynal, who in 1770 published a huge book, *Histoire philosophique et politique des Etablissements et du Commerce des Européens dans les Deux Indes* (Philosophical and political history of the settlements and trade of Europeans in both Indies). America, these scholars of quick pens and universal knowledge maintained, was a late creation, still incomplete and unfit for human life, let alone civilization. Europe was incurably infected by this contagion and had to pay the price for its colonialism with diseases and bankruptcies.

Vehement debate flamed up. Another protégé of Frederick the Great, the Benedictine Dom Pernety, disputed De Pauw, and others became involved in the futile quarrel. Even a truly able historian like the Scot William Robertson was influenced by Raynal's affirmations, and there was widespread belief in the inevitable backwardness of the Americans. But this superstition was swamped just as it reached its high point by the wave of sympathy for the American Revolution, which so obviously proved the contrary of these abstractions. Raynal even repented, and he testified to his change of heart at great length. The phantasms vanished like mist before the sun, but they left visible traces for a long time, even in the debates in the Netherlands, where no one had ever been completely carried away by the French errors. Observations about the weakness, superficiality, and childishness of the Americans found their origins in these theories, which the Dutch knew from a constant flow of translations.[14]

All this indirect information, however unreliable, nonetheless aroused curiosity, but the Dutch became really caught up in the debate over America only when the news of the revolt came in 1775. Then a flood of new publications began to appear, for and against American independence, for and against the Dutch taking sides in the conflict. Although objectivity was ordinarily hard to find in them, all this excitement meant at least that more direct, less mythic reports about America were reaching the Netherlands. It was probably not mere chance that among these were the religious works of Jonathan Edwards, the deep-thinking pietist from New England, published in Dutch translations. They were no doubt directed at a special public, one that sought intense religious experience and adapted Lockean empiricism to the promptings of the pious soul, but they were put out by a Utrecht bookseller, Van Paddenburg, who soon became one of the most important publishers of Patriotic literature.[15]

As the debate continued, the Dutch began truly to be informed about American reality. Travelers' accounts that included political commentary were published. The extensive reportage on America by the Swedish botanist Pehr Kalm appeared in Dutch translation in 1772, less than a decade after its first publication in Swedish; for the most part it was an objective work filled with information about flora and fauna, although it was here and there afflicted with strange notions about the backwardness of the New World; the reader learned more about tobacco and Indians, however, than about the white colonists. The Dutch could read in their own language a travel book by an English preacher, Andrew Burnaby, who had visited all the colonies from Virginia to Massachusetts in 1759 and 1760. He wrote an entertaining if somewhat condescending account which became a bestseller, and in 1775 published a new edition with comments on current events, which was translated into Dutch the next year. His informative book was highly tendentious. He repeated the French argument that climate in the New World made men listless and indolent, so that they might become happy but never stalwart: "America is formed for happiness, but not for empire." The country was too big ever to be united, "the difficulties of communication, of intercourse, of correspondence, and all other circumstances considered." If it gained independence, it would fall into civil war. And it could not be defended, for its long coastline laid it open to any foe. His highly significant conclusion was that "America must first be mistress of the seas, before she can be independent, or mistress of her own." In other words, the country was still far from ripe for independence.[16]

Publication of this book in the Netherlands was probably the work of English propaganda, launched by one of the most interesting defenders of the English cause in the Dutch Republic, Isaac de Pinto. Businessman, economist, philosopher, and pamphleteer, he was a fiery Orangist. He had been an adviser to the English government during the peace negotiations in 1763 and had been rewarded with an English pension; his numerous enemies therefore accused him of being a hack writer in English pay. He furiously denied it, but confirmation comes to us from no less a source than James Harris, who tells how Dumas and De Pinto—whom Dumas in his letters frequently spoke of in contempt as "the Jew Pinto"— argued in the coffeehouses. The "Jew Pensioner of England," wrote Harris, is a very learned man; "he is very lame, and very deformed, and hence he is sometimes called *Le Diable Boiteux*.* His pension makes him entirely English as to politics. He is of Sophia's mind, *Que le vrai Amphitrion est celui ou l'on dine*."**[17]

If De Pinto was paid, he earned his wages, for he published a large number of pamphlets and translations in defense of England.[18] Naturally, he was the butt of rejoinders, and a full-scale paper war ensued. Translations of English advocates and antagonists of the American struggle poured from the presses. The favorite skirmishers were clergymen. The

---

* "The Lame Devil," after the principal character's in Le Sage's novel of the same name [translator's note].

** "That the true Amphitryon is the one who is your host at dinner," a famous phrase in Molière's play *Amphitryon* [translator's note].

English position was defended by Dr. Josiah Tucker, the dean of Glouces-
ter, and by John Wesley himself, and it was attacked by Richard Price and
American preachers such as William Smith and Samuel Cooper.[19] As the
wrangling grew, so did the public's interest, and propaganda speeded the
supply of information. Sometimes a work tried to be objective, like the
*Observations upon North America and the English Settlements There,
Based on Oral Reports from Mr. Franklin*: this work was translated from
German, and its author was Gottfried Achenwall, professor of public law
at Göttingen. It gave, though scantly, a picture of the colonists' life. Probably the most partisan, but also the best reading, was the translation of
Paine's *Common Sense* (into French!) that appeared in Rotterdam in
1776, the year of its publication in Philadelphia.[20]

It is striking that virtually all of these works about America were of
foreign origin. The first, and for some time the only, Dutchman who un-
dertook a more extensive study of the American question was a political
philosopher with an eminent name, Louis Theodore, count of Nassau,
lord of De Leck and Odijk. He was a descendant of Prince Maurice and
a councillor in the court of Vianen, a sinecure that provided him with
all the time he needed for his political dabbling, for that is really all his
studies amounted to. In 1777 he began to write a series entitled *Letters
on the North American Troubles, the Likely Outcome of the War, and the
Influence that These Events May Have upon the Interests of Europe in
General and of This State in Particular*, which he signed with the name of
Nassau la Leck. They appeared, eighteen in number, under the imprint of
the bookseller Van Paddenburg.

He was writing, the count declared at the very start, because he had no
other profession. He wished to be objective, to be ruled neither by English nor American interests. His relatives withheld from him all interces-
sion and protection in "the Courts of this Republic," and to be useful he
devoted himself to these studies. Besides the *Letters*, he published a play,
a number of pamphlets, and a journal, *De Staatsman* (The statesman),
which was a kind of general continuation of his American letters and appeared between 1779 and 1784, first in Utrecht at the press of Bartholomé Wild (the man for whom Cérisier worked) and later in Amsterdam at Allart and Holtrop's.[21]

Nassau la Leck is a very interesting and almost unique figure in the
Dutch world of the eighteenth century. A political philosopher of broad
interests and great knowledge, he also, like most philosophers of his time,
possessed a fair measure of the power of abstraction. His arguments are

ingenious, though sometimes too long winded, and not unimaginative. He was essentially a kind of political commentator on current events; in our time he would certainly be on television. In hindsight, we can point out many wrong prognostications, but it was still an achievement to have been so broad in his approach and so objective in his commentary. That did him no good, of course—how could it, in such a conflict? He got a reputation as a Patriot and was one of those who found it safer in 1787 to leave the country. He returned later and died in 1795 at Ravestein.

· IV ·

It would lead us too far afield to discuss here the whole complicated debate on America in all its aspects, especially the economic. At the heart of the matter, however, we find essentially two arguments used over and over again by opponents of closer relations with the rebels. First, America could never become an independent and prosperous nation because it was too large and too divided to form a single country. Second, thanks to its immensity, it might become such a powerful empire that it would constitute a fundamental threat to Dutch trade, especially in the colonies. In other words, America would be both too weak and too strong. These two contradictory contentions were used constantly; sometimes they rubbed shoulders in the same piece. They were invoked to prove that the hope that Dutch trade would prosper when the English mercantilist monopoly was broken and navigation to America was free was nothing but an idle dream, "the fancies of the overheated minds of those who promised to win us gold from America," as Amsterdam burgomaster Rendorp wrote.[22]

America was too strong and too weak. "Assuming that the rebels finally gain the upper hand, I cannot understand how the twelve colonies could form one Republic when they are so different in their feelings about religion and other matters that they cannot easily agree about a fixed form of government," wrote Fagel to the Prince of Orange in 1776.[23] Nassau la Leck presented the same notion in his *Letters*: there were too many different kinds of people in America, he averred, too many Germans, in particular (he thought they were a majority), who were not at all ready for freedom, for they had "been brought up in the deepest subjection and bondage." In his *Collection*, Van der Kemp repeated the nonsense about a majority of Americans being Germans, but he held that this was no problem, for although they were "ambitious, insufferable and proud in high places, and slavishly obsequious when kept low," in America they lost those harmful traits. De Pinto explained just what the differences were and came to exactly opposite conclusions: for him the inhabitants of Pennsylvania, the Germans, that is, were peaceful and tolerant, but the Puritans of Massachusetts were the true evildoers, a fanatic, superstitious, and narrow-minded people.[24]

An extensive country simply cannot exist in freedom—that was the principle, honestly accepted as truth, that lay behind these objections. It had been learned from Montesquieu, whose echo we hear repeatedly among our controversialists. The Americans would be able to keep together so long as they were fighting, but once they were free, they would certainly split apart. If strong authority was necessary, as Nassau la Leck wrote, why not maintain that of the English? asked De Pinto. "The essence of Political Liberty consists in a Constitution which grants power only to the wise and the intelligent and freedom to all." De Pinto used these words with the English constitution—the best form of government to an Enlightened man of the eighteenth century—in mind. Soon the Americans would build their own political order on the same notion. But the foes of America did not see that country's future in such rosy colors; they expected the spirit of rebellion and popular omnipotence to create anarchy and ultimately lead to dictatorship.[25]

At the same time these same writers argued that America would become a mighty empire and then—oh, horror!—would form a threat to the Dutch colonies. Behind all this contradictoriness lay the same uncertainty that had made Raynal's work so ambivalent. The unsuspecting Dutch reader who plunged into the translation of that almost all-encompassing book would meet Buffon's full ideas in volume 6 (book 17): America was a backward country where climate wore out and consumed people. But in the following volume (book 18) he would come up with exactly contrary information: America was the land of the future; it would build up an expansive empire once it had been loosed from its colonial ties; and it was therefore not wise to work against England, for that was to exchange an enemy close at hand for an "even more formidable foe" far away. But there was not much that could be done about it really. Raynal described the future wholly deterministically: "The more our peoples one by one weaken and succumb, the more the population and agriculture of America will increase; the Arts, brought there by our endeavors, will speedily take root; that country, having come up from

Nothing, burns with the desire to make a show upon the face of the Globe and in the History of the World." [26]

A French lawyer active in London, Simon Linguet, spread similar ideas in his newspaper *Annales politiques, civiles et littéraires du 18e-siècle* (Political, civil and literary annals of the eighteenth century), and he too was widely read in the Netherlands. De Pinto also readily adopted these ideas and gave them a foundation in another typically eighteenth-century notion, that northern countries are always stronger than southern: "Northern nations, thanks to their large populations and their bodily vigor, have always invaded and subjugated Southern nations." What would happen to poor Europe when it no longer received the riches of Mexico and Peru because the Americans had got the whole continent into their hands? Nassau la Leck reasoned in the same way: Driven to expansion by the "cruel climate" and infertility of their land, the Americans would sail to the south "upon the always favorable winds" and take over the Dutch colonies, which were so close, for their own use, and they "will soon be in a position to decide our fate, yes, to lay down the law to us." They will "become wealthy all of a sudden. . . . They will be all the more formidable and terrifying. . . . Then they will crush Europe by means of the Arts and Sciences which they will have raised to the highest perfection; they will subject the Mother Country, timid now before the luster and the prosperity of her former children." [27]

Eighteenth-century thinkers had a fondness for seeing large lines and fixed patterns in history, like the regular expansion from north to south. Even more favored by many was the belief in the movement of civilization from east to west, and they saw a kind of Great Circle, in which the ancient cultures of Asia and Egypt were followed by that of Greece, the Greek by the Roman, the Mediterranean by the Western European; now civilization was on another westward journey, which would close the circle and bring history to completion. This could be given a positive interpretation, of course, as Crèvecoeur had done in his well-known *Letters from an American Farmer*: "Americans are the western pilgrims who are carrying along with them that great mass of arts, sciences, vigour and industry which began long since in the East; they will finish the great circle." Van der Kemp wrote in similar vein to Adams: Europe was doomed to go under, as Asia had, and civilization would find refuge on the coasts of America. But that picture of the future struck terror to the hearts of many. The Dutch stadholder, with his usual insight, impressed upon Amsterdammers who came to an audience with him that America would take away Dutch trade as the Dutch had that of Venice.[28]

America would be the Dutch undoing—that weighty argument gave quite a bit of trouble to the ardent enthusiasts for the American cause. It was even proclaimed in poetry:

> Weep, you Dutch Merchants! your own demise bewail!
> America's flag it will to topmast nail!
> Thirteen new-born states you've need indeed to fear!
> Weep! when *they* PROSPER, *your* OWN FALL IS NEAR.* [29]

· V ·

It was hard for these pessimists, these realists—call these foes of America what you will—to row against the stream of yearnings, fantastic notions, and dreams about the New World which Dutch merchants nurtured. Greed had touched them, and greed makes men quick to believe. Adams described them well in a letter to Franklin: "There is an appetite here for American trade as ravenous as that of a shark for his prey." America was still the land of gold in the imagination of many, and the Dutch attitude was determined in large part by fear of being too late. What if England became reconciled with America and kept a monopoly of some kind? What if France should win a favored position thanks to its treaty with America? Either way, too much prudence would hurt Dutch trade. "To declare the North Americans rebels and treat them as such was no different, if the fortunes of war turned in their favor, than to abandon a Branch of Trade whose golden fruit, so long harvested by England, would now fall into the laps of Neighbors."[30]

It was not too difficult for those who shared these fears for the future of Dutch trade to refute the arguments of their opponents. Nassau la Leck became his own harsh critic. Had he maintained that America was too weak and divided? This could be granted, but it was still no obstacle in the way of good commercial relations. The disunity that must be anticipated was still far off and in any case would mean not the loss of independence but the creation of "thirteen different smaller Powers," and in

---

* Ween, Neerlands Koopmanschap! ween, hijs de treurvlag op!
  Straks klimt de Heilzon van Amerika ten top!
  Vrees vrij voor d'opkomst van die dertien Wingewesten!
  Ween! want *haar* voorspoed is *uw* ondergang ten lesten.

the meantime there was much profit to be made. Van der Kemp contended that there was no need to fear anarchy and resulting tyranny in America, the country had a healthy constitution. "But America will suffer the fate of all other empires. True, but that holds for everything in this world. America indeed may prosper for centuries before misfortune strikes, and then the inhabitants of the coast will be the first to be affected. So long as the nation does not lose its character, a Brutus will be able to rescue them from a General or a presumptuous Citizen who trampled on the Liberty of their Fatherland, and then they would find in their constitution the balm to heal the new wounds." What a fine example of eighteenth-century thought Van der Kemp treats us to here, and how gladly people listened to him.[31]

But such optimism meant running the danger of avoiding Scylla by sailing into Charybdis. If America grew so prosperous and powerful, would it not become a threat to the Old World and to its colonies, just as the antagonists were quick to argue? A "Letter from an American Gentleman to his Friend in Europe," reprinted in the newspaper *De Vaderlander*, neatly indicated the dangers to be faced. Europe was at this time at a height, the anonymous letter writer held, but it was wearing itself out, America had reached the point "where we can do without Europe more easily than Europe can do without us." The Americans would become traders themselves "and deal the death blow to your trade, which is already in decline." "The Lord who governs all therefore has something splendid in mind for us." Dutch merchants had reason to be frightened of such a Providence; they wanted America to succeed, but not so completely.[32]

The apprehensive friends of America asked for answers from the man who had to know them, John Adams. They importuned him with speculations of every sort, he wrote to Franklin. "Every one has his prophecy, and every prophecy is a paradox." There were those who maintained that America would "become the greatest manufacturing country, and thus ruin Europe." Others added that America would become so strong that it would threaten Europe. But not in a thousand years, Adams told them, would America manufacture enough goods for its own use, and Americans so hated war and loved peace that they were hardly able to raise an army to defend their freedom, "and therefore, while we have land enough to conquer from the trees and rocks and wild beasts, we shall never go abroad to trouble other nations."[33]

Even the friends of America were not entirely confident that Adams

was telling the whole story when he so easily waved away their difficulties. They used the appearance of a strange pamphlet to warn him of
their concerns. Adams gave the pamphlet, which was his own adaptation
of an article by Thomas Pownall, a former governor of Massachusetts
then living in England, to Luzac for his judgment. Luzac found it a fine
piece, but had "one small scruple." The author presented the growing
commerce of the United States as a bit too successful, which might well
frighten off its readers. A general free trade was probably a great good,
and the possession of colonies an evil. But prejudices were deeply rooted,
and, Luzac wrote, when he pleaded the cause of America, he was often
told that a free America would one fine day lay down the law to Europe
and seize its colonies, swallow up Mexico, Peru, Brazil, and Chile, and
repay Europe's good deeds with ingratitude. It would be a pity to change
the pamphlet, Luzac wrote, but a foreword might put the matter in a better light, and he offered to write one.

Adams gladly accepted and told Luzac to write what he pleased. Of
course it was nonsense to think that Europe had anything to fear from
America, he added. It would remain an agricultural country for centuries,
dependent upon European industry. It would supply raw materials, nothing more, until the entire continent was populated, and that would take
several hundred years. He wrote to Van der Capellen, who had raised the
same difficulties, that Pownall had written his little book to create fears in
the Dutch Republic, for he was certainly no friend of America.[34]

Luzac wrote his introduction at once. He argued that the commercial
benefits to be expected from the opening up of America were much
greater than the disadvantages of competition. The little book appeared
in November 1780 under the title *Pensées sur la Révolution de l'Amérique Unie* (Thoughts about the Revolution of United America). Feelings
calmed down.

Adams had not, however, been wholly candid in the affair. He did not
really mean the pretty picture that he had painted of America as an economic colony that would remain dependent upon Europe. For, not long
after, he wrote to a member of his family, not without bitterness, that
America should never expect anything good from Europe. "I wish we
were wise enough to depend upon ourselves for every Thing, and upon
them for nothing. Ours is the richest and most independent Country under Heaven, and we are continually looking up to Europe for Help! Our
Riches and Independence grow annually out of the Ground." But this private outburst resulted from professional fatigue; in his official capacity

the American envoy continued to tell the Dutch what a splendid future awaited them in American trade.[35]

The happy faith that this was so was also put into poetry:

> Joy takes in Village and in City,
> Each river exults that runs into the Sea.
> One shout resounds: AMERICA IS FREE!
> Fountainhead of Holland's prosperity.* [36]

* Elk Landschap, elke Stad kan nauw zijn vreugde bedwingen.
  Hoe juicht de Maas en Waal, hoe juicht het scheeprijk Y.
  Elk roept met éénen stem: AMERICA IS VRIJ!
  En ieder speld hieruit een bron van zegeningen.

CHAPTER 10

Henry Laurens's Papers

*It looks as if England would force the Dutch into
the War: but if they take a Part it will
certainly be for us—Oh, that Laurens was there.—
Oh, that Laurens was there!*
JOHN ADAMS

HEREAS the said Henry Laurens has, by unavoidable accidents, been hitherto prevented from proceeding on his said agency; we therefore reposing especial trust and confidence in your patriotism, ability, conduct, and fidelity, do by these presents constitute and appoint you, the said John Adams . . . our agent for and on behalf of the said United States, to negotiate a loan with any person or persons, bodies politic or corporate, promising in good faith to ratify and confirm whatever shall by you be done in the premises, or relating thereto." With these words, Adams had been authorized in June to borrow money in Amsterdam.

By the time Adams received the report in September, Laurens had sailed, been caught up by fate, and was already locked up in the Tower of London. The provisional American agent in Holland could not yet know that, and he took up his task with his usual energy. He went to work at once, he wrote to Congress; he could not give the names of the persons with whom he was in contact but they deserved the confidence of Congress. They had told him bluntly that he was badly informed; there was not as much money available as he thought, and concluding loans was not easy either. Nor did America have as many friends as he had believed. They found it strange, Adams added, that Congress should send an envoy to conclude a loan without at the same time empowering him to reach a political agreement and conclude a trade treaty. He suggested that Congress send a plenipotentiary to The Hague to present himself to the Prince of Orange and the States General—that would make a loan far easier.[1]

Thus Adams's enthusiasm ran aground immediately upon the caution of the Amsterdam bankers. They considered him a friend and treated him with courtesy, but would give nothing without first being given greater assurance. The persons whose names he would not give were eminent figures in the money world of Amsterdam. His principal adviser was Hendrik Bicker, a member of "one of the most ancient, opulent, and respectable families in that city," as Adams wrote years later. "He was to me a sincere friend and faithful counsellor, from first to last." Bicker warned him against De Neufville and recommended the house of Van Vollenhoven. But it refused, and other efforts had as little success. Not only were the bankers cautious, but there existed a rivalry between the banking houses. Adams was ready to draw a historical lesson from the experience. Once more it was apparent that "emulation" ruled all, and produced "the same passions and effects among capitalists and mercantile houses, as it does between admirals, generals, ministers of state, and rival nations."[2]

Great patience was needed, Bicker wrote him, "and a person properly accredited." Adams persisted, made specific proposals, and inquired after reliable brokers. But toward the end of the year he began to see that his chance of success was slender. As he wrote to Alexander Gillon, who was also attempting to pry money loose and having as little success: "I have left no measure unattempted that prudence could justify, but have neither procured any money, nor obtained the least hope of obtaining any." All his hopes had been dashed. And to the president of Congress he wrote that he could not fail to remark that all declarations of friendship for America were nothing more than "little adulations to procure a share in our trade." Truth commanded him to say this. Americans in Holland discovered "the politeness of the table, and a readiness to enter into their trade," but they did not obtain real help, political or fiscal. The Dutch were too afraid of England and the English party. In his private correspondence he bared all his disappointment and bitterness: "Avarice and Stingyness" ruled the Dutch, and they worshiped Mammon.[3]

Early in the spring of 1781, Adams, yielding to despair, began to talk business with De Neufville. Everyone warned him, he tells us in his recollections, "that a loan was desperate," but De Neufville was confident that a substantial sum would come in. A loan of one million guilders was floated, in bonds of one-thousand-guilder denominations at an interest rate of 5 percent. Pamphlets designed to drum up sales were published. Now it would be seen whether America had any friends. "My business," Adams wrote to the banker, "is to try the experiment, and to know whether we have credit and friends or not." The experiment failed. "This Borrowing went slowly at first, but soon more quickly, to the great assistance of the Americans, who continued to yearn for a closer Relationship to this Country with its surpassing Riches," wrote Loosjes, gratefully but utterly incorrectly. The whole affair became a fiasco; no more than five bonds were placed, and three of them were with faithful Luzac. Adams was not disappointed by this result, he wrote later, for he had expected absolutely nothing.[4]

Another loan floated soon afterward by France on behalf of America left him quite unimpressed. In the first place these bonds were not taken up so long as the United States was even named in them; in the second place, the funds that were eventually received, five million guilders in all, did not go into American hands but were used to pay off Congress's debt to France.[5] It was all too plain that these prudent, fearful Dutchmen did not have much confidence in America.

· II ·

Yet, during that same uncertain winter, the Dutch Republic finally found itself in open conflict with England and, in a roundabout way, the ally of the American rebels. The story of this rupture begins with an American, the very man on his way to the Netherlands to replace Adams, Henry Laurens. What happened with Laurens became the occasion for the Anglo-Dutch War, and we must therefore go into it more fully. But then we must begin with a deep-lying cause, the question of the League of Armed Neutrality, as it was formally called, capital letters included. It was a complicated affair, for it involved the use of the most secret channels of diplomacy and the most contradictory interpretations of international law. It was also a kind of political fairy tale, for probably no diplomatic affair had ever caught the popular imagination as this one did. In the unbridled fantasizing of the Dutch people, the empress of faraway Russia became a kind of Princess Charming who would ride to their aid and save them in their need.

To the initiated, the empress of Russia, Catherine II, was not quite a character out of a nursery tale but was, on the contrary, as one member of the stadholder's court told another, "a Messalina so lustful that she could scarcely be satisfied." She was in any case a powerful and self-willed ruler; early in 1780 she had issued a decree in which she championed the rights of neutrals and invited them to enter an armed league. The Netherlands, at that very moment about to introduce unrestricted convoy, was all ears for this proposal. Merchants were enthusiastic, and the government saw a way out of its problems. The empress, said the elated grand pensionary, is now "our only sheet anchor." In the summer an embassy was sent to St. Petersburg to discuss the situation. Other countries, such as Denmark and Sweden, had already gone ahead of the Dutch, and it was important that they take part. But there were also those who gave warning: Would England really allow the Dutch to act so directly against her interests and against their own obligations under the treaties of alliance? The warnings were echoed by the English, and Yorke began to put on pressure. Van Hardenbroek, a member of the stadholder's court, warned: "If the Republic makes a declaration to England like that which Russia, Sweden and Denmark had done, then she would at once declare war upon the Republic, and that in that event orders already lay ready and preparations had been made to seize several of our most important settlements in the East Indies." [6]

The Dutch therefore found themselves trapped between two fires. The two special envoys sent to St. Petersburg, Van Wassenaar-Starrenburg, a member of the order of the Nobility in the States of Holland, and Van Heeckeren van Brandsenburg, a member of the States of Utrecht and one of the Prince's chamberlains, were instructed to demand a guarantee for the Dutch colonies as a prerequisite for the Republic's participation in the league. It was a condition impossible to grant, and this created many problems for the negotiations. Exactly at this moment, in September 1780, England put her hands on the weapon with which she hoped to force her will upon the Republic.

Which brings us back to Laurens. On 3 September, reported George Keppel, captain of H.M.S. *Vestal* (His *British* Majesty, of course), while cruising off the coast of Newfoundland, he "fell in with a Brig or Brigantine or Vessel bearing or carrying a flagg or Colours [this sounds as though a lawyer were writing Keppel's report for him] with thirteen Stripes and thirteen Starrs." He found one of his prisoners to be an American gentleman who introduced himself as Henry Laurens and soon admitted that he was on the way to Holland to conclude a loan "for the use of the persons calling themselves the United States of America." (A naval captain's language or a lawyer's?) Captain Keppel also reported that a bag with papers had been thrown out of the captured ship into the sea, but had been recovered by members of his crew. [7]

This bit of bad luck for an American diplomat turned out to be the beginning of the history of disasters that the Dutch are accustomed to call the Fourth English War ("Anglo-Dutch War" to the English). Laurens, an eminent and very wealthy planter from Charleston, South Carolina, was a hesitant revolutionary who had enrolled under the banner of Independence only in 1776, then had become president of Congress for a year (1777–78). In October 1779 he was named envoy to the Netherlands with the task of concluding a treaty and getting a loan if possible. Private business delayed him for months, to Adams's great impatience, and only on 13 August 1780 did he at last sail from Philadelphia in a small packet, the *Mercury*. For the first five days the *Mercury* was escorted by a warship, but then it had to risk the crossing on its own. The sad result we already know. Laurens himself admitted that his papers "had been inclosed in a bag, accompanied by a reasonable weight of iron shot, and thrown overboard, but the weight proved insufficient for the purpose intended."

This was an odd thing to admit, and it raised much doubt at the time. In a later statement, Laurens changed his account slightly, saying instead that only at the last moment had he realized that there were several important pieces among his papers. How extraordinary the story seemed in general is illustrated by a conversation of Van Hardenbroek with Prince William V. He found it strange, the Utrecht baron said, "that Laurens was carrying papers that he did not need and threw them in the water yet they did not sink." We find among others the same distrust about the intentions of the captured American. The French ambassador in Philadelphia, La Luzerne, reported to his government on rumors that Laurens had not been caught against his will, that behind the whole scene was a secret plan to renew peace negotiations with England. Laurens had good friends in the British Parliament.[8]

In any case, Captain Keppel had had a stroke of luck. The papers that so narrowly escaped vanishing into the depths were of the greatest importance. They were the documents that Laurens had hoped to use in his mission. They included letters from various persons, Van der Capellen among them, but the key piece was a copy of the secret treaty that William Lee and Jean de Neufville had drafted two years earlier in Aachen. Rumors of what had happened soon spread, and in the middle of September, De Neufville's son Leendert went to London to ask the Dutch ambassador, Van Welderen, whether he could get back from the English the letters addressed to his father that they had intercepted. The English government obviously turned down the request, for now they had at their disposal a corpus delicti, or at least a stick with which to beat the dog, and they used their opportunity with frenzied delight. On 11 October, after the affair had been checked into and the papers put in order and copied, Lord Stormont wrote to Yorke that his long-held suspicions that

Amsterdam had had direct contact with the Americans had now been proved true. Such conduct was "to all Intents and Purposes, equivalent to actual Aggression." If the States General had had a hand in it, he continued, it would be considered a declaration of war. The best way of proceeding was probably to speak first to Fagel and then to lay the documents before the stadholder, who, if he were "really capable of steady manly Exertion," could make splendid use of them against the opposition, the French party. But was he vigorous enough? And what if the French faction should still win out and the Republic joined the League of Armed Neutrality? In that case the English government would have no alternative. The papers that had been recovered could justify before the whole world any measure they wished to take, "and give the properest Direction to the War, by making it a particular Quarrel between Great Britain and Holland, in which no Neutral Power has any concern."[9]

This letter makes England's intentions clear. If the English government was not thinking of immediate war, the "Laurens papers," as the unhappy documents came to be called, would serve as a prod to keep the Netherlands out of the Russian camp. If this did not work, there would be war. Yorke received his superior's letter two days later (13 October) and strode at once with it to old Fagel. The *griffier*, Yorke reported to Stormont, was very outraged but also satisfied, for now the eyes of the Dutch would be opened and the country, already at the brink of the precipice, could be saved. And, yes, the Prince would have to be informed at once; weapons had been put into his hands. But it would be best, Fagel argued, to bring the duke of Brunswick into the secret beforehand. When Brunswick proved to be in agreement with Fagel, Yorke went to William V and laid the papers before him. He too reacted with anger and satisfaction—and, as usual, with hesitancy. The Prince realized that he would have to bring the grand pensionary into the business, but he would do everything he could to halt the drive to join the Armed League.

Yorke was satisfied for the moment, and publishing the papers would have a good result by rousing the burghers' fears. "The Affair cannot fail to occasion a wonderful Alarm in the Country, and as far as I can judge, will thoroughly cool the Ardour for the Northern League." Indeed, the stadholder himself would now regain his power and be restored to his former position, which had been, alas, so sorely weakened.[10]

This was the ambassador's program of action to frighten the Dutch out of their wits, and it was put into effect with vigor. The Prince made the first move by appearing in the meeting room of the States of Holland and telling the deputies what had happened. As was usual, he was thanked "for the continued demonstration of his care and vigilance, as Father of the Country, for the interests of the State," and then the deputies turned to discuss the situation. The Amsterdammers were called to account, but they naturally excused themselves with a host of arguments. Burgomaster Temminck responded at once in a talk with the Prince, and the burgomasters (four in number) and town councilors made an official reply a few days later (25 October). The jealousy of neighboring countries, the fact that the agreement at Aachen was only a provisional treaty, a "Preparatory Plan" as it was called, the imperative duty to protect the interests of trade, not just of Amsterdam but of the whole country—these were adequate motives for their innocent deed.[11] A long-winded debate began.

But England had no intention of loosening the noose around the Republic's neck. On 31 October, Stormont insisted that Yorke take strong action, and the ambassador was only too ready. He had had to abandon quickly his first hope that the Prince would show some spunk. Early in November he told De Larrey, William's secretary, that the Prince "was weak, vacillating, lacking firmness and indeed was sometimes inconsistent . . . and gave his attention to trifles and trivialities that were better left alone." It was apparent, Van Hardenbroek commented when De Larrey told him what the ambassador had said, that Yorke's intention, in view of the memoir which soon followed, was to "bring everything here into a commotion." The memoir arrived on 10 November, and it did not avoid the issue. His Majesty's Government had to conclude, it ran, that there existed in the Republic an "unbridled Cabal" which had entered a conspiracy "of which there is no example to be found in the Annals of the Republic." "Prompt satisfaction" was demanded; Van Berckel and his accomplices had to be given exemplary punishment as "disturbers of the public peace and violators of the Law of Nations." Otherwise the king would be obliged to take his own measures to uphold his dignity.[12]

There was an explosion of excitement. Adams, who kept a close watch on what was happening, reported the situation to his government. There was wide expectation of war, he wrote, and cargoes to St. Eustatius could not get insurance for less than 20 to 25 percent. The arrogant English were treating Amsterdam exactly as they had Boston; Yorke's language had the very sound of that of the English governors in Massachusetts, and Van Berckel was in the position that Otis or Hancock had been in, or Adams (for John Adams seldom forgot himself). The Dutch nation had fallen into indescribable disturbance, "a state of astonishment, confusion, and uncertainty," and therefore he could not get a penny from them. The English were attempting to split the country, to bring down on Van Berckel the fate of "Barnevelt, Grotius or De Witt." The Americans needed to have a minister with full powers at The Hague.[13]

The members of the governments, high and low, were in a state of perplexity, to be sure, but they did their best to ride out the storm. First the States of Holland and then the States General strongly censured the conduct of the Amsterdam burgomasters, and Fagel presented their resolutions to Yorke in the hope that they would be satisfactory. But the decision to enter the League of Armed Neutrality had been taken a few days earlier.

The commotion of which Adams wrote was indeed unprecedented, as was very evident from the flood of pamphlets and prints that appeared. "Many anonymous pamphlets appear on both sides," Adams wrote. It seemed to him that in such confusion the stadholder would still win out, but nothing could be said with certainty. Adams himself could do nothing. The warning that the acidulous English minister sent Yorke in these days, "It will be necessary to watch Adams as narrowly as possible," was superfluous. For what was at stake in the fierce pamphlet war was not America but Amsterdam. It was what one of the most celebrated defenses of the city called in its title *The Political System of the Government of Amsterdam* that was being challenged—and with it the whole Dutch system of government. Was it possible that a single city could drag the whole Republic into war, as there was now reason to fear? *Seven Villages Aflame thanks to the Imprudence of a Sheriff and a Secretary, or History of the Fritters* was the title of the most savage of the satires aimed at Amsterdam, one which came from the pen of the fiery Orangist R. M. van Goens.[14]

In the opinion of the English government, the Dutch talked but did nothing. The censure of Amsterdam's conduct did not satisfy the king, and the English decided upon war. A second memoir by Yorke presented to the States General on 12 December spoke no less sharply than the first about the "transgression of the very Constitution of the Republic," "which the King had guaranteed." This reference to a guarantee aroused surprise and anger in The Hague. What in heaven's name did it mean? It sounded as though the Netherlands were a kind of protectorate of England's! That was going too far, the Prince said to Van Hardenbroek. It was rumored in The Hague that Brunswick and Fagel had had a hand in writing Yorke's memoir. Actually, the English did not even expect a reply to this new declaration. When the States General informed the belligerents on 10 December that the Republic had entered the League of

Armed Neutrality, Yorke was recalled to London and a declaration of war was drawn up. There was, of course, no mention of the league in it, but numerous old sores were reopened. These included the charge that "an American pirate had spent several weeks in one of their [the Dutch] harbors and that they even permitted a portion of his crew to stand guard in a fort on Texel. . . . In the West Indies and in particular on St. Eustatius every protection and help was given to Our rebelling Subjects. Their privateers were openly received in Dutch ports [and] permitted to undergo caulking." His Majesty's Government would welcome having to take measures only against Amsterdam, the declaration of war continued, but that was not possible unless the States General declared that it would not stand by the city.[15]

In extreme distress the appalled regents made a last attempt to save the situation. The cases of the Amsterdammers, especially of Van Berckel, were sent to the Court of Holland for examination and possible prosecution. Fagel brought this news to Yorke just as the ambassador was about to leave, but he found it a "dilatory and completely unsatisfactory reply." He refused to stay, but departed for his homeland by way of Antwerp.

Caught in a trap, the Dutch thrashed about desperately. In his letters, Adams gives a fascinating account of the unfolding events. On 14 December he was still reporting to Congress how "the Dutch are now felicitating themselves upon the depth and the felicity of their politics" because they had joined "The Neutrality." They were in deadly fear of England, more "terrified than I ever saw any part of America intimidated in the worst crisis of her affairs." They thought of only one thing, their money, and therefore wanted peace at any price. "No Resentments of Injuries or Insults, no Regard to national Honour or Dignity will turn them out of their pacific Course," Adams wrote a friend. "Such a Nation of Idolaters at the Shrine of Mammon never existed, I believe, before." As a result, there was no chance whatever of getting a loan from them.

He explained the situation further in another letter to Congress: "War is to a Dutchman the greatest of all evils. Sir Joseph Yorke is so sensible of this, that he keeps alive a continual fear of it by memorials after memorials, each more affronting to any sovereignty or delicate notions of dignity than the former. By this means he keeps up the panic and while this panic continues I shall certainly have no success at all. No man dares engage for me; very few dare see me." In a later review of the situation, he put it even more strongly: "All this had such an effect, that all the best men seemed to shudder with fear. . . . I was avoided like a pestilence by every man in government. Those gentlemen of the rank of burgomasters, schepens, pensionaries, and even lawyers, who had treated me with great kindness, and sociability, and even familiarity before, dared not see me, dared not be at home when I visited at their houses, dared not return my visit, dared not answer, in writing, even a card that I wrote them. I had several messages in a roundabout way, and in confidence, that they were extremely sorry they could not answer my cards and letters in writing, because '*on fait tout son possible pour me sacrifier aux Anglomanes*' [they do all they can to sacrifice me to the Anglomaniacs]." [16]

Yet Adams also saw a possibility that some good might emerge out of all this unrest. The anti-English feeling was so strong in Holland, he thought, that in the event of war the nation would restore itself and a new situation arise. On Christmas Day, when he wrote twice to Congress, Adams prophetically reported that the "violent struggle" that gripped the Dutch Republic had all the signs of "an agony that usually precedes a great revolution. The streets of the city swarm with libels of party against party." Ably written pamphlets, he continued, had appeared in favor of the burgomasters. "Thousands of extravagant and incredible reports are made and propagated. Many new songs appear among the populace, one particularly adapted for the amusement of the sailors, and calculated to inspire them with proper sentiments of resentment toward the English. A woman who sung it in the streets the day before yesterday sold six hundred of them in an hour and in one spot. These are symptoms of war. But it is not easy to conquer the national prejudices of a hundred years' standing, nor to avoid the influence of the stadtholder, which is much more formidable. In this fermentation the people can think of nothing else, and I need not add that I have no chance of getting a ducat of money." [17]

In spite of everything, Adams did not lose hope. On New Year's Eve he wrote again, more optimistically. The neutral powers would not let themselves be bamboozled by England; they would give assistance to the Republic and before long come into the war themselves. And even if they did not, Holland now had been driven into the arms of France, Spain, and America. But the king of England, with his empire collapsing, would set all Europe aflame, rather than make peace. "Patience, firmness, and perseverance are our only remedy; these are a sure and infallible one; and, with this observation, I beg permission to take my leave of congress for the year 1780, which has been the most anxious and mortifying year of my whole life." [18]

Many years later, in his reminiscences which appeared in the *Boston Patriot*, he reviewed the events of 1780 and drew a lesson from them. Reconsidering the English aims, he found them to be a thoughtless departure from England's traditional balance-of-power policy. The Dutch Republic had simply been surrendered to French influence. He also gave an acute description of the old Dutch dilemma of how to stand their own ground between England, an ever more powerful commercial competitor, and France, a menacing neighbor. In the beginning they had held their own extremely well by maintaining a fleet that was the equal of or even better than England's, and later by the establishment of the Barrier fortresses in the Southern Netherlands. But gradually they became so dependent on their English ally that they let their fleet fall into neglect, and they also allowed the Barrier fortresses to crumble away. The war of 1780 confronted them with a desperate dilemma—either they abandoned their independence or they joined with their former enemies against England. The old system of balance of power had come to an end, as was evident from what happened afterward (Adams was writing in 1809). At the moment the question before the Dutch was how to bring about a new international equilibrium.[19]

No one doubted that the true reason for the English declaration of war was the adherence of the Netherlands to the League of Armed Neutrality. But that did not make the alarm any the less. The Prince asked Van Hardenbroek if he had ever thought things would turn out as they had, and Van Hardenbroek answered: "No, Your Highness! It is still my conviction that the English are taking a hard, unreasonable, and imprudent line of conduct toward us, and that they are in so doing playing into the hands of their foes." The Utrecht nobleman, who was himself bewildered by the course of events, wondered silently whether an "extremely sly policy" did not lie behind the English actions, a secret understanding between the Dutch court and England to hold Amsterdam down with a "decided superiority."

The question then was why England had taken such "violent measures," and the answer, again, was "to keep us by violence from joining with Russia." But Van Hardenbroek could not still all his suspicions. In his confusion, as in that of the Dutch in general, we find the same amazement that we find in Adams. What interest could England have in making an enemy of the Dutch? The diplomat Hendrik Hop, the Dutch envoy in Brussels, used words that remind us of Adams's: "The end of it would be that we would have to throw ourselves in the arms of France and Spain, and so we would be wholly lost to England, which is neither to their advantage nor to ours, or it will turn the Republic upside down, which will mean of course the downfall of the Prince and of all of us."[20]

In all these comments overestimation of the importance of the Dutch

Republic rings out. England knew what she wanted: she badly wanted war because over the years her rancor against the Dutch had grown very deep. "The only fear one hears expressed," wrote Lord Beauchamp to Sir John Vaughan on 29 December 1780, "is that the activity of our preparations may induce the republic to make such concessions as to prevent a continuance of hostilitys." The British acted with extraordinary speed and harshness. The first attack was against St. Eustatius, as we have seen, but the Dutch merchant fleet was another immediate target. In the first month of the war, January 1781, a full two hundred ships fell into English hands, and Dutch shipping was at once totally paralyzed.

In the Netherlands agitation and impotence went hand in hand. In the Amsterdam theater actors who worked in anti-English remarks got cheers, Adams recounts, and a new play called "De Ruiter"—after the great seventeenth-century admiral who had so often beaten the English—was put on the boards to applause *a tout rompre*, that is in plain English to make all split." Van Hardenbroek tells a similar story about a play at The Hague theater: The words "*l'Amitié d'un Anglais fut toujours incertaine*" (an Englishman's friendship was always fickle) brought applause that lasted for minutes, while many looked up at the box where the Prince and the Princess sat. Would the old Dutch spirit revive now?

From America, Abigail Adams wrote to her husband that the fall of St. Eustatius had to bring to new life the spirit of freedom of the Dutch, who had been able to resist Philip II. Jefferson's friend, the half-American Philip Mazzei, saw the situation in a more gloomy light. If there was anyone who could get the Dutch back on the right track, he wrote Adams, it was he. Adams would probably get some money out of them, Mazzei continued, but it would not be as easy to arouse their "martial spirit." And Mazzei spoke to Jefferson of St. Eustatius's fall as "Rodney's success against the most vile jews of Europe (I mean the pusillanimous still unarmed Dutch)." The Dutch were wealthy and cowardly, intent on nothing but profit, a people who understood only the language of "Kicks and Slaps." [21]

The picture of the Netherlands that we meet here was a widely held one. In the prints of the time the money-hungry but timid Dutchman is a favorite character. Rightly or wrongly, the Dutch were in fact very perplexed. The Prince of Orange might look all "firmness," but he was quite aware of how pitiable the Dutch situation was. "There is a shortage of everything, ships, sailors, troops." There was much wisdom, too, in his musings: "It is the usual consequence of a long peace that many things are neglected and allowed to run down. That is mainly what has happened in the Republic, which seldom returns to the required level of activity unless something extraordinary happens." Only in his dreams did he himself achieve great things. "I feel better today than yesterday," he told Van Hardenbroek on one occasion. "It was all past by yesterday evening, I slept well and dreamed that the English had made a landing and that I went to meet them and beat them off. Dreams can be so nice."[22]

The only hope that existed in reality, or rather that the Dutch hugged close in their utter lack of realism, was help from the armed neutrals. This is most evident in the prints that appeared now in large numbers. The figure of the noble empress Catherine is to be seen many times, young, beautiful, and strong, repulsing the English. People there, Adams wrote to Francis Dana, a young friend, could hardly believe that the English were at war with them. Instead of relying upon themselves, they looked to Russia and the Northern powers. But his own hopes were not different. He wrote to Dumas that Russia, Sweden, Holland, France, Spain, and America would soon form a grand alliance against England, but the agent of America in The Hague warned him not to be too optimistic. The government at The Hague likewise had its doubts, as did the Prince of Orange. When Russian help was mentioned to him, the Prince shrugged his shoulders and said: "Ay, Russia, I don't know what to say about Russia." Would it not be better, he persisted, to attempt a reconciliation with England? To his secretary he said, as if conversationally: "Couldn't we somehow forgo the trade with North America to satisfy England?"[23]

Bewilderment gripped the merchants of Amsterdam. The division of opinions was described by old Burgomaster Hooft in a letter to Van der Capellen. As for himself, he said, "I cannot imagine that great-hearted Catherine will tarnish her reputation and leave us in the lurch. Now, when the waterways in Muscovy are still frozen, what can the eminent Princess do but offer her mediation in order to prevent the spilling of blood and other misfortunes; if England will listen to her advice by releasing, with costs and damages paid, our ships, which have been taken into English harbors in complete violation of law and propriety; by recognizing the independence of North America and granting the right of free navigation to all, then the whole world and future generations would speak of the Great Catherine with respect and veneration." This was the whole program of the Amsterdam regents to be achieved by the dea ex machina, Catherine II, and she would even earn her epithet of "Great" so far as they were concerned.[24]

The anxiety that had seized the leaders of Amsterdam soon led to a radical, if temporary, change in the municipal government. In this moment of crisis, it suddenly appeared that Van Berckel had no real friends. It was obvious that the Prince of Orange wanted him on the gallows, but his own burgomasters, even Temminck, were fed up with his arbitrary and high-handed conduct and were turning against him, and that meant his downfall, even if only for the time being. Only Hendrik Hooft remained loyal to him, but he could do nothing against the new burgomasters elected in the beginning of February 1781, Joachim Rendorp and Jacob Elias. Rendorp in particular was a politician of strong character, a friend of the Prince of Orange, and a moderate conservative in his views, but totally opposed to Van Berckel. In his letters, Adams wrote that the Amsterdam pensionary was marked out for the fate of Grotius or De Witt (the victims of the Orangist party in the seventeenth century), and Van Berckel himself shared Adams's fear for him. Later he denied it, saying it was his wife who had been afraid and did not want him to go to The Hague with the Amsterdam delegation to the States of Holland, "since she predicted and feared that I would be taken to Loevestein" (the castle where Grotius and De Witt's father had been imprisoned). Whether it was Van Berckel or his wife who really was frightened did not matter; with the change in burgomasters, he could not go on in any case, for they had no further desire for his services.[25]

As it happened, he escaped a judicial sentence. The Court of Holland privately considered him guilty, according to a widely believed rumor. But at the end of March it decided to drop all proceedings against him. This was politically wise, in view of what a sentence of guilt would have signified after England's declaration of war. He was, however, excluded from all political power, which meant, among other things, that the American cause had lost a very important base of support in the city of Amsterdam. Adams would find this out, painfully.[26]

· CHAPTER 11 ·

Raising a Dust

*Mr. Adams seems to think a little apparent Stoutness
and greater air of Independence and Boldness
in our Demands will procure us
more ample Assistance.*
BENJAMIN FRANKLIN

 HE new year at once brought Adams what he wanted. On 1 January Congress decided to name him plenipotentiary minister, the official envoy of the United States to the government of the Dutch Republic. He still had to obtain diplomatic recognition, of course, and that would not come easily. But at least he had taken a small step forward on the rocky path that led to recognition.

News of his appointment was rushed off to him at once, but it was the end of February before he received it, and the credential letters did not come for almost another month. It was an ordeal for such a quick-tempered man as Adams to live in a time of slow communications. He could barely stick it out. Even before he received the report of the appointment, he chafed impatiently to begin to do something, although he was not quite sure what. He sounded out his friends. Would it be prudent, he wrote to Dumas on 15 January, to attempt to make contacts with the Dutch government by being presented, for example, to the grand pensionary or members of the States General? Certainly the time was ripe now.

But Dumas, taught wisdom by his own many disappointments and imbued with the notion that the Dutch, like peat, were slow to catch fire, warned him against it. Hopes were still held in The Hague, he said, for aid from the League of Armed Neutrality, and there were those too who still desired a reconciliation with England. England, Dumas went on, would no longer accept reconciliation, and then the empress of Russia would have to come to the aid of the Dutch. That would be the time for Adams to act.

But, Adams wrote back hurriedly in a letter that, with full self-knowledge, he began with the words "*Nulla dies sine linea*" (no day without a line), would it not be good, even wise, if Their High Mightinesses gave Dutch ships permission to bring their prizes into American ports and, inversely, permitted American ships to enter Dutch harbors? It might still be too soon, he added a few days later, to act in an official way; people's minds had to be prepared by "hints and ideas" for what was about to happen. In a crisis everything happened of itself, but such a crisis had to be prepared; it had to be made, as a midwife carefully worked to avert danger. "And the Corps Diplomatique, with all their superb pomp, are but a company of grannies." Peace with England in any case was no longer possible, he continued. Most of all, the Dutch ought not flatter themselves with the vain hope that the neutrals would help them. Many shots would still have to be fired before England would back down.[1]

Adams also, on 20 February, asked Bicker for advice. Were the instructions that he had received from Congress to conclude a loan not broad enough to include powers to conclude a treaty? But Bicker did not agree. It was not in Adams's powers to do so: the words *with any person or persons, bodies politic and corporate* could not be interpreted to apply to negotiations with a sovereign body. Five days later, Adams, beaming with satisfaction, could inform the Amsterdam banker that he had just received a letter from Congress with the ardently desired instructions to negotiate with the States General and to conclude a treaty if possible.[2]

The impetuous "militia" diplomat was not to be held back any longer. The first point to which he gave his attention was the idea of reciprocal opening of harbors, which he had already discussed with Dumas. Congress had declared in October that it stood fully behind the principles of the League of Armed Neutrality, and Adams was instructed to work for the American acceptance in its ranks. On 8 March he submitted a memorial to the States General informing Their High Mightinesses that Congress had adopted a resolution on armed neutrality. Now that the American Revolution had led to the great reform in maritime law represented in the principles of the league, it was not unreasonable for America to take part in the league, accepting the privileges and obligations of a member state. Would Their High Mightinesses deliberate upon this matter and consult their neutral friends about it? In this way, Adams, basing himself upon the principle of free but protected navigation, attempted to get the harbors of Holland opened to American privateers. Copies of the memorial went to the envoys of Russia, Sweden, Denmark, and France, as well as to the government of Amsterdam. In The Hague, Dumas delivered the copies in person.

It all came to nothing. La Vauguyon let it be known that he could not support Adams's step without instruction from Paris. The deputy of the States General who sat as president for the week accepted the memorial and asked where it came from, but that was all. The Prince immediately acted to block consideration. He wrote to Van Bleiswijk: "It has further been my intention to inform you that Mr. van Wadenoyen [the president for the week] has communicated to me a memorial in the English language from one John Adams, who takes the character of Minister Plenipotentiary of the so-called united States. It is my thought that, as this person is not recognized in this character, no memoires should be accepted from him." [3]

It helped little that the towns of Holland reacted favorably to Adams's initiative. The pensionaries of Amsterdam, Dordrecht, and Haarlem— the trio of Van Berckel, De Gijselaar, and Van Zeebergh, who were to become so famous later, is here mentioned as such for the first time—were very grateful for the opportunity to see the memorial, they told Dumas, but, to their great regret, they could not reply officially. De Gijselaar indeed was willing to go to Leiden with Dumas to make the American's acquaintance, but even that visit fell through, because he unexpectedly had to return to Dordrecht. That same day, Adams wrote to Dumas to ask what happened to his memorial. "Has it been laid before their High Mightinesses, or not? and what was done with it? Pray, has the president, by the constitution of this country, a right to pocket, suppress, or deliver to the Stadtholder papers addressed to Their High Mightinesses? Is the delusion almost over? When will mankind cease to be the dupes of the insidious artifices of a British minister and stockjobber?" [4]

The situation there remained impenetrable, he wrote two days later to Congress. No task ever given him had required greater patience, tenacity, and caution. The Dutch nation had fallen into a crisis and was very divided. There were "stadtholderians" and "republicans"; investors in English funds and merchants; adherents of an alliance with England, and those of a league with France, Spain, and America, and then those of a third kind who wanted to follow Russia, Sweden, and Denmark in everything. Some wished to recognize America and to conclude a treaty of trade and friendship with her; others found that an appalling idea because it would make any reconciliation with England impossible. Some did not want to strengthen the navy unless the army too were improved; others would rather neglect the navy than make the army stronger. There was a "perfect chaos of sentiments and systems," so that it was no wonder that general weakness and indecisiveness ruled. Everyone was afraid of unrest and rioting, whether for or against the war, for or against England, for the Prince or for Amsterdam, for or against America. There was no chance of a loan at this time. He had presented the memoir, but his proposals had lain upon the table for a long time, and were then sent *ad referendum* to the different provinces, towns, and nobles, who were the real sovereignty. They, he wrote desperately, "deliberate and deliberate and deliberate," and some were for and some against concluding a treaty. "Statia [St. Eustatius] is gone, and the Dutch yet dead," he wrote pithily in a letter to Dana; "when they will come to life I know not." To Jay, he wrote: "I have been in the most curious country, among the most incomprehensible people, and under the most singular constitution of government in the world." And to Congress, he exclaimed: "The councils of this people are the most inscrutable of any I ever saw." Adams in truth was utterly baffled, discouraged, and embittered by the Dutch political system. But he was still John Adams, and when the right time came, he became, as he had written, a veritable lion. He would do everything now in grand style, against the current, like a prince.[5]

In the beginning of the year he had given up his lodgings with Widow Schorn, for it had no longer been fitting for America's representative to reside on the Achterburgwal, and besides there were rumors about the disreputable neighborhood. For a few months he traveled back and forth between Amsterdam, Leiden, and The Hague, but in April he moved into a house that still stands on the Keizersgracht at number 529, close by Spiegelstraat. He had set his requirements: it had to be a stately house, with a large reception room, four bedrooms for gentlemen, two for servants, all beautifully furnished. The rent could be as much as three thousand guilders a year. In addition he would need a coach for four persons, with horses and a coachman, who like the two other servants had to be attired in blue livery with a red cap and red waistcoat. He chose everything, even the table silver, tea service, and linens. For now he was a man of standing, whether they wanted to recognize him or not. "I have taken an House on the Keysers Gragt near the Spiegel Straat and am about becoming a citizen of Amsterdam—unless their High Mightinesses should pronounce me a Rebel, and expel me from their Dominions, which I believe they will not be inclined to do." He gave Abigail his new address: Keysers Gragt, which means Emperor's Canal, near the Spiegelstraat, the Looking-Glass Street. He was established there now, he said, and had a house. "Alas, how little like my real home.—What would I give for my dear House keeper. But this is too great a felicity for me."[6]

He had left home a year and a half before.

· II ·

As Adams described the situation years later, it was as though a black cloud were hanging over the seven provinces. And he believed that he could break through the darkness, ripping it to shreds by going over to the attack, by his "militia" diplomacy. Now that he had been named minister to the Dutch government, he had to press himself upon the powers at The Hague and demand recognition. In the worst case they could expel him from the country, and what was lost then? In the best case, he would be accepted. Most probable however was that his proposal would be given to the provinces *ad referendum*, and that in itself was no small victory.

It was just at this time, in mid-April, that his young friend Francis Dana came to him at Leiden and asked his advice. Dana told Adams that he had been appointed American minister to St. Petersburg, in the same one-sided way that Adams had been appointed to The Hague, and he was probably equally unwelcome. What should he do? he inquired. Go to the Russian capital prudently, as a private person, explore the situation, and sound out whether he would be received? Or present himself in his "real character" and proclaim publicly what he was seeking?

Adams gladly replied, orally and in writing. Of course Dana had to go to Russia in the most official way possible. America, after all, had nothing to hide, no need to be ashamed of anything. She had risen up in the cause of mankind, and if foreign governments thought otherwise—which was up to them to decide—then they should say so honestly, and no harm would have been done. "America, my dear sir, has been too long silent in Europe. Her cause is that of all nations and all men; and it needs nothing to be explained, to be approved."[7]

Adams himself, undaunted, took this path of open challenge. At the end of March he began to draw up another memorial demanding much more than just open harbors. He worked hard on it and was not satisfied until he had drafted a third version. He wanted to have Luzac translate it into French, but Dumas pleaded to be allowed to do it. Luzac helped by having his brother-in-law Wybo Fijnje in Delft ask to do the Dutch translation. Dumas, who was not independent, also advised informing La Vauguyon, so that France would be brought into the affair. Adams thereupon wrote to the French ambassador that he had received his credentials from Congress, and the Frenchman replied with equal promptness that if Adams planned to submit them to the Dutch government, he, La Vauguyon, would like to meet with him in order to give him his own vision upon their common business.[8]

The discussion took place the next day and had to be resumed the second day because Adams and La Vauguyon were utterly at odds and all their talking did not bring them to agreement. Their meeting was an excellent example of the European and American styles of diplomacy in conflict. Perhaps we ought to say, "Adams-style diplomacy," for it was a sample of Adams's unyielding character at its very best, his *"entêtement"* (stubbornness), as the French duke called it in a letter to Vergennes. From the start the American minister understood what the French government was up to. "I had my apprehensions," he recollected, for he knew that Vergennes was opposed to him and that therefore La Vauguyon had to work against him. But he understood also that to act without informing the French ambassador would have caused many complications, and he therefore went to the embassy.

The discussion the first day lasted two hours and was continued the following day at eight o'clock in the morning at Adams's hotel in The Hague—which, we may note, was called "At the sign of the Parliament of England"—lasting another four to five hours. We have two accounts by Adams of this extended discussion, one written a year later in a letter to Livingston, the other in his reminiscences of 1809. La Vauguyon also made a report in his dispatches to Vergennes, but less completely. If we may believe the American—and there is no reason not to, although the exact words spoken were probably not the same, since Adams lamented that he had not written them down at once—the conversation ran something like this: "Sir," said La Vauguyon, "the King and the United States are upon very intimate terms of friendship. Had you not better wait until we can make the proposition in concert?" "God grant they may ever continue in perfect friendship," said Adams, "but this friendship does not prevent your Excellency from conducting your negotiations without consulting me. Why then am I obliged . . . to consult your Excellency?" And so it went, neither giving an inch. La Vauguyon inquired whether the loan that France was floating on behalf of America was in danger. Adams replied that he did not know, but added that recognition or a treaty could only expedite the loan. The Frenchman suggested that recognition would anger the empress of Russia, but Adams did not see why. Holland was now at war with England, like the Americans, he said, and the Northern powers were not. La Vauguyon thought it would be better to wait until they knew Vergennes's opinion. "I know already beforehand," Adams replied, "what that opinion will be." "Ay, what?" "Why, directly against it." "For what reason?" "Because the Count de Vergennes will not commit the dignity of the King or his own reputation, by advising me to apply, until he is sure of success, and in this he may be right; but the United States stand in a different predicament. They have nothing to lose by such a measure and may gain a great deal."

But what if Holland were reconciled with England? was the Frenchman's final argument. Adams's rejoinder was that if there was any chance of that, then there was all the more reason for acting at once. But Holland was too afraid of a French invasion to do that. "God," said he, "you have used an argument now that you ought to speak out boldly and repeat peremptorily in all companies, for this people are governed very much by fear."

That is how Adams's first account went. A quarter of a century later he repeated it with embellishments. "Monsieur le duke, I must speak out in plain English or plain French. I know the decision of The King's Council will be directly and decidedly against me; and I am decidedly determined to go to the president [of the States General], though I had a resolution of the king in council against me; and before my eyes.". . . "What!" said the duke. "Will you take the responsibility of it upon yourself?" "Indeed, monsieur le duke, I will, and I think I alone ought to be responsible, and that no other ambassador, minister, council, or court ought to be answerable for anything concerning it." "Are you willing to be responsible then?" "Indeed, I am, and upon my head may all consequences of it rest." "Are you then determined?" "Determined and unalterably determined I am."

There is a third version from the American side, also from years later. It is to be found in a letter of Benjamin Waterhouse, an American student, who evidently followed closely the account that Adams gave him. La Vauguyon and Vergennes, in his opinion, "deceived and duped that honest patriot [Adams]." But they failed. "I never shall forget some of his paroxysms of patriotic rage." "The explanation of all this was to keep Adams under French influence, and by all means prevent Holland from acknowledging our Independence, and receiving John Adams as our minister." In a way, Waterhouse was right. But there were, of course, other aspects of the French attitude. France was at this time, in the spring of 1781, hoping for a Russian mediation in the war, and it had fears that Adams's impetuous action would endanger the Russian efforts.

La Vauguyon gave his own version in a dispatch to Vergennes: "You will not be astonished, monsieur le Comte, since you are familiar with the stubbornness of Mr. Adams, that he offered much resistance. I have informed the government of the Republic that Adams's step was not taken in consultation with the French ambassador, and I left them without any doubt in the matter. Mr. Adams wanted to give more '*éclat*' to his step and had his Memoire printed. I am convinced that you disapprove as much as I this new proof of his inconsiderate impetuosity." Of course Vergennes agreed with him and La Vauguyon tried again to persuade Adams; but he would not listen, and to the French diplomat the publication by Adams of his memorial was further proof of his obstinate character.[9]

Adams pushed ahead; nothing and no one could hold him back. With all the pomp and circumstance at his disposal, he would storm the fortresses of government in The Hague. Waterhouse has left us an absolutely delightful description of how the day of the great happening began. Adams was in Leiden at the time, where his sons were attending school. "I shall never forget the day," Waterhouse wrote, "and the circumstances of Mr. Adams going from Leyden to The Hague with his Memorial to Their High Mightinesses the States General. . . . He came down into the front room where we all were—his secretary, two sons and myself—his coach and four at the door and he full dressed even to his sword, when with energetic countenance and protuberant eyes, and holding his memorial in his hand, he said to us, in a solemn tone—Young men, remember this day—for this day I go to The Hague to put seed in the ground that may produce good or evil—God knows which—and putting the paper into his side pocket, he stepped into his coach and drove off alone— leaving us his Juniors solemnized in thought and anxious for he had hardly spoken to us for several days before—such was his inexpressible solicitude."[10]

This glorious scene, all ready for the stage, took place on 1 May. Adams's memorial was officially dated 19 April—accidentally or by design, he did not know, Waterhouse wrote—19 April being the day when the first shots of the American Revolution had been fired at Lexington and Concord six years before.

The piece was written out in a neat hand and translated, and accompanying letters to the stadholder, the grand pensionary of Holland, and the secretary of the States General were provided. It ran sixteen pages in the Dutch version, which appeared in print soon afterward and was officially entitled *Memorial To Their High Mightinesses the States General of the United Netherlands.* Neither the publisher's name nor the place of publication was given on the first page. At the end stood the name of the author: John Adams.

It was a piece of authentic propaganda, and it can be respected as such. The author began by telling who he was—the official plenipotentiary of Congress. He then described how the rebellion in America began. The country was a part of England, but England denied her own character— it was, after all, still seen as the true land of freedom, even by Adams— and "conceived the design of subverting the political systems of the Colonies; depriving them of the rights and liberties of Englishmen; and reducing them to the worst of all forms of government." All the misdeeds of the English were reviewed: They had blocked the ports and sent troops, mercenaries, even Indians against the Americans. At last nothing was left to the Americans but to rise in rebellion. The "immortal Declaration of the fourth of July" was the foundation of the legitimacy of the new government. Although the English maintained the contrary, most Americans were fully decided to defend their independence; only a few had turned away from "the standard of virtue."

Then Adams addressed the Dutch. Congress had long hesitated to send a minister, not wishing to sow discord between the Dutch Republic and her allies. But now that the British had broken all treaties and had declared war on its ally Holland, the time had come for joining hands. No more natural alliance could be conceived. Adams named all the historic ties—the Pilgrim Fathers, the foundation of New Amsterdam, the "similitude of religion," the "similarity in the forms of government," "in general usages," and so on. "The originals of the two republics are so much alike, that the history of one seems but a transcript from that of the other; so that every Dutchman instructed in the subject, must pronounce the American revolution just and necessary, or pass a censure upon the greatest actions of his immortal ancestors; actions which have been approved and applauded by mankind and justified by the decision of heaven."

After all these pious and patriotic considerations came the pièce de résistance. Adams had by now gotten to know the people he was dealing with. The best reasons for an alliance were economic interests. The Netherlands was rich in trade and funds; America in products and raw materials. The English had good reason to dread such a natural alliance. This was the purpose behind their Navigation Act, so harmful to the Dutch and to the colonists. "There is now an opportunity offered to both, to shake off this shackle for ever." It was just such a trade treaty as this that would throw fear into England and compel her to make peace. And what advantages flowed from the trade! Indeed, "there has seldom been a more distinct designation of Providence to any two distant nations to unite themselves together." The fear of competition, used as an argument by the English, was nonsense. America's products for use in shipbuilding—tar, turpentine, and lumber—would never become major imports in Europe, in view of the costs of transatlantic transport and insurance. Not enough hemp, sailcloth, and cordage were made in America, and they would have to be imported from Amsterdam. The United States would continue to be a market for Baltic trade for centuries.

Moreover, there was no need to be afraid of other colonies following the American example. Other countries did not treat their colonies as badly as England had hers. These, to the contrary, had good governments, "founded deep in the hearts, the passions, the imaginations, and understandings of the people." They had nothing to fear for "it is not in human nature to exchange safety for danger, and certain happiness for very precarious benefits." So the revolutionary agent adapted himself to his conservative audience and certainly also to his own deepest conservative inclinations.

The pamphlet concluded with a paean to free commerce. It appealed to the model treaty of 1776, written by Adams himself, when it declared America's desire "to form equitable commercial treaties with all the maritime powers of Europe, without being monopolized or governed by any. . . . If such benevolent policy should be adopted, the new world will be a proportional blessing to every part of the old." [11]

It is interesting to see how skillful propaganda and honest convictions merge in Adams's arguments. We have already observed that Adams himself did not really believe that America was all that dependent upon Europe; it was quite able to save itself, this proud Patriot and economic nationalist thought. But at the same time he sketched a course of policy that would be typical for America in the future, the quest for an open door in all countries, for a system of sincere reciprocity. And who was readier for that message than the merchants of Holland, who passionately believed in free trade and who were so fond of having their portraits painted showing them with a copy of Grotius's *Mare Liberum* in their hands?

The problem now was to obtain from the memorial the results that Adams expected, or at least cautiously hoped for. In the last paragraph he had informed Their High Mightinesses that he had credential letters that he wanted to present to them and to the stadholder. To Congress he reported fully the progress of his diplomatic assault: he went to The Hague on 1 May, and informed the grand pensionary, Van Bleiswijk, that he had something of importance to communicate to him. "I proposed to do myself the honor to wait on him the next morning at half past eight, if that time should be agreeable to him." Dumas brought Adams's letter to the grand pensionary, and Van Bleiswijk agreed to receive the American at that hour. The next morning Adams paid his call upon the grand pensionary and told him that it was his intention to offer his credentials to the States General and the Prince of Orange on 4 May. Van Bleiswijk replied in a friendly tone; personally, he supported Adams, but it was a delicate matter. Adams had his reply ready at once: He hoped that it would not be so delicate as to form an obstacle for closer relations now that war had come between England and the Netherlands. Van Bleiswijk echoed his words: "One thing is certain, we have a common enemy." The conversation ended with civilities.

As a matter of course, the grand pensionary communicated at once with the Prince and the "president of the week" of the States General, Baron Van Lynden van Hemmen. The very first day after Adams's visit, William V wrote that he had serious objections to receiving the American: "I find the matter so critical that I am opposed to advising Mr. Van Lynden van Hemmen to accept the alleged credentials of the said Adams, but think it would be better that he say to him that he is not authorized to accept them but would inform Their High Mightinesses of his visit." This is just what happened on 4 May. Adams first returned to Van Bleiswijk, who explained to him that the president of the week had declared he could not accept any papers because America had not yet been recognized, but that he would report the visit to Their High Mightinesses. The matter would then go to the provinces for discussion because of its great importance for the Republic. Adams thanked him and informed him that he would have the memorial printed.

Van Lynden van Hemmen reported the same day that "a certain person calling himself Adams" had come to him and stated his request and that now the question could be sent to the provinces. As was to be expected, Adams had even less success with the Prince. He was indeed received by "Baron de Ray" (he meant William's secretary, De Larrey), who promised to give his letter and the memoir to the Prince; but two hours later he returned the documents, unopened, to Adams at his hotel. The road to recognition was therefore not open, but it was not closed either. There were those, wrote the historian Loosjes, who surmised that "Their High Mightinesses wanted to clear the way for negotiations with the North Americans." There were certainly many who favored delay, despite all the rumors that "the Country's Fathers would recognize the Independence of America and that the Stadholder held frequent conversations with the North American envoy." Loosjes quoted this from the *Post van den Neder-Rhijn*, and he deemed it to be proof that "however much envy bespatters the House of Orange with its foul slime, . . . he [the Prince] took to heart the salvation of the Republic."

It was not unreasonable either, wrote the *Post* shortly thereafter, that Van Lynden van Hemmen had not accepted Adams's letters, for a government cannot receive an envoy before it has recognized his principals, "unless, as the saying goes, we want to put the cart before the horse." When even a Patriot newspaper like the *Post* was so scrupulous about recognition of America, the road that Adams still had to travel was long and difficult.[12]

But he was not easily daunted, either by Dutch uncertainties or by French opposition. Nothing could tame him, and in that we see his greatness. He was not deterred even when his own government left him in the lurch, although he took advantage of the slowness of communications to hold to his path. Opponents in Philadelphia made many difficulties for him. Vergennes had the French ambassador to Congress, Chevalier de la Luzerne, use all his influence to restrain Adams, and La Luzerne's influence was not small. The New York politician who became secretary of foreign affairs in October 1781, Robert R. Livingston, was under the spell of the French ally and strongly opposed Adams's audacious diplomacy. The first letter that he wrote after taking office on 21 October was a warning against Adams sent to John Jay, who had been the minister in Madrid since 1779 and was now appointed a member of a special peace delegation, together with Franklin, Adams, Laurens, and Jefferson. Livingston's words were harsh: "Holland claims your particular attention. Our minister there is zealous and laborious but"—and here he continued in code—"I will not answer for his prudence. His memorial, his ridiculous display of his public character when everything was against it cannot be accounted for on principles that will do him honor."

He also wrote repeatedly to Adams himself to rap him on the knuckles for taking the side of the Patriot party in the Netherlands. Aristocratic governments, Livingston argued, were especially afraid of popular movements, and hence it was precisely the unrest that Adams helped bring about that contributed to reconciliation with England. He emphatically advised Adams "to be well with the government." It was all right to be on civil terms with the friends of America, but not so much as to kindle the wrath of the government. It would be better, he advised, to reside in The

Hague, where he could make contacts with the envoys of other countries, instead of staying in Amsterdam. More rebukes followed in a second letter almost a month later. He had not received Adams's report about the memorial, but had heard the whole story indirectly from Dumas. Why, he demanded, had Adams taken such a step, so humiliating to the United States? And why had he had his piece printed? Livingston told him to be more prudent and to work in closer agreement with the French envoy. "Your business, therefore, I think lies in a very narrow compass." He advised him "to be, in your language and conduct, a private gentleman." He crossed out an even harsher passage in this letter, in which he warned Adams against acts of imprudence which "serve to throw an air of ridicule on your mission." [13]

Adams, as we would expect, did not take these reprimands lying down. He replied at length in defense of his conduct. By this time it was already February 1782, and he had gone much further down the path of bold deeds, as we shall see. He made it clear that he had contacts in both parties in the Republic, and was treated courteously by both. He naturally stayed out of intrigues, he said; that was not his way at all. He had had good reasons to stay in Amsterdam, but things had so changed that he was about to move to The Hague. The envoys of other countries, in any case, hardly dared to enter into relations with him, being afraid and surrounded with spies. The situation was delicate, to be sure, but that did not disturb him "as my whole life, from my infancy, has been passed through an uninterrupted series of delicate situations."

In a subsequent letter he said that he had obtained the advice of America's best friends in Holland before he went into action, even though the French ambassador found the time too early. He had had the memorial printed precisely because the sovereignty in the Netherlands was so divided, with a good four to five thousand regents—members of the governing bodies—in the country. The president of the States General had told him he could not accept the memorial, because he was not yet recognized "by our constituents and sovereigns; we are not the sovereign." In that case, he had replied, it was his duty to issue the memorial in print "because I have no other possible way of addressing myself to the sovereign, your constituents."

The results, furthermore, had proved him right. Thanks to publication of the memorial, his position was no longer ridiculous, and he had to be reckoned with. It was precisely by coming out into the open that he had protected himself against the English party. He would not have taken this step in an absolute monarchy, he said, but in a political system like that of the Republic it was necessary. In fact, what he had done had even saved Holland by drawing it out of its uncertainty.

That was what he had written also to Dumas, shortly after he submitted the memorial: If it were not accepted, future generations would blame their ancestors for aiming too low, "for it is no rash opinion, that not only the prosperity, but the existence of this Republic, depends upon an early connection with America." He repeated his opinion in a letter to his wife: "I know not what this People will do. I believe they will awake, after some time. Amsterdam, Harlem and Dort [Dordrecht] have represented the Necessity of an Alliance with America but when the rest will be of their Mind, I know not. If they neglect it, they and their Posterity will repent of it." This exaggerated conception of the situation, as though the Dutch towns had already argued for recognition of America, was not repeated by Adams two days later in a letter to Congress. In it he included a copy of the proposal by Amsterdam and the other towns to the States of Holland in favor of seeking closer relations with France, and he added his own comments that Amsterdam represented the true Batavian spirit. His memorial had given the regents an opportunity to discover what the public was thinking.[14]

Adams underestimated neither his own importance nor that of the cause which he upheld. Dumas saw to the printing and distribution of the memorial, which he could report on 11 May was all ready. His French translation did not remain the only one, however. Cérisier published his own version in *Le Politique Hollandais*, and a classic translator's debate ensued. Dumas's version might be more literal, Cérisier admitted, but that did not make it more accurate. "For, when one translates the work of a genius from one language into another, one must often depart from the letter in order to reproduce better the elegance, the energy and even the spirit of the original."[15]

The memorial drew a variety of reactions, chiefly about its economic arguments, as can be easily understood. The discussion dwelled on the same points that had been made before. America was or was not a good credit risk; it would remain an agricultural country for a long time, or it would soon become a strong trade competitor of the Dutch; and so forth. The most original contribution to the debate came from one of the best known of the pro-English party, the former university professor turned pamphleteer, Rijklof Michael van Goens. It was desirable and realistic, he asserted, to discuss only interests, not the abstract ideals involved, for "a sovereign not only has no duty, it has in fact no right to act with such *generosity* [aid to America on the basis of love of freedom] if such action

is inconsistent with the *advantage* of its subjects, and indeed would probably be *disadvantageous* for them." The entire piece, for all its partisanship, breathes this same spirit of independent realism. Van Goens understood quite well that France and Spain had no interest whatever in aid to
the United States as such, but that their real purpose in continuing the
war was to weaken England and to tie her down. He did not believe that
Dutch commerce would pluck all the promised golden fruit of the New
World, and he correctly anticipated that the New Englanders would become competitors of the Dutch in the carrying trade. In general, he held,
the Dutch did not have much to hope for from America, and meanwhile
they were fools to mess up their relations with England.[16]

But, in actuality, it was Van Goens who was rowing against the current,
not Adams, although for a while it seemed to be just the opposite. Adams
wrote at this time, on 16 May, the bleak letter about the "melancholy
situation" of the Dutch nation that we cited in the prologue of this book.
But he went his way with undiminished energy. By early June he had to
submit another paper to the ruling gentlemen at The Hague, who did not
want to recognize him. He had to inform them of the completion of the
American union, now that Maryland, the last of the thirteen states to do
so, had ratified the Articles of Confederation. Now the country was one,
from New Hampshire to Georgia, as Adams proudly wrote. He sent the
relevant documents to Dumas, asking that he convey them to the president for the week and to the Prince, by the post or by hand, as seemed
best to him.

On 5 June, Dumas went in person to call upon the president, who was
that week Baron Palland van Glinthuizen, and upon the Prince's secretary, De Larrey. Both accepted the papers that he brought them and asked
him to come back on the next day. When he returned, they were handed
back to him, and the president even gave him a scolding for having deceived him: He had not said that they came from Adams in his capacity
as plenipotentiary minister of the United States. This, however, was how
they were signed, and no such person was officially recognized in the
Netherlands. Dumas defended himself at length, testifying to the honesty
of his intentions, but the baron ended the discussions by putting the papers in Dumas's hat. He had no choice but to leave. De Larrey was courteous, as always, but he too returned the papers, as the Prince could do
nothing in a matter that had been sent to the provinces for decision.[17]

For the moment, Adams had to stand still; all he could do was wait. He
remained convinced, however, that he was right, although he had moments of despondency. As with any action in politics, only the outcome

would prove him right or wrong. Some eight months later, in February 1782, with the advantage of hindsight, Adams expressed his satisfaction with what he had done. In a truly lordly way he made history dance to his tune. His memorial, he wrote, had been the start of a total transformation of European politics. Not only had it safeguarded his personal position in the Netherlands—"If it had not been presented and printed, I am very sure I could not long have resided in the Republic"—but it had also called back to life the true spirit of the Dutch, inspired Van Berckel to demand his rehabilitation and prompted the burgomasters of Amsterdam to propose giving the Prince an advisory council and resisting Brunswick's influence, and aroused the whole nation to new zeal, as was evident in the battle of the Doggers Bank. All Europe was changed. The French had sent their fleet to America, and that had made Yorktown possible; the Spanish had opened negotiations with Jay; the king of Sweden had quoted from the memorial in a letter to the king of England; and the Holy Roman Emperor had undertaken his reforms under the influence of the spirit of freedom that spoke in the memorial.

One might say, he raged on, that his imagination and vanity swept him on. But when one has to defend oneself, one has to look at every aspect of things. He claimed only that the memorial did no harm and probably much good, more perhaps than could be proved. He asked to be forgiven; a man who was defending himself always looked a bit odd. It was easy enough to say that he was losing his reason, that he was vain, full of himself, and more such immodest things. Old hands in diplomacy and politics, wrote Adams, looked upon him as a kind of militiaman and sneered at him. Wise men, however, knew that militia sometimes won victories over regular troops by departing from the rules.

How many weeks after publication of his memorial, Adams continued, was it that the Emperor made his memorable journey to Brussels, Ostend, Bruges, and Antwerp? How long after that that he made his visits to Holland and Paris? Did not the contents of the memorial give him matter for reflection while on his trip? Did he not undertake his negotiations with France about dismantling the Barrier towns after that? Was France not induced in the same way to conclude an agreement with him, as was shown by the evacuation of those towns soon thereafter? If the Republic thereby was more tightly bound to France, to the advantage of the American cause, was the memorial not worth the trouble? And so on—all Europe changed to the good by the memorial!

Adams defended his own conduct magnificently, overexcitedly, and improbably, in this piece of fiery and emotional writing; it was a distortion of history that has no match in partiality, self-confidence, and swagger. Of course what Adams described was not exactly what happened, and the *propter hoc* does not so obviously follow from the *post hoc*. This will become evident as soon as we pass in review the events that Adams mentions. But we have Adams here in all his impetuosity, folly, and strength, the Adams of whom Franklin once wrote: "He means well for his country, is always an honest man, often a wise one, but sometimes in some things absolutely out of his senses." We see here the passion and the energy that made him what he was. We see too, with surprised entrancement, his feeling for the relativity of the human situation. For after having summarized all this with such overweening and bellicose conceit that he makes us think of the immortal Mr. Toad in Kenneth Grahame's book *The Wind in the Willows,* he suddenly concludes with a few sentences of clarification that bring everything, and especially himself, down to earth again.

It is possible, he wrote in closing, that the plans contrived by courts and princes and nations gradually come to a kind of ripening and then need only the slightest push to put the whole machine into motion; it was possible therefore that his memorial had given the final impulse to all the transformations he described. And then these surprising words: "What a dust we raise, said the fly upon the chariot wheel!" [18]

· CHAPTER 12 ·

Two Students at Leiden

*You are now at an University where many of
the greatest Men have received their Education.*
JOHN ADAMS
to his son John Quincy

 N all probability it will do more for your education to go back to France with your father than to prepare for college at Andover." This is what John Quincy Adams, sixth president of the United States, remembered that his mother had told him almost fifty years earlier when he was twelve years old. He had made the great journey to France with his father in the winter of 1778–79, and they had returned safely during the summer, rejoining his mother, his two sisters, and his younger brother Charles. His father had hardly recovered from the adventure of that journey when he received a second mission to cross the Atlantic, and again he faced the question which of his children he would take with him. It was Charles's turn to make the journey, which was strenuous, even dangerous, but very educational. Johnny did not want to go again; he was a studious child and wanted to go to school, first to Andover and then to Harvard. But his parents wondered whether the crowded school of life would not do him more good than learning from books at home. One Sunday afternoon after church his mother took him aside, had a serious talk with him, and convinced him of the unique opportunity that lay ahead for him.

The whole awareness of the significance of what they, the American rebels, were doing echoes in the words that she wrote him in farewell: "These are times in which a Genious would wish to live. It is not in the still calm of life, or the repose of a pacific station, that great characters are formed. . . . Great necessities call out great virtues. When a mind is raised, and animated by scenes that engage the Heart, then those qualities which would otherwise lay dormant, wake into Life, and form the Character of the Hero and the Statesman." The child must eventually become a statesman, a hero—this was from the start the ideal of his demanding parents—and the lad sailed a second time to Europe, with his father and his brother Charles.[1]

They arrived in the Netherlands in the summer of 1780. The boys had read about the country in the books that their father had assigned them; now they had to put their knowledge to use and learn from what they saw. John Thaxter, their father's secretary, who was still in Paris, exhorted Johnny: "As you are fond of keeping a Journal, be very particular in your description of the capital Towns you pass, of their Curiosities, their Manners, Customs, Dress, but more particularly of their Religion and Governments. This will be of great Advantage hereafter.—Omne tulit punctum qui miscuit utile dulci [he has carried every point who has mingled the useful with the agreeable (Horace)]." The useful with the pleasant, that was the standard set for an ambitious young man, and in that order! "Master John," Thaxter wrote to the lad's anxious mother, "sends me now and then small portions of his Journal which is very judiciously written. . . . They are indeed both fine young gentlemen and conduct themselves with great propriety."[2]

But the time came, as it had to, when the boys had to cease their sightseeing and go to school. At the end of September, Adams reported to his wife that he had placed them in the Latin School on the Singel near the Mint (the building still stands, although it is now a police station). John Quincy had attended the "Commencement," the opening of the school year, where the students delivered Latin orations and received their prizes, "which set his ambition all afire." But Charles was a friendlier, more winning personality, and he won the hearts of all the ladies. With the title of Burke's book in mind, the proud father proclaimed: "One of these Boys is the Sublime and the other the Beautifull."

The initial enthusiasm did not last long, however. The boys knew not a word of Dutch, and although their father believed they could learn Latin and Greek without knowledge of Dutch, the school thought otherwise. Adams wrote a note to the rector asking that his older son be placed in a higher class so that he could continue with his Greek, but he did not send it. He discovered that the educational practice was strict and oppressive and that corporal punishment was in common use. The boys did not like the school. Studious Johnny found no work for his ambition and became troublesome, the rector complained. At the beginning of November he wrote to the father asking him to take his son out of school: he was disobedient and impertinent, he spoiled his "*aimable frère*" (charming brother), and he merited a thrashing. Adams received this report "with astonishment and regret." "Send my Children to me this Evening," he answered, "and your Account, together with their Chests and Effects tomorrow." He was furious and blamed the teachers. "The Masters," he wrote to Abigail, "are mean spirited Writches, pinching, kicking, and boxing the Children, upon every Turn." [3]

Another school had to be found, and Adams, as he asked around for suggestions, must have thought of the American student in Leiden, Benjamin Waterhouse, whom he had met in Paris. Hoping that Waterhouse might be of help, he wrote him from Amsterdam to ask what schooling was available at Leiden for his children. Waterhouse, who knew the university very well—he had just received his M.D. there—gave him a full report on the courses and the tutors. He assured him that life in Leiden was cheaper than in Amsterdam and that he did not have to worry about his sons being teased because they were Americans. (Adams must have raised the question, as it was just at this time that he was afraid that the imminent war with England would lead to his own expulsion.) The Dutch, Waterhouse declared, were not troubled by their principles when it came to making money. Turk, Christian, Jew—it was all the same to them. Adams made up his mind swiftly. A few days later Thaxter, who had joined Adams in the fall, left for Leiden with the two boys. They were able to find two rooms in the house on the Long Bridge where Waterhouse lived, at a rental of fifteen guilders a month. Shortly afterward, early in January, they were enrolled as students in the university, where their names are still in the books; *Rectore* (under the rectorship of) Ewaldo Hollenbeek (1780–81); Johannes Thaxter, *Americanus*, 25 years; Johannes Quincy Adams, *Americanus*, 14 years; Charles Adams, *Americanus*, 10 years (with special permission because of his young age).

The father swelled with pride. This was something other than the paltry school in Amsterdam. To Abigail he reported: "I have this morning sent Mr. Thaxter, with my two Sons to Leyden, there to take up their Residence for some time, and there to pursue their Studies of Latin and Greek under the excellent Masters, and there to attend Lectures of the celebrated Professors in that University. It is much cheaper there than here: the Air is infinitely purer; and the Company and Conversation is better. It is perhaps as learned an University as any in Europe." And he impressed upon his children that they had to take advantage of their opportunity, study hard, and faithfully report their progress to him. "You have now a Prize in your Hands indeed. Such as if you do not improve to the best Advantage, you will be without Excuse. But as I know you have an Ardent Thirst for Knowledge and a good Capacity to acquire it, I depend upon it, you will not do no Dishonour to yourself nor to the University of Leyden." [4]

More fatherly admonitions followed. Adams wrote almost every day, even while he was sending long dispatches to Paris and Philadelphia. He corrected names that little John misspelled, and he allowed him to buy skates and a pair of riding breeches and boots, but these had to be long enough for him to grow into. He instructed him to attend the church (the one where the Scots dominie preached) twice every Sunday. And he gave a list of the names of the professors he had heard about. There were Valckenaer and Ruhnken for Greek—"This Mr. Ruhnkenius had published an edition of an Hymn to Ceres (found in Russia, and supposed to have been composed by Homer) with a Latin Translation and Notes. I would have you purchase that Hymn." There were Pestel for international law and Voorda for Roman law. "Pray, enquire whether he reads Lectures upon the whole Corpus Juris, the Digest, the Code, the Novells etc., whether he takes any Notice of the Feudal Law, that is of the Consuetudines Feudorum, and whether any Mention is made of the Cannon Law." And so on. There was nothing that Adams did not want his son to turn his mind to. He should study the whole system of the universities as a model for American universities. [5]

The lad John Quincy did his best, and he fitted better in Leiden than in Amsterdam. His reports to his father breathed pride, and to his mother he wrote: "I am now at the most celebrated university in Europe which was founded here for the valour of its inhabitants when it was besieg'd, when they were at war with Spain, it was put to its choice whether to be exempt from all taxes for a number of years, or to have an University founded here, and they wisely choose the latter." He taught himself Dutch from the Leiden newspaper and read Dutch history in Cérisier's book. And he threw himself into the study of the classics, as his father naturally demanded most of all from him. Adams himself became enthusiastic again during the first months of 1781, when he spent much time in Leiden, eagerly observing his sons' education upon the ancients. Van der Kemp, at this time Mennonite minister at Leiden, reminded him many years later how together they had discussed the merits of Demosthenes at the Golden Lion inn. [6]

The children had lessons every day for two hours in Greek and Latin from a tutor named Wensing. It is difficult to gauge the worth of this introduction. Waterhouse was very satisfied with it; the teacher did not use a book but had the boys write down their own grammar—John Quincy in Greek, Charles in Latin—from his dictation and in the evening they did the exercises. "The Young Gentlemen have been very steadily employed since they have had an Instructor, and their Improvement is in proportion," wrote Thaxter on New Year's Day, and he continued to report on the progress of their studies. John Quincy wrote that he had copied out the whole of a very rare essay on Greek by Hemsterhuis. His father wanted to send him a copy of Terence, a fine edition with the Latin text on one side and a French translation on the opposite page, but worried that it would be too easy and that the teacher would not approve. The son replied virtuously that it would be better not to send it, "because when I shall translate him he would desire that I might do it without help." After a few months he could report that he had read the fables of Phaedrus and Cornelius Nepos's book on famous men, and that each day he transcribed and learned a Greek verb in the active, medium, and passive voices. His father encouraged him to begin Sallust, saying that he was one of the best Roman historians and always worth reading. With Sallust, Cicero, Tacitus, and Livy, he declared, his son would learn wisdom and virtue. The aim of all study was to become a good man and a useful citizen. And John Quincy should read better writers than Phaedrus and Nepos. He should read Demosthenes and Cicero. If need be, John wrote, he would teach them to him himself.

But nothing, not even the great Classics, could be viewed as an end in itself. Adams drummed into his son—John Quincy, of course, for Charles gives the impression of frolicking along behind; he was not cut from the same hard wood as his brother—pure eighteenth-century thought: "These great Masters of Antiquity, you must sooner or later be able to judge of critically. But you must never imitate them. Study nature, and write accordingly, and you will resemble them. But it is nature not the Ancients that you are to imitate and copy."[7]

In all of this, Adams received a great deal of support from his friend Luzac, who had the boys come to his home and helped them when he could. He shared the father's enthusiasm over young John Quincy. Do you still remember, he wrote Adams many years later, "that you thought fit to leave him under my supervision and to entrust him to my teaching? . . . And what a lad he was! no unteachable, play-loving, indolent boy, but a lad . . . who modelled himself on his most excellent father."[8]

Fortunately, the youngster so full of promise was one who needed relaxation too. The winter of 1780–81 was a hard one, and his father permitted him to buy skates. Yet, even skating was not to be thought of as mere pleasure. It was good that he give himself to it just a few hours and in moderation, his strict father wrote. "Skating is a fine Art. It is not Simple Velocity or Agility that constitutes the Perfection of it but Grace." But that grace was developed by self-control. The sport helped one to learn self-restraint, to hold one's passions and impetuosity within bounds. Everything in life had to be considered and done with judgment fitting into the large "Plan of Happiness and Utility."

As we read Adams's exhortations, we get the impression that he was preaching at least as much to himself as to his son, who was actually much more reserved and disciplined than the father. The boy outshone him in virtuousness. When summer was near, he declared that he did not desire too long a vacation, lest his studies be hurt. "It is with no small pleasure," Waterhouse wrote two days later, "I inform you that John adheres to his studies with a constancy rarely seen at that age."[9]

Young John took after his father; that was clear to everyone. Banker Grand's wife had earlier written to his mother from Paris that the boy "inherits the spirit of his father and bids fair to be a Roman like him." Charles was different. He did not enjoy life far from home; he became homesick in the spring, and after much searching his father found an opportunity to send him back to America, where he arrived in January 1782 after an adventurous voyage.

Meanwhile John Quincy also left on another journey, but in the opposite direction. Francis Dana, who had been named the minister of the United States to Russia, as we know, needed a secretary and a translator (not for Russian but for French, the court language in St. Petersburg). And who would be better, Adams mused, than his son? John Quincy was willing, although he regretted leaving his studies, and early in July he left for the East with Dana. It was exactly his fourteenth birthday when his father sat down to write his mother: "John is gone, a long Journey with Mr. Dana:—he will serve as an Interpreter . . . and the Expence will be little more than at Leyden." The lad remained in the Russian capital for fourteen months. Dana's mission did not achieve much, but John did better with his studies. There were moments when Adams had second thoughts about so hastily permitting his son to go away. "I regret your Loss of the glorious Advantages for classical Studies at Leyden," he once wrote. But his industrious son reported to him that he had read all of Nepos, translated Cicero's first oration against Catilina, read Hume's *History of England*, and was now busy with Mrs. Macaulay's. He was not bored at all.[10]

During these months, John Quincy became a young man. In the autumn of 1782 he left alone on a long journey through Sweden, Denmark, and Germany, and turned up in The Hague in the spring of 1783. At the moment his father was in France, but Dumas took him in. They spent pleasant hours in scholarly conversations. As Dumas wrote John Adams, "Your son conducts himself in comprehension and manners like a grown, well-educated man. He is my wife's darling." "We enjoy ourselves reading together the Caligula of Suetonius, the Pseudolus of Plautus, and the amorous Dido of Vergil." Dumas enjoyed catering to the youth's interests, and he gives a most charming and romantic description of an outing they made to Scheveningen, then just a fishing village across the dunes from The Hague. "Yesterday we all went to picnic in middle of the Scheveling dunes. One dune served as table and chairs, the sound of the sea as a symphony, the endless horizon as a dining room and the pure air as a cook adding unusual spices to the flavor of the food we had brought."[11] After a few months of this life of learning and idylls, John Quincy went to Paris to become his father's secretary. Adams was then in the midst of the peace negotiations.

Adams was and remained for his son the very model of devotion to duty, self-sacrifice, and the other Roman virtues then held in high esteem. It is difficult to imagine what the late-eighteenth-century people really felt, what they were really behind their stern Roman masks, what pains of separation from their beloved ones John and Abigail Adams suffered. Not that they did not write about it; the letters of this remarkable couple, so happy in their marriage, are full of it. But they never gave way to sentiment; they controlled all emotion, wrapping it in the forms and images of the times. Romanticism had not yet broken through, which is probably why they were able to bear their pain. John confessed his "horrid Solitude . . . amid Courts, Camps and Crowds." Love of country, Abigail asserted, "is the most disinterested of all virtues." "The Letter of the 10 I read over and over without End—and ardently long to be at the blue Hills, there to pass the Remainder of my feeble days," wrote Adams.

"I shall assume the Signature of Penelope," she wrote, "for my dear Ulysses has already been a wanderer from me near half the term of years that that Hero was encountering Neptune, Calipso, the Circes and Syrens. In the poetical Language of Penelope I shall address you

> Oh! haste to me! A Little longer Stay
> Will ev'ry grace, each fancy'd charm decay:
> Increasing cares, and times resistless rage
> Will waste my bloom, and wither it to age."

She was willing to use his health as an argument for his return, but she tinged it with patriotism: How could he serve his country if he fell ill and lost his strength in Holland's damp climate? But duty came before everything else. Her letters are splendid examples of the eighteenth-century consciousness; reading them one understands why the people of that time found David such a great painter and why they so disliked Gothic cathedrals. Strict simplicity poured into the mold of classical art forms was the pattern of their lives. That too was the heritage of their children. They would have no expectation of wealth; they would not be spoiled in foreign lands by the reigning luxury; the example of their homes led them along the path of "universal Benevolence and good will to Man." In the evening they did not play cards but used their free time to read useful books. Thus they became "usefull and ornamental Members of Society."[12]

· CHAPTER 13 ·

A Year of Tension

*I shall carry Holland
in my veins to my grave.*
JOHN ADAMS

HE year 1780, Adams had complained, was the most difficult of his life. But 1781 would surpass it in setbacks, confusion, and despair. It had begun full of hope, with his appointment, his vigorous memorials, his enthusiastic "militia" diplomacy, and it would end so brilliantly for the American cause. But in between came long months of uncertainty and opposition. Independence was in greater peril than most of the American leaders realized. The United States was on the verge of becoming a football in an extremely complicated game of European diplomacy, and the Americans were too far away and too dependent on their French ally to see it clearly. It was the particular achievement of Adams that he saw it clearly from the very start and that he resisted with all the indomitable courage characteristic of him.

The heart of the problem was the attitude of France. For the fact was that the French government was not at all eager for an American victory. France's intervention in the struggle had been quite ambivalent; her purpose was more to oppose England than to help the American rebels, toward whom she displayed an overweening paternalism, and she conceded to them scarcely any role of their own in the diplomatic struggle that in these years 1780 and 1781 became steadily more intense and especially more complex. America was no more than one small piece in a true eighteenth-century conflict over the balance of power. This became all the more evident as talks on an eventual peace got under way.

A steadily growing desire for peace began to take hold among all the warring parties. The war was costly, and success seemed to be beyond anyone's reach. In America the British armies controlled large territories after their most recent victories; yet they were in no position to reconquer the whole country. The European countries at war with England all had their own interests. France, Spain, and the Dutch Republic formed an unsteady alliance, and two of them had not even extended diplomatic recognition to their American ally. It was realized on both sides that there was no prospect of an adequate military solution to the war. The problem was to find a diplomatic solution that would not inflict too great a loss of face on any of the combatants. It was therefore not surprising that offers of mediation found a ready ear.

The full story of the diplomatic complications of the years 1780 and 1781 is too long to be told here, and besides it has already been superbly done by several historians. What it came down to was this: Russia and Austria offered to act as mediators in the struggle, and proposed a peace congress to be held in Vienna. They were after their own advantages and had almost no interest in the American cause in itself. The Russians put forward a suggestion that each of the thirteen American states be consulted separately about what kind of relationship it wanted with England. The English government showed some interest in the Russian idea, which could cause dissension among the Americans; it saw in the mediation of the Holy Roman emperor and the Russian empress a real chance to save its situation. It even hoped to bring them to its side by making them tempting offers: The island of Minorca was the bait for Russia and the opening of the Scheldt for Austria. France could not wholly abandon her American ally—and this would become an insuperable stumbling block in the course of discussions—but at the moment she thought she had found a middle way in a proposal for a provisional settlement, an armistice in which the belligerents would hold what they controlled, *uti possidetis*, as the diplomats solemnly called it.

Vergennes set forth his ideas in a secret memorandum in February 1781. The English would stay where they were in North America, which meant keeping the South and the far North, where they controlled Maine by occupation of the mouth of the Penobscot River. The West, including the Great Lakes, would also remain in their hands, but there would have to be further talks about the future of New York, still held by British troops. Because of its alliance with America France could not itself make these far-reaching proposals, but the mediators were the obvious powers to do so. The Americans would simply have to realize that this temporary arrangement was the best they could get. The historical example to prove it lay before them in the Dutch Revolt which they so admired—the truce of 1609 had given the Hollanders their freedom, but they had had to leave the Southern Netherlands in the enemy's hands. There was another point as well where Vergennes failed the Americans, or, more precisely, made them dependent upon French policy. At an eventual Congress in

Vienna, he proposed that France look after the Americans' interests, and if they were allowed to send a representative, he would have to be under French supervision. Furthermore, the presence of an American representative would not at all imply recognition of the independence of the United States. No wonder Vergennes liked the idea of consulting the American states separately.

During the spring Austria and Russia jointly put forward other conditions for the proposed peace talks. All parties at the Congress would discuss their proposals together, but England and her American colonies would conduct parallel talks, and the other powers would guarantee the terms of their agreement. At the same time the warring powers would put down their arms for a year upon the basis of the territorial status quo. These were, however, nothing but figments of diplomats' imaginations, plans that had no real chance of success. The English were not at all ready to enter such negotiations with the rebels; nor would it be easy to get the Americans to accept a policy that would put their independence in mortal danger.

Nonetheless, it seemed during the spring that things would actually go this way. Vergennes did everything to bend the American Congress to his will. He gave detailed instructions to the French ambassador in the United States, A. C. de La Luzerne, to compel the Americans to pass through the strait gate, as he wanted "to prepare the Americans, to be led, if necessary, in the last extremity, to the abattoir at Vienna." The first thing that had to be done, therefore, was to put the troublesome Adams in his place. La Luzerne almost brought it off, with much pressure and much bribery. It was his work, he boasted in a report to his court, that Livingston was named "secretary of foreign affairs" in August. As we have seen, Livingston was an opponent of Adams's "militia" diplomacy, and he was selected instead of Arthur Lee, the candidate of the anti-French party. French money turned the scales in the election. The next step was to persuade the Americans to accept the French demands, with France guaranteeing their independence, but they would have to drop their own demands for expansion into the Mississippi Valley and for fishing rights off Newfoundland, and their peace delegation would have to work in complete cooperation with the French and accept the mediation of Russia and Austria. Lastly, the delegation would have to be expanded to five members.

This final proposal was specifically directed against Adams, until then the sole official peace representative of the United States in Europe. La Luzerne directed his fire against Adams in particular. Adams, Vergennes informed his ambassador, was not suitable as a negotiator; he was a pedant, obstinate and too much taken with himself. He had not been willing to adapt himself; he had not realized that his country needed the French alliance, and how unmanageable he was had just been shown in his presenting himself on his own to the States General as the American envoy and in submitting the memorial to them. If it was not possible to get him recalled, Vergennes continued, he still had to be taught to keep step with the French. The man was blind; he served only the interests of New England with his insistence upon American fishing rights. The general interests of America were safe only in French hands, and Adams had to be restrained by naming several other negotiators alongside him.

Congress did not know how to get out of the French snare. For many of the members the belief that French help was necessary for victory was an honest conviction, but French money and French propaganda also played a role. Congress gave in to most of the French demands, and John Jay, Benjamin Franklin, Thomas Jefferson, and Henry Laurens were named as negotiators along with Adams. Because Jefferson, whose wife was ailing, did not accept, and Laurens was still bewailing his fate in the Tower of London, the negotiating team in practice was reduced to three—Adams, Franklin, and Jay. They were furnished with new instructions quite different from those that Adams had taken with him in 1779. The territorial demands were no longer stated absolutely but became only the optimum gains to be sought. There was a special provision requiring collaboration with France. Fishing rights no longer were central; a motion to make them a prerequisite had been rejected, and because the instructions to Adams in the 1779 instructions to make a treaty with England were withdrawn, he was no longer able to get his way in this matter. The anti-French party muttered its objections and introduced various countermotions, but it was repeatedly defeated. It was necessary, the majority reasoned, to sacrifice national self-esteem to the national interest in the French alliance.[1]

The American position was dependent and pitiable, although the great victory was just in the offing. France's shrewd diplomacy held the rebels in a velvet grip from which they could not break loose. But in the long run the rancor against France which remained after the war would do more harm to French than to American interests and would contribute to the American mood of isolationism. Adams had seen from the beginning what was happening, but in the summer of 1781 he himself was the victim of the French triumph.

The news took some time to reach him, and it was his wife, Abigail, who had to absorb the first shock. In a letter to a friend she expressed her indignation over the way her husband had been treated. This man of honest zeal who had no sinister purpose whatever, she said, who did not make politics a game of personal friendship, who had no ambition to win riches at the expense of his country—"this, this man must be crushed, he must be calumniated and abused." He was a good man, she continued; would that Heaven would give them more like him in the service of the country. As she told her friend, he was a man of principle, and he would not do violence to his conscience in order to gain the favor of a minister or of Congress. "Yes," she wrote, "it wounds me Sir—when he is wounded I blead."[2]

· II ·

Whether or not he wanted to, the French minister of foreign affairs, Charles Gravier, count of Vergennes, a *grand seigneur* of the Old Regime, could not get around involving in the preliminary discussions for preparation of the Vienna congress the one American in Europe who had powers to negotiate for peace. That was, of course, no one other than that crude peasant from Braintree, that tactless Puritan John Adams. It was he and not the suitable, easy-going Franklin whom, in .the end, Congress had chosen for the task. And as long as Vergennes was unable to get him excluded, he had to work with him, willy-nilly. At the beginning of June, Adams received from the French chargé d'affaires in The Hague a courteous note informing him that the interests of the United States required his presence in Paris. He should come as soon as his business in Holland permitted. Adams replied from Amsterdam that he would like to know what was involved so that he could form a firm judgment. He heard many things in Holland that gave him but little pleasure, but before he left for Paris he was informed about what was brewing there.

The Dutch awaited with tense impatience the news from Russia. The special mediation that Empress Catherine had offered to England and the Netherlands—she excused herself from giving assistance to the Dutch Republic because the formal entry of the States General into the League of Armed Neutrality had arrived too late, after England had already declared war—aroused much vain hope in the Republic. There was still an entire party of those who wanted reconciliation with England before all else, and it was not the municipal government of Amsterdam, dominated since the fall of Van Berckel by Burgomaster Rendorp, which took the lead. Rendorp, who was, according to Adams, "secretly in the interest of the stadholder and the English," really desired a middle course between England and France, and he therefore took a middle position between the Prince and the States party. He turned against the duke of Brunswick and supported the notion of setting up an advisory council alongside the stadholder. Rendorp negotiated in secret for peace with England, but he wanted to save Holland's honor.

There was no real chance for peace, however. With regard to the Netherlands and with America, the English government was not ready to make any concession—Yorktown was still in the future—and it discussed conditions for a peace congress only in order not to offend the Russian empress. Catherine favored mediation, and she would go ahead and mediate; so London had to meet her at least part of the way by setting out certain conditions. No one in the Netherlands could take those conditions seriously. There was not a word about reparations for damage done to the Dutch, and return of their conquered colonies was made dependent upon Dutch readiness to rejoin England in opposition to France. In any case, the English insisted, Adams had to be expelled from the country and all American loans forbidden. On the other side France pressed steadily harder for the so-called "concert," that is, common action against the now common English foe, a policy which would bind the Dutch, like the Americans, to a foreign policy completely dominated by France.

Caught between these two fires, William V fell into confusion. "The best that could happen would be for me to be away from here; I should go to my hereditary lands to plant cabbages," he whimpered repeatedly, and felt himself to be up against a blank wall. Fagel, stubbornly defending the established order, thought that everything would eventually work out: "If France would renounce the independence of America," then the mediation of Catherine II and Joseph II could succeed. Did Fagel know how close to the truth he was? And how far from it? For whatever thoughts were on the minds of the French and however easily they sacrificed their friends, events never got that far. There was a vague yearning for peace on every side, but all the parties disdained a "peace without victory" as long as they thought they could come out of the war with victory. Little could therefore emerge from a congress in Vienna or from the mediation of Catherine II between London and The Hague. A secret English agent, Paul Wentworth, had to return from the Netherlands having accomplished nothing.[3]

Adams followed all these developments with close attention. He feared without exception all mediation and all efforts for peace, for he understood that the independence of his own country was always at stake. Like the Dutch Patriots, he hoped that the English secret talks would fail. In the spring he began to realize that neither his country nor the Netherlands had any chance of gaining the assistance of the League of Armed Neutrality, for which they had hoped. He did not know just what was being cooked up in St. Petersburg, but he wanted no part of the mediation of the Russian empress. When reports from the Russian capital reached The Hague in mid-June and it became clear just how meaningless was the friendly help offered by Catherine with her mediation, Adams drew his own conclusions. He was still guessing, but he anticipated a general mediation, and he at once sent a sharp warning to the president of the American Congress. There must be no negotiations until England first recognized the independence of the United States, and that it did not plan to do. "I regret that this idea of a negotiation for a general peace is upheld, for I am convinced that it is only a cunning maneuver of the British government and that many powers in Europe, especially Holland, will fall victim to it." Such a negotiation would obviously be held upon the basis of *uti possidetis* and would therefore place the American union in grave danger. If he was invited to take part in these negotiations, he added, he would attend with all patience and tact, as though he believed that they were honestly intended.[4]

There was a bit of tragicomedy in Adams's visit to Paris in July. It is clear that the French ministry was intent upon deliberately humiliating him, but they still did not quite know what to do with him. His first audience, with Secretary of State Rayneval, went badly. Was he a British subject? he was asked. What was his actual status? The next day, when he saw Vergennes himself, he at last got to hear what the plans were for the Vienna meeting, and he was even allowed a glance at them, but he was not permitted to make a copy of them. Nonetheless he reacted vigorously and to the point. He was not against mediation, he declared, but a temporary suspension of arms upon the basis of the status quo was completely unacceptable. A peace, even an armistice, was only possible if England first evacuated all thirteen colonies. As for himself, he was ready, if need be, to go to Vienna, but not without an official invitation that recognized his status. Moreover, he would go only as the representative of the federal Congress; the plan for separate delegates from the thirteen states was utterly out of the question.

Adams thus canceled out all the French plans with one sharp, challenging stroke. Vergennes might badger him and insult him—he was addressed as "Agent of the United States"—but he could not manipulate him, he could not bring him round, and what La Luzerne had secretly cooked up against him in Philadelphia was not yet known. For the moment the lack of rapid communications furnished Adams with many advantages. He was able to stand firm and set his style of action, his "militia" candor, against all the tricks and traps of Old Regime diplomacy. The tone that he took with the French minister was that of the virtuous American faced with corrupt Europe: "The dignity of North America does not consist in diplomatic ceremonials or any of the subtleties of etiquette; it consists solely in reason, justice, truth, the rights of mankind." How the lordly French minister must have been irked by such Puritan preaching! Just as Clemenceau a hundred and forty years later would be irked by the exalted moralizing of Woodrow Wilson.[5]

Adams, as it turned out, succeeded. It would of course be going too far to say that he, and only he, was responsible for the dropping of the Vienna mediation. He would claim later that it had been his work alone, but there were in fact other forces at work. For all that, this was a moment to be proud of in his life. The vigor, perspicacity, and swiftness with which he reacted to plans that so greatly imperiled his country are admirable still. And it is at least understandable that in his reminiscences years later he should have maintained that his resistance in July 1781 had "defeated the profound and magnificent project of a Congress at Vienna, for the purpose of chicaning the United States out of their independence."[6]

It was already August, when he was back in the Netherlands, before he heard what had been decided in Philadelphia behind his back, that his original instructions had been withdrawn and that four additional negotiators had been appointed to join him in order to open negotiations on much more flexible conditions. The report came from Franklin, and Adams answered him at once. He was afraid, he wrote, that the new instructions would be just as useless as the old ones. It would be better for them to return home and wait until the last British soldier in the United States had been killed or captured. Until then England would want no peace. "Upon my word I am weary of such roundabout and endless negotiations as that of the armed neutrality and this of the congress at Vienna."

He would not have been John Adams if he had not felt the humiliation strongly and deeply; in his later letters and reports he repeatedly returned to it. Naturally, he tried to put a good face on what had happened. Some men, he wrote to Dana, would have been annoyed by these innovations (the withdrawal of his instructions and the appointment of five negotiators), "but I am glad of them. They have removed the cause of envy, I had like to have said; but I fear I must retract that, since J. A. still stands before B. F. in the commission." And then, pointing his finger toward France, he said: "You know from what quarter this whole system comes. They have been obliged to adopt our systems of war and politics in order to gain influence enough by means of them to lessen us. But I will consent, upon these terms, to be diminished down to the size of a Lilliputian, of an animalcule in pepper water. There is no present prospect of peace." Vergennes was behind it all, he believed, and in his diary he explained that the count had tried to get him removed by "negotiating very artfully with Congress." But happily, he had failed: "No Wrestler was ever so compleatly thrown upon his Back as the C. de Vergennes."[7]

He still had his sense of honor, he wrote to Abigail, and his "sentiments of Delicacy, as exquisite as the proudest Minister that ever served a Monarch." "Don't distress yourself about any malicious attempts to injure me in the Estimation of my Countrymen. Let them take their Course and go the Length of their Tether. They will never hurt your Husband, whose Character is fortified with a shield of Innocence and Honour ten thousandfold stronger than brass or Iron."[8]

· III ·

Did the proud Adams return so hurriedly to Holland in order to forget as quickly as possible the vexations he had suffered in Paris? He rode day and night, and was back in Amsterdam at the beginning of August. He dispatched at once to the president of Congress a report of his conversations with Vergennes and repeated that it was useless to expect peace because England was intent on going on to the very end. He also gave an interesting account of the incognito visit of Emperor Joseph II to the Republic. Joseph had actually asked after the American envoy, who unfortunately had been in Paris at the time. In another letter not long after, Adams reported that the Dutch fleet had fought well in the battle of Doggers Bank. Did it mean that the general apathy had been broken through? he wondered. At last, he wrote to Franklin, the Dutch had discovered the only effective method to negotiate with the English, which was to fight. And he continued to believe that the credit for their renewed spirit belonged to him, that by his memorial he had brought back to life the old Batavian spirit that had lain slumbering so long.[9]

This was his last letter before he was laid up by a serious illness at the end of August. He had to remain in bed for more than a month and was not able even to pick up his pen. In the first letter that he wrote after his recovery, on 9 October to his wife, he ascribed his sudden ailment to the hot summer and the "pestilential Vapours" of the stagnant waters in the canals. What had brought him down was "a nervous Fever, of a dangerous Kind, bordering upon putrid." He had been wholly unconscious for five or six days and had not even observed what the doctor and the surgeon had done to him. He had been cured by a medicinal herb, and he had everything to thank for the skill of his doctor, Osterike (he meant the Leiden professor of medicine, N. G. Oosterdijk). But his recuperation was not yet complete, he wrote. He continued to complain about the aftereffects of his illness, and he doubted whether he could fully recover "amidst such cold damps and putrid Steams as arise from the immense quantities of dead Water." [10]

The Dutch waterways were probably partly to blame, but are we going too far if we suppose that the "breakdown" (as we now call it) of this highly temperamental man was also due to the bitter disappointments that he had just undergone? It is not impossible, and it is certain that he was more deeply hurt than he was willing to admit to himself.

Once he was back on his feet, he noticed that little had changed in the Dutch Republic. The situation still aroused the same sickness at heart. Indecisiveness reigned. The brief flickering of hope after Doggers Bank had died down. It was still impossible to borrow money for America and the discussion of diplomatic recognition was still being endlessly debated in the provinces. It was impossible to predict what the States General would do. Adams lost himself in reading history, especially the negotiations of the seventeenth-century French diplomats in the United Provinces, Jeannin, Torcy, D'Avaux, and D'Estrades, all of whom had suffered the same uncertainties that he knew. It was, he wrote, a national trait of the Dutch to delay all decisions as long as possible and then to make them suddenly, out of fear. Years might pass before he would be recognized, but it might also be next month. The party conflict had blazed up again, he continued. The English party still hoped for reconciliation, but that was impossible, for a number of reasons. First, there was still a national pride in the country and a general conviction that the English were in the wrong and the Americans in the right. The actions of the Americans resembled those of their own forefathers too much for the Dutch to be able to take up arms against America. His memorial had made that clear, he stated. Second, the hope for American trade remained strong. Third, for the Republic to join with weak England against strong France, Spain, and America would mean her downfall. But for the moment there was nothing to be hoped for, and little for him to do. "My prospects both for the public and for myself are so dull, and the life I am likely to lead in Europe so gloomy and melancholy" that he pleaded for his recall.[11]

But just at this moment, in the bleak autumn of 1781, signs of new life seemed to be appearing in the apparently moribund society of the Republic. Adams reported them as soon as he saw them. "There is at present a fermentation in this nation," he wrote to the president of Congress. Pamphlets were being put out by the hundreds, and a remarkable excitement was taking hold. He noted in particular a "large pamphlet" that was distributed everywhere and discussed by everyone. Its contents were best indicated by the edicts issued against it; he sent a copy of that issued by the States of Utrecht. A week later he reported that an English translation of the pamphlet had already appeared, and he sent another edict, this time by the States of Holland, to make clear what was up. He himself was enthusiastic about the little book: "I consider this libel as a demonstration that there is a party here, and a very numerous one, who are proselytes to democratic principles."

The pamphlet which drew such rapturous praise from Adams was *Aan het Volk van Nederland* (To the people of the Netherlands); it appeared anonymously, and its authorship remained secret for a century, when it was proved that it had been written by Joan Derk van der Capellen tot den Pol, as some had suspected at the time. Adams's letters are only one more piece of proof of the enormous excitement that this pamphlet stirred up. Adams even devoted an entire letter to the significance of the work. It was the American Revolution, Adams maintained, that had shaken the people out of their slumbers and spread a new spirit among them. The roots of the democratic principles that were now spreading throughout Europe could be found in the American uprising. But he also had to raise a warning finger: "When I say democratic principles, I do not mean that the world is about adopting simple democracies, for these are impracticable; but multitudes are convinced that the people should have a voice, a share, and be made an integral part." Government must be a mixture of the one, the few, and the many, he contended, the *imperium mixtum*, the balance of the three powers of monarchy, aristocracy, and democracy, all working together in one democratic system; the aim of all government was the happiness of the people, the greatest happiness of the greatest number.[12] Adams's phrasing here might remind one of Jeremy Bentham, but is more probably derived from the same source as Bentham's, the writings of Joseph Priestley.

The ideas of Adams closely paralleled those that were held by Van der

Capellen and his Patriot friends; no more than Adams were they radicals who believed in direct government by the people. The people—and in their eyes that meant the burghers whose property gave them an interest in good government—should receive a right of indirect participation in government, but no more. We will have to return to this point later.

Other signs of the new spirit soon followed. In mid-October, Robert Jasper van der Capellen van de Marsch, a cousin of Joan Derk, appealed in the States of Gelderland for recognition of the United States. The time had come to put an end to the "cowardly indulgence" of England. "What is holding us back from . . . making the closest ties with this virtuous and powerful People?" Adams immediately sent a report to the president of Congress, giving copious quotations from the speech of the Gelderland nobleman. It was, he observed, the first public statement in favor of American independence, but it would take a long time, a very long time, before the Republic would follow his example with unanimity. A few weeks later, in early November, similar voices were heard from the Oostergo quarter of Friesland. Everything could be expected from recognition, the Frisians argued: restoration of trade, return of the lost colonies, and "the confidence of the Most-Eminent Powers France and Spain." For the moment these were the only ones who spoke out. The affair would "drag on to the next year," as a contemporary historian wrote.[13]

Things had finally begun to move more rapidly because of events on the other side of the ocean. There the protracted and uncertain war suddenly ended with a miraculous, glorious victory. On 19 October at Yorktown an English army of eight thousand men under the command of General Cornwallis, encircled by the armies of Washington and Rochambeau and the fleet of De Grasse, laid down its arms. The bitter conflict was coming to a close. The great news was rushed to Europe by a special ship, and it reached Adams on 23 November. He was elated, but did not immediately believe that all problems were solved. To be sure, there was no more talk of a congress at Vienna. But would the English government really give in? he wondered. "The rage of the nation is still too violent." And as for the Dutch, they were not blind, but they sat imprisoned by their fear. Cornwallis's capitulation made them a little bolder; all sorts of people came to congratulate Adams; and there were calls for an alliance. They were starting to think about the Americans, but they mulled things over for a long time. And there were "invisible fairies, who disconcert in the night all the operations of the patriots during the day."[14]

· CHAPTER 14 ·

A Flood of Petitions

*It is strange to see how the American Revolution
has excited these phlegmatic Dutchmen.*
DUMAS

 E can see from the varying instructions given to Adams how wobbly and changeable the attitude of the American Congress was in the summer before Yorktown rang down the curtain on the last act of the Revolution. Where he had been put sharply in his place in June, with his powers strictly limited, a new set of instructions was sent to him in August specifically for what he should do in the Dutch Republic. The debates in Congress were extensive, and from one day to the next opinions shifted and Adams's powers were increased. What finally resulted on 16 August was orders to Adams to conclude if possible an alliance with the Dutch government, preferably as part of a triple alliance with France as the third partner. A precondition for this alliance would be the Republic's recognition of American independence. Both parties would be required to continue fighting until this independence was officially recognized in a peace treaty. It was emphatically prescribed that Adams maintain close contact with the French ambassador in all his negotiations.

This may not have been the fulfillment of all that Adams desired, but he was pleased nonetheless when he received the new instructions at the end of November, together with the news of Cornwallis's capitulation at Yorktown. If French supervision would be annoying, at least he had approval for going ahead with his own aggressive diplomacy. Furthermore he was still on good terms with La Vauguyon and therefore hoped that he would succeed. He at once informed the duke of his new instructions, but sought Dumas's advice in an optimistic letter: "My new instructions are very well timed, and we shall make it do to get an answer I hope, and to cement a triple or quadruple alliance in time, which may set all the fools in Europe at defiance." [1]

La Vauguyon responded very favorably. He wrote Adams that he too believed that the moment had come for taking the big step. On 18 December he came in person to visit Adams and suggested that he pay a visit to the president of the week to ask for a reply to his memorial. "He thinks," Adams later reported to the president of the American Congress, "that I now may assume a higher tone, which the late *Cornwallization* will well warrant." Once he had seen the president of the week, La Vauguyon added, Adams should go on to visit the deputies of each of the towns of Holland at their official residences in The Hague, in order to broaden his support as much as possible. Adams traveled to The Hague the next day to confer with Dumas and to consult with friends. They gave him the same advice that La Vauguyon had offered: visit the president of the week, the secretary of the States General, and the pensionaries of the towns of Holland.

But as Adams got down to work, there once more stood in the shadows a threatening censor—the French foreign minister. La Vauguyon, who had another extended discussion with Adams on 21 December, might have been enthusiastic, but Vergennes was not. The French ambassador left before Christmas for Paris to consult his superior, and even before the new year began, he wrote to Adams that Vergennes had no objections to his visiting the members of the Dutch government, providing that he put his questions orally and confined himself to the question of the memorial. But Adams was not kept in line that easily. Other friends encouraged him; Van der Capellen tot den Pol, in particular, urged him to ask for a categorical reply to his memorial in a tone fitting the greatness of America and the indignation she felt about how the American envoy had been received.[2] Orally or in writing, it did not matter; Adams was on his way.

Early in January the time was favorable. President of the week of the States General was the Holland deputy, Bartholomeus van den Santheuvel, burgomaster of Dordrecht, who was a moderate. On Wednesday, 9 January, Adams called upon Van den Santheuvel and asked, in so many words, for a categorical reply to his memorial of the previous May. He next went to see the grand pensionary, who excused himself on grounds of illness (he actually was sick, as it happened). The next morning Adams visited Fagel, the *griffier*, who assured him that the matter had been given to the provinces *ad referendum* in May but that no reply, favorable or unfavorable, had yet been received from them. Fagel, wrote Adams, although a very good friend of the stadholder's court and of England, was extremely courteous and accompanied him through all the rooms and hallways to his coach.

Then, guided by Dumas, Adams journeyed round the various official residences for the deputies from Holland's eighteen towns. He explained to Congress the value of these visits in winning the support of the towns, each of which was like an independent republic. In their governments the burgomasters, who possessed the executive power, were like kings, and they shared the limited legislative power with the town councils. The aldermen were the judiciary and the pensionaries the ministers.

The house of Dordrecht was first on the list to be visited, and there Pensionary De Gijselaar, a Patriot, received him warmly and promised his support. The rest of the circuit went off no less successfully, with one exception. When they came to the door of Amsterdam's house, Burgomaster Rendorp sent out word that no one was present who could receive them; it was several days before the new pensionary, Visscher, who had replaced Van Berckel, permitted them to enter.

His visits, Adams told Congress, had made a big impression, and the public spoke of them with approval. This was not quite true of Their High Mightinesses. Van den Santheuvel, the president of the week, informed them "that N. [*sic*] Adams, accompanied by one Dumas, had come to see him." This Adams had asked for a categorical reply to his request of May to be permitted to present his credential letters. "Which being deliberated upon," the resolutions of the States General tell us, "the Deputies of the respective Provinces accepted copies of the aforesaid declaration to be communicated to their constituents for further discussion."

For the moment all Adams could do was wait. But, as he wrote to Van der Capellen, he had been encouraged by his reception. A favorable decision could not be too long in coming. How sad therefore was the attitude of "one big town," dictated by the "private ambition" of a single person. Adams probably had Rendorp in mind, the ambitious burgomaster who, as we have seen, sought a reconciliation with England and therefore opposed recognition of the United States. The Overijssel nobleman read the letter attentively, and wrote a lengthy commentary upon it to his cousin Van de Marsch, in which he gave vent to all his bitterness. He had become so suspicious, he wrote, that he could scarcely dare to share Adams's hopes, and he was "completely unable to expect anything good from that cowardly and evil troop." He would exclude only a few regents, a couple of Frieslanders, and the aged Amsterdam burgomaster, "Father" Hooft. But most were worthless: "*Almost* all our nation, and *all* the Regents, consist of fools and knaves. . . . These damned Periwigs, I can't stand them, even less than the Pr[ince]."[3]

At that moment, Van der Capellen was closer to the truth than Adams, although he would soon be proved wrong. The bewigged gentlemen in

The Hague did not plan to go so far as yet as to recognize America. The Dutch political scene early in 1782 remained the same as before: hopeless indecisiveness, endless timidity, ambivalence, waiting upon Russian mediation. There were hopes for reconciliation with England; yet because the country had already been at war with England for more than a year, there were hopes too for collaboration with France. It was as though they were in a coach drawn by four or five horses, each pulling in a different direction, and they could only hope that they would not run into anything, whichever way they went.

One of the most skilled diplomatic talents possessed by the Republic, the Arnhem burgomaster Gerard Brantsen, who would soon be the Dutch envoy to the peace negotiations in Paris, drew up a peace plan early in January which was an effort to find a solution, but it did not rise above half-heartedness. The first of his five points was a sensible one, to strengthen the navy. The second point stated his desire for the "concert" with France, but without declining the proposal "to make a separate peace with England." His third point was acceptance of Russian mediation, with emphasis upon the unconditionality of neutral rights. The fourth point was to inform Denmark and Sweden of this in the hope that they would give diplomatic support.

The fifth point repeated the old uncertainty about America. "Neither to conclude at once a treaty with the Americans nor to show ourselves averse to it." The art was to be so circumspect that a "separate honorable reconciliation" with England was not made impossible, but, on the other side, not to disdain the American request, presented by Adams, "so that the Republic, in the eventuality of declaration of the independence of the North American colonies, would not be deprived of the important benefits which in that case naturally could and should flow from an alliance with them for the extension of the trade of this country." The intentions were as devious, and as impossible, as the prose was prolix. Brantsen admitted to Van Hardenbroek that he was so depressed by the sorry state of the country that often even at banquets he "lapsed into stillness." But the plans that he had concocted did not have much chance, he feared, so long as the Prince was so inadequate and, together with the *griffier*, conducted such an anti-French policy.

Brantsen put the attitude of the Dutch government toward America quite accurately. It was also the attitude of the indecisive majority of the Dutch regents. Thus, it was therefore not likely that American recognition would soon be given. All this hesitation was not at all strange, however, for there was suspicion that France was not enthusiastic about recognition. Such suspicion was fed left and right by warnings from Joan Cornelis van der Hoop that "France itself would not like to see the Republic ally with America or enter any treaty with her." His remarks carried weight because he was not only the able and ambitious new "fiscal" (administrative secretary) of the admiralty of Amsterdam and therefore, in practice, the informal navy secretary of the Republic as a whole, but also because he was a confidant of the Prince of Orange and was well informed about political developments. He based his warnings, he said, upon letters from Vergennes, although at the same time La Vauguyon was still telling De Gijselaar that he hoped the Republic would form an alliance with America.

It was a baffling situation. A Utrecht nobleman, Van der Capellen van Schonauwen, told a friend that Adams, for his part, did not speak in favor of France; on the contrary, he "had once argued to him, Schonauwen, that the Republic would act unwisely and against its constitution if it entered into closer ties with France, but that it should form a closer alliance with America." "This was all the more incredible," Van Schonauwen said, "in view of the fact that De la Vauguyon argued that the Americans acted wisely in addressing themselves to the Republic, and that even Adams himself had once sought to do so upon the instigation of France"; yet Vergennes did not want it. How was that all to be reconciled? he wondered. The Dutch regents were as puzzled as the members of the American Congress by what they saw: "There seemed to be either a paradox, or something was happening behind the scenes that was being kept very secret."

A few days later Van Schonauwen lifted the corner of the curtain a little after he had pressed Van der Hoop for an answer to his questions. Vergennes, Van Schonauwen now understood, had written to the fiscal that if La Vauguyon "had gone too far in what he said in certain matters, it should simply be reported to him, Vergennes, and he would take care of it; and he also let him know that he [La Vauguyon, that is] had no instructions to express himself about the Americans as he had done, and this appeared very strange, since he, La Vauguyon, had written in exactly the contrary terms to Gijselaar."[4]

The Prince hoped that this confused situation would enable him to hold off recognition of America. Otherwise he feared, as he said, that the national hatred between the English and the Dutch would grow too great. He thought that even Brantsen's cautious fifth point went too far. He therefore stood more upon principle than did the majority of the regents, who wanted to keep all paths open. In the short run he was able to get his way, especially because Amsterdam, like all the others, continued to waver. Burgomaster Rendorp laid down the line for his city: Adams could not be received as an envoy, but he should not be rebuffed outright either. He should therefore be given a hearing, just as during the Dutch revolt against Spain, Dutch envoys had been given a hearing in France and England in 1575, 1578, and many subsequent years. But, wrote Rendorp in his memoirs, this cautious policy failed, for "most members [of the States] became so over-excited that this moderate proposal found little acceptance." [5]

Rendorp's words describe the situation in that curious spring of 1782 very effectively: people were "over-excited." A closer examination of what was happening in those months can only confirm what Rendorp wrote. The Dutch, battered and dismayed by the incomprehensible events occurring about them, fell into a funk. As usually happens in such a crisis, they sought culprits and found them everywhere, each party finding its own set: on the one side, the Prince was seen as the source of all evil, or at the least the duke of Brunswick; on the other, it was the regents who opposed them on whom blame was put. Nowadays we would describe a situation like this as "polarization." In the gloom that swallowed them up, the Dutch began, as the prophet wrote, to dream dreams and see visions. One of these visions, and the most obvious because so far away, was the New World. The will-o'-the-wisp of America worked like a magical spell, surprisingly enough with greatest effect upon the merchants and traders, who are ordinarily considered to be the most sober and businesslike of people but who have often been the greatest dreamers—and is that not just where their greatness has lain? Dutch pettiness and covetousness have often been described in tones of contempt, probably rightly so; yet in this particular case there was something fine, foolish, and unreal in their excitement. We may say, with Hamlet, that there was a "method in their madness."

That spring, confusion, impotence, frenzy, a romantic mood reigned in the Netherlands. It was sadly obvious how little the Republic counted when in April the report came that Emperor Joseph II—to whose hereditary lands the Southern Netherlands had belonged since 1713—demanded the withdrawal of Dutch troops from the Barrier fortresses. It is true that this defensive belt no longer had any meaning, that it made no sense in the changed relationships of the powers, but it was the heritage of a great past directed against France. Still, it was humiliating that Dutch rights should be swept away by a flick of the hand, and the Dutch smarted under this humiliation.

The strangest rumors went round. There were people who even said that the Republic would revive its old rights in New Netherlands and assist the Congress with troops, and then, when the English had been driven out, exchange these rights for free trade and unlimited fishing rights in the Newfoundland banks. Hopeless discussions went on with a special Russian delegate, Arcadius Markov, and a secret English agent, Paul Wentworth, but who really believed that these talks meant anything? What were they but straws for a drowning man? The Prince of Orange might have retained some hope in them, but it was an "illusory hope," as La Vauguyon correctly wrote to Vergennes, because "unlimited freedom of the seas" would never be conceded by the British government; yet that was what the principle of neutrality to which Their High Mightinesses were bound came to in the end. What was at stake was again the old bone of contention, the treaty of 1674, which the British government wanted to revise by all means, whereas the Dutch desperately clung to it: The doctrine of "free ships, free goods" was almost the constitution of their international trade. That was clear enough even for outsiders, certainly for France, which did not worry too much about an eventual British-Dutch reconciliation. The English and Dutch principles of *Mare Clausum* and *Mare Liberum* were too far apart. Rendorp admitted as much to Wentworth, saying that if he could not promise free trade, return of the Dutch colonies, and reparation, he might as well return home.[6]

While the unrest was rising higher, the government at The Hague remained ambiguous in its policy. Early in March the States General adopted a resolution which accepted both the "concert" with France and the mediation of the two emperors. The only opposing vote came from Friesland, which wanted no mediation until recognition of the United States had been accorded. The bewildered and fearful Dutch did not know which way to turn. Their policy in this period has been differently judged by two outstanding historians of the period, Colenbrander and Geyl. The former, with all the haughty self-assurance of hindsight and the certitude of his Orangist convictions, poured out the vials of his wrath upon them. At the very time, he emphasized, when the fall of the obstinate North ministry was expected any day, the Dutch bound themselves "to continue for an entire year the pernicious war, in order to cater to the people's delusions." The Dutch government neglected the interests of the country, and it was inevitable that, "being looked upon as the branch office of a firm with its main offices elsewhere, it would lose everyone's respect." This is too harsh a judgment, however. As Geyl said in rebuttal of Colenbrander's condemnation, the Dutch had to be committed to France, which had reconquered various of the Dutch colonies and threatened not to return them. "It is absurd to imagine," Geyl wrote, "that the leaders here were only puppets and that the French ambassador pulled their strings."[7]

Still, I think we must not overly praise the reasonable Patriot program, as Geyl calls it. Even if it was not the slavish obedience to La Vauguyon that Colenbrander considered it to be, it was less a program than an expression of uncertainty and bewilderment. What it came down to in the end was that eighteenth-century rationalists were just as irrational as the people of any other time, that unlike the historians, with their advantage of hindsight, they were very much in the dark about many of the factors that controlled their situation, and that therefore they were blind men groping for their way—politicians, dreamers, in a word, simply men. The more difficult their situation became, the more they wanted to believe in a miracle, and they believed they had found that miracle in the New World. It was exactly because they did not want to be completely dependent on France that the Patriot leaders began to hope for an American connection. This lay beneath the remarkable upswell of the petition drive in March that called on the government to recognize America. They saw such action as a panacea for all evils, a charm to cure the country.

In general it must be said that there is some danger in judging the Dutch situation of the late eighteenth century by looking only or primarily at its foreign relations. The temptation is understandable. No less a scholar than Colenbrander yielded to it, and some modern historians are following in the same track. But the motives of the Dutch cannot so easily be reduced to impulsions and manipulations from abroad. The interplay of internal and external factors is apparent. Adams had a very good understanding of this interaction, and any evaluation of his role in Holland must take it into account.

It is not easy to discover why the movement for recognition began so suddenly and assumed such vast proportions. In the nature of things the Patriots played a large role, and Adams was delighted to feed the flames. They spurred the campaign because they recognized in it a splendid way to block reconciliation with England, true, but also because they believed in it. They saw not only economic benefits glittering before their eyes but also, in the petitions, the practical application of a principle, the winning by the people of their right to have a say and a share in government. Van der Capellen emphasized this idea in a letter to his friend Valck: "It is deemed best to present to the Magistrates by means of petitions *the wishes of the nation*." It would also be the way to avert "the embitterment of the Americans," who would otherwise exclude the Dutch from sharing in the benefits of trade with them. He even used Adams and his firmness of attitude as a threat. "This danger is not imaginary. I know the unflinching character of Mr. Adams. I know that His Excellency has long been unhappy over the partiality displayed by our nation and over the reception he has had here. I know that it has been a sore point with him to be shunned as if he had the plague, and I shudder for the consequences if we embitter a man of this influence, one of the principal founders of American freedom—the legislator of Massachusetts Bay (for he drew up its admirable constitution)."

Later the baron became less enthusiastic about the use of petitions in this way. He called it "a temporary expedient that does not work well in the long run. . . . It was a disguised Democracy, indeed of the worst kind, in which the People says what it feels *in person*." Now he wanted to move toward a more regular representation of the people, but he admitted that he himself had more than once favored recourse to petitions. Others, however, continued to see them as the first expression of democracy in the Netherlands, where the voice of the people was the voice of God. It was for them the start of the whole Patriot movement. There is an element of truth in this observation, for the campaign was a model of a people's political movement. When we call attention to the irrational element in all this agitation, we are really only saying that the roots of the rational system of democracy lie in the people's emotions. This is in itself certainly no condemnation.[8]

Beyond question, Adams himself had a hand in the whole movement. The first petition presented, that of the merchants of Leiden, was drawn up by his friend Luzac, and we have seen how they together made use of the pamphlet by Pownall to promote the myth of America as a permanent market. Adams was always ready to spread the idea. Van Hardenbroek, the Utrecht diarist, recorded hearing "that Adams, while at Leiden, had said to various manufacturers and merchants there that he could assure them that they could not produce and supply enough cloths, kerseys, etc., to meet America's needs." In Amsterdam it was another close friend of Adams, Hendrik Calkoen, who drew up the petition. From these two cities the movement spread over all of Holland and then swiftly to the other provinces.

In reading these documents, we are struck by an optimism born of necessity; they describe the dark clouds that had piled up over the country and the golden future that American trade would usher in. It was not at all true that Americans would create their own trade and industry. Listen to the words of the joint petition of the merchants of Leiden, Haarlem, and Amsterdam: "For, in truth, anyone who has the slightest knowledge of America and its huge size knows that the number of its inhabitants is not at all proportionate to the extent of its territory, and that both Banks of the Mississippi, the most fertile part of a region so fertile in every way, have still to be brought under cultivation; and because many hands will be required for this, there is no reason to anticipate that they will be able or willing to concern themselves with the establishment of new Factories." Equally, they do not have sufficient numbers of men "to serve the Fisheries of their own Country" and "therefore are compelled . . . to leave the transport of goods to us."

The consequences of recognition would be great for every part of the Netherlands: "Gelderland and Overijssel cannot distribute enough of their Linens, Striped Cloths and other Manufactures; indeed, even the Shoe factories in the district of Den Bosch will have a considerable market; virtually all the factories of Utrecht will become prosperous, and also at Leiden. Haarlem will see a revival of its ailing Twining mills, and its Cloth, Lace, Ribbon and Cordage factories. Delft will see the activity of its Potteries and Gouda of its Pipemakers increase to an amazing extent." This is a long quotation, but it does show clearly that the merchants' dreams were down-to-earth in their concerns, if unbounded in their anticipations.

Excitement was everywhere. "Never was more Ardor and Zeal discovered than in signing the Petitions," wrote Thaxter to Abigail Adams. And an Overijssel businessman reported on his observations while traveling: "In most of the Cities that I passed through, as in Utrecht, people were hard at work drawing up and presenting petitions. . . . In the meanwhile I spent some cash on hand in buying coarse linens . . . and ordered several hundred pieces more, in order to send them to North America as soon as the treaty will be concluded. A cousin of mine in Delft has had several thousand woolen blankets prepared for the same purpose."[9]

With such intense feelings, no one wanted to listen anymore to those who held opposite opinions. A cautious man like Van de Spiegel, then still secretary of the States of Zeeland, employed as warning the contrary arguments that had been made for a long time: Dutch trade would be endangered by American competition; the free-trade system of the Americans would give the Dutch no preference. Did the Dutch have to make friendship with England forever impossible? he asked. But the party that continued to favor Russian mediation and reconciliation with England was unable to resist the flood that broke loose and was overwhelmed by the patriotic sentiments of a majority of the nation. The last efforts on behalf of mediation, made in late March and early April, were wrecked in this tidal wave of utopian hopes, as we shall see in a moment.[10]

Hindsight would eventually show how vain all these dreams were. Rendorp wrote in his memoirs, not without a certain self-satisfaction: "But anyone possessing an impartial eye and a cool mind who observed the case could anticipate what happened, namely, that these splendid chimeras, of which the notorious Baron Van der Capellen tot den Poll was one of the principal peddlers, would vanish into thin air like broken bubbles." This was the voice of a conservative delighted to have been proved right. But Loosjes, the Patriotic historian, had to admit that it was true: "The Trade with the new and great Republic in *America*, which men had imagined would be the rich source of Prosperity for this country, by far failed to correspond to expectations." It was the American states which grew in "strength and prosperity," while the Netherlands "dried up." The "enterprising character of American Merchants" would "not easily accept bounds."[11]

· II ·

"The proposal comes from the Oostergo quarter, but I cannot think that the other quarters will be mad enough to follow the same idea," William V remarked to Van Hardenbroek in the summer of 1781. He was commenting upon the readiness of Oostergo, one of the constituent parts of the province of Friesland, to give a favorable reply to Adams's memorial, and he was right about the others to the extent that they did not come around to Oostergo's view until early the next year. Then, on 26 February 1782, the States of Friesland officially instructed its deputies in the States General to "take action to win approval for at once admitting the said Mr. Adams as minister of North America." This was called "recognition" by Friesland. Adams described it in such terms in a jubilant letter to Dana: "Friesland has already done it. This is the second sovereign state in Europe that has done it." The reality, of course, was that this was not diplomatic recognition at all, for no matter how divided sovereignty in the republic might have been, none of the provinces had the power to conduct an independent foreign policy.

Still, it was a great victory for Adams, and he crowed right and left about it in his letters. He wrote Livingston that Friesland was said to be "a sure index of the national sense." The Frieslanders were persistent;

they finished what they started. And he could also explain why they took the lead. They had never accepted the feudal system in their own country and had preserved all their privileges; they knew what true freedom was. He thanked the States at Leeuwarden, telling them that Friesland would have the honor to have ushered in a new policy of neutrality and friendship with the United States, for which future generations would be grateful to them.[12]

But he did not yet dare to believe that the other provinces would soon follow its lead. For the time being, he wrote in another letter to Livingston, the Americans must not expect too much. Gradually, one after the other, the Dutch provinces would recognize America, but a general treaty was far off. He therefore believed that it was necessary to exert new pressure, and he put a way to do it before La Vauguyon. Relying upon the support from Friesland, he proposed that he again call upon Their High Mightinesses for an answer to the memorial in even more categorical terms, demanding to know "whether they consider the United States as an independent State or not; whether they consider their inhabitants as friends or enemies." The duke did not find such fighting talk to his liking, and as usual he applied the brakes. The effect would be to slow up things and not to hasten them if Adams acted in this way, La Vauguyon wrote to him, and he was ready to explain why in detail. The French ambassador was not ready to burn his fingers again; without Vergennes's approval he would not give him any assistance, and Adams could not go ahead on his own, as he had done a year before, because of the reprimands from Congress.

Vergennes informed La Vauguyon that he did not believe that the Dutch would really recognize America, for what interest did they have in doing so, as France had had? It would be wise to act with greatest prudence, not to work against Adams and the Patriots but also not to encourage them. Then France would not have any responsibility for what would happen.[13]

Thus, the uncertainty continued. A few desperate Patriots contrived a plan by which the individual provinces would recognize America but the Republic as a whole would not publicly confirm their action. Adams rejected the plan with "utter detestation," suspecting that Van Bleiswijk lay behind it and that La Vauguyon would concur, but Dumas informed him that it was the work of men who themselves considered it to be only "their *pis aller*." Dumas himself was for deeds. On the advice of a friend, whom he did not name, he suggested to Adams that he establish contact through Van Berckel and Bicker with Amsterdam's burgomaster, Hooft, who was very favorable to America. Adams did so, but received the reply that it would be better to wait some more. Dumas wanted to press on. He suggested that Adams use the threat of an American navigation act that would open the ports of the United States only to Frisian ships. He clearly had in mind the French example of a few years before, when Amsterdam and Haarlem had been exempted from import dues in France because of their acceptance of unlimited convoy.[14]

At the moment the attitude of Amsterdam was in fact the great stumbling block. Dumas warned Adams about Rendorp's "ill will." Van der Capellen complained about the regents of Amsterdam in a letter to Valck. Would that they were all like "worthy Father Hooft," he wrote to him, but, "alas, the situation is bad." In the town council there was no majority for recognition, despite the fact that La Vauguyon had visited them. He "had taken much trouble to bring over the members. I know this from close at hand [Van der Capellen was staying with Hooft when he wrote this] and can therefore with reason contradict the rumor, probably deliberately spread by the English faction to make us hesitate, that the Court of Versailles is jealous of our connections with America and that it is secretly working to oppose them." La Vauguyon had said that this was completely untrue; France was strongly in favor of Dutch recognition of the United States.[15]

It is difficult to determine whether this was what La Vauguyon actually said. It would come out that he was still going beyond what Vergennes desired, and the discrepancy between their ideas continued to puzzle the leaders at The Hague. In mid-March the resistance to accepting Adams crumbled further. The stream of petitions suddenly swelled, and the opponents were greatly perplexed.

Adams meanwhile made his presence a challenge by buying a house in The Hague and setting it up as his embassy. He was continuing undaunted on the path of his "militia" diplomacy. He wrote to Livingston that it had seemed necessary to him to have the American envoy present in The Hague, "for which reason, having the offer of a large and elegant house in a fine situation on a noble spot of ground at The Hague at a very reasonable rate, I have . . . purchased it, and shall remove into it on or before the first of May." It was the first American embassy anywhere in the world: in France the cautious Franklin had not yet dared to take this step.

We shall have more to say about the house itself later on; here we need merely report that this bold step made an impression upon the Dutch public. A passionate conservative like Nicolaas ten Hove, the mintmaster general of the United Provinces, wrote to his friend Van Goens: "It is true, and particularly remarkable, that Eve's Husband has, take good note, just bought a house in The Hague, that whether or not this was true, he, Adams, would never be admitted to the Republic as an envoy." The fierce Orangist J. le Francq van Berckhey, a university lecturer at Leiden and an active pamphleteer, published a whole poem about Adams to tell him that he was not welcome:

On the American Adam

Tell us, Adam, what you're doing here in Holland's Paradise!
Do you want to make an Eve out of your own rib?
Do not be so foolhardy, oh Adam, be wise.
Think not that the Orange fruit is for worms like you.
But if your Eve wants some forbidden fruit to eat,
Let her eat a lily bulb, and you can eat it too!
Then you'll forget your Eden in America
And, an exile and in danger, roam this land of ours:
Go, you who dare anger God and your own King,
To your desert land of thistles and thorns.[16]

By his proud attitude, however, Adams actually won the respect of the political leaders in The Hague. We see in Van Hardenbroek's memoirs what was being said in their private conversations. A particularly important role in this development was played by Jan Elias Huydecoper van Maarseveen en Neerdijk, a member of Amsterdam's town council and a former alderman. In early March he wrote to Brantsen that opinions in Amsterdam were beginning to change, and he asked whether it was not now necessary to give Adams a reply on his memorial. A week later he wrote again that the American business seemed to him "more serious and important each day." If the special Russian mediator Markov could not promise a peace with England within a short time, it would become necessary to form closer ties with France and to talk with Adams. Brantsen agreed with him. He had already heard "that Mr. Adams would not be satisfied with a dilatory answer but would definitely insist upon a *yes* or *no*." The Prince of Orange remained opposed. It would be a sorry state of affairs if the Americans negotiated with England apart from the Dutch; "then we are totally lost, for afterwards the Americans themselves would be able to rob us of our possessions in the West Indies at some time."[17]

It is obvious that the Amsterdammers veered round out of fear. Even Rendorp could not stand up against the arguments of dangers to trade. A deputy to the States General from Overijssel, the burgomaster of Zwolle, Lucas Gijsbert Rouse, also received a letter from Van Maarseveen, informing him that the Amsterdam town council would present a proposal for recognition of Adams to the States of Holland. The pressure was mounting. Rouse had heard Van Lynden van Hemmen, the Gelderland deputy, say in *griffier* Fagel's own room "that now that the petitions concerning Adams are about to come in from every side, we shall have to give in." Fagel had been so upset "that it was worth money to see the Griffier's mug when he heard proposals of this kind, all the more because he had just said how happy they would be if he, Adams, just went away." Even the grand pensionary, whose attitude was always up in the air, now took a firm stand; he was nettled "because there had been such joy in England over his illness and hope that he would die."[18]

But there was also a strange rumor—Van Maarseveen had heard it from the Dutch merchant Van der Oudermeulen, who was still resident in London—that an Englishman had arrived in The Hague in order to have talks with Adams. There were good grounds for the rumor, for the English government, in one of Lord North's last acts of desperation, had sent a secret agent, an American by birth, to Holland to persuade Adams to support a separate peace. The agent, Thomas Digges by name, acted in great secrecy. He wrote to Adams from a hotel in Amsterdam with a request for an interview with "the gentleman who arrived this night, and lodges in room number ten." He enclosed a letter from David Hartley, an English member of Parliament who was a friend of Franklin's and a well-known advocate of reconciliation with the colonies, in which Hartley asked whether Adams was empowered "to *conclude* as well as to *treat*."

But Adams was on the alert; he was willing to receive Digges, but only in the presence of his secretary, Thaxter. He gave an appointment for the next morning at ten o'clock. It came out that Digges had been sent to sound him out about a possible armistice and an eventual separate peace, but Adams was fully prepared. He replied with his usual aplomb: "If the King of England were my father, and I the heir apparent to his throne, I would not advise him to think of a truce, because it would be but a real war under a simulated appearance of tranquillity, and would end in another open and bloody war." And he added that he would take no step without Franklin.[19]

Why should have Adams entered into such talks just then when the American cause looked so good, even in the Netherlands? Holland, mighty Holland, was on the point of granting recognition. The work, the intense work of years, first by Dumas and then by Adams, against the steady stream of Dutch doubts, caution, and fear, seemed finally about to yield results. Is it any wonder that both were deeply moved? The day after

Adams sent Digges away empty-handed, Dumas wrote to him. He was as lyrical as a medieval Franciscan: Now they could say "their sister Holland," as they said "their sister Friesland." And then he turned classical, singing, like Ovid, a song of triumph: "*Dicite, Io Paean!*"

Adams heard about the turnabout in Amsterdam from Burgomaster Hooft in person: The council had voted for recognition with "sufficient unity." (Did this mean that only Rendorp had voted against?) Hooft also told Brantsen—who in turn told our priceless informant Van Hardenbroek—that Adams "was so moved and touched by what he heard that he broke into tears." What a marvelous scene that was in the Amsterdam townhall! People thronged about, and everyone asked Titsingh, the bookkeeper of the East India Company, who accompanied Adams, "seeing that he had a stranger with him, whether this was Adams." The conclusion was evident, Van Hardenbroek noted in his memoirs: Although Adams was still not well known, this meant just "that the inclination of the nation for the Americans was more the result of their own movement and convictions than of a cabal or secret operations, as is so often suspected in The Hague."

This must have been the scene that Adams described with enthusiastic pleasure in a letter to his wife: "Your humble Servant has lately grown much into Fashion in this Country. Nobody scarcely of so much importance, as Mijnheer Adams. Every City, and Province rings with De Heer Adams." If everything worked out, they would be received within a few weeks in The Hague "in awfull Pomp." He prophesied truly. The dike had been broken through, and no one could hold off recognition now. The Prince himself, Adams wrote to Franklin, "has declared that he has no hopes of resisting the torrent, and therefore, that he shall not attempt it." Van Hardenbroek used almost identical words in his memoirs: "The Prince said to Rouse when they entered the Princess's circle: 'Now we're all becoming Americans'. To which Rouse replied: 'Yes, we should have expressed ourselves with prudence about that matter some time ago.'" His Highness grumbled to Van Hardenbroek that recognition was still not in line with Russian mediation, but since everyone wanted it, he would have to go along with it.

The argument with which the leaders of the government harassed and stymied the stadholder was that Russia had not brought about the promised peace with England and that postponing recognition had already been debated at length in Brantsen's plan, which William had quite forgotten. Why had Wentworth disappeared so suddenly last June? they asked him. Did His Highness know about his visit? England did not accept the Dutch conditions, they told him, yet she was herself on the point of recognizing America. In the event that "the case of a new sovereignty existed," it was in the highest interests of the Dutch, they argued, "to be on good terms with that power and to profit to the greatest extent possible from the advantages of trade with it." It was not easy to persuade the Prince, however, for he seemed as obstinate as his cousin George III. As Baron Van Nagell, a deputy to the States General from the nobility in the Zutphen quarter of Gelderland, said to Rouse: "It was as if these two cousins—the king of England and the Prince of Orange—were banging heads to see which of them could hold out the longest in his own country against the will and wish of the nation." [20]

A crucial step was taken on 28 March. The States of Holland adopted a resolution like that of Friesland calling for recognition of Adams. It had been preceded by a hot debate. The deputies of the Nobility, no doubt instigated by the Prince, had again argued in favor of Russian mediation, and they had been furiously denounced by Dordrecht's pensionary, De Gijselaar. Van Bleiswijk, the grand pensionary, came to their defense; an excited exchange of words followed, but in the end there was unanimity for recognition.

The grand pensionary was instructed to communicate the decision to Adams. But the fickle Van Bleiswijk balked. How strange it was, a number of members said, that he had defended the standpoint of the order of the Nobility so vigorously during the meeting of the States, and now was embarrassed to call upon the American envoy. He tried to settle the business through Dumas, who declined, "saying he had received no instructions from Mr. Adams to do so." So, finally, Van Bleiswijk himself had to write to Adams. Dumas reported the incident at length, and he displayed some self-satisfaction that it was now he who refused to take a letter from Van Bleiswijk and not the other way around. It is not clear why the grand pensionary suddenly balked; his whole attitude in the affair was fluctuating and impenetrable. [21]

Recognition by the States General seemed within reach, but there was still time for a hitch to occur. When the North ministry fell at last late in March, it was followed by Rockingham's government, in which foreign affairs were in the hands of Charles James Fox, the eccentric Whig statesman and great champion of the people. Fox at once informed the government in The Hague, through the Russian mediators Markov and Galitzin, that he wanted to make peace with the United Provinces. It was too late. The ties with France and the recognition of Adams had been decisive; the whole attitude in the Republic had changed, and no one had any confidence left in a rapprochement with England. The Prince and Fagel, however, still had hopes of turning the tide. Fagel quoted what the American envoy had said in his letter of thanks to Van Bleiswijk: "I flatter me that it [the recognition of the United States] will be of the happyest effect for the Republicq, for all the nations of Europe, yet for England itself." Fagel concluded that England was serious about peace, and even "this American seemed to know it." But there was no real interest in England's peace initiative anymore.[22]

Franklin heard about the affair in Paris and used a folksy example in the style of his Poor Richard's *Almanack* in his comments to the Dutch envoy, Mattheus Lestevenon van Berkenrode. The Dutch, he said, would make a laughing stock of themselves if they accepted the English offer. "A has a stick in his hand and attacks his neighbor B, who happens not to have one, takes advantage of the situation and gives him a bad beating. When B finds a stick and returns to take revenge, A says, 'My old friend, why should we fight? We are neighbors, let us be good neighbors and live together peacefully as we used to do.' If B is satisfied that easily and puts down his stick, then the other neighbors, as well as A, will laugh at him."[23]

The new English government also made an approach to Adams. On the basis of a misreading of Digges's report, they believed that something could be undertaken with the American envoy in Holland, and they brought up their big guns in support. They sent Henry Laurens, who had been let out of the Tower, to Holland to see if he could persuade Adams. Tempted by the promise of complete release, Laurens made the attempt without himself believing in it. He met Adams in Haarlem in the inn *De Gouden Leeuw* (The Golden Lion). "He told me," Adams reported to Franklin, "he was come partly for his health and the pleasure of seeing me, and partly to converse with me." He had acted at the request of the new ministry. Adams was wary and gruff: "I asked him if he was at liberty? he said, No; that he was still under parol, but at liberty to say what he pleased to me." Adams thereupon made it plain that he could not negotiate with him, and that he should tell the government in London bluntly that nothing would come of efforts for a reconciliation, an armistice, or a separate peace. For his part, Laurens told Adams that no one in London trusted Digges, and that he himself did not trust the new cabinet, which was as corrupt and unreliable as the one before. This was the last attempt to get Adams to change course.[24]

The movement in the Netherlands for recognition of America rose to new heights. During the first weeks of April one province after another declared in favor, Zeeland on the fourth, followed by Overijssel on the fifth, Groningen on the ninth, Utrecht on the tenth, and Gelderland on the seventeenth. There was extended debate in all these meetings of the provincial States over the advantages and disadvantages of recognition; the mediation of the empress of Russia was balanced against profits from American trade. Everywhere the conclusion was reached that recognition must be given. The change of government in England was not taken to be a chance for reconciliation with Britain but was seen as a threat, for if there were a quick peace between England and America, the Dutch would be too late. Fox's offer was "no sincere inclination," as the committee of the Utrecht States expressed it, and, on the other side, it was clear that "the Prince could take a warning from the king of England, who now at last had been compelled to bow."[25]

In all the excitement, everything was interpreted as everyone wanted to believe. There was no holding back recognition.

· CHAPTER 15 ·

Recognition and Imagination

*I Hope Mrs. Warren will give my Dutch Negotiation a
Place in her History, it is one of the most
extra-ordinary, in all the diplomatic Records.
But it has succeeded to a Marvel.*
JOHN ADAMS

HOSE who have the honor of making the acquaintance of Mr. Adams see that his visage bears the unmistakable signs of candor and honesty." These were the flattering words used early in 1782 by Cérisier's newspaper. Adams, it went on, was just as taciturn as William the Silent, but he became eloquent when his great principles were concerned. He lived modestly, as befitted a republican, and he had written the constitution of Massachusetts, without doubt the best in the history of mankind.

Adams became the fashion. People paid attention to him, respectfully or suspiciously as the case might be. The French ambassador wrote to Vergennes early in April, when things had moved far along, that he would keep an eye always on Adams and report the slightest irregularity in his conduct. For what would happen now that this audacious soloist had a chance to blow his own horn as loud as he pleased? This was the question that raised serious concern principally in France. There was a long way ahead on the road to peace.[1]

But in that spring month of April 1782, Adams could set all such worries aside and enjoy with a light heart the victory he had finally won in Holland. At last his exertions had paid off. The resolution of the States General, dated Friday, 19 April 1782, completed what the provinces had begun:

> After resumed debate upon the Memorial and second Memorial of Mr. Adams, dated May 4, 1781, and January 9 of this year, addressed to the President of the assembly of their High Mightinesses, desiring in the name of the United States of America to pre-

sent his Letters of Credential to their High Mightinesses, and in the second Memorial seeking a categorical reply in order to inform his principals thereof:

It is decided and understood that Mr. Adams will be admitted and recognized as Envoy of the United States of America, and he is so admitted and recognized by these presents.

[Signed]
W. Boreel.
[Confirmation]
In conformity with the above
Resolution
[Signed]
H. Fagel.

Willem Boreel, who was president of the States General for the week, went at once to inform Adams of this decision. The American came to the assembly of Their High Mightinesses on 20 April to present his letter of credential:

High and Mighty Lords
The United States of America in Congress assembled impressed with a high sense of the wisdom and magnanimity of your High Mightinesses and of your inviolable attachment to the rights and liberties of mankind, and being desirous of cultivating the friendship of a nation eminent for its wisdom, Justice and moderation have appointed the honorable John Adams late a delegate in Congress from the State of Massachusetts, and a member of the council of that State to be their Minister Plenipotentiary to reside near you, that he may give you more particular assurances of the great respect they entertain for your High Mightinesses.

The letter continued with a prayer for the protection of God and was signed by Samuel Huntington, president, and Charles Thompson, secretary.

The reply came the following Monday: Mr. Adams was acceptable to Their High Mightinesses. He in turn informed them the next day that he also had instructions to propose a treaty of friendship and trade.[2]

At last! "*Non tanta molis erat Romanam condere gentem!*"* wrote a relieved Dumas to Franklin. The time had come to celebrate. The days

* Not even the foundation of the Roman Empire had cost such exertions.

that followed were filled from morning to evening with visits, audiences, and dinners. The triumph was complete, and every day Adams gave a beaming report in letters to Livingston. He had proved what he could do with his "militia" diplomacy. In one letter he reported a visit to "His Most Serene Highness, the Prince of Orange." He asked the stadholder if he might speak in English, and the Prince replied, "If you please, sir." The American Puritan was not embarrassed to use a bit of flattery, telling William that the American people had a deep veneration for the House of Orange. But William was a bit embarrassed by the visit. He read the letter of credential and replied in such an indistinct murmur that Adams understood only his last sentence—that "he had made no difficulty against my reception." The rest of the audience was filled with the usual chitchat. How long had Adams been in Europe? William inquired. Had he bought a house in The Hague? Had he not lived for a while in Leiden? This small talk must have been quite a burden for the Prince.

The next day there was a dinner at the French ambassador's, to which the whole diplomatic corps was invited to meet their new colleague. Stiff as Adams could sometimes be, he enjoyed himself. He sought to persuade Livingston, but himself even more, that no harm had been done: "There is nothing, I suppose, in the whole voluminous ceremonial nor in all the idle farce of etiquette, which should hinder a minister from making a good dinner in good company, and, therefore, I believe they were all present, and I assure you I was myself as happy as I should have been, if I had been publicly acknowledged a minister by every one of them."

He paid a round of other visits, and noted in his diary the names of all those upon whom he called. If he actually visited them all, he must have been a very busy man for awhile. Most of the eminent personages in The Hague and all the representatives of the cities of Holland are on the list. In good diplomatic fashion the diplomats of other lands received only a visiting card. A high point, but one not without its difficulty, was a visit to the Princess of Orange. Adams had written down beforehand what he would say—at least this is the impression we have from his words—and he sent a copy of them to Livingston, probably to display for once that he too could talk like a diplomat, and in French: "Madame,—Je suis ravi d'avoir l'honneur de présenter une république vierge, un monde enfant, à la bienveillance et à la protection de votre altesse royale," * and more of the same. The words sound as though they were written by Dumas.[3]

---

* "Madam, I am delighted to have the honor to present a virgin republic, an infant world, to the benevolence and the protection of your royal highness."

All in all, these days gave him great satisfaction. There was also the extra coincidence that 19 April was a special day, the anniversary of the Battle of Lexington. The members of the government in The Hague had probably not realized it, but some of the newspaper writers did call attention to it, sometimes much later, however. Adams wrote down in his diary a news report in the *Rotterdamse Courant*, copying out the whole sentence in Dutch (which we translate here, leaving the Dutch for the footnote): "It is remarkable that the States General recognized the independence of the United States just on April 19th of this year, which was the seventh anniversary of the Battle of Lexington, and what makes this affair even more remarkable is that the first Memorial of Mr. Adams, which made such a great impression upon the Dutch nation, was signed April 19, 1781."* Luzac had discovered the coincidence at once. In the number of his newspaper for 26 April 1782, he called attention to the fact: "Thus it happens that, precisely seven years after the first hostilities at Lexington . . . our Sovereign Government has recognized the Republic of the *New World*, whose *birth* we predicted more than seven years ago." Luzac was truly proud, as is apparent from the report in his newspaper, which was usually so objective. He had in truth said back in 1775 that the struggle in America would mark an epoch *"in the General History of the Human Race."* And he paid tribute again to Van der Capellen, who had urged Governor Livingston in 1779 to send an envoy to Holland, which was how the ball got rolling.

The baron received the tribute with pleasure, and he repeated it in numerous letters to friends. It was he who had given to Congress the wise advice. It was a blessing that he had done so, he continued, "for if Mr. Adams had not been in the Republic, there would never have been a question of his first or second memorial and hence not of the petitions either, thanks to which alone recognition of independence resulted. I think I can say without boasting I was in all of this an instrument in the hands of Providence." And he told Luzac it would be a good idea to say all this in the *Gazette de Leyde.*[4]

---

* "Het is opmerkelijk dat de Staaten Generaal de Onafhanglijkheit der Vereenigde Staaten juist op den 19 April deses Jaars erkend hebben, zijnde die dag de zevende Verjaring van den Veldslag bij Lexington, en wat deze zaak nog opmerkelijker maakt is dat de Eerste Memorie van den heer Adams, die zulk een grooten Indruk op de Hollandsche Natie gemaakt heeft, gedagteekend is den 19 April 1781."

· II ·

The recognition of America and the reception of Adams as envoy, wrote La Vauguyon to his superior, "arouses the liveliest transports of joy, and the triumph of the Patriot party is that of the nation." There is other evidence of this general joy. Recognition was celebrated all around with the customary festivals, fireworks, and banquets. A flood of topical poetry, which has a rather pompous ring to our ears, was published in extensive collections. The titles were characteristic, for example, "Crown of Honor upon the Heads of the Illustrious Statesmen, City Fathers, Naval Heroes and Other Personages" and "Commemorative Column upon the Occasion of the Declaration of Independence of North America." In translating this doggerel, there is no point in even attempting to match the limping verse; but the ideas and the feelings expressed, even conveyed in an almost literal translation, are significant. Here is the Leiden theological student J. J. Harttenroth pouring out his soul:

> Who makes me pluck the bold strings
> Of my joyful cither,
> And pair my song with others?
> You, oh free American!

And many more verses followed in the same strain.
   A lady who knew English reworked the English anthem:

> God save the thirteen States!
> Long rule th'United States!
> God save our states!

And so on, with a host of exclamation marks.
   Another poet published a pamphlet of his own to spill out his heart:

> In Franklin, Adams and Laurens
> We see the *Colonists'* wish,
> Of whom they may gaily boast,
> And thankfully call their Saviors,

and on and on, interesting to note but not to read.
   Most of the poets wrote unabashedly about what most inspired them and the Dutch nation:

> Rejoice, Merchant, rejoice! Broad America
>   Now is declared independent,

And already yearns for your wares,
  Load your ships, and anchors weigh.

Rejoice, rejoice with right! you Pillars
  Of the Republic, rejoice! Manufacturers:
America calls for your wares,
  Work on, work on, refill your Purse.

In this song—for such it was; it could be sung to the tune of "Hier
heeft mij Rozemond bescheiden"—the treaty of Aachen was commemo-
rated again:

Rejoice! Amsterdammers, your Regents,
  Whose fine draft treaty made to our good,
Which others seek to make hateful to you,
  Rises Phoenix-like from its Ashes.

Hand in hand with the poetry went prose that had its gaze fixed on
Parnassus.

Schiedam, the city that owed its fame to the stills that made Dutch gin
and happy Dutchmen, sent Adams an invitation to be its guest at a grand
banquet for more than a hundred diners. If he had accepted and had acquired a taste for it, who knows what market America might have become for Schiedam's fluid joy! But the newly established diplomat declined the honor. There were other things on his mind, the loans which
now had to be concluded as quickly as possible and reports coming from
Paris about peace negotiations just in the offing, for which he certainly
had to be present. He therefore had Dumas offer his excuses to the Schiedam distillers, and he decided not to attend other festivals.[5]

Even without him the merriment went on, especially in Friesland, where
the celebrations were even more ebullient than elsewhere. The old saw
Frisia non cantat (Friesland does not sing) was proved false again. On the
occasion of a mere fireworks show produced by students at Franeker, a
number of poetical works appeared. One of them was a song:

Mr. Adams was asked here too
To gaze upon Freedom's fire,
Ha ha, ha ha, ha ha,
Friesland loves Adams so, ha ha,
It gives him greatest pleasure, oh, ha ha,
But he is much too busy
To come up to Friesland,
Ha ha, ha ha, ha ha.

Other poems were more solemn. One ended in this sprawling stanza:

Then rejoice, rejoice to Britons' spite,
Batavians, Rejoice with me,
Let your Joy be heard resounding,
Rejoice! America is free.[6]

The stream of verse flowed easily, fed solely by excited imaginations. What strikes us in all these effusions is that America had become a word for something the people did not really know. It was their fine, vague dream. We have already seen how little people usually knew about the New World, and how Adams did his best to provide good, even if partisan, information. But in the outburst of joy in the spring of 1782 we meet again the preeminently romantic picture of America that had always prevailed. We see repeatedly the favorite theme of the unspoiled Western Hemisphere, in contrast to the wealth of the Old World, but in conflict too with more commercial fantasies. The picture of the Americans as simple farmers living with nature and in nature was already familiar, probably from reading Voltaire; for it was the noble Quakers, whom he had praised, who were respectfully named, and Penn's treaty with the Indians was of course described as a model for mankind. The simple Americans had to live together with the noble savages, and they "made every effort to elevate them through Friendship and Philanthropy, and to bring them in close contact with the more civilized Societies of the white people."

The honest Americans were very popular in Dutch Patriot writings. According to one Patriot author they knew true equality, these "peaceable and virtuous Inhabitants . . . under the shadow of the Laws . . . and all the happiness that this world, with its imperfections, can provide." Another author held that they were "a more Sober, Upright, Loyal, Peaceable and Humble People" than the English. The inhabitants of the New World were proud, robust people, enlightened and patriotic. Between their periods of toil upon the land, they discussed the rights of man and the citizen, and after they had plowed their furrows straight, they put on helmet and cuirass in order to do battle for their country—true Romans who must inevitably triumph over a nation so enslaved to debts, wealth, and vice as the English. It was now evident, wrote *Le Politique Hollandais*, what nonsense the idea was that the human race would degenerate in America. On the contrary, one could well believe that "the human race, far from sinking into decline, is being improved in that land."[7]

There were still a goodly number who dreamed of going off to that wonderful world: "Oh my Dear Friend! If I go to America and help defend its rights under the banner of Freedom, would this not confirm both my happiness and my fame?" were the words of the young poet Jacobus Bellamy to a friend. Luzac was almost persuaded to become a citizen of that free republic and to enjoy the friendship of the wise men who governed it. The Frisian Patriot Coert Lambertus van Beyma claimed that he had prepared his wife for the journey, "and she is fully determined to follow me to America, leaving our possessions behind." But none of them actually made the trip, with the sole exception of impetuous Van der Kemp, as we have seen, and he really only because he was virtually banished from the Netherlands.[8]

America was to remain a dream which embodied the Patriots' enthusiastic hopes. There, it appeared, some portion of the untainted past still lived on that just then was being glorified in the Batavian myth. A primal Golden Age was being made reality to the west across the Ocean. The dream also incorporated an eager comparison with the other forefathers, the rebels of the sixteenth-century Netherlands. This comparison was of course bitterly rejected by the Patriots' opponents, especially by the Prince of Orange, who indignantly described the American Declaration of Independence as "the parody of the proclamation issued by our forefathers against King Philip II." "If our forefathers," wrote De Pinto, "had taken up Arms only over a tax of three pennies on a single Pound of Tea, or over a Tax upon Stamped Paper, we would never have been able to uphold the justice of their uprising. . . . And for such a case they too would not have been able to pray and hope for Heaven's blessing, except if they wished to make mock of God and Mankind."[9]

But that made the adherents of America only the happier with the comparison. The same spirit animated both rebellions, and whether oppression was greater or less in the Netherlands or in America only the oppressed themselves could determine. There were numerous correspondences, Cérisier exulted, even in the persons: he compared George III with Philip II of Spain, Thomas Hutchinson, the English governor of Massachusetts, with Philip's chief minister in the Low Countries, Cardinal Granvelle, and General Thomas Gage, the English commander in America, with the duke of Alva, Philip's army commander in the Netherlands. But Cérisier considered Washington to be far nobler than William the Silent, who had only wanted to replace the king's power with his own. The entire uprising in America he saw as purer than the Dutch revolt because it was untarnished by religious fanaticism.

Bellamy reached for his cither again:
Just look back over the two hundred years
To the time when you threw off the Spanish yoke.
Now America wants to match your lofty spirit,
America, too long oppressed by British might.

And so on and on.[10]

· III ·

When the time came to face the reality of all these vague notions of these sweet utopias which made men deaf and, as Rendorp said, heated up their brains, when the time came, that is, to take the dream literally, the dreamers had to take refuge in allegory. They turned to pictorial representation. The happy event of the recognition of American independence would be immortalized in prints and medals, and America shown to the world in all its glory. Falling back on a two-hundred-year-old tradition of artistic symbolization of the meaning of America, they showed America as a beautiful nude woman, wearing at most a few feathers on her head and loins; surrounding her were strange beasts and, not to be forgotten, the rich fruits of the land. Nowhere is this to be seen more impressively than in the grandiose ceiling that Tiepolo painted in the palace of the bishop of Würzburg.

It is probably an error to evoke such a magnificent painting here; everything done in the Netherlands on the same theme is thin and weak by comparison. What was done in Holland in the depiction of America is but a very small part of the vast work of portraying America's image that occurred in those years. It was so small, indeed, that it was not even included in the magnificent exhibition *The European Vision of America*, which was held in 1976. We must therefore give it some attention ourselves.

The Dutch political prints of the period from 1780 to 1783 usually present the figure of America as a more or less dark-skinned Indian with an apron and a feather headdress, exactly as Gillray was doing in England in his earliest prints, although with somewhat greater skill. In another print a couple of boys who are stealing the breeches of the king of England are marked as Americans by a single feather in their caps; in another the American can be distinguished only by his feather. But the naked Indian boy was more popular; we see him in various prints, on a sketch for a wallpaper by Jurriaen Andriessen, and, even more characteristically, on an engraved glass, where a young Dutch merchant takes his wares from him and keeps him happy with a string of beads. In a print in praise of the Peace of Aachen, America is shown as a stately woman, again with a feather in her hair; more charming is the young lady in the print *The British Leopard Brought to Reason*, who is dressed in the colors of the new nation, and literally sits upon the bales of goods that constitute her wealth. The accompanying caption describes her as "America, in the image of a young woman with a moderately wild visage, who sits upon weapons and bales of merchandise, and holds a sheaf of thirteen arrows." Her "wild visage" is not very well drawn, but the little figure as a whole is quite delightful. We see similar little dolls in the "perpetual calendar" constructed a short time later by a sea captain from Ameland who was obviously an enthusiast for the American cause.

The whole idyll of the New World is beautifully portrayed in a print probably made in 1781, after Cornwallis's capitulation at Yorktown. It was intended as a sequel to a print of 1778, which had been made in England and had become extremely popular, as is evident from its reproduction in several European countries. In the first print England is represented as a cow which is milked by a Dutchman, while an American is busy sawing off its horns. The English lion is asleep, an English lord desperately wrings his hands, France and Spain take the milk from the Dutch farmer, and in the background the brothers Howe are asleep in Philadelphia. In the second print the cow is completely emaciated, the English treasury is empty, lord and lion are looking up in despair to a cloudy heaven, and in the background an English embassy approaches a canopy under which America—our Indian lady—is sitting. The text reports: "On the other side the Commissioners approach the Congress, which is represented in the shape of a sitting American surrounded by twelve other persons. The Congress shows the Commissioners the Liberty Cap and has before her feet a broken yoke and broken chains. At Congress's side stand Justice, Wisdom, Strength and Prudence, and a ray of Heavenly Light shines upon them, while another American is busy putting Goods into barrels for shipment to various Places." One could scarcely present the utopia of America in more delightful fashion.[11]

It was difficult to depict the lofty ideals of liberty and independence in popular prints without resorting to allegorical abstractions that needed lengthy explanations. We can see how difficult it was by examining the materials preserved in the Leeuwarden archives dealing with the preparation of a medal to mark the recognition of America. The Leeuwarden Society for Freedom and Industry decided, with permission of the States of Friesland, to eternalize the happy event in a medal "chiefly and principally concerned with the reception of Mr. Adams as minister of the united States of N. America and the rejection of a separate peace with England." The society drew up a description of what they wanted on the medal. There had to be a free Frisian "dressed in the old Characteristic garb of the Frisians," with his right hand extended toward "the figure of a woman, the new Republic of the 13 united States of N. America," who was crushing the scepter of England under foot. "But since she is not yet in the tranquil and assured possession of the freedom she has won, she turns her eye upon a descending Angel who offers her the Hat of Freedom as a special gift of Heaven, while in his descent he pours rain with an open hand upon the Head of the Frisian." The members of the Society ingeniously raised advantage and principle to a higher level. England was to stand on the right, offering a peace plan which was rejected because the free Frisian glimpsed in time the snake hidden in the grass. On the other side of the medal there would stand the arms of Friesland, held up by a divine hand.

The problem remained of how to depict America. The artist who was invited, Jacobus Buys, was well known as an illustrator. He prepared a number of sketches that were discussed at length: "There is an objection to the *feathers* on America's Head; some consider that this is the usual way to depict South America, others feel on the other hand that it is adequate for North America: the Society therefore accepted the idea that it would be best to show no *feathers* at all." The artist agreed, for these were small changes that could be done by the engraver. When we look at the drawings, we see that he used every possibility afforded him by these narrow specifications. He sketched some of the figures of men and women in more or less symbolic style, others realistically. Frisians were variously shown as an inhabitant of Hindelopen, a Frieslander of the seventeenth century, a Roman Frisian—anything wanted. Buys also drew Englishmen and Americans in various poses: the former sometimes with a dog (or tiger, or leopard, which received different interpretations), the latter in noble classic mold, with a shield where the name could be placed, and a liberty hat and feathers, male or female as desired.

The medal was ready within the year. In December a special committee under the chairmanship of Wopke Wopkens was able to draw up a list of the persons to whom it would be sent as a gift: the members of the States, Adams and Congress one each (a member proposed sending twelve to Adams, but that was thought to be too extravagant and was rejected); the

French ambassador, two; and one copy each to such eminent Patriots as Burgomaster Hooft of Amsterdam, Van der Capellen tot den Pol, and Dumas, for once not forgotten. They all sent their thanks, each according to his own style and temperament—Adams in a friendly tone, Hooft with ceremonial pomposity, Van der Capellen passionately and anxiously: "My pleasure would be considerably greater if I had more reason to rejoice in the domestic and foreign position of our Fatherland. . . . I would rather see the whole Republic go under with honor than remain half alive with dishonor."

Such pessimism was exceptional among the Patriots, however; the future then seemed so beautiful and full of promise. It was the spirit of the poem "On the Silver Medal of Honor," by Theodorus van Kooten, rector of the Latin school at Middelburg, in Zeeland, who returned not long afterward to his birthplace, Franeker, as a professor. In it we read these lines:

Your friendship delights the People of the Thirteen free lands,
Who already offer you Peace to the advantage of you and them.
Open your land wide to them, and your trade will flourish,
There you see a Treasure from abroad unloaded at your wharves,
And abundance flow again into your treasure houses;
And your fleet sets sail, as of yore, for the open sea.[12]

Men's imaginations now knew no limits; they looked to the future with eyes shining with commercial heroism. A fine example of such true eighteenth-century classical fancies was provided by the banquet that was given during the following year, on 26 April 1783, in honor of Van der Capellen and the whole triumphant cause of the Patriots, at the hall of the Nieuwe Doelen in the Garnalenmarkt in Amsterdam. "The banquet consisted of 70 places," wrote the *Nieuwe Nederlandsche Jaarboeken*. The climax came with the dessert, which consisted of five splendid tableaux: the temple of freedom, Oldenbarnevelt, the free sea, vanquished tyranny (specifically the abolition of corvée services), and "the Tie with North America." "The North American Maid, clad in a Lion's skin, and in her left hand Hercules' Club, presses down a crowned man in a princely attitude, lying before her with a broken sword but still threatening, while she extends her right hand to the Dutch Maid across an altar standing between them, on which Independence rests. . . . Behind this Piece there stands a Palm tree, to which the national flags of both Republics are tied with these words: *Indissolubilia vincula jungo*, that is: I unite them with unbreakable bonds."[13]

· I V ·

These festivities succeeded, in the words of an opponent unburdened with factual knowledge about where Adams lived in America and what he did but with a sense for what was happening in the Netherlands, "in metamorphosing John Adams from a Notary in Philadelphia to the Minister Plenipotentiary of the 13 Free States of America."[14]

Now is the proper time, therefore, to close our description of all this work of imagination with Adams's own conclusions. Months after his success he was still peppering his letters with outbursts of triumph. He informed Dana that recognition by the Dutch Republic had occurred "with a solemnity and unanimity, which had made it, in a peculiar sense, the national act." The origin lay, of course—he could not believe otherwise—in his memorial, which had set the newspapers to writing and the people to thinking. He described to Livingston the scope of the victory: a country that had been tightly bound to England was now "torn from her bosom." To Abigail he declared that the American cause had triumphed in Holland without money or friends, despite the flood of intrigues, "by the still small Voice of Reason, and Perswasion, Tryumphantly against the uninterrupted Opposition of Family Connections, Court Influence, and Aristocratical despotism." Men must know that what had happened was of high historical significance; therefore, he kept all his letters, copies of all conversations. History would teach how important his role had been, and it would be evident how truly the Spanish ambassador had spoken when he said to him: "Sir, you have struck the greatest Blow in all Europe." That compliment recurs in various letters of Adams and also of Dumas; he must have told it boastfully everywhere. This deep satisfaction remained with Adams for his whole life. From the day he was born until that day, he wrote in 1814 to Van der Kemp, his sojourn in Holland had been the most important period of his life. The exultation was nowhere higher than in a letter that he wrote in September 1782 to Dumas. He quoted again what the Spanish ambassador had said, as well as numberless eulogies, and he viewed his triumph, *sub specie aeternitatis Johannis Adamsensis,* in the light of his own glorious immortality: "The standard of the United States waves and flies at The Hague in triumph, over Sir Joseph Yorke's insolence and British pride. When I go to heaven, I shall look down over the battlements with pleasure upon the stars and stripes wantoning in the wind at The Hague."[15]

CHAPTER 16

The Complete Diplomat in The Hague

The Hague draws cries of admiration from all visitors.
GEORG CHRISTOPH LICHTENBERG

OTHING is left of the house, not a stone or a picture of any kind. The archives have been ransacked without result. We know no more about the first American embassy established anywhere in the world than what we find in the contemporary descriptions. We shall probably never know what the Hôtel des Etats-Unis, as it was called, actually looked like. We might be tempted to say with the Psalmist that the place thereof shall know it no more, but it would not be true: the thorough searches of the best Adams scholar, the editor of the great modern edition of his works, Dr. Lyman H. Butterfield, have at least thrown some light on the problem. He came to the Netherlands in 1959 to collect materials, and in his very first letter he wrote: "By six o'clock I had made some progress. Among other things I found the site of J. A.'s house." But that was all, a house number on the street called the Fluwelen Burgwal in The Hague. The only picture we have dates from 1844; it is a lithograph showing a canal, since filled in, and a low wall where Adams's house had stood until it had been demolished twenty years earlier. The editor, at his wit's end, nonetheless used it as an illustration in reprinting John Adams's diary.[1]

We must be content with the written sources, and they at least are ample. On 23 February 1782, Dumas wrote to Adams that he had completed his task: Since the previous evening the house had belonged to him; it was transferred into his hands in the presence of the notary for the sum of 14,052 guilders ten cents free and clear, and he could enter into possession on 1 May. Dumas would handle the remaining practical details; he had bargained for the best possible price, he wrote Adams, and hoped for a quick reply "that you are satisfied with me." From this letter it is evident that Adams had already seen the house and that he was in fact satisfied with Dumas. To open an embassy in The Hague before he was recognized fitted in neatly with Adams's aggressive diplomacy. His opponents were greatly exasperated, as we have seen. He would never be received, whether or not he had a house, it was said in The Hague. Was it really true, one of these Anglomaniacs asked Dumas, that Adams was coming here to The Hague to live? "Oh! Yes," the loyal Dumas replied jauntily, "and the instigator and the perpetrator of the crime stands here before you."[2]

Three days later, Adams wrote to Livingston that it seemed to him of the greatest importance for America to have an envoy in residence at The Hague, "for which reason, having the offer of a large and elegant house in a fine situation on a noble spot of ground at The Hague at a very reasonable rate I have . . . purchased it, and shall remove into it on or before the first of May." Dumas added a bit extra in his own dispatch to Livingston on the significance of what had been done. The purchase of a house had had immediate results "politically," for only France and Spain had their own embassies at The Hague; other envoys had to take up residence in expensive hotels. And he concluded with pride: "Our best address in the future will be *at the Hotel d'Amérique, in The Hague, Holland.*"

Recognition came, as Adams had scarcely dared hope, even before he moved from Amsterdam. He could begin work with complete diplomatic status. Thaxter was in charge of the packing of all the glassware, the china, and the large cabinet and the shipping of all the furniture by canalboat to The Hague. Adams himself went on 12 May, a proud, happy man for personal reasons as well: "I hope the air will relieve my health in some degree from that weak state to which the tainted atmosphere of Amsterdam has reduced it." In letters to Abigail after his arrival he told her that the air at The Hague really made him feel better. He rejoiced with his usual enthusiasm: "You can scarcely imagine a more beautifull place than The Hague."[3]

Although we can no longer have any idea of how Adams's house looked, with some imagination we can see the interior with our mind's eye, for we have the complete list of the inventory preserved in the neat handwriting of Dumas's wife, who took her place as the mistress or, more modestly, concierge of the new household. Fourteen folio sheets list all the crystal, porcelain, and copper; all the goblets, carafes, and cuspidors; all the mattresses, sheets, and carpet. The furniture is noted by room: in the antechamber, sixteen chairs and two armchairs, all in green damask, a new Turkish rug, two curtains of grey silk and two lace curtains hanging on copper rods; in the drawing-room, a sofa of red damask with cushions, six chairs of the same cloth with down cushions and six chairs without cushions, four damask curtains with cords and tassels, a large mirror with a golden frame, and so forth—a houseful of furniture. Unfortunately, we do not know what hung on the walls, except in Adams's own room, where there were portraits of himself and his two sons, all "in a golden frame," while in his son's room Washington was displayed in the same manner.

What the whole catalogue of furnishings makes quite clear is that Adams, however much a plain Puritan by origin, was convinced of the necessity to make an impression as the representative of the new nation. Everything had been done in a grand style. America had to take her place among the nations not timidly and diffidently but in her full glory, as a full equal. That is the true reason for these "30 Bocale Goblets," and "22 English Wine Glasses flat," "19 Rhenish glasses," a dinner service of blue porcelain and one of Dresden china—the whole show. He would be second to no one, not even to the duke de La Vauguyon.[4]

It all cost money, but the financial horizon began to brighten. The time had come to conclude the long-awaited loans. Even then, however, things did not go smoothly; the Dutch merchants were cautious and harsh in their terms. Moreover, as Adams himself realized full well, as a result of the disastrous war there was not too much money around. He complained to Livingston that the greed of America's friends was as great an obstacle as the opposition of her enemies: "I can represent my situation in this affair of a loan, by no other figure than that of a man in the midst of the ocean negotiating for his life among a school of sharks." Still, an agreement was reached in May. Three Amsterdam banking houses, Willink, Van Staphorst, and De la Lande and Fijnje, came to terms with Adams on a loan of five million guilders with interest at 5 percent, plus another 5 percent costs. It was not an impressive beginning, but still it was a beginning. One of those who subscribed eagerly was Van der Capellen, who put in sixteen thousand guilders. But in general there was no great enthusiasm, and Adams was very nearly right in his cautious prediction that it would be excellent if one and a half millions came in of the five million.

He was a bit on the somber side, however, for by the end of September he could report that he had "at least one million and a half in cash." In any case that was enough to provide him with days full of toil, for he had to sign all the bonds personally. "Spent most of the day in signing Obligations for the United States. It is hard work to sign ones Name 1600 times after dinner." The same remark occurs over and over again in his diary!

But he had to complete the task and wrote with satisfaction to Arthur Lee: "The mijnheers have overcome most of their terrors, and are now well fixed in the good system."[5]

Thus began, in a cautious, businesslike way, the lending of money that would help the new nation onto its feet and provide the basis for a great future. Now and again the Americans would remember it. In 1841 at a reception given by President Tyler in the White House, the Dutch chargé d'affaires, E. M. A. Martini, reported, Tyler had a fitting compliment for each guest, "for me, that the people of the United States would never forget that their first loan had been given by my country."[6] A little over a hundred years after that America reciprocated with the Marshall Plan.

· II ·

Among many other things the house newly acquired in The Hague meant a new future for the faithful servant Dumas. Because he plays a principal role in our tale, we must again turn our attention to him. As one reads his letters, it is easy to become somewhat irritated by the regularity with which, over the long run, self-pity and pleas for recognition appear in the letters that he sent to his principals in Paris and Philadelphia. But we should also take account of his situation. In the first place, he had given of himself with great devotion to the cause of the rebellion, which for him was the cause of mankind. In the second place, his position had remained legally uncertain so long as he had received no regular appointment from the American side. As we have seen, he had hoped to assure himself of such confirmation by taking an oath of allegiance to the fatherland of his choice, but that had not made him an American: laws and juridical definitions stood between his dream and its fulfillment.

He complained about his hardship to every American he knew, but never more movingly than in a letter of February 1781 to Livingston. Why, he asked, was he always fobbed off with the necessity to "consider" his case? When Congress had asked him to enter its service—and he had not asked first—"I did not take time to consider, but with an exalted soul, threw myself into the flames of the burning house of the virtuous people, dearly beloved by me, which I saw struggle for liberty." He trusted them; he devoted himself to them; he brought down upon his neck the hatred of a powerful faction in the country. And what was his reward? He was almost forgotten, thrown aside; others would reap what he had sowed, and his own family looked at him reproachfully, believing that he was ruining them. Could he wait quietly, trusting in Livingston's cool assurance that "they will take time to consider"? "Consider!" he replied. "What? My very numerous official Letters and correspondence with Congress, and with all the servants of the U.St. in Europe?—or my mortifying and wretched situation here? . . . But I fear my case may be that of poor Joseph, Exod. I.8." ("Now there arose a new king over Egypt, which knew not Joseph.") What losses he had suffered, and how he was forgotten!

The fear of being forgotten must have sat relentlessly upon Dumas. He found every kind of image for his plight: Joseph in prison, a chicken that disappeared in the pan, or a man eaten by cannibals. Who was still thinking of him? Had he not been given a promise of a salary of five hundred pounds sterling? Had it gone awry because Laurens had been captured? His was a frightening fate: "I am abused, shunned publickly as an infected and dangerous person." And so on. He was doomed; he was forgotten. "In a word, I am looked on by much the greatest number as a romantic fool that has discredited himself and his family."

Dumas personified, in spite of himself, romantic fears and yearnings. He dreamed of a security that was not granted him; he dreamed because he was afraid, and he found no rest. In America he was respected and used, but not given what he asked for. He remained a stranger at the gate. They knew his problem, and they gave him sops. Livingston, immediately after becoming secretary of foreign affairs, wrote him with sympathy, but without understanding, that Congress was sensible for his "attention to their interest." He was treated as if he were engaged in some kind of incidental charity, when in fact he had become their servant at their request. In any case, in the sorry state of their finances, they had no money with which to increase his allowance.

Dumas was near to despair. The war made everything more expensive, but his income remained small and, worse, irregular. Early in 1782 he decided to break up his household. He wrote to Franklin in grief that his wife and he had had to leave the house where they had lived for twenty years; his wife and daughter had gone to live in the countryside in Gelderland, where they had a little land, and beginning in May he was renting a few rooms in The Hague. It was a bitter separation, but a necessary one. Sometimes, he confessed, he almost lost courage. Where could he go?[7]

Precisely at that moment of uttermost despair came salvation. Fourteen days later he bought the house upon the Fluwelen Burgwal in the name of John Adams, and that meant a happy solution for his problems. At Adams's suggestion he and his wife came to live in the stately house as its stewards: they found refuge under the wings of the United States. When diplomatic recognition of Adams immediately followed, it seemed to Dumas that the time had come when his case could be settled for once and all. On 4 April he wrote to Livingston that it was necessary to accredit him to Their High Mightinesses as secretary of the legation and chargé d'affaires of the United States. This was the practice of other countries. "Without it, I would face many difficulties in my actions." Diplomatic status was therefore a first requisite.

Adams supported his request. Dumas had already pointed to his services and his selfless loyalty; now Adams threw himself behind those demands. It was in the interest of the United States, he told Dumas in black and white, to name him secretary of the legation and chargé d'affaires with a salary of five hundred pounds sterling if there was a minister in residence, and one thousand pounds if he had to manage all the business by himself. He could write that to Congress in his name, Adams told him, and he would also write to Congress himself, as he had already done. Fourteen days later he asked Livingston to give Dumas diplomatic status: "He is a man of letters and a good character; but he is not rich, and his allowance is too small at present for him to live with decency."

In his subsequent letters to the American authorities, Dumas continued to harp on this theme. He sent Livingston a copy of Adams's letter, pointing to his uninterrupted service since 1775 and to the sacrifices that he had made for the American cause. He had given seven years of "faithful and painful labor . . . in the service of humanity, of the United States." When, he continued, at the moment of death he could add to this testimony of his conscience the knowledge that he had gained the respect and friendship of the American leaders—and in particular that of Livingston— then he would end his life with the words of Horace on his lips, "*Non ultima laus est principibus placuisse viris* [my highest praise is not to have been pleasing to princes]."

During the summer he pleaded his cause again with Robert Morris, the director of the American public finances. He was afraid, he wrote, that he would be considered a "*Nouvelliste*" (news-writer), while he was really a "*Négociateur*" (negotiator). Alas, his enemies knew this better than his friends.[8]

But there was no readiness in Philadelphia to honor Adams's suggestions and Dumas's appeals. The essential point was that, despite all his hopes, Dumas was not an American. For what concerned Dumas's business, Livingston wrote him in September, Congress was very sensible for his zeal and devotion, but he did not yet know what its decision would be. For his own part, he said, he hoped heartily for Dumas's promotion. The foreign secretary concealed the heart of the matter from him, but told Adams a few days later: "The request of Mr. Dumas is now in Congress. They will probably name him secretary of the legation, which I heartily wish, for he is certainly a diligent and loyal servant. But there is no chance that they will go any further, for they would certainly not name anyone other than an American to so important a post as that of chargé d'affaires. And the present economic system does not permit so great an increase in his salary as you mention." That was where it rested for the moment; Dumas was esteemed, kept on the string, and underpaid, but he would never become an American, although he would turn his soul inside out. His position therefore remained ambiguous, and if the tide turned, that could have painful consequences for him.[9]

· III ·

If we compare the portraits of Adams done in 1782 and 1783, before and after his recognition as American minister, we can see what the triumph meant for him and how it changed him. The portraits of 1782—there are two of them, virtually identical, intended as illustrations and engraved by Reinier Vinkeles—show a friendly man, almost Dutch and with a touch of the countryman, quite modestly presented within the frame (see Figure 10). But what a difference between this little print, less than eight inches high, in black and white, and the life-size, full-length portrait painted a year later by no one less than the American John Singleton Copley. The plain rebel has been suddenly raised to the high society of the Old Regime; the American countryman has become a European courtier.[10]

With all his Puritanism and his "militia" diplomacy, Adams was superbly equipped to play his new role when the time came. La Vauguyon reported the change with a touch of astonishment: "With regard to me, Mr. Adams has conformed with the established usage and has asked me for a time when I can receive him." From one thing others followed: receptions, dinners, the whole diplomatic life unrolled for the brand-new envoy. Inevitably, this vain, eager man enjoyed it, in spite of himself. He had a happy romp with his own sins. Typical is what he writes about his big painting: It had to be placed in a golden frame that could be taken apart, so that it could be shipped to The Hague (it was painted in London) or Boston. "Thus this Piece of Vanity will be finished. May it be the last."

Fig. 9. *Political cartoon on Van der Kemp, showing him half as a minister, half as a soldier.* Around him are symbols of his revolutionary goals. On the pulpit are quotations from the Bible and from Hobbes's *Leviathan* (part 4, "Of the kingdom of darkness," chapter 44: "Of spiritual darkness from misinterpretation of scripture").
(Collection of the author.)

Fig. 10. *John Adams, envoy of the North American States in the United Netherlands.* Engraving by Reinier Vinkeles, 1782. (Collection of the author.)

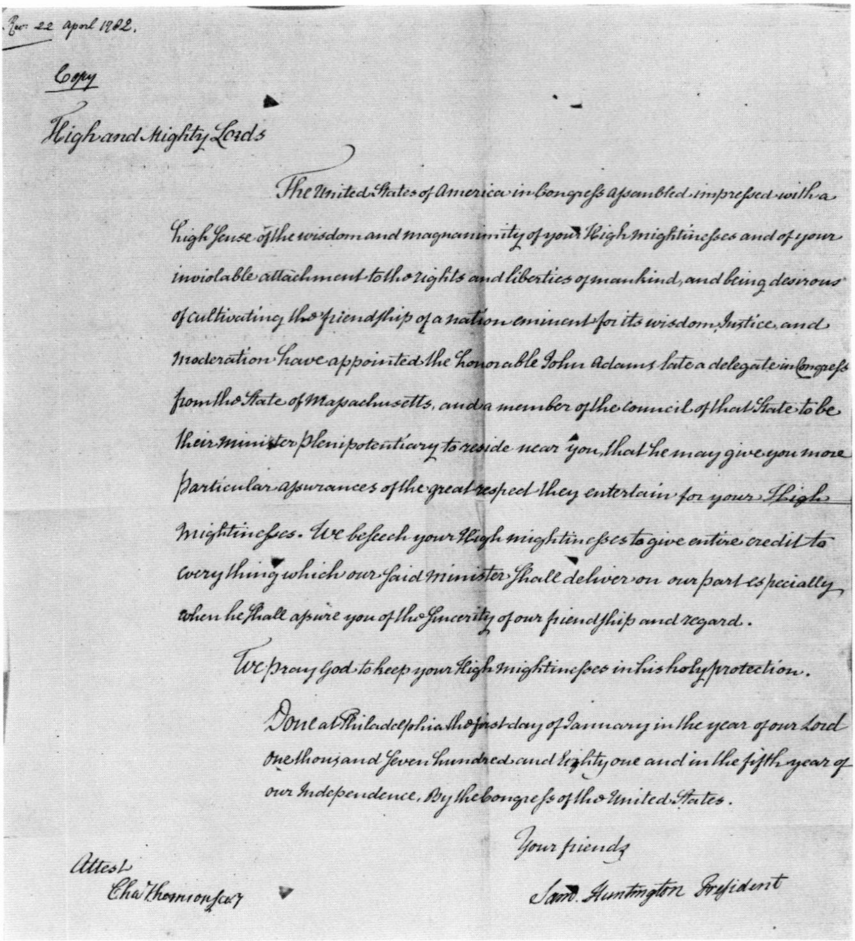

Recd 22 April 1782.

Copy

High and Mighty Lords

The United States of America in Congress assembled impressed with a high sense of the wisdom and magnanimity of your High Mightinesses and of your inviolable attachment to the rights and liberties of mankind, and being desirous of cultivating the friendship of a nation eminent for its wisdom, Justice, and moderation have appointed the honorable John Adams late a delegate in Congress from the State of Massachusetts, and a member of the council of that State to be their minister plenipotentiary to reside near you, that he may give you more particular assurances of the great respect they entertain for your High Mightinesses. We beseech your High Mightinesses to give entire credit to every thing which our said minister shall deliver on our part especially when he shall assure you of the sincerity of our friendship and regard.

We pray God to keep your High Mightinesses in his holy protection.

Done at Philadelphia the first day of January in the year of our Lord one thousand seven hundred and eighty one and in the fifth year of our Independence. By the Congress of the United States.

Your friends

Attest
Cha Thomson Secy

Saml. Huntington President

Fig. 11. *Credentials presented by John Adams to the States General.*
(Algemeen Rijksarchief, The Hague.)

GEDENKZUIL,

TER GELEGENHEID DER

VRY-VERKLAARING

VAN

NOORD-AMERICA,

DOOR

A. LOOSJES P.Z.

TE AMSTERDAM,
Bij W. HOLTROP, 1782.

Fig. 12. *Title page of a book celebrating the recognition of the United States, 1782.* Engraving by Reinier Vinkeles after J. Buys. (Atlas van Stolk, Rotterdam.)

Fig. 13. *The Netherlands and America in their commercial relation symbolized by two little boys.* Wine glass with stipple engraving. (Museum Boymans–Van Beuningen, Rotterdam.)

Fig. 14. *Allegory on the recognition of the United States.* Engraving by
C. Brouwer after P. Wagenaar. 1782. The poem explains the meaning:

America tramples down angry Albion,
While the British crown is crushed by Bourbon,
And sees itself by Holland, after the example of the
     citizens of Amsterdam,
According to the preparatory plan, declared free in Adams.

(Collection of the author.)

Mr PIETER JOHAN van BERCKEL
MINISTER-PLENIPOTENTIARIS VAN DEN STAET DER
VEREENIGDE NEDERLANDEN BIJ DE STATEN VAN
NOORD-AMERIKA, RAED IN DE VROEDSCHAP EN
OUD-BURGEMEESTER DER STAD
ROTTERDAM. enz. enz. enz.

Fig. 15. *Pieter Johan van Berckel, the first minister plenipotentiary*
of the Dutch Republic in the United States.
Engraving by L. Brasser after F. J. Pfeiffer.
(Collection of the author.)

Fig. 16. *Cornelis de Gijselaar, pensionary of the city of Dordrecht.*
Engraving by L. Kobell after a painting by L. Temminck. Stipple engraving.
(Collection of the author.)

He enjoyed his new life in the same way. Your husband, he wrote to his wife, has been completely transformed, "he begins to be a Courtier, and Sups and Visits at Court among Princesses and Princes, Lords and Ladies of Various Nations." But he hastily added that he would not go far in these courtier's goings-on; he had to remain an independent man, and the question was how could he combine that with the character of a courtier. But he was not weighed down by his dilemma; he recorded with obvious delight in his diary how he was received at Huis ten Bosch, the Prince of Orange's residence at the northern edge of The Hague, whom he met, and what was said.

There was a bit of a fuss over his reception by William V during the summer. The pensionary of Amsterdam, Carel W. Visscher, wrote His Highness a long letter to remind him that he must not overlook Adams when he received the diplomatic corps, and Van Bleiswijk, the grand pensionary of the province of Holland, made fun of the Amsterdammer's meddling, for Visscher came to him "to inform him in great haste and as a matter of the highest importance" that the French ambassador had also complained that Adams was the only diplomat not invited. Van Hardenbroek, the memoir writer who heard everything, tracked the whole affair down to the last detail and decided it was just one more instance of the grand pensionary's unreliability. But Visscher's demarche worked, for in the end Adams was invited.

Adams led a pleasant life. In the morning he would go riding in the dunes, sometimes with General Van der Dussen, who wanted to know everything about the Indians; then he would work and receive guests; sometimes he would go out in the evening, attending the French Comedy or having dinner with a colleague. But the Dutch mijnheers were not free with their invitations, except for Boreel, a deputy of Holland to the States General. The others, Adams wrote, never invited anyone, neither foreigners nor each other. "Hospitality and Sociality are no Characteristicks here." He himself asked to his home various persons, especially from the circle of the Patriots, such as De Gijselaar and Visscher. Another guest whom he lists in his diary is the count of Sarsfield, a Frenchman of Irish origin, who instructed him in etiquette, table arrangements, titles, and formulas. Adams realized he had to know this French art "of living with people." Thus he became a respected diplomat.

A special problem was presented by language. Adams could speak some French, but far from perfectly, and he knew very little Dutch. When *Mevrouw* [Mrs.] Boreel asked him at table whether he understood Dutch, he replied that he knew only a little, but was beginning to learn it. In the morning at breakfast, he said, he tried to read the newspaper with the help of a dictionary. "Mr. Geelvink called out to me, pleasantly enough, leese Mijnheer de Diemer Meerche Courant [read the *Diemer Meersche Courant*, Sir]," he wrote his wife. "Yes well, Mijnheer, says I, en de Hollandsche Historische Courant oke [and the *Hollandsche Historische Courant* too]." He did not find Dutch easy going, however. "Adams sat very still," Visscher told Van Hardenbroek, "not that he lacked all comprehension, but his silence came mostly from his speaking only English well."[11]

· I V ·

What kept Adams in Holland for the whole summer was not the status and pleasures of diplomatic life but the problem of getting a treaty. As we have seen, he had presented a proposal for a treaty immediately after his recognition, and the negotiations took up another half year. Although there was agreement on the main lines of a treaty, there were differences about details. Peace and friendship, mutual most-favored-nation treatment, including the colonies, protection for shipping—all these were completely in accord with the model treaty that Adams had drawn up years before while still in his own country. But the Dutch wanted to know what the provision that the treaty would not prejudice the treaty already in existence between France and America meant. They also asked why Spain had to be invited in the following clause to join the alliance. And what did Adams have in mind, they continued, with the provision that Dutch consuls must support the Americans in an eventual negotiation with the Barbary pirates?

During an interview that Adams had in June with the grand pensionary, the latter, in his usual manner, waved aside all these queries as not really important. But the months crawled by with the customary deliberations. In August, Adams wrote to Jay: "The march of this people is so slow, that it will be some time before the treaty of commerce can be finished." At the end of the month the reports came in from the provinces, and Adams was invited to meet with a committee of the States General. In September they completed their work, and Adams went over the text of the treaty with Fagel word by word. "We have now, I hope, agreed upon every word, if not every point," he wrote in some annoyance to Livingston. That it had taken so long was due to the lukewarm, if not down-right hostile, attitude of the court. The Prince of Orange, Adams accused, was evidently as incurable as his cousin George III.

The actual signing of the treaty did not take place until early October, in the Trèveszaal (the chamber where the twelve years' truce with Spain had been signed in 1609) of the Binnenhof, the buildings of state in The Hague. It proceeded with some ceremoniousness. Van den Santheuvel and Van Lynden tot Blitterswijk awaited Adams at the head of the stairs and escorted him into the chamber. Things moved so slowly that he had a chance to look about him and admire the paintings. Fagel explained that they represented scenes from the life of Claudius Civilis as reported by Tacitus; Fagel's father had studied it all and written his findings on the backs of the frames.

Afterward, Adams wrote his thoughts on what had been achieved. It was Dumas, he began, who should be thanked that everything went so well, for he was always at hand and translated everything into French. The treaty as a whole was as close to the instructions that Adams had been given as was possible. Only a few points were at variance. Friesland had proposed inclusion of an article assuring to subjects of the Republic the right to buy land in America, but he had been able to keep it out. The rights of France and Spain were adequately guaranteed, although not in the exact wording he had proposed, and La Vauguyon was satisfied. The clause in which the Americans pledged to respect the Dutch colonies and their rights was superfluous, to be sure, and even revealed some envy, but still it implied a compliment to American power and importance and he had therefore kept his objections silent. Finally, there was the article on religious freedom. The Dutch had insisted that the limitations on public demonstration of religions (other than the official Reformed religion, of course) in the Dutch Republic be expressly included in the treaty. He was opposed to it, Adams wrote, for he was an enemy of any appearance of compulsion in so sensitive and sacred a matter of religious freedom, but the laws in the Netherlands did not permit Roman Catholics to have stee-ples on their churches and those laws could not be changed.[12]

Thus Adams's last major task in the Netherlands was accomplished. In a little over two years he had succeeded in obtaining everything he wanted, and he could be satisfied. As required by the customs of the time, the treaty had to be celebrated and portrayed in medals and prints. The usual symbols were employed, and Liberty and Trade shone in all their glory. Honor was paid to America, but no less to Amsterdam, which, in truth, had shown the way in the secret treaty of 1778. Fame was shown with her trumpet, "while the Lion's Skin and the Club of Hercules lay next to her on the clouds, as a sign that these two mighty Sea Powers, armed with strength and courage, will be able to enforce their mutual treaty, and to make it enduring and in every way advantageous for both States." Around it was written *"Faustissimo Foedere iunctae,"* united by an alliance promising everything good. The dream could not come to an end; there was symbolism enough to make it true.

Now the time had come to bid farewell. There was so much still to do. Adams spent his last days in The Hague signing bonds, with intervals for walking in the Woods (Haagse Bos) and visiting. He paid a parting call upon his friends from Amsterdam, who gave a banquet with him as guest of honor. His host, Christiaan Everard Le Vaillant, toasted him with a specially engraved glass. The lip showed *Aurea Libertas* (golden freedom), and Le Vaillant, raising his glass, declaimed a Latin poem, which Adams proudly copied down in his diary. "Never was Bumper quaffed with more good will," he reflected with pleasure.

The final visits were made to government officials and to friends. Adams told Van Bleiswijk, in an extended metaphor, that he went to Paris with an olive branch in his mouth, in his heart, and in his hands. To Fagel he explained the composition of the American peace delegation: Franklin, Jay, and he himself were the members, he said. Franklin was old, suffered from gout and the stone, and could not sleep. Fagel asked how old he was, and Adams replied that he was all of seventy-six, having been born in 1706. Fagel said that he was that age also, but that there was nothing the matter with him. Adams commented that he was not surprised, for Fagel had walked in the dunes the day before for four hours. During Adams's visit, the Prince of Orange showed great interest in the peace negotiations. Had the king of England carried through the recognition of American independence without a decision of Parliament? he asked, amazed and sarcastic.

Adams next went to dine with La Vauguyon, who urged him vigorously to propose Dumas as chargé d'affaires to the Dutch authorities. Although Adams hesitated—after all, Dumas had "no other character than that of Correspondent of Mr. Franklin"—he still did so when he paid a visit of departure to the president of the week, Count George van Randwijck. He had long confidential talks with his friends in the government, Pensionary Visscher of Amsterdam, who confided to him that the stadholder was "the g.T. in this Country—stubborn as a mule" ("g.T. is probably 'greatest Tyrant,'" Adams observed in his diary), and Pensionary De Gijselaar of Dordrecht, who discussed with him at length the foreign involvements in the party struggles in the Republic. Thulemeyer, the Prussian minister, had warned La Vauguyon about French support for the Patriots, but if Prussia gave its support to William V, where, De Gijselaar asked Adams, could the Patriots go for help but to France? And he wondered whether Adams could be of assistance to them in France.

Adams must have given a noncommittal reply, but he made no mention of doing so in his diary. He had no real interest in the Dutch party conflict, certainly not now that he had won his own battle. He just wanted to be off to Paris without delay. Accompanied by his young friends Thaxter and a second American who had just arrived, Charles Storer, who served him as personal secretary, he traveled up through Haarlem to Amsterdam, and then down to Utrecht—where he admired the canals with their high banks and warehouses—thence to Gorcum, with "a fair view" of the prison fortress of Loevestein, and Breda. They arrived there at about nine o'clock in the evening, but a messenger who had been sent ahead had the gate, which was usually closed at half past six, kept open "to admit Mr. Adams the Ambassador of America." The next day they rode out of the Dutch Republic, their first stop Antwerp.[13]

CHAPTER 17

Traveling Diplomacy

*Indeed, as I perceive by the papers that Mr. Adams
is gone over to Holland I am not
without hopes that his object may be
to procure supplies of money.*
THOMAS JEFFERSON

T was a cold and rainy fall, and the roads were so
drenched that it took the party of Americans no less
than four days to reach Antwerp. But the energy and enthusiasm of Adams were not so easily deadened, and he
found time to admire the works of Rubens—"Beautiful
beyond description"—before traveling on to Paris by way of Brussels and
Mons. In general, Belgium seemed to him a dismal, impoverished country; the villages had decrepit houses and people were wrapped in rags—
"What a contrast to the Villages of Holland." But he had no reason to
linger, for he had to rush on to Paris to take part in the negotiation of
peace, and except for an occasional bit of sightseeing—Fénelon's grave in
the church of Cambrai, the château of Chantilly—there was not much to
hold him. In all the journey from The Hague to the French capital lasted
ten days.[1]

There the gathering in of the harvest began. That the American Revolution would be brought to a glorious conclusion in a peace that was extremely favorable to the new nation would be in no small measure the
result of Adams's stubbornness and discernment. William Lee had predicted it all when he met Adams in Brussels and told him that he was the
swallow that heralded the summer. The story of the negotiation lies outside our theme, but one aspect of it does concern us. The American negotiators, Franklin, Jay, and Adams, decided to disregard the explicit instructions of Congress and go their own way instead of following the
lead of the French diplomats. Adams, long convinced of Vergennes's per-
fidy, was principally responsible for this shift, and history has justified
him, for there is no longer any doubt that America would not have gained
so advantageous a peace if it had trailed at the French apron strings. In

1783 the peace terms were ratified and a new country came into existence as a member of the international community: the United States of America. In the spring of 1785 Congress officially named envoys to France and England. Jefferson went to Paris, and the first recognized revolutionary at the Court of St. James was none other than the triumphant Adams. There had been rumors of his appointment for a long time. Dumas had given Adams his congratulations back in March 1783, and Adams had replied with some annoyance that he himself knew nothing of such an appointment and had no desire for it; but he thought he had a complete right to it. On 1 June 1785 he was received in audience by King George III, an event whose quality of historical drama did not in the least escape him. "I was the focus of all eyes," he wrote to Jay, who had become secretary for foreign affairs, and the king "listened to every word I said, with dignity, but with an apparent emotion."[2]

Pushed, perhaps we should say shoved, on to the great stage of the world, our hero might easily have forgotten Holland, which had been his dressing room. There were, it appeared, so many greater matters at stake now. But the material source of all activity continued to lie in Amsterdam, and therefore Adams returned almost every year to the Low Countries to discuss loans and payments with the bankers. From the start he was aware, conscientious New Englander that he was, that the new nation must be a reliable client, able to repay its loans when they fell due. This, in turn, made him a convinced nationalist. The United States, he wrote to Livingston in the summer of 1783 on the eve of his departure for Holland, had to show that they were trustworthy by acting "as one people, as one man, in their transactions with foreign nations."

In the beginning some of this trustworthiness was lacking; the mutual divisions and uncertainties of thirteen undisciplined states were too great, and payment of interest in tobacco and other products was not very acceptable to creditors. Could he not see to it, Adams wrote to Robert Morris, the financier of Congress, that American products were sent to Amsterdam in a common balanced endeavor, rice and indigo from South Carolina and Georgia, tobacco from Virginia and Maryland, wheat and flour from Pennsylvania, fish from the Northern states? In 1784, Adams succeeded in obtaining a new loan of two million guilders, but at an interest rate of no less than 7 percent. The bankers of Amsterdam, says the Dutch historian P. J. van Winter, who has studied this matter so closely, "made use of the need for money to obtain the top profits, which was justified by the low creditworthiness of the weak American nation." This was the plain reality of business life, he goes on, but admits "a feeling of satisfaction" that there was more lively interest in the American bonds among Patriots than other Dutchmen.[3]

As time passed, things went better. In 1785, Adams could report that the credit of the United States had improved considerably and that the loans, which had reached a total of seven millions, had been just about fully subscribed. In the years that followed he was able to make arrangements for payments and new loans, but not without difficulty. In 1787 a new loan could be concluded only at a still higher interest rate of 8 percent. Jefferson in Paris was brought into these later negotiations, and in the spring of 1788 the two friends met in Holland for discussion of the financial problems with the Amsterdam moneylenders. They finally succeeded, but not without much wariness on both sides. In our own day, the Dutch have congratulated themselves that it had been their bankers who had helped the American nation to its feet financially, and there were even those who spoke of a first Marshall Plan in the other direction. At the time, Adams was not so full of gratitude. He wrote to Jefferson to warn him against the "immense greed" of Amsterdam. But then, he asked, what could one expect in business relations? Lending and paying back rested upon terms, and trustworthiness upon security. The final success of the loans said more about the viability of the Americans than the kindness of the Dutch. By 1794 the total of loans to the new nation had risen to thirty million guilders, and the Dutch investments formed the entire public debt of the United States. Fifteen years later, in early 1809, the last debts were paid off. America had proved its viability.[4]

· II ·

A journey to the Low Countries, especially from London, was quite an operation. Adams knew something about it, certainly after his winter crossing in January 1784. It belongs, with his voyage across the Atlantic in 1778, among his deeds of particular heroism, and he wrote at length about what he had experienced. The wintry weather and his own delicate health, he wrote, meant that he ran the risk of not surviving the trip, but his conscience commanded him to go. So he set out for Holland, accompanied by his son. They had to wait for three days at Harwich before they could sail, and they were at sea for three days, flung this way and that by the storms. Hellevoetsluis, the usual port inside the delta, could not be reached, and they finally had to go ashore on the forsaken coast of Goeree Island. In biting cold they walked half a dozen miles to the little town of the same name, then rode in an open peasant's cart to Middel-harnis. There they hired an iceboat to take them, sometimes in the water and sometimes on the ice, to Hellevoetsluis, where they again rode on a wagon to Den Briel. The journey across the South Holland islands had taken them three days. On 12 January, nine days after they had left London, the two Americans, chilled to the bone, reached The Hague. There, under Dumas's good care in their own embassy, they were able to regain their health and strength.[5]

During his stays in the Netherlands, Adams took up residence at the embassy. He went out from the house on the Fluwelen Burgwal to pay his official visits, including one to the stadholder in Huis ten Bosch, who was courteous as always, and he kept up his relations with old friends, especially the leaders of the Patriots. He was always ready too to receive visiting compatriots.

We have an interesting description of one such visit by young Elkanah Watson, from whose book *A Tour in Holland* about his travels in 1784 we quoted in our prologue. He made his call, he tells us, at "the grand hôtel . . . lately purchased by Mr. Adams, for the residence of our future ambassadors. It is decently furnished, has a large library, and an elegant little garden." Adams received him cordially, made a short excursion with him to Scheveningen, and took a long walk with him in The Woods, where they went into the little palace of Huis ten Bosch on an unofficial visit and gazed with admiration upon its furnishings and paintings. According to Watson, the American livery worn by the embassy servants was held in high honor by the population of The Hague. On their ride to Scheveningen, all the passers-by took off their hats to the Americans. Our visitor spent the evening with his host and "the famous Monsieur Dumas, his secretary, who eminently distinguished himself in the early part of our contest, at the court of France, as well as by gaining us weighty friends in this republick." The fame of poor Dumas obviously always remained somewhat hazy. The following day, Watson and Adams made another excursion to a palace near Rijswijk, clearly Honselaarsdijk, a splendid house but in complete disrepair, Watson wrote.[6]

Although Adams had won his place in the Netherlands, his curious traveling ambassadorship was not wholly to the taste of the government in The Hague, and not at all so when they learned that he had been named American ambassador in London. How could that be? old Fagel asked Van Lynden, the Dutch ambassador at the English court. The *griffier* then called Dumas on the carpet to give a further explanation. A whole exchange of letters followed. Adams wrote in person to explain why he had not been in touch with the authorities in the Netherlands. It was not an act of discourtesy; he had not received a "letter of recall" from America and hence could not make any move. As soon as he had his official dispatch, he would of course come to The Hague to take his departure in due form. The question was brought to a calm for the time being, but it was not until 1788 that the official ceremony of departure took place at last.[7]

Adams's most enjoyable visit to Holland during these years was certainly that of 1786, when he was accompanied by his wife Abigail. The couple had been reunited in 1784, after a separation of almost five years, and the subsequent years must have been among the happiest of their lives. In August 1786, when Adams had to go to The Hague to ratify with the Prussian envoy Thulemeyer the treaty between Prussia and America, he decided to have his wife see at last the country from which he had written so many letters full of love and pain, and which she herself had dreamed about in raptures. She was very contented with what she saw. It might be a frog land, but the inhabitants were a well-fed, well-dressed, satisfied, and happy kind of people. There was no other land like this, so wide, so flat, so clear.[8]

As we have said, it was not until early 1788 that Adams finally, after ten years of diplomatic service in Europe, received permission to return to his homeland. At first, in January, he was afraid that he could not go in person to The Hague to take his departure, but the discussions about the loans in Amsterdam, which compelled him and Jefferson to journey to Holland in March, provided him with the opportunity to see once more the leaders in The Hague and his friends with whom he had gone through so much. The States General gave him the usual farewell gift, a gold medal and chain worth thirteen hundred guilders. It showed on one side the arms of the Dutch Republic, on the other those of the stadholder and each of the seven provinces. The legend on both sides was the motto *Concordia res parvae crescunt—Discordia maxime dilabuntur* (Through unity small things grow—through disunity they collapse; the first part of the phrase was the official motto of the United Provinces). It was wisdom with which Adams agreed with all his heart, but which he had sadly failed to find in the Republic.[9]

CHAPTER 18

Dutchmen in America

*I can now affirm that I found America different from
what I had expected and that the word liberty
has acquired another meaning for me.
In America I changed my mind about America. . . .
American liberty has had a bad influence on our own.
This much I have learned and that is
better than seeing a heaven on earth.*
GIJSBERT KAREL VAN HOGENDORP

HE time came at last when even opponents acquiesced in recognition of America. Left with no choice, they made the best of it and took part in doing what needed to be done. Recognition meant not only receiving Adams but also sending a Dutch ambassador to the United States. His instructions had to make clear everything he would have to do and what he would have to watch closely. The questions that he would have to answer were those that Europeans in general had on their minds: Would America become a welcome commercial partner or a dangerous competitor? How strong in fact was the country? Was her democratic constitution a good or a bad thing, and in what ways? He would have to inform himself about "the internal constitutions" of each of the thirteen states and "the essential form of their mutual association and the form of their General Government." These were problems that fascinated the Dutch; after all, they had been themselves seeking answers to them in their own country for more than two centuries.[1]

The next question was whom to send. There was thought, briefly, of Robert Jasper van der Capellen van de Marsch, the cousin of Joan Derk, Baron tot den Pol. But when Van de Marsch hesitated, the post was given to Pieter Johan van Berckel, the brother of the pensionary of Amsterdam. He was a year older than Engelbert François, but had not kept up with him. Unassuming, insignificant, and full of good will, he was glad to accept the appointment at a salary of twenty thousand guilders plus another twenty-four thousand for travel costs, outfitting, and insurance.

Whether he fulfilled the high requirements of the office, as an enthusiastic article in the *Post van den Neder-Rhijn* asserted, whether he was "a man of vigorous understanding, acute judgment and deep insight," "of lively mind and terse, natural eloquence," "learned in modern History" and with "an intimate knowledge of everything concerned with the essential interests of his Fatherland," and many other such fine qualities, is open to doubt. He was, claimed the historian Loosjes, a very capable man, one "whose morals would not be corrupted by pomp or play." But the reports that he sent home once he was in America do not give us as high an impression of him.[2]

His departure for America was accompanied by the usual pompous orations and high-flown versifying. He sailed with an entire squadron, a sign of the high expectations for his mission. His flagship was the *Overijssel*, a warship, and it was accompanied by three other ships. One of these, the *Erfprins*, had aboard the young traveler Gijsbert Karel van Hogendorp (who was later to become one of the great statesmen of his country, founder of the Kingdom of the Netherlands in 1813), who had received permission for the journey only after some resistance from his mother; he wanted to see the New World, to observe how a new state comes into life, and to draw lessons for his own homeland. He was the only one who would really be a perceptive observer and achieve a real, if one-sided, understanding of America.

The voyage, through storms and contrary winds, was extremely difficult. It lasted from June until October 1783. The *Erfprins* became separated from the rest of the squadron and finally was wrecked on the coast of Massachusetts; among the few survivors was Van Hogendorp. Van Berckel himself reached port safely and presented himself to Congress in November, while it was meeting in the little town of Princeton, in New Jersey. He was received with many signs of respect. He spoke to Congress in French (a report by a Dutch historian that he spoke in Dutch is improbable); his high-flown phrases were matched by those of the American reply. The days that followed were filled with dinners, visits, and repaying visits, and even the grand man of the War for Independence, General Washington, was present. The young Patriot from Drente, Carel de Vos van Steenwijk, a member of Van Berckel's retinue, was enthusiastic about a noontime banquet offered by Congress: "There were more than sixty places."

The reports sent to The Hague by Van Berckel during the five years that he was the Dutch minister do not show much intelligence or insight, as we have noted. They include lengthy descriptions of all kinds of unim-

portant externals: a triumphant arch erected in Philadelphia in honor of
the winning of the war; the insignia of the order of the Cincinnati; and
the like. He complains over the high cost of living, which makes it impossible "to get by with the salary that Their High Mightinesses grant me."
He sends sensational accounts of widespread criminality and avers that it
is not safe to walk through the streets in the evening: "Among others, two
Ladies were . . . badly slashed in the face and bosom during the same
evening, and one of them has already died." He recounts with pleasure
how "an air-ball [balloon] thirty-five feet in diameter" was sent up in
Philadelphia and caught fire. He repeats without comment newspaper accounts of the frontier fighting with the Indians, and other such matters.
But nothing of any essential importance. Even so fundamental an occur-
rence as the adoption of the Constitution in the summer of 1787 is reported in a matter-of-fact way, without a single comment that would
show some understanding of what it meant.[3]

It is hard to see any good reason why worthy Van Berckel was sacked
after the revolution of 1787 in the Netherlands. His dismissal is another
example of the extreme reaction that was running riot in The Hague,
when an effort was made to purge everyone with a Patriotic past. It is all
the more curious because he was succeeded by his son, Pieter Franco van
Berckel, whose dispatches were just as uninteresting as his father's, if
somewhat longer. Fearing the reaction raging in his homeland, the dismissed diplomat did not return to the Netherlands, but settled in the
countryside near New York and spent his last years there until his death
in 1800. His son remained the Dutch minister until the next revolution in
his homeland, in 1795, when it was his turn to be dismissed. He was followed by another Patriot as envoy, Rogier Gerard van Polanen, whose letters are of more importance, and shall shortly receive our attention.[4]

· II ·

If there is at least one thing that is clear and still of interest in the small-
talk reports of Van Berckel, it is his disappointment with the land of his
dreams. But in this respect he is not very different from many others; it
may even be said that he represents a pattern. So many Europeans, so
many Dutchmen, had vague, high-strung expectations about a country
they did not really know. So many of them hoped to find a better world,
an almost perfect world even. What could follow from a real meeting but
disenchantment, which often turned into disgust?

A very good example of such a process is to be found in the rather extensive correspondence of the Dutch merchant from Rotterdam Adriaan Valck and his wife Johanna Dros. This couple sailed to Baltimore in 1783, where Valck planned to set up a commercial firm with a special interest in the tobacco trade. In Holland he had been a close friend of the great Van der Capellen, and of course like him an ardent Patriot and full of admiration for America. He had tried when still in Rotterdam to obtain a post as commercial agent of the United States, and Van der Capellen had recommended him to Adams. But Adams, who already had the problem of the Americanization of Dumas on his hands, replied that it was impossible to employ foreigners in the service of the United States. Clinging to his plans, Valck then decided to emigrate to the much-admired but unknown world in the West.

The letters that he and, even more, his wife wrote from America to their relatives in Holland are extreme examples of the great frustration that uprooted people sometimes have to suffer when their dreams are confronted with reality. Their whole correspondence is nothing but one long litany, one complaint about the evil world in which they are caught; nothing, absolutely nothing, is to their taste, not the people, not the climate, not the daily needs of life. The roads are unpaved, the vegetables expensive and bad, the summers full of flies and the winters full of snow, et cetera, et cetera. "How beautiful a picture was dangled before our eyes, about this land of promise, but if this is the land of promise I wish I had never seen it." There is too much freedom and too much equality for the taste of these middle-class Dutchmen: "It is an insolent, useless nation, freedom knows no bonds here; it is possible that this beautiful land will survive but we don't believe it; luxury, pride, licentiousness, laziness are the dominant features of this people."

Also evident in these letters is the Dutch disappointment over the English competition in trade: "We should like to see one of those fanatic supporters of America come over here, one who understands the language and is able to travel around, we have no doubt that he would sing another tune when he came back. The worst of all is that they have thrown off the English yoke and now that they are free there is nothing they can appreciate if it is not English; for no other nation do they have any respect."

In the end the Valcks, like so many other European progressives who came to the land of progress, took the side of the conservative party in America; the Federalists were their only hope. Early in 1787, Valck wrote home that the situation seemed to have changed for the better; new laws were expected: "This is the result of the fact that the best and richest part of the inhabitants of this country deplore the disorder and want to do all they can to restore their society. The great mass of speculators and debtors, aided by the power of too many lawyers, try to prevent this restoration."[5]

· III ·

The prejudices and sympathies that most travelers brought with them from home were tested in the reality of America. Often that reality was found wanting, but not always. Sometimes it came up to expectations. But that depended not only on the reality itself, but also on its interpretation, on the perceptions of the visitors.

An interesting example of this was one of the favorite pastimes of travelers in the New World: watching General Washington. For Washington embodied America. To Europeans he was America and all humanity in one person; he had no equal in history. The image of Washington among the many European dreamers who never had a chance to cross the Atlantic Ocean and see him with their own eyes was a religious one. Two aspects were emphasized: he was the true Roman, the general who left the plow to take up the sword and then, having won the battle, returned to his simple farm; he was also the living proof that it was possible for mankind to attain perfection. To be proud of him meant to be proud of the human race. His glory shone upon all who honored him.

The poet Jacobus Bellamy dedicated a poem to him, which contrasted him to tyrants like Caesar and Alexander:

> I read their name upon the page, and weep:
>   I scream: O woe! I too am a man, like them!
> Then I see your greatness and delighted shout:
>   Victory! I too am a man, like you.*

And Bellamy's friend A. Vereul, in a panegyric upon the poet, asserted: "With Washington we honor Bellamy, as we honor a sculptor with the gods whom he portrays." Other Patriots—Van der Capellen, Van der Kemp, Dumas, Luzac—indulged in the same kind of glorification. Luzac

---

* De stervling zegt, bij ' lezen van hun naam;
  Hij gilt: helaas! 'k ben ook een mensch!—
 Doch roept, verrukt daar hij uw grootheid ziet,
  Triumf! 'k ben ook een mensch!

proclaimed that Washington was as great as all the heroes of antiquity together, Themistocles, Aristides, Cato, Solon, the whole crew. The fiery Patriotic preacher in Diemen, Bernard Bosch, put an entire poem into the mouth of the great American, in which he spoke to the American people as he put down his command:

> After all your pains and troubles,
> Live happy now and be Free!
> But be Independent too of me.*⁶

It is interesting to see how the Dutchmen in America who got the chance to look with their own eyes upon this god on earth almost all displayed the same veneration. Here is the description of "great Washington" by P. A. Godin, another Patriot who emigrated to America, with the intention to start farming and live a truly bucolic life. He saw his hero at a reception: "He is a tall, handsome man who seems between fifty and sixty years of age, speaks and laughs with everyone, and so easygoing and obliging that when it comes time for us to leave, he goes himself to look for our hats." Even more striking in their adoration for the American leader are the letters of Gerard Vogels, another young Dutchman who came to America in 1783 to try his fortune. He got an opportunity to gaze with his own eyes upon "the greatest Man who ever appeared upon the face of this Globe," and he rejoiced: "And then this Excellent Hero came in person, riding a horse of uncommon beauty which seemed so proud of his burden that I had the feeling of seeing Germanicus's horse, while we, enthralled at the sight of the Hero, seemed in doubt whether we should admire more greatly the simplicity of this splendid Heroism or the friendliness of the best and greatest of Heroes." What a man this was! He would soon retire to his estate in the country, Godin continued, leaving the bustle of the world, "while his pious Christian Sentiments assure him Immortality now and Hereafter." When Vogels had a chance to meet the general a few days later, his joy ran over: "If I do not become haughty now, I do not fear that I shall ever be."⁷

Carel de Vos van Steenwijk, who kept a detailed account of his American trip in a diary, was not so worked up; that was not his style, for he was a cool, almost dull observer who set down his geographical materials in careful order. But even he was impressed when, in the company of

---

* Gij moet na zoo veel ramp en pijn
Gelukkig—heel in Vrijheid leeven—
Van mij ook onafhanglijk zijn.

Godin, he was received by Washington: "This admirable man received us in a very friendly and distinguished way in every respect."[8]

In the whole chorus of jubilant and adoring voices there is only one voice singing out of harmony. This was Van Hogendorp, a mere stripling of twenty years, but hyperintelligent and all too self-assured. His visit to Washington was an act out of a tragicomedy, exquisitely revealing of both guest and host. The young man set off with the highest expectations; he had indeed been warned that the general was aloof, but he thought that only made his character more admirable. When in the distance he saw Mount Vernon, to which Washington had just retired, his heart pounded with excitement. What followed was an anticlimax that brought him down with a bump.

His reception was chilly, almost unfriendly. The general, obviously bored by this latest in a long line of inquisitive visitors, displayed no interest whatever in his guest and did not even reply to his questions. "I tried to explain to the general that I doubted whether the lands which Congress planned to sell [Van Hogendorp meant the western territories] will bring in very much money. He did not understand me very well, perhaps not at all. He was unable to state his thoughts clearly, elegantly, or even with some taste." Suddenly, Gijsbert Karel lost his balance; he was no longer the rational, critical observer, but a pure-blooded romantic, all *Sturm und Drang*. He wrote to his mother in an agitated French: "This scene which I had so little expected threw me into a profound reverie and I had to go outside to abandon myself to my reflections. A hundred times I repeated the passage from Hamlet: 'What a piece of work is a man! how noble in reason, etc. . . . and yet to me what is this quintessence of dust? man delights not me.' I had indeed broken with the whole human race."

When he had calmed down, he concluded that his god had fallen and that Washington was not a genius, not even a man of great talent, drawing an almost Marxist conclusion that it was not the hero who led the crowd, but the other way around, that he was only its representative. "I consider Washington as the instrument of independence, the source is to be found in the genius of the people who inhabit America." We are tempted to say that Van Hogendorp, in his meeting with Washington, or at least in his reactions to it, runs through the entire gamut of intellectual development from the eighteenth to the nineteenth centuries, starting with the Enlightenment and passing through Romanticism to Marxism. This would be an exaggeration, however. It would be safer to say that this curious encounter tells us something about Washington—there are other accounts of his cool and reticent personality—and a great deal about the eager, opinionated, and self-assured young Dutchman. What really happened was that he measured the general against himself; his ambition and self-overestimation were in fact the signs of his own immaturity.[9]

· IV ·

The judgment of the youthful Van Hogendorp not only upon Washington but upon America as a whole is more interesting, penetrating, and idiosyncratic than that of any of his countrymen who came to the country, indeed than that of most European visitors of his own time. In his powers of observation and vision he is at least the equal of such far more romantic Frenchmen as the marquis de Chastellux, Abbé Robin, Brissot de Warville, and so many others. The only other Dutchman who traveled through the country, in fact even more widely than Van Hogendorp, was Carel de Vos van Steenwijk, whom we have already met. He too was a young man, just twenty-four years of age, and he too came with Van Berckel and had introductions to important people. But De Vos van Steenwijk lacked Van Hogendorp's power of mind and insight. His voluminous diary is rich in detail but has not a single reflection of substantial judgment upon the problems of America. Although he traveled far to the south, all the way to Charleston, South Carolina, he did not come to any conclusions about the problem of slavery, even though, unlike Van Hogendorp, he was a progressive, an ardent Patriot.

We have a different kind of man in Van Hogendorp, one who holds our attention far more closely. It is fascinating to watch him on his travels through America; he is open to everything he sees and yet so full of himself, so intent upon using his experiences in America in order to reform his own country, to "make the good cause triumph and with it to impress my name imperishably in the memory of my country as long as it lives." In this he succeeded, it may be said, although much later, when he became the founder of the modern Kingdom of the Netherlands. His American journey was only a small part of his preparation for that role, a first start. The young man did not find what he was looking for in America; for him American democracy and equality went too far—the constitution seemed impractical and the federal system too ineffectual. In the end he admitted he was disappointed: "I can now declare that I found America to be different from what I expected, and that the word freedom took on another meaning for me. In America I changed my mind about America. . . . People in America are no more virtuous than those here in the same circumstances, but until now these circumstances are better." [10]

As he went along, he gave his judgment upon everything of importance that he saw in notes and letters home, and later he put his views into essays and published articles. He asked the eternal query of European visitors: Was there more equality in America than in the Old World? He thought there was indeed, but still true equality could not exist, and he began with a clear contrasting of the classes. "There is a general division here between 'gentlemen' and 'persons in lower life'. The root of this distinction lies in affluence: independence of others is based upon possession of property, so that the richer and more independent one is, the 'genteeler.' Coach and horses, fine clothes, banqueting, are stared at here as everywhere. The poor step back willingly." The difference from Europe was really that the ranks were not fixed and that wealth and reputation were so fluid and changeable.

As for the constitution, he believed that it was absolutely necessary that the rich gain greater influence. He eagerly adopted the opinions of the rising Federalists and believed with them that there had to be a stronger central government. But he was not at all sure that this would come about: "The merchants are the most eminent Inhabitants, they are not taken with the idea of a pure democracy, and they would prefer to see The Great Public Officers with greater power, because they are familiar with their influence, which always goes in partnership with Wealth. But the Country-People are proud of the power they have gained and they will hold on to it as long as possible." It is not surprising, therefore, that when Van Hogendorp heard a few years later of the adoption of the new Constitution, with its strong federal authority, he broke out in rejoicing. Now America had a future, he thought, and what a difference from what was happening in France. [11]

Another American problem that Van Hogendorp viewed very closely was slavery. When he was in Annapolis while Congress was meeting there, he became a good friend of Thomas Jefferson, if only for a short time, and Jefferson's conceptions, as we know them from his *Notes on the State of Virginia*, find their echo in the observations of the young Dutchman. But although Van Hogendorp repeated the familiar stereotypes that blacks were children, submissive and musical, he did not stick to those prejudices. He wondered if they were really as docile as they seemed, and he expected that a time would come when they would get more rights and liberties, when they would be better educated and want their share in government. What would happen, he asked prophetically, if for instance one of the political parties took their fate to heart and supported their demands? How would it be possible then to keep black and white apart? Or were his white informants right that the blacks were too weak ever to raise themselves up and would never possess the whites' powers of discernment? He hesitated to come to a conclusion.[12]

In many ways, Van Hogendorp embodied the European ambivalence about America. There is a pattern in his experiences that we meet often. Initial expectations turn into disappointment and fault-finding. Two sheets in Van Hogendorp's papers contain very characteristic observations: one has "Advantages of America. According to Americans"; the other "Disadvantages of America. According to me." These were written while he was still in the New World, in Philadelphia, on 1 and 2 March 1784. The Americans, he reported, believed in their isolation, their simplicity, their freedom. But he saw the jealousy between the states, the scarcity of natural resources in the North, the dependence upon Europe in taste and therefore in industry, the indolence of many, and finally the "despotism of a few Masters over many Negroes in the South."[13]

So he foresaw a bleak future. For the moment things seemed to be going well, but what would happen as America developed? A time had to come when there would be an end to the boundless possibilities of the country, whatever optimists might claim. Prophetically, our conservative explained:

> But, since the population increases daily, the land will finally become scarce, people will have trouble earning a living, one man will depend on another, the poor will have to work more, mutual dependence will increase, money will be concentrated in a few hands instead of being widely distributed as now. Then there will arise at last, as with us, a class of men who have to spend every hour of the day in hard labor, using their children to help them, without time to spare, either for them or for themselves, for acquiring or even keeping knowledge, but rather whose intellectual powers, religious impressions, and good habits of life, will decline from father to son, becoming at last that pitiable portion of the nation known by the name of dregs of the people.

In brief, America, like Europe, would become familiar with a proletariat; it would not escape history in its dream of freedom and equality.

With such gloomy but prophetic insights, Van Hogendorp was far ahead of the ordinary observer of his own time. For him America was not a paradise beyond the horizon but a chapter in the tragic history of man-kind, in "the march of men across the world, in turn loathsome, friendly, laughable and sublime."[14]

· V ·

The choice of Rogier Gerard van Polanen as envoy of the Batavian Re-public to the United States in 1795, was not a wholly happy one for the new revolutionary regime. He was a Patriot, to be sure, but a moderate, not of the revolutionary stamp that had just triumphed; on his death the *Christian Register* of Boston would write that he "inclined somewhat to aristocracy." What clinched his appointment was probably that he was already on the scene, having arrived in the United States in 1790.

His judgment of the New World was not too favorable. Like Van Hogen-dorp, he found many flaws in the American Constitution; even after 1787 the people, in his opinion, had too much influence. Not much of the dream remained for a Dutchman who looked about him and saw the re-ality of America. Van Polanen, as a matter of fact, went so far as to assert that the American states had been much happier before the Revolution: "People from every station" had told him so.[15]

"America already provides an eloquent example of how precarious must be the State of a Country in which the common people have a direct influence upon the choice of the executive power," he commented on the occasion of Jefferson's election as president in 1800. As was to be ex-pected, this representative of Batavian freedom chose the side of the con-servative Federalists. Although he swore an oath in 1798 against the stad-holdership, federalism, aristocracy, and anarchy, he completely favored the conservatives in the United States. Like them, he found Jefferson, the champion of increased popular influence, the devil incarnate, the man "who with his collaborators has destroyed respect for government and has encouraged the birth of popular delusions." He thought all law and order would cease: "The administration of justice will be wrung from the clean hands of commonly acknowledged learning and respect and given over to the President's partisans." Respectable men were being reduced to beggary. The land was on the path to destruction.[16]

"The seeds of an impending civil war have already been sown," he re-ported in a later dispatch. Jefferson was a disciple of the French philoso-phers, "all that was lacking to bring a Nation already fallen into the most profound immorality and intoxicated by unparalleled prosperity into total profligacy." The Federalists gave warning in vain; the people supported Jefferson. Soon elections would be held in which "Democracy will show herself in her true, horrid shape. Every means, however low or shameful, will be used to inflame the enthusiasm of the people and to bring them over to the interest of a single party. Taverns and public houses are the principal stages upon which the popular leaders play their role and instruct the people under the favor of strong drink."[17]

The spectacle of an authentic democracy, with all its evils and imperfections as they could be seen then in America, was for a Dutch observer, even one with the official Batavian principles, just too much. The distant example became a warning when seen close up; this is made amply clear from the eyewitness account of Van Polanen. He was scornful and fearful of America. With his nose pressed down upon reality, he was afflicted with the same ambivalence that was present in observers from afar. America would not do; it seemed to be falling apart in party strife. But at the same time it threatened to become a country of colossal strength. The Dutch envoy reported in 1799 that a representative from Virginia, Josiah Parker, had declared in Congress that a day would come when America would be a mighty land and lay down the law to the whole world, thus assuring the happiness of mankind. Van Polanen wrote down this observation: "Who, taking into account the important results that the present commotions in Europe may have, which already threaten the outworn Old World with total upheaval, will declare these prospects to be unfounded?"[18]

· CHAPTER 19 ·

America: An Example and a Friend

*But what is there to oblige a citizen of the
United Provinces to consider Americans as
friends of the Republic?*
JOHN ADAMS

 HE decade of the eighties in the eighteenth century may
be considered the prelude to a new age in the Netherlands. With its unrest, its mutual struggle of Dutch
against Dutch, its yearning for both a greater unity and a
more genuine, if still far from complete, influence of the
people upon the government, it forms the period during which the old
order was attacked at its heart and the new sought to come into being.
And the whole spectacle was in truth not a puppet play—on this Dutch
historians are now virtually agreed—in the hands of managers in London, Paris, and Berlin. The thesis of the Dutch historian Colenbrander
that Dutch weal and woe were determined abroad, and with it his contempt for the Dutch forefathers of the eighteenth century, has been overcome now. The Republic was not a province dominated by mighty neighbors; it was a country struggling for a new future and therefore open to
what was happening in the world at the time. Put in other terms, the fate
of the Dutch was decided not only by ministers of state; there was also a
spiritual, national movement. It was bourgeois in character—could it
have been otherwise?—and therefore ambiguous in its attitude toward
the ideals of the age. The words that were used could mean many things,
as was true wherever else the new ideas broke through, in America, for
example.

Popular influence, equality, representation—all these fine words were
spoken at the height of men's voices. But as the leading Dutch historian
of this period, Dr. C. H. E. de Wit, has shown in his broad and thoughtful
studies, we must listen carefully to who is actually doing the trumpeting.
The same thing said by two different persons is not the same thing.

What is clear in any case is that the American influence upon the events
of these years in the Netherlands was of fundamental importance. It is
true that there was an old democratic tradition in the Dutch Republic,

and we must agree with De Wit when he observes that the principle of inalienable rights of the people, which the popular party now made its slogan, not only betrays the influence of America but also has its roots in the history of the Netherlands. All the same, the influence of America was a great stimulant, he adds, and we have seen in these pages various examples of its action.[1] To establish causal connections is always a risky business for historians, but there seems to be no reason to doubt that the American Revolution wakened men's minds in the Netherlands, that the whole interrelated history of the Patriotic consciousness, the struggle with England, the intensification of partisanship, and so many other turbulent events of the time would have been unthinkable without what was going on in the New World.

As we have seen, the Dutch were slow to grasp the significance of the American revolt. America was a dream for them before it became a reality. American slogans were gladly used, but there was little comprehension of their import in America itself. In all the Dutch relationship with the New World there remained something vague, a faraway shape dimly seen. We have seen already how Dutch pamphleteers and even Dutch travelers could fall victim to misunderstanding. It came over the Dutch only slowly that freedom and popular rule were words that meant different things to different persons, in America as elsewhere; how could it have been otherwise when only in the course of time did the Americans themselves begin to form parties? The revolutionaries John Adams and Thomas Paine had little in common, but in the beginning, seen from afar, they looked like brothers in battle.

Only after a number of years did the Dutch begin to have a keener understanding of which Americans they really wished to follow, and in those same years many of the Americans—John Adams is a good example—began to calm their revolutionary zeal and to steer a more conservative course. The initial enthusiasm for the American ideals that we found in Van der Capellen, Van der Kemp, and so many others was still broad and blurred, without real direction. They admired a freedom and even an equality that they wanted only in moderate form in their own country. As the years sharpened the powers of discernment, the situation changed.

A good example of this uncertain admiration is what was written in the Netherlands about the federal system in the United States. A topic that had a background for the Dutch in their own history, it was "food for philosophers," who gladly served up their philosophical disquisitions upon it. We have already seen that Pieter Paulus, while still young, praised the American Articles of Confederation as almost equal in perfection to the Union of Utrecht, although he soon came to the conclusion that such a loose federal system in the Netherlands would inevitably lead to its downfall—as it did during his own lifetime. Many in America were coming to the same conclusion about their Confederation. But how tightly the Dutch provinces should be bound together in their union was a bitterly disputed point in the Netherlands. Where in the United States it could be considered a proof of conservative attitude to work for a strong national government—a conservatism to which, as so often, the future belonged—and Jefferson's adherents upheld "states' rights," the situation in the Netherlands was exactly the opposite.

There also resulted in America a shift in the meaning of words. The word *federalism*, which really referred to the Confederation, was adopted and expropriated by the men who wrote the Constitution of 1787 and made the Confederation (Dutch *statenbond*, German *Statenbund*) over into a federal system (Dutch *bondsstaat*, German *Bundesstaat*). They began to label their opponents, the original federalists, with the contemptuous name "Anti-Federalists"; they named the essays in which they defended their achievement the *Federalist Papers*; and in that brilliant work they sharply condemned all European federal systems because they were too loose. Essay 20 of the *Federalist Papers*, written by James Madison, is wholly devoted to the Seven Provinces of the Netherlands— "United," as they were usually called, but Madison's point is that they really were not—and Madison has not a single good word to say for them. On paper the constitution embodied in the Union of Utrecht might look very fine, but the reality was bad: "Imbecility in the government; discord among the provinces; foreign influence and indignities; a precarious existence in peace, and peculiar calamities from war." The Dutch example taught the Americans that more unity was needed to hold a number of provinces ("states," as the Americans called the members of the federal system) together. Thus American federalism became centripetal, while the Dutch was centrifugal.[2]

There is no reason to be surprised, therefore, that Dutch observers were somewhat confused in their reactions to this complicated reality. Admiration for the loose federal system that was in force before 1789 (the year that the new Constitution replacing the Articles of Confederation went into effect) was loud and vague. What did it really mean when a cautious reform plan like that offered in the *Grondwettige Herstelling* of 1784 praised the American confederal system as a model? "By means of such a bond, the Swiss, the United Netherlands and the United States of America gained their independence and thus rose to be notable Powers." Is there anything in such praise beyond emphasis upon the greatest possible provincial autonomy? And must we not add at the same time that such emphasis does not at all imply increased popular rule? America was an example from afar.

Furthermore, what should we mean by "popular rule"? Does it include anything more than that the people should speak up from time to time, but not too loudly, as had occurred during the petition campaign in the spring of 1782 on behalf of recognition of America? "We see clearly that this is the voice of the People and that in a free Republic vox Populi is Vox Dei . . . : this has often been considered to be so in this Republic," wrote the *Zuid-Hollandse Courant* at the time, and many would have agreed. For who were the people who spoke with God's voice other than the prosperous bourgeoisie? This was the clear argument in reply to those who feared radicalism. "The shouting of some Preachers against the presentation of Petitions, who called it *a turbulent passion of an unrestrained Populace, a Break-in of the Common Folk in the Council Chamber*, and the complaining Merchants *the Dregs of the People*," was contradicted, Loosjes wrote angrily, by the names of those who signed the petitions, for they were all prominent persons. It was Mandrillon's opinion that the whole movement of protest had begun with those petitions; it was then that the protesters began to be concerned with "the affairs of Government."[3]

But more conservative spirits, even in the ranks of the Patriots, were still shocked by the method of petitions. Van der Capellen himself, as we have already seen, was scandalized by it. The moderate Patriot and educator J. H. Swildens found the whole movement to be mistaken. "Didn't the Petitions frequently become Tippler's Plea? You grasp what I mean. One signs because he has been threatened, another to ingratiate himself, a third to get customers, and a fourth for a bribe."[4] Even if the method of petitions was a good one when applied in 1782—at least it had a good aim and a good outcome—it was not one that could properly be used all the time.

Opinions as to how much the people should have an influence upon government and how it should be exerted were very divided. It is evident that there was a gradual radicalization, at least among the bourgeoisie, during the decade of the eighties. Where some shrank back from the quite limited method of petitions, others went further and demanded representation. But that, in turn, is a concept that has many meanings and one that had its own past in Dutch history. In England it had been "virtual representation" that the Americans had confronted; in the Republic of the United Provinces that same notion of representation without participation had many defenders. In the United States, too, there was much division over this problem. The constitution of Pennsylvania provided for far-reaching popular participation in government, but traditional prudence controlled that of Massachusetts. It is probably characteristic that it was the Massachusetts constitution that was most influential in the Netherlands—its author, John Adams, had of course seen to that—while the Pennsylvania one had almost no echo.

We find this reflected in an avowed conservative, Van de Spiegel, the Zeeland councillor pensionary who, after the Prussian intervention and Orangist revolution of 1787, was put at the helm of Dutch politics as Holland's grand pensionary. Van de Spiegel, a typical representative of the Dutch Old Regime, a powerful man, intelligent, well-read, and conservative to the core, wrote several extensive defenses of the Union of Utrecht. In one of them he was happy to use a quotation from the French Enlightened writer, Abbé Mably, whose *Letters on the Form of Government and Laws of the United States of North-America* had been published in Amsterdam, first in a French edition in 1784 and the next year in a Dutch translation. Mably had criticized the constitution of Pennsylvania and heaped much praise on that of Massachusetts, written by his friend John Adams. "The political thinker Mably," Van de Spiegel wrote, "when asked for his opinion about the Constitution of the United States, has correctly said that such democracy was an excellent government for a country no larger than Sparta, and with the customs of Sparta, but he was not so favorable to democracy as a government in larger states and 'with different customs.'"

The best example is undoubtedly the doctoral dissertation defended at Leiden University in 1784 by a young man from Deventer, in Overijssel, by the name of Rutger Jan Schimmelpenninck (who later, during the Napoleonic period, would become one of the most important leaders of the country). Its title was *De Imperio populari rite temperato*, that is, "A Well-Organized Popular Government," but in a second edition he obviously thought the title too radical and put *caute* in place of *rite*, so that it became a "carefully" rather than rather than "well" organized democracy. The little book, only eighty-four pages long, was translated at once into Dutch, with the purpose, according to the introduction, mainly to make clear how great was the difference between liberty and license, between a free popular government and anarchy. Indeed, the translator observed that the same principles underlay both Schimmelpenninck's book and the work *Grondwettige Herstelling* (Constitutional restoration).

The work by young Schimmelpenninck much pleased Adams. It begins by controverting Rousseau's idea of "the purest Democracy" and notes at once that the great mass of the citizenry are not at all governed by reason but are ruled by their passions. These were ideas that touched Adams to the quick. The entire little book is filled with the spirit of Adams: the people possesses *Majestas*, sovereignty, but not *Imperium*, government. It entrusts government to its representatives in free elections. There should be a council, neither too large, which results in confusion, nor too small, which gives rise to oligarchy. A radical element in Schimmelpenninck's conception is that the election must be public. But the young doctor of laws, like Adams, finds that natural differences between men must continue to exist, that government should be in the hands of the best people, and that of course only those who own property have an interest in the social order and therefore should receive the right to vote. Property, age, independence, and knowledge—these are the criteria for the suffrage in Schimmelpenninck's dissertation, as they were in the constitution of Massachusetts. Universal suffrage would bring confusion and decline. The "lowest order of the people," those who pay no taxes, have to be excluded.

The voters should elect those who govern them, the book continues, and they should also be able to recall them. In this proposal, Schimmelpenninck is somewhat more radical than Adams and clearly shows the influence of Rousseau. There is no necessity, he held, to state reasons for recall; it is simply withdrawing the delegated right to govern. But representatives do not have the right to resign their offices, for they are in the service of the community. (It is interesting to note that the same argument was made with regard to the kings of France by royalist writers.) If they fail, they may be punished, but not if they merely err. Every crime requires punishment, as in America, where the article on impeachment of the president in the new Constitution reflects the same attitude.

In the second chapter of his little book, Schimmelpenninck seems to fall more strongly under Rousseau's influence. This is where he exalts the general will of the people, to which all must submit, even those who oppose. As a citizen, then, one approves what, as a person, one rejects. All citizens may be called to all offices, and therefore they will be zealous in striving for the good. The author waves away all objections that popular government brings with it partisanship and unrest; these are excesses, the result of wrong specific arrangements of government but not inherent in democracy itself. He ends with a romantic touch: a republic is indeed possible, but only if opulence is combatted, for the difference in possessions must not be too striking. And how can this be more easily achieved than in farming, the ancient warranty of equality and virtue?[5]

What Schimmelpenninck proclaimed, for all its moderation, was still radical in the eyes of most Dutch Patriots. His acceptance of real instead of "virtual" representation, if it had been adopted, would have meant a genuine renewal of the Dutch constitution. A straight line ran from this program of 1784 to the declaration that citizen groups presented to the States of Holland in August 1787. De Wit tells us that the principles of the modern state are already present in this Declaration. "Although these demands arose in the first place out of Dutch conditions, the influence of the American [state] constitutions is visible in it. . . . Especially the constitution of Massachusetts, drafted by Adams himself, had made a strong impression in the Netherlands, and it was defended by R. J. Schimmelpenninck in his dissertation as a model for a democratic state. The American experiment provided proof in the debate with oligarchy that a moderate democracy was feasible." But we should add that what was relatively conservative in America was quite radical in Dutch circumstances.[6]

How far Schimmelpenninck himself went remains a question. He had collaborated with such authentic radicals as Wybo Fijnje and Pieter Vreede in drawing up the so-called "Leiden Draft," another programmatic statement in which the Patriots demanded "Democracy with Representation." But caution was called for, within the country as well as internationally. French support for the Patriots could be obtained only if they did not proceed in too radical a manner. We also find Schimmelpenninck's signature under the "Draft of a Plan for an Aristo-Democratic Constitution," drawn up by a number of Amsterdam citizens in May 1787 "to prove to the Ministry in Versailles that good Citizens do not intend by reform or improvement of the Government of the Republic, particularly of [the province of] Holland, to introduce a purely Democratic Government." The plan included a demand for "democracy by representation," but that meant that government would be conducted by those "whom it has pleased the People from time to time to choose and appoint as their Representatives: whereby we, the Undersigned, demonstrate that we are averse to complete Democracy, in which the Citizens together and individually perform the work of Governments."

No adventures *à la Rousseau*, therefore. There would be no election of the members of the city government. There would be election only of a double list of candidates by the citizens in their districts; from it the town council would select a permanent "Board of Citizen Delegates," with the task of informing the city government of the wishes of the people by means of "petitions, remonstrances, memorials, etc." This board would also have the power to convene the citizenry from time to time "to learn and get to understand their Opinion and Wishes."[7]

This was how cautious and moderate the radicalism of the Amsterdam Patriots really was. The American example that they wished to follow, once they understood something of the American reality, was definitely not that of Thomas Paine but at most that of John Adams, the conservative revolutionary who did not really believe in human perfectibility.

· II ·

If there was a single point where the Dutch clearly and noisily profited by the American example, it was that of arming the people. In this, as in other things, it was Joan Derk van der Capellen who showed the way. Back in 1774 he had translated into Dutch an English pamphlet of 1698 by Andrew Fletcher, under the title *Political Discourse upon the Necessity of a well-ordered Citizen's Militia*. Fletcher, an extreme radical, had wanted to abolish the whole standing army and replace it by an armed citizenry. There was repeated discussion of this idea during the eighteenth century; it was very popular among the Enlightened philosophers, and in the final decade of the century it would culminate in the levée-en-masse of the French Revolution.

But Van der Capellen, as always ambivalent, radical in feeling and prudent in mind, significantly moderated Fletcher's ideas. As in the business of democracy, he wanted change, but only by adding to what existed, not by replacing it. There would have to be citizens' militia, but only alongside the standing army; by themselves, an armed citizenry could not meet the needs of war: "I am not foolish enough to recommend the *Spartan* Plan of Mr. *Fletcher* to any European People, as some people have imagined I intended. This would not be endured by our bodily and spiritual constitutions, which have been enfeebled by opulence." Nonetheless, he called in martial language for arming the people, citing the examples of Switzerland and America. The farmers and burghers all had to own their own muskets and bayonets, and they could train with them—is there anything more Dutch than this?—on Sundays after church services. But that was what the Union of Utrecht had prescribed in its eighth article: arming of every man from eighteen to sixty years of age.

In any case, Van der Capellen was himself too weak physically and spiritually to accomplish much of this in person, and he experienced a bit of ridicule when he played soldier. "I have been compelled to take command upon myself," he wrote to his cousin Van de Marsch, "I could not refuse it. What each man will try in order to get promoted out of the ranks is incredible. . . . There is more trouble in this Militia Society than in leading an entire regiment of regulars."[8]

The radical quarter Oostergo in the province of Friesland made the same appeal to the Union of Utrecht and the American example when it proposed organization of a citizens' militia. "Without such a means, it is probable that the honorable, exemplary, and wonderful nation of North America would never have reached the position it holds at present, in which we pay it so much respect and admiration." A commentary upon the Oostergo proposition in the *Post van den Neder-Rhijn* reads like a treatise by Mao Tse-tung on guerrilla tactics. No enemy can defeat a citizen's army, it is "too well positioned, an army of militia heroes avoids danger by dissolving and becoming plain citizens again; ready at the first wink to take advantage of a more favorable opportunity and to gird on their swords. The North Americans repeatedly provided examples of this Tactic in their War and so frustrated their enemies."

The *Grondwettige Herstelling* advocated a similar approach when the Dutch Barrier fortresses in the Southern Netherlands came into peril. The Emperor was "obliged, as the English were, to wage war at a great distance from his principal possessions." The Dutch would therefore be "in the same situation that the States of North America were in recently, . . . Let us then . . . follow in the footsteps of the Americans, who themselves took our own Forefathers as an example to imitate. Let the whole Republic become an army camp. Let all inhabitants become accustomed to weapons to be used in the defence of the Fatherland." And so on. It is all just romantic over-excitement, however, without any real importance. The truth of the matter was that the Barrier fortresses could not be defended, and they fell to Joseph II during the next years without a blow being struck.[9]

As a weapon in foreign policy, the citizens' militia was completely worthless. But within the country it appeared to have great importance at least in the eyes of the impassioned Patriots. Soon the Patriotic appeals were all full of martial demands and ideas. To resist "internal tyranny," armed groups should be established, divided by lot in three classes, "as was undertaken in North America." The members would be obligated to report in case of need, either in person or "making another available in their place." That sounds cautious enough, but as the political conflict grew more tense over the years, there was a very impressive amount of military activity—parades, uniforms, banners, training. At least it looked impressive, as we can still see in the innumerable colored prints of this activity which have come down to us. We see them in formation, swearing noble oaths, unfurling banners, muskets at the ready, a play performed with the highest seriousness. For that is how they must have felt it; in all that display there speaks an awakened civil consciousness, a passionate nationalism, that must not be underestimated, even though in the hour of danger it would not all be as bold a display as it looked at the rehearsal. According to the *Nederlandsche Courant* of 13 April 1786, the civil guards would grow to eighty thousand men, "the bravest and boldest part of the nation," by summer. Even children took part in military training, and when they hit the target during firing practice, they were rewarded with silver medals.[10]

There is hardly a more charming commentary upon all this activity than the writings of the romantic poet and disillusioned Patriot Gerrit Paape. With much sympathy and a good deal of irony, he describes the parades, the banners, the drums, the bucklers, and especially the celebrations: "Here they ate and drank, in the plain taste of the old Batavians; while always at hand were Poets and Orators, who explained the purpose of the meeting, and had the Patriotic throng sing Patriotic songs." Did all that singing help very much? Probably just as little as in church: "The Songs were gloriously sung;—but how many glorious Songs have been sung through the centuries in Church, where the senses remain sober, and how much good has it done?—The civic, that is, the Patriotic virtues, can be aroused in the hearts of men, even less than Religious Virtues, with lips wet by drink, let the song be as fine as it can be."[11]

Paape seems to have understood the impulse of patriotism and, it must be said, also the importance of the singing. For the significance of the Patriots continued to be that they gave a new impulsion to Dutch national feeling. Like the Americans, as they cheered for humanity, they became aware of their own identity. And they kept it lively with much Dutch gin, much Dutch song, and much honest conviction.

· III ·

The Americans who watched the spectacle of Dutch party strife felt a tie of kinship—and could it have been otherwise?—with the Patriots, and at first made as little distinction between left and right, radical and conservative, as the Patriots for their part had when they looked at America. Eyewitnesses like Adams and Jefferson, the two most important American observers of the Dutch political scene, only gradually perceived the deep differences and tensions that existed; then they ceased to find it obvious which side they favored. On his return visits to The Hague, Adams reported on the increasing controversy in the Republic. In an important letter of the summer of 1785, he described the two parties: The Patriots were the party of the middle classes; the Prince's adherents that of the highest and lowest classes. For the Patriots, the stake was to limit the power of the stadholder, and they had won the game very nicely; they were now the dominant party, led by two very able men, Van Berckel and De Gijselaar. Adams stressed that they felt closely bound to America, whose revolution had roused them from their lethargy. They were forming volunteer corps everywhere and even children paraded on the streets. No wonder that everything made him think of America in 1775: "This Party views America with a venerating partiality, and so much attached are they to our opposition, that they seem fond of imitating us wherever they can, and of drawing parallels between the similar circumstances in the two countries." An army officer who had gone over to the Orangists was instantly branded a Benedict Arnold.[12]

Abigail Adams, who visited the Netherlands the next year with her husband, reciprocated with fondness, but also with concern, the friendship shown her by the leaders of the Patriots. The old spirit of freedom had been reawakened, she wrote, not least by the connection with America, but whether they would succeed in achieving their great ideals without the spilling of blood was very much a question. John and Abigail together attended the ceremony of oath-taking of the new, very democratic members of the town council in Utrecht, and they were very happy at what they saw. "In no Instance, of ancient or modern History, have the People ever asserted more unequivocally their own inherent and unalienable sovereignty," wrote Adams to Jefferson. He regretted that he did not have enough time to tell him more at the moment. The regret is also ours, for we are of course struck by the question why Adams had such admiration for an act of democratic politics that went quite a bit further than he himself favored. The seizure of power by the popular party with the use of force in truth contradicted Adams's own fundamental principles of balance in government.[13]

Even more remarkable is that it was Jefferson, so much more democratic in his thought than Adams, who viewed the democrats in Holland and Utrecht provinces with much greater mistrust. In fact, we must draw the conclusion that Jefferson, certainly in his view of the process of European radicalization in France and the Dutch Republic, was not at all as democratic as we usually believe. Admittedly, the American historian R. R. Palmer has made the same point very clearly in an article with the significant title "The Dubious Democrat," which discusses Jefferson's attitude toward events in France; but Jefferson's observations in the Netherlands are of the same character. The Dutch, he wrote in August 1787, were busy cutting each other's throats. The stadholder's party was winning. A few days later, he explained the situation precisely to Jay: There were three parties, "Stadhoulderians, Aristocrats, and Democrats." The aristocrats were divided into "Violent and Moderate" factions; the first wanted to maintain the power of the regents intact, but if they had to, they would rather switch to an agreement with the stadholder than with the common people. The moderates were ready if necessary to accept a "temperate mixture of Democracy," that is, election of the members of government by the people. But their moderation shattered on the extreme demands of the Democrats, who spoke of people's tribunes, annual accountability, and the recall of members of government when the people desired it. Thus a break had to ensue between them and the moderates, who also went over to the stadholder's party. Unless the Democrats became wiser, the stadholder's influence would grow great again. But nothing was certain, for foreign intervention of course became ever more probable in the face of so much unrest in the Netherlands and such greed on the part of her neighbors.[14]

Adams's hindsight judgment was cooler too, as is clear from his reactions to the events of the fall of 1787 in the Dutch Republic. What happened in the United Provinces in that September and October was that Prussia and England put an end to the Dutch disorders, reestablished the insulted Orange dynasty in their rights—the Princess of Orange had been detained by a citizen militia corps at the border of the province of Holland at Goejanverwellesluis—and approved a fierce reaction against the party of the Patriots, who hastily fled to safety in France. Adams felt great pity for his old friends, but he warned Jay that the United States should now follow a policy of strict impartiality. His argument was a blueprint for true American isolationism, in phrases that would later be used by many American leaders, not least by his own son John Quincy Adams in the formulation of the Monroe Doctrine: "That our country may act with dignity in all events, that she may not be obliged to join in any way without the clearest conviction of the justice of the cause, and her own honor and real interest, it is indispensably necessary that she act the part, in Holland, of perfect independence and honest impartiality between the different courts and nations which are now struggling for her friendship, and who are all, at present, our friends." For this reason the excessively pro-French attitude of Dumas and the Van Staphorsts, however appealing it might have been, had to be rejected.

In a later letter his tone became sharper. The Patriots had bet upon the wrong horse in hoping for help from France. He had indeed the highest regard for many of the leaders who had fled the Netherlands, but the fact was that they had failed. He doubted that they really understood "the nature of government." Furthermore, and this was an accusation of the most serious sort, they had lost contact with the common people.

The next spring, during his last sojourn in Amsterdam, he pronounced a judgment of extraordinary bitterness upon the men with whom he had worked so closely, who had supported him so strongly in the difficult years before recognition. "The Patriots in this country were little read in History, less in Government: knew little of the human heart and still less of the World. They have therefore been the Dupes of Foreign Politicks, and their own undigested systems."[15] With these words, Adams said farewell to the Dutch period of his life, and also to his own revolutionary past.

CHAPTER 20

America: An Example from Afar

*In fact what a crowd of lessons do the
present miseries of Holland teach us.*
THOMAS JEFFERSON

HAT, we may wonder, would have happened if the essentially moderate American Revolution had not been followed by the French Revolution, which was so much more radical? Would the influence of America upon developments in the Netherlands have proved lasting? Would the movement toward greater democracy have been able to continue gradually in the Netherlands, as it did in the New World?

What is the use of such "iffy" questions in history? As the English poet John Masefield has written, "time pours and will pour, not as the wise man thinks, / but with blind force to each his little hour." The French Revolution, with all its violence, came like a force of nature. Ever since contemporaries and historians have explored in their minds and debated with each other what the true relation was between these two revolutions in America and France, and whether they were essentially kindred or contrary in character. There is no need to resurrect that debate here. We need only examine how far the eruption in France changed the Dutch relations with America and their vision of that country, how the American revolt, once so admired, was shoved aside and neglected because of the far more spectacular events so much closer at hand in France.

A confusion of thought and feelings resulted. A debate among the Dutch about the causal relations between the two revolutions was inevitable. True conservatives did not doubt that they were related as cause and effect, but the supporters of America were divided among themselves, depending on how radical they were. Some wanted to find an identical spirit at work in both America and France; others strove to play one revolution against the other. In the long run some conservatives too began to change their minds, as they saw how the American Revolution was steered into the channels of law and order. Adriaan Kluit, the thoughtful conservative historian of law and political institutions, had originally had no doubt that good King Louis XVI had nurtured a snake in his bosom: "The efforts to raise the Americans to the level of a *free Republic* . . . had to be the prelude of what would later be undertaken and hatched in France." Another outspoken conservative, Van Goens, saw one long chain of events, a single sinister plan behind everything. "It is not in France, it is in Holland, and originally in America, that the French revolution is to be studied, and the true key and means of it . . . to be look'd and traced back to. . . . Whatever horrors were committed in France, on a large scale, had been plotted in miniature and tried in shew in Holland. . . . It is in Holland and ultimately in America, that the Demon of Revolution has served his prenticeship."[1]

But when they studied events more carefully, some of these antirevolutionaries became less sure. When the Revolution came to a halt in the United States, when the Constitution of 1787 restored "law and order," they took a new look at the situation. When Kluit turned to pour the vials of his wrath against the French Revolution, he gave the Americans a passing rap on the knuckles—his principles were as firm as a rock—but he was glad to notice that "a new Structure of Government has been laid down and happily brought to completion" in America. What a difference there was from France, where the heresies of Thomas Paine were all the rage. He could blaze out for pages on end against "the chimerical plan of reform" of the American radical, who was "praised to the skies." His writings were "eagerly read in the Netherlands," Kluit observed bitterly, and "a huge fuss was made over them."[2]

The French Revolution also changed Van Hogendorp's judgment of America to a more friendly one. On his return home in 1784, still disillusioned, he had reported to the stadholder that the United States had absolutely no future. He began a career in Dutch politics and almost completely forgot about his progressive friend Jefferson—Jefferson, to be sure, did the same with him. When the great explosion of violence occurred in France, however, Van Hogendorp began to view what he had seen in the New World in a more favorable light. He reflected upon the difference in the long, and unfortunately still unpublished, essays that he wrote in the years 1792 and 1793, in a bold, flowing hand. Sure of his cause and of himself, he praised with verve the new Constitution of the United States, which established equilibrium, not equality. He abhorred the principle of equality: "North America has indeed known this doctrine but has rejected it. It was not able to take root there any more than elsewhere. It has remained in the speculative brains of conceited philosophers or in the pages of pamphlets which have long since been forgotten. But this wise and good nation, the people of North America, have built upon a different foundation than the chimerical doctrine of equality." The Americans were united, while in France only the guillotine "has become the impulse behind all service to the Fatherland and the *Gouvernement Révolutionnaire* has replaced unanimity."

The French dream could not exist, equality could not exist, unless "every citizen does by himself what is good without the prescription of the laws or the Compulsion of the Government," but this could never be "so long as men are not angels, that is, so long as men are men." When Van Hogendorp was writing these lines, had he read the *Federalist Papers*? It seems very probable, for he is repeating almost word for word Madison's famous statement in essay number 51: "But what is government itself but the greatest of all reflections on human nature? If men were angels, no government would be necessary." For Van Hogendorp the American Constitution was a reaction against the Revolution, and he was the first in the Netherlands and probably in all Europe to defend America upon conservative grounds, as the land of conservatism. His admiration was great because the Americans followed the English example, because they were not unique, not a model for others, but traditional. In a piece entitled *Omwendingen* (Turnabouts), written in 1793, he devoted a special chapter to America. In it he praised the "spiritual temperament" of the American people, which was responsible for the excellence of their Constitution. About the future, we have noted, he was not so certain, but be that as it may, in the present America was for him a model for the good, in glaring contrast to ill-starred France.[3]

The Orangist Van Hogendorp's praise for the American Constitution was matched by that of the Patriot Gerhard Dumbar. In Dumbar we meet a man typical of the moderate, erudite burghers of the small cities outside the province of Holland, especially Overijssel. Zwolle harbored Van der Capellen tot den Pol, Deventer produced Schimmelpenninck, and Dumbar came out of the same Deventer circles. His Scots forefathers had landed long before in the city on the IJssel River. His grandfather had been a scholar of some renown and had played an important role in the cultural and social life of his city and province; the same was true of the grandson, who was the traditional scholar in politics, cautious and moderate, his ideals always tempered by his prudence. He wrote long discourses upon such topics as "the right of majority voting in the meetings of the States of Overijssel," but he also took an active part in politics. In 1785 he was a delegate to the meeting of the Patriots in Utrecht, and the next year he was elected colonel of the citizens' militia corps in Deventer. In 1787 he was dismissed from his post as secretary of the city.

With more time to write, more than ever before, he devoted himself to a study of the American Constitution. In the three volumes of a book published from 1793 to 1796, he discussed at length the changes made by the Americans in their political institutions. It is interesting to see how close Dumbar is in his judgments to those of Van Hogendorp. True, he is more favorable in the abstract to the old Articles of Confederation, which demonstrated that the Americans "did not consider it beneath themselves to consult the wisdom of our forefathers, displayed two hundred years before on the stage of statecraft." But the Articles were lacking in something indispensable in any civil society, a clear sovereignty. For this reason a better constitution with more central power was absolutely necessary. Dumbar cited with strong agreement the arguments of the American defenders of the Constitution, Hamilton, Madison, and Jay, in their famed *Federalist Papers*. Indeed, an entire volume of his work consists of a translation of these pieces.

Dumbar's work is certainly the most thorough and important about America that appeared in the Netherlands in the eighteenth century. It gives a good historical background, borrowed from David Ramsay's *History of the American Revolution*; it describes fully the struggle around the Constitution in the years from 1787 to 1789; and it deliberately stresses the contrast between the American and French revolutions. There is, Dumbar holds, a striking similarity between the United States and the Republic of the United Provinces. Despite all the differences, it still has to be said that "there does not exist now and never has existed any country to which more or closer resemblances to our own can be found than in the State of the United Americas." The French Revolution was a lesson to the Dutch of how easy it was to demolish everything, how likely it was that concentration of power would give rise to "all the horrors of despotism," while "the American form of government is built upon the sound foundations which support the freedom, tranquility, prosperity and independence of the nation." There has never been a political system "that can better withstand the probing examination of the philosopher or of the Statesmen informed by history and experience." It should be an example to the Dutch. It guarantees in an ideal fashion the balance of powers and yet achieves "the unity and indivisibility of the common government."

Holding such principles, Dumbar could only be unfavorable to the developments in the Batavian Republic. Although he was restored to his offices in 1795 and elected as a member of the National Convention the next year, he held them only briefly because he refused to take the oath of fidelity to the principles of popular sovereignty. He was even more hostile to the coup d'état of 1798 by those who favored a unitary state, with the traditional provinces swept aside. For a considerable time he was held a prisoner with other recalcitrants in Honselaarsdijk. When reaction triumphed again in 1801 and a new government was established, Dumbar returned as a member of the Legislative Body. He died in 1802.[4]

A very similar lot befell Luzac, the editor of the *Gazette de Leyde* and John Adams's loyal friend. He too was an admirer and propagandist of the American cause and, measuring what later happened in France against the American example, condemned the Revolution there. He had become a person of authority in the Republic, since 1785 a professor of Greek and Dutch history at the University of Leiden. He followed closely the events in France, the homeland of his ancestors, and he grew increasingly opposed to what he saw. He expressed his views to the American chargé d'affaires at The Hague, William Short, after the French Republic was proclaimed in Paris. Why, he wrote to Short, had the cause of liberty, which was so honorable and worthy in America, become in France a cause of which one was ashamed? His answer, he said, was simple: The mass of the American people were virtuous, of pure morals, enlightened in religion and hence ready for freedom. But the majority of the French people was fundamentally corrupt, possessed neither good morals nor religion, and could therefore not be free, could not keep to the proper mean between slavish subjection and unbridled and unbounded license.

It was in the year of the Batavian Revolution, 1794–95, that Luzac became the rector magnificus (chancellor) of the university. In January 1795 the armies of the French Revolution had invaded the Dutch Republic and installed a new revolutionary government (events to which we will come back soon). Shortly after these sweeping changes the anniversary of the foundation of Leiden University was celebrated in customary fashion with an oration by the rector. On 21 February (the actual day was 8 February, but the celebration had been put off two weeks because of the recent revolutionary events) Luzac delivered his oration. It was delivered in Latin, as always, but had so much immediate significance that it soon appeared in Dutch. It was entitled *De Socrate Cive* (About Socrates as a Citizen), and it was dedicated, in a demonstration of political likemindedness, to his friend John Adams.

You in America, he told Adams in the dedication, have been able to avoid the mistakes of the Dutch Republic, "thanks to which our Fatherland, over a period of two hundred years, has been flung in its woe hither and thither, convulsed and finally hurled to its utter ruin." America is a country "where the Laws, holding the State to a most salutary leniency, protect the Freedom of the People but also hold them in bounds."

Like Adams, Luzac believed in a balance between aristocracy and democracy in a political triad, such as was defended in antiquity by all the sages. Solon "tempered *Popular Government* by the *influence of the rich*. He established a *Democracy*, whose mischiefs were kept from their worst consequences by the counterweight of a fair and salutary *Aristocracy*." The "best people" had to have the daily administration of government in their hands, but aristocracy should not degenerate into timocracy. There was always an elite and always had to be. Antiquity always thought well, not ill, of what was excellent, the best in man. It was precisely aristocracy that maintained a just mean between democracy and monarchy. Even Rousseau, whose work "contains so many striking truths alongside so many false and dangerous positions . . . remarks very well that they [the aristocracy] are of three kinds, a natural Aristocracy, an Aristocracy by choice, and an hereditary Aristocracy, and he says that the second is the true and the best." The mixed form of government, *imperium mixtum*, is the best, and Luzac feels compelled to declare openly "that I consider a Country where the *will of the People* is the *highest law* in ordinary government, the MOST UNFORTUNATE OF ALL."

Exactly like Adams, he based himself upon the essential conservative assumption that men are after all only men, that in the governance of the state one must take men not "as they ought to be" but as they really are. They are defined by "self-interest, self-love and other unrestrained passions." Whoever builds on ideals creates chimerical Utopias.

Such talk was certainly not particularly welcome in the joyful honeymoon of the Batavian Republic. The Committee of Vigilance soon smelled heresy and called the attention of the board of governors of the University of Leiden to the rector's troubling oration. Its specific accusation was that Luzac in his oration on Socrates had said that democracy contained the danger of an overthrow of all salutary institutions and had to end in a complete tyranny. The governors, crying with the pack, dismissed Luzac from his post in national history, and he was proud enough to lay down his Greek post as well.

John Quincy Adams, who returned to the Netherlands in 1794 as the envoy of the United States, reported the whole episode in letters to his father. Immediately after his arrival he went to see Luzac, and his old teacher received him warmly and explained his political position. Both parties in the country were against him, he said; the Tories called him a Whig and the Whigs a Tory.

Shocked by the news of Luzac's dismissal, John Adams passed it on to his friend Van der Kemp, who had fled to America in 1788 and was now living in northern New York state. Luzac was in difficulties, he wrote, because he was a man of sound understanding and education.

Luzac had also sent his oration to Washington, and the president replied comfortingly that the future would be better. In times when passions are in control, he continued, calm reason is driven out by extremism. When sound understanding returned, however, the man of principle regains his influence. And so would it be with Luzac, Washington assured him.[5]

The wise American president was proved right; Luzac's future was better. In 1802, like Dumbar, he benefited from the restoration of a moderate government and took up again his posts at Leiden. In the meantime he had poured forth all his gall in very erudite fashion in a work, published in 1800, that is one of the most curious writings that has ever appeared in print in the Netherlands. It was called *A Short Sketch of the French Revolution by a Society of Latin Authors*. It was published in Rome, according to the title page, *Prope Caesaris Hortas* (Near Caesar's garden), and in Paris, *Nabij den tuin der Tuileries* (Near the garden of the Tuileries). The date was given as "III Kalendas Septembres, A.U.C. MMCLIV" (meaning 30 August *Ab Urbe Condita* [since the founding of the city, Rome] 2554, which is 1800 A.D., for Rome was founded in 754 B.C.). The little book consists of nothing but a series of citations from the great historians of Rome—Livy, Tacitus, and others—each piece so chosen and arranged that altogether they form a complete history of the French Revolution sharply exposing all its cruelties and terrors with the authentic words of authors who had lived almost two thousand years earlier. Nobody could blame Luzac for classical quotations: he had become cautious, yet in his circumspect way he was able to be more critical than ever. With these clear, bitter words of the Roman historians the eternal martyrdom of mankind was recounted, emphasized, and branded by one of its most deeply hurt victims.

· II ·

With the story of Dumbar's and Luzac's fortunes we have entered the history of the Batavian Republic. In January 1795, when the country was gripped by intense cold, the armies of revolutionary France crossed the frozen rivers. They were accompanied by Patriots returning from exile. The poor stadholder fled with his family to England, the "true freedom" of rule without a stadholder was shouted from the rooftops, and a period followed of confused struggle for a new system. A National Assembly came into existence, and clear party groups were soon formed. The criteria around which they took shape were, just as in America, the relation between central and provincial authority and, even more important, how much direct influence the people would possess. In Holland, where the petty bourgeoisie was strongly represented in the local governments and where there was weariness and worse over the chicanery of the landward provinces during the preceding two centuries, advocates of a strong unitary system dominated; but elsewhere, as we have seen with Dumbar, provincial interests brought support for maintaining the federal system. Thus Unitarists and Federalists came to face each other. But this contrast was intersected by another involving how much democracy there should be, whether there should be complete or limited sovereignty of the people. It was this question that divided men most of all. Naturally, all sorts of intermediate positions were possible. In particular there were those who vigorously favored a strong central authority but wished to reserve it for a governing elite, with democracy kept very much under restraint. Thus there arose a middle party of moderates, led by no one less than Schimmelpenninck.

This is, of course, not the place to write the history of the Batavian Republic. We are concerned only to see how much was left of American influence in a period during which the Netherlands was more and more dominated by France. American influence meant little in practice, to be sure, because it was too far away. America itself swiftly ceased to have any further interest in the satellite state that the Netherlands became. In 1797, John Quincy Adams was recalled because his position in The Hague had little meaning left. He had settled the financial arrangements as well as could be expected and helped to solve a few remaining problems concerning ships captured at sea before 1795; but he had a great deal of time left for commenting upon the increased influence of France in Dutch affairs, and indeed in all Europe. His reports, which his father, who was then vice-president, passed on to Washington, had an essential influence upon the preparation of Washington's "Farewell Address," the first formal expression of American isolationism.[6]

For their part the Dutch "Democrats" could give little attention anymore to America. Their tussles with their French friends, who were only too close at hand, took up all their time. But the American example was still cited to some extent in the debates over a new form of government, especially over a new constitution. It continued to carry theoretical weight. We meet references to America repeatedly in the interminable debates in the national and provincial assemblies over the future of the country, and Dumbar's book was beyond question their most important source of information.

The idyll of a common awakening of a civic revolution in America, France, and the Netherlands was proclaimed and upheld as the point of departure for Batavian freedom. During the civil festival of 3 March 1796 in The Hague, upon the occasion of the opening of the National Assembly, spectators could admire an allegorical parade led by heralds "holding the Batavian, French and American flags, with National Ribbons." But in the debates that followed, in the day-by-day reality of politics, this linkage of the three countries did not proceed so idyllically. It soon appeared that the Federalists more and more called upon the American experience in defense of their moderate, conservative position, while the Unitarists took France as their example. Perhaps this is too simple and coarse a division, for there were many other tensions and antagonisms. An idealist complained: "I see with repugnance and sorrow the disastrous *lutte* [French for "struggle"] between two opposing parties which tear each other apart: I see self-interest, cabals, and cheating on both sides."[7]

But on the whole this party division dominated political life, and those who admired the Americans continued to be the Federalists. We have a clear picture of their circles from the reminiscences by C. L. Vitringa of his father Herman Hendrik Vitringa. The elder Vitringa was a Federalist much like Dumbar: he too came from the eastern provinces and therefore opposed the domination of Holland; he too was a fiery Patriot who became more moderate all the time; and he too was an admirer of America. His father, Vitringa the son relates, read a great deal about the American rebellion, such as Ramsay's *History* and Dumbar, and he was also a faithful reader of the *Gazette de Leyde*. His admiration for Luzac brought him into contact with the editor-professor, who in turn introduced him to John Quincy Adams. This demonstrates the existence of a direct American influence upon the Federalists. In any case, it was sufficiently strong so that the French government felt it to be a threat. The representative of the Directory in The Hague, François Noël, was emphatically warned against the American in his instructions.[8]

There appears to be something contradictory in these appeals of the

Batavian orators to the American experience. It was the conservatives, the Federalists, who called upon the American Federalists for support, but actually American federalism was exactly the opposite of Dutch federalism: the former called for unity, not for variety. It rejected the idea of states' rights, to which the Dutch Federalists clung so desperately. A few Unitarists, such as J. G. H. Hahn, perceptively called attention to this discrepancy. Hahn remarked in the National Assembly that he was in favor of the American system of federalism, "which is vastly different from the justifiably hated Federalism of the United Netherlands, for there [in America] the provincial government is purely local and cannot interfere in any way in the decisions of the general Assembly."[9]

But it was not the tension between central and provincial authority that decided the choice for or against America, with all due deference to the party names, but the question of democracy. The Dutch Federalists felt a kinship with their American namesakes, despite their differences about unity of government, because like them they were afraid of too much democracy. What they particularly admired in the United States— we have seen this already in Dumbar and Luzac—was the principle of balance, in which the elites were not brought down to a level of general equality. They were very cautious in their appeal to the American example because they did not want to be accused of conservatism—then, as nowadays, progressivism was the ruling fashion—and they denied that they wanted the Dutch republic "to be cast in the American mold," as the Amsterdam lawyer Johannes Gerardus Luyken expressed it. But, Luyken added, he did wish to resist the radical notion that it is "monstrous to put bounds upon the supremacy of the people." What is there monstrous about it? Was the American Constitution a political monstrosity? Just read what Dumbar wrote about it, he told the National Assembly.[10]

Cornelis Willem de Rhoer, another man from the eastern Netherlands, born in Deventer, a professor of Greek and history at Harderwijk, came forward with a different argument. He admitted that federalism could lead to tensions, but asked whether it was not true that the driving force of freedom had to be sought in the principle of balances and counterweights. He presented a report about it: Freedom is lost by an excess of freedom; popular sovereignty leads easily to despotism. Therefore there should be not one chamber in the legislature but two. In his support, De Rhoer cited not, as one might think, the great defender of the bicameral system, John Adams, but Thomas Jefferson. He had read in Jefferson's *Notes on the State of Virginia* that the "enterprising spirit of the Legislative Assembly [had] exceeded the limits of its power and had substan-

tially encroached upon the rights of the other Powers." Balance was the
saving word. "We want contrariwise to have the powers work together
for the happiness of the nation"; that was the true harmony that was possible, and America had returned to it after first wandering from the right
path.[11]

Another East Netherlander, the Zwolle lawyer Willem Queysen—like
Dumbar and Vitringa, he became one of the victims of the coup d'état of
the Unitarists in 1798, and he sat in prison for half a year—called the
French philosophes to support his case. Did Montesquieu and Rousseau
not advocate federalism? Did Mably not praise federalism "as one of the
happiest and wisest institutions in the Constitution of the Americans"?[12]

The Federalists were delighted that the Revolution in America had
been turned to the path of moderation. Like Luzac, they really believed
that there was a deep difference between America and France in religion,
in morals, and hence in the possibility of freedom. Dominie Ysbrand van
Hamelsveld, who preached the gospel for years in the pleasant little fishing village of Durgerdam and then became a professor at Utrecht, was
dismissed from his chair during the reaction of 1787 and returned to his
fishermen. He too placed stress upon this difference. He loudly praised
the American Constitution and added: "Yes, Citizen Representatives, I
declare openly that I join with the Americans in considering Religion as
one of the first rights and duties of the man and the citizen. . . . No, I am
not an ant, nor a lion either, but a rational Being raised far above all
beasts without reason, and as such I rejoice in the privilege of Religion. . . . Heavenly Father! [Here the journal of the National Assembly
records in the margin: "Here the speaker raised his eyes and hands to
Heaven."] whom I publicly confess, oh! may all my fellow-men acknowledge and feel with me this privilege and duty." Our preacher friend continued with the contrast between pious America and godless France, with
its murderous scaffolds.[13]

The Unitarists, still on the ascendant, were not ready to be persuaded
by the example of America, not even with such rhetoric as this. They did
not think the two nations could really be compared. America was so
large, and it had, too, such an extraordinary leader in Washington, who
held the country together. But they wondered what would happen when
he left the scene. Schimmelpenninck himself, holding cautiously to the
middle, used such arguments. "Don't present me with the example of
North America, and don't point out to me the happiness and the aston-
ishing prosperity which are enjoyed in those Provinces thanks to a Constitution built on a federalist principle.—Really, who can compare the

American States with the Netherlands? Who doesn't get lost in the immense difference of territory of these two countries? Who compares these Netherlands of ours, this little dot of ours on the Globe, with a country where a single province, Georgia, is larger in territory than the entire country of France?" As for the American Constitution, it had not yet passed the test. Time had been too short. How would it work when before long the great men would be gone? And then he made a prophecy, as others, like Van Hogendorp, had done: "One ought to wait for the time when, thanks to the increasing prosperity and amazing increase in population, a struggle of the many interests will be felt." Only then "and not before will experience put the seal of approval upon it, and only then may that model be put forward with the force of authority." [14]

America was not an example for them to follow, Schimmelpenninck repeated a short time later when the problem of the executive power came up for debate. In this respect he seemed to be closer to the Americans, fearing too great a popular influence and feeling that the executive power must not be a mere creation of the legislative power. But neither did he want the executive power to be chosen by the people. The Americans went too far in that respect. The people were not competent, "if left to themselves, to choose the most capable persons for posts of this kind." America seemed to have been able to do this, but there the right to vote was not all that widely distributed, and in any case Washington had been a generally beloved figure. [15]

True radicals went much further. They forthrightly and vigorously rejected the American example. Take the example of fiery dominie Bernardus Bosch, a wanderer and seeker, always in conflict, always overwrought. Why, he exclaimed, had the Americans lacked the courage "which the French later displayed to destroy all distinction of provinces and to organize and bring together the whole Nation in one body?" Federalism, he averred, would probably bring about the downfall of America, and it would show its strength after the death of Washington. When we think of the separatist tendencies in American history before the Civil War, this was not such a crackbrain prediction. The Rotterdam wine merchant Johannes Henricus Midderigh was at least as sharp in his statements as Bosch. He described the two parties that had arisen in the Netherlands: One really wanted to begin anew, to clear away all inequality; the other attempted to preserve the old order and put a veneer on it. The former honestly wished to make men free and happy; the other "wishes to remain as much as possible with the old order, and swears by nothing else than Roman Law, the Union of Utrecht, or moves Heaven and Earth to make the American Constitution more attractive than the French." [16]

This was plain language, a simplification of the contrast that was not without some justification. We can employ it as a sort of conclusion of our argument. In the imagination of the Batavian Patriots, America acquired a stronger and clearer image of conservatism, and authentic radicals preferred to seek their salvation with nearby France. And they were in fact saved by France. But in the end they discovered that they had been more fully "saved" by overpowering France than they really wanted.

America's image of conservatism was further strengthened by another question that came up for discussion in the National Assembly, that of slavery. During the debate over the article on colonies in the draft constitution, Pieter Vreede—who was an old friend of Van der Kemp and an extreme radical who was later to lead the coup d'état of 1798—raised the question. He was astonished, he told the assembly, that there was not a single word about slavery in the whole document. He admitted that it might be wrong to move with haste, but still abolition of such an abhorrent system ought to be adopted in principle. America, he observed, had at least set a term of fifteen years "for the cessation of the use of slaves and the slave trade." (Vreede must have had in mind the date of 1 January 1808, before which date the slave trade could not be ended, as part of the compromise of the Constitutional Convention. At the time that he was speaking, there were about eleven years still remaining before the date of the abolishment of the slave trade.)

There was agreement in principle with Vreede, but also emphasis upon the practical difficulties in abolishing slavery in the Dutch colonies. Schimmelpenninck, conservative as always, noted that Vreede himself admitted that it was not possible to achieve everything that was desired. Who gave Vreede the assurance that fifteen or even twenty years was enough? he asked. The president of the assembly, Jacob Abraham Uitenhage de Mist, a Federalist from Kampen (again, a town in the eastern Netherlands), remarked that the American readiness to abolish slavery existed only on paper. He could assure the assembly that just the year before, fourteen ships loaded with slaves from Guinea had landed in the United States. That was to be blamed, added the Groningen deputy B. W. Hoffman, upon "the intense selfishness of some American Cantons [the term *states* for what Europeans thought of as *provinces* or, as in Switzerland, *cantons* still remained a bit odd to most ears] which had threatened never to accept the Constitution if this did not remain open to them." [17]

· III ·

Thus, the American example was repeatedly employed, but with little practical effect. The picture of America was ambivalent, and remained so during the nineteenth century. Everyone sought what was to his own taste in America, but that was in fact not of essential importance. What really mattered was that America was far away and France close by. The irony and tragedy of history for the Batavians was that, yearning for freedom, they were compelled to follow the French models of the Directory and the Consulate, which, to put it mildly, limited freedom. The American example grew dim beyond the horizon, and many years would pass before it was rediscovered.

Epilogue

*Although I can not say with Jacob that my years
have been few and bad—yet, was it possible,
I could not wish to run once more
the same course.*
FRANÇOIS ADRIAAN VAN DER KEMP

 HAT remains to be told? The historian who realizes that his work is a story, a story he has loved to tell, must of course bring it to an end. Isn't that what every story is meant to have, an ending, a conclusion? But, on the other hand, history never ends. As Ecclesiastes said: "The thing that hath been it is that which shall be, and that which is done is that which shall be done." Even if we believe in more change than the Preacher in his wisdom was allowing for, it is clear to all of us that there are things which remain.

Perhaps we might say that the friendship between the Netherlands and the United States is a story that is not over, a tale of wonder and misunderstanding and friendship and mutual help for two hundred years. To tell it all would require another book, or many books. Here we have been dealing only with its beginnings, and as to the end, "who shall bring us to see what shall be after us?" May it be far away!

But there is something still to say about the people in the drama that I have recounted, the players on that broad stage, what happened to them, and to their work, whether it was preserved or destroyed.

First, to the nobleman with whom we began our tale, Joan Derk van der Capellen tot den Pol. Only a short time was granted to him, or rather, he wore himself out. He was always busy, always passionately involved in the events of his time, and yet always yearning for a peace that was elsewhere. He played with the suggestion of his friend Valck to come to America as a visitor. "Do not reckon it chimerical that I may come to visit you in your new Fatherland—I remark more and more that I need a change of subject. My ailment lies chiefly in the soul." But nothing came of the suggestion. He found no rest and tortured himself without end, wrote twelve to fifteen hours a day even while he was weak and ill, and worked himself up over everything, as his letters reveal to us. Even shortly before his death he wrote to a friend to tell his plans. He was thinking of writing another pamphlet about the people of the Nether-lands—but wondered whether he had the strength to do it. "Never has my health been bad for so long. A complication of ailments has held me down until now." He suffered from rheumatism and gout; his feet swelled up; there was an intermittent pain in his side; he was "painfully weak in the head." Therefore he had to limit himself, he wrote, "to taking note of the dawdling, the errors, the botched work, that we have seen every day since the war began, are either a fault of the constitution or of the per-sons who govern. Wherever the fault lies, it must be corrected or the Re-public will go to its downfall. As for me, I begin to believe with many others that our country is beyond saving, that the sickness has gone too far."[1]

A week after he wrote this prophecy, he died, on 6 June 1784. His death brought an explosion of Patriotic sentiments. He was mourned and adulated in a superabundance of rhetorically florid sermons, pamphlets, and poems. He was laid to rest, with his wife, who followed him in death a year later, in a beautiful sepulcher in an open field near Gorssel, for he did not want to be buried in a church. A poet wrote:

> Rest, my Capellen, rest! at last your pain halts,
> Safe here your mortal remains, your lifeless bones,
> Ev'ry Patriot your glory exalts,
> While God your heroic Soul brings to his thrones.[2]

But his bones were not safe. Three years later came the Orangist revolu-tion, and the fierce reaction against everything Patriotic did not spare Van der Capellen's grave. In September 1787 craven men destroyed the family coat of arms on the commemorative column, and a year later, in August 1788, they blew up the whole monument. The bodies of the Van der Capellens were then taken to a safe place and probably rest now in the Reformed church in Gorssel.

Another tribute to the memory of the great Patriot was made impossi-ble by the revolution of 1787. This was a monument to their hero that admirers had planned to erect in the choir of the Great Church in Zwolle. They commissioned an Italian sculptor to make the monument, and he completed a statue of the Overijssel nobleman, flanked by two allegorical figures and with the Netherlands lion before it. When the tide of power turned, however, the sculptures were never delivered, and they still stand, separated, in the gardens of the Villa Borghese in Rome. The beautiful choir of the church in Zwolle was spared the sculptor's pompous classicism.

· II ·

The counterrevolution of the fall of 1787 struck not only the dead Van der Capellen but also the living Dumas. This loyal, fervent man had devoted himself since the recognition of the United States in 1782 to his task as chargé d'affaires in The Hague, and his zeal had not flagged. But whether he was in fact chargé d'affaires was, as we have seen, an open question. In letter after letter, he pressed for legalization of his position. Adams supported his requests and urged Congress to let him know "in what light I am to consider this gentleman, and what relation he is to stand in to me." Dumas had been indefatigable in the American service, he added, and he should be rewarded.

So long as the Patriot party appeared to be dominant in the Dutch political struggle, Dumas could count upon a recognition of sorts in his relations with the government at The Hague. At one time he was even presented, as he reported without pride, to Princess Wilhelmina. And he intervened in the political controversies with a good deal more partisanship than was proper in a diplomat; he had very close contacts with such men as Van Berckel and De Gijselaar. At least partial recognition came from the United States in 1785, when Congress decided "that in consideration of the valuable services of Mr. C. W. F. Dumas, of the city of Amsterdam, in the United Netherlands, he be allowed and paid a salary of thirteen hundred dollars per annum, that the said salary commence the 19th day of April 1775, and continue till the further order of Congress, he continuing his services." That was very good indeed, but not good enough. Congress seemed unaware even of where he resided, and his position was paid but not settled. He was in a better position financially, because the French government contributed its mite with a pension (annual allowance) of fifteen hundred livres. Unfortunately, payment fell short of what was due him, and in October 1786 the poor American agent was still pressing the government to pay its arrears.[3]

Meanwhile, the continued absence of Adams meant that the Hôtel des Etats-Unis stood empty. Returning to his own home on the Wagenstraat, Dumas urged that something be done about keeping up the embassy building, which was falling into disrepair. Finally, during the tense summer days of 1787, Congress decided to fix up the house and to permit Dumas "to occupy and reside in the House of the United States." Early in September he was able to report that the work of repair had begun; a carpenter named Duyfhuys was hired, and he went to work with his helpers. But in the same month the Prussians marched into the Netherlands, occupied the country, and brought the stadholder back to his residence at The Hague in triumph.[4]

The fury of the Orangist populace at once broke out against everything at all Patriotic. Dumas, in fear of his life, fled to the French embassy and began to send out cries of distress. "I place my fate in the hands of God and the United States," he wrote to Jay, and he gave Jefferson a vivid description of his situation: "The situation in which I find myself with my wife is dreadful. Chaos rules everywhere. The civil administration here at The Hague obeys both the military and the people, who foam with rage. We were able to save our poor lives by seeking refuge in the French embassy, without our having even the necessities. . . . Our house is guarded by sentinels who live at our expense. I cannot go out for fear of being attacked on the way and assaulted with impunity, as almost happened yesterday when I was shouted at and followed."

In a later letter to Jay, he told of being accused of having supported a Patriotic volunteer corps and concealing weapons in his house. He was hooted at as "Kees," "The nickname they give here to Patriots, as they give them in America that of Jan Kee."[5] (Pronounced "Yan Kay," this was presumed to be the origin of "Yankee" by foreshortening from Jan Kees, "John Nick." Etymologists consider the derivation dubious.) Both Adams and Jefferson went into action. The former sent a memorial to the secretary of the States General, informing him that Dumas, whatever his status, was entitled to reside in the American embassy and therefore had a right to protection. He pressed Congress again for a settlement of Dumas's position. The attack upon the agent, who had been too closely attached to France, had not surprised him, but he would still regret it deeply if anything should happen to him.

Jefferson, for his part, went to the Dutch envoys to Paris, Lestevenon van Berkenrode and Brantsen, to protest against the threats to Dumas. The States General replied through Fagel with a promise that Dumas would be protected. But the tone of Fagel's letter, characteristic of the counterrevolutionary attitude in The Hague at the time, was extremely unpleasant. Adams's memorial about Dumas, he wrote, had not been taken "into formal discussion" because it was written in English and not in French. The States General would not happily see Dumas or any other citizen come to harm, but it would not conceal that in its opinion Dumas "little merits its protection, having conducted himself in a way which was improper in several respects." Therefore, Fagel concluded, he must press for the quickest possible replacement of Dumas by another chargé d'affaires.[6]

The American authorities were embarrassed by the Dumas question. Now their failure to recognize him while they kept him in their service was exacting its price. They wondered what they should do. It is evident from a letter from Abigail Adams to her son John Quincy how shocked she and many others were by the fate of the Patriots in Holland, but also how helpless they were to do anything for poor Dumas. That a country that once had withstood the Spanish Empire should now be humiliated by a few Prussians! "Poor Dumas and family have lived in a state worse than death; since to exist in constant dread of being dragged a victim to an enraged mob . . . is worse than death." But "as he never had any public character, or, rather never was commissioned by Congress," America could do nothing for him. Furthermore, he had made himself very hated by joining the anti-Orange party.

Even John Adams, for all his sympathy for Dumas, was ready to sacrifice him if need be for the interests of the United States. The United States, he wrote, would become much too easily involved in war if its agents concerned themselves with the domestic policy of other countries. In other words, Dumas endangered American isolation. What was left to the Americans, Adams continued, was either to dismiss Dumas or to ask the States General to explain their objections more fully. But Jay, who had become secretary for foreign affairs in 1784, did neither; he did not want to give way under pressure, but neither did he want to ask The Hague for more information about a man who held no official position. He drafted a full diplomatic reply and then did not send it. Thus the affair came to an end.[8]

But not for poor Dumas. In the fall he attempted to save himself and his position by proposing that he go to Brussels as an American envoy in order to conclude there a treaty of trade and friendship after the model of that with the Netherlands. But Jefferson, to whom he sent his request, would not hear of it. Dumas continued his activity. He saw to it that the new American Constitution was reprinted in Luzac's newspaper and had the coat of arms of the United States, which had been prepared on Adams's order, hung from the gable of the embassy. In the spring of 1788, Adams came to The Hague for his final visit, accompanied by Jefferson, whom Dumas met for the first time. Adams bade farewell to the government and received the customary medal, but Dumas wrote Jay that he received nothing, not even the same medal in a smaller size, as was proper.[9] He was tolerated, no more, and other unpleasant experiences were in store for him.

His marriage began to break up under all the blows that he had received. His wife talked of leaving him; she was tired, we may assume, of so many years at the side of so much excitement and selflessness. Dumas wrote to Jefferson shortly after the American's departure—and how characteristic this letter is of Dumas's illusions and his lack of human understanding: "I had hoped that personal acquaintance with Your Excellency would persuade my wife to pardon me for all that she has suffered in these troubles."[10]

In July he had to report to Jay that the side wall of the embassy had been painted orange during the night by miscreants. He had had it painted over but had presented no complaint; the culprits could not be found. He became depressed when he thought about the chaos in Europe; the situation was hopelessly confused. With Cicero he had to say: *Nihil simplex, nihil in politicis honestum, nihil illustre, nihil forte, nihil liberum* (nothing was simple or honest in politics, nothing great, or strong, or free). What a difference from the New World![11]

He got himself into new troubles by having "Agent of the United States of America" painted on his door. In no time there appeared a bailiff of Their High Mightinesses, who handed him a letter over the signature of *griffier* Fagel enquiring "why he had arrogated to himself to place on his door the Title of agent of the united States of America" and requesting a reply in writing. It was a bitter grudge that the powers in The Hague bore against him. He sent as an answer copies of the documents in which Congress granted him a salary and the right to reside in the embassy. In a long letter he argued that he had been in the service of America since 1775 and had been recognized by the States General in 1783, when they arranged the ratification of the treaties with him. At the end of September a decision came from Their High Mightinesses: Dumas had indeed functioned as Adams's secretary, but now that Adams had departed, no one could be in charge of his affairs. Since then he had never addressed himself to the States General with a request to be recognized as an agent. Yet he had been protected during the troubles of 1787, although he had not deserved it. The conclusion in any case had to be that he was only a private citizen and therefore had to see to it that the title was removed from his residence.[12]

Dumas had to obey, but he thought of a way out of the order. He reported to Jay that he had placed upon the embassy "Correspondent of the United States" in order to avoid difficulties, since the word *agent* was forbidden. But of course the ruling powers did not let him be. Early in October he was summoned to the Delegated Councilors, the permanent executive arm of the States of Holland. The chairman, Baron Van Wassenaar Starrenburg, ordered him to remove this new sign, and also the arms of the United States. "Obey!" the baron told him in gruff French. But the Hôtel des Etats-Unis did not belong to him, Dumas replied; the plenipotentiary minister had had the coat of arms made up and instructed him to have it hung up. How could he remove it now? He was willing to paint out the word *correspondent* if he had to, but no more.

But the chairman wanted the whole inscription removed and thundered again, "Obey!" He became angrier and finally told Dumas that he knew very well why his person was distasteful to the government. "I replied to Mr. Starrenburg that I did not know why and implored him to tell me. He remained silent and I withdrew."[13]

Dumas remained in the embassy for the time being, while his wife and daughter went to reside in the house on Wagenstraat. Probably damaged but not broken, he had withstood the shock of the first outburst of "Yankee, Go Home!" feeling in history. He sat all alone in the big empty house and read the newspapers. The year that followed was 1789. The great news of the French Revolution penetrated into his silent house and reawakened his buoyant spirit to life. If now all "papimania" and "feudamania" were really rooted out, he wondered, would that be the dawn at last of the great day of the "triumph, gentle, progressive and finally worldwide, of civil and religious freedom"? In 1790 he rejoiced at the great transformations in France. An incurable optimist, he now believed in "a citizen king, more solidly powerful than any of his confrères." A new age was dawning, *novus rerum nascitur ordo.* He, a seventy-year-old, would still see it, he said; he, a little Diogenes, all alone in the great barrel of the American embassy, asking nothing from all the Alexanders than that they ceased to block the sun with their shadows.

He now added to his signature "citizen of the United States." He fiercely took the side of Paine in his debate with Burke, that "Don Quixote of violence and deceit." He was enthusiastic about the French constitution of 1791, with its "truly representative" monarchy. But his personal life remained black. In 1792 he had to report that his wife, suffering from melancholy, wanted no more of him, and in April there was a legal separation of bed and board, which was still not settled in May because of the difficulties made by his wife.[14]

His despair drove him to writing poems in which he brought his yearnings out in words:

> When will the veil be torn away
> That keeps the world in darkness gray?
> Spirit of truth, must your light descend unbidden?
> Until what time shall you stay from us still hidden?

There was solace, however, in the thought that civilization was moving from east to west, where there still was a worthwhile future. With all his emotionality and insecurity, Dumas remained a man of the eighteenth century. In one of his last letters to Adams, he proclaimed again his belief in progress: "I firmly believe that Providence will finally turn the troubles of our moral world to good purpose, just as it does earthquakes and volcanic eruptions. While I wait and witness that the Americans are happy, you make me as happy as possible, considering where I am. May God continue his blessings upon the best possible representative Democracy." [15]

Two months after this confession of faith with its fullness of hope, he experienced for the last time another great revolution. The French came, and the liberty tree was erected on the public squares of Holland. This was the fulfillment of his life, and he rejoiced: "Providence has shattered the despotism of the hated oligarchy by freezing the waters of the flooded countryside and making them a roadway for the French." But he was still a child of misfortune, and no rest was granted him. Everything looked fine, and even his wife returned to him. During the spring they were sitting together, an old couple now, when—as Dumas related in a letter of protest—a man and his wife presented themselves and informed them that they were being billeted on the Dumases. If they refused, a detachment of grenadiers would be sent. Dumas became furious, but his wife, "even more incapable than myself of facing scenes of tumult," calmed him down, and they let their strange guests come in. They soon suspected that the guests were imposters and had not at all been sent by the Committee on Housing. The man was not a French soldier but a Dutchman. Dumas complained to the authorities, and there is every reason to believe that his protest was accepted, although no documentary proof of it remains. In August, Dumas received official reparations for all the obloquy he had suffered under the old order, and with such honors he certainly would have been molested no further.

Thus his life moved to a close in a major key. Thankful and satisfied, he wrote one last hymn in justification of his life: "Thanks to the King of

Ages (the only one I revere and love because he is the only one who is good and wise), what was my constant solace amid the persecutions now constitutes my victory." The false rulers from before 1795 who had wished to destroy him were now themselves destroyed, and he felt like one of the blessed of the Bible, with a reference to the Beatitudes: Blessed are those who are persecuted for the sake of righteousness. Less than a year later, he died at the age of seventy-five on 11 August 1796.[16]

· III ·

A few of the most important figures in this book—Luzac, Van der Kemp, Adams—still require a bit more of our attention. The first, Luzac, we have already followed until 1796, when he was dismissed by the new authorities. Like other "aristocratic Patriots," he was carried along by the movement of events, low and high. He devoted himself after his dismissal to scholarly work—he counts as one of the most important representatives of the "Graecophile renaissance" of the period—and continued to work for his newspaper. But the *Gazette de Leyde* was banned during the first coup d'état of January 1798, to reappear during the second coup of June. The restoration of 1801 rang in better times for Luzac. He was restored to his professorship in 1802, this time in national history and literature, in the university of his beloved Leiden.

"This city has been named Leiden from time immemorial but never knew why until January 12, 1807," the great storyteller from Swabia, Johann Peter Hebel, wrote in his almanac. He, like all of Europe, must have been deeply moved by the disaster that struck the city—hence, his tragic pun upon the German word *Leiden* and its Dutch equivalent *lijden* (pronounced the same as "Leiden" in Dutch) for suffering. On that day a canalboat carrying a load of gunpowder blew up in the center of the city on the Rapenburg Canal, on which the university is located. The disaster took many victims, among them Kluit and Luzac. The two adversaries—but were they really that far from each other?—died at the same time. Luzac, on his way to visit a colleague, was hurled into the water by the force of the blast and drowned. His body was found six days later. Only a few weeks later, Adams, in far-off America, still unaware of the catastrophe, replied to a letter from Van der Kemp telling him that Luzac's wife had died. He expressed his sympathy for Luzac and in grateful recollection praised him as a special friend, "a large Portion of the Salt of the

Earth." Not until late April did he learn that Luzac himself had died in
the disaster, and he sent word of it to Van der Kemp: "Alass! Luzac! Alass
Leyden! . . . Luzac has not left upon Earth a worthier Man"[17]

· I V ·

Among all the Patriots who waxed enthusiastic about America, Van der
Kemp was one of the very few who finally ventured across the Atlantic
Ocean, and he did so only under the force of circumstances. During the
turbulent decade of the eighties he had thrown himself with ever greater
fervor into the political struggle, giving up his peaceable Mennonite
pulpit and spending both Sunday and almost every other day of the week
in uniform. He became the commander of a citizens' volunteer corps, first
in Leiden and then in Wijk bij Duurstede, a little town in the province of
Utrecht. When the Prince of Orange's troops entered the province in
1787, Van der Kemp was taken prisoner. After several months he was
released after bail of forty-five thousand guilders, no mean sum, was
posted by a friend, but he was required to quit the city and the province.

It is quite remarkable to read how these not too heroic exploits of Van
der Kemp were later embellished by his friend John Adams. In a letter to
Jefferson he wrote, by way of introduction, what might be called a short
biography of Van der Kemp in which he especially emphasized his behavior in the crisis of 1787:

> In 1787 when the King of Prussia threatened Holland with Invasion, his Party insisted on his taking a Command in the Army of
> defence and he was appointed to the Command of the most exposed and most important Post in the Seven Provinces. He was
> soon surrounded by the Prussian Forces. But he defended his Fortress with a Prudence Fortitude Patience and Perseverance, which
> were admired by all Europe, Till, abandoned by his Nation, destitute of Provisions and Amunition, still refusing to surrender, he
> was offered the most honourable Capitulation. He accepted it. Was
> offered very Advantageous Proposals, but despairing of the Liberties of his Country, he retired to Antwerp determined to emigrate
> to New York.

What a beautiful example of Adams's inveterate inclination to exaggerate! The town that Van der Kemp commanded was certainly not "the
most exposed and most important Post" in the Netherlands. It was not

surrounded by Prussians but by the provincial militia of that area, and our hero surrendered without one shot having been fired. He was imprisoned, and he did indeed reject attractive proposals to go over to the Orangist party and was then banished from the country. How do we explain Adams's embellishment of history? What was his source? The letters from Van der Kemp himself? They are, as a matter of fact, a bit more modest. Or was it Adams's own memory that failed him after so many years? (The letter is dated 9 August 1816.) The chief cause must, I think, be found in Adams's predilection for the superlative. He is really in many of his letters a representative of the Romantic movement.

What is at least true in his report is that Van der Kemp went to Antwerp and decided to emigrate to America. In Antwerp he was joined by his wife, who had remained in Leiden, and they traveled on to France. Early in 1788 he took ship in Le Havre for the New World. Armed with letters of recommendation from Adams and Jefferson, he hoped to build a better life in America. After arrival, he went first to visit the leading figures of the country. Hamilton, Knox, Clinton, the Livingstons, and even great Washington himself—whom he found cold and haughty, like Van Hogendorp before him—and then settled temporarily at Kingston, on the Hudson. He was pleasantly surprised to find the Dutch language in common use and delighted by the generous hospitality with which he was met. He was in high spirits: "I flatter myself that I shall be able to earn a modest livelihood at first and then a more prosperous one as I become a better farmer."[18]

Nonetheless, he continued to be restless and felt uncertain of himself despite all his work upon the land. He was probably not as good at it as he thought, and he soon contracted the American fever of believing that a better future awaited him somewhere in the West. In 1792, just after he turned forty, he made a long journey into the wilderness near Oneida Lake in upstate New York. He described the trip in an utterly charming diary, which is a typical example of the romantic travel report of the period. He was delighted with the fat eels in the lake—at least as good as those in Holland!—and was very moved by the majesty of nature. One would have to be a brute, he wrote, not to feel one's bosom glow with love for the great Creator who had made everything so wisely and well.

Van der Kemp, of course, was the very opposite of a brute; he was rather an idealist of tender feelings, and therefore he decided in 1794 to settle in this splendid countryside. He managed to hold on for three years on a farm near the just-founded town of New Rotterdam, but despite the help from one or more black slaves, probably a family that he brought from Kingston, he did not have much success. He might think in idyllic terms about the calm life of the peaceful farmer and sing its praises to other settlers; he even delivered a speech in which he described the happy farmer who took his noonday rest under a tree and read Thomson or Milton and in the evening studied the laws of political science in Sidney, Locke, Montesquieu, and Adams, and then ecstatically exclaimed: "I am a free American!"

But reality was less gentle. Finally he had to give up, and he moved to the settlement of Barneveld (later also called Trenton), somewhat further east in land owned by the Holland Land Company, just to the north of the town of Utica. The settlers were under the leadership of an agent of the Amsterdam directors of the company, Gerrit Boon, and his assistant and successor Adam Mappa. Like Van der Kemp, Mappa was a Patriot who had fled the Netherlands, and Van der Kemp would become very close to him in the years ahead. Boon began to build a large and stately home with an interior decorated with lovely and costly wood carvings, a house which still stands. Van der Kemp took up residence in a simple cottage just behind Boon's house, and it too stands, partially rebuilt. "It was a service of love," writes Van Winter, "that provided him with a life free of cares." [19]

Not quite that carefree, however. It was difficult for him to earn his daily bread, and this novice pioneer found work in the garden hard. It was thanks to the solicitude of his children, in particular his eldest son, who was more practical than he, that he finally obtained a modest security of livelihood. "The bread that I eat," he wrote to his old friend Pieter Vreede, "is generously provided us by a worthy son. Our home is humble, 20 by 30 feet, two small rooms and a little kitchen. Yes, it is confined. . . . But we are considered to be happy, healthy and satisfied, because we seek nothing but tranquility and oblivion." And a few years later he wrote: "Our situation remains the same. We have no basis for expecting it to improve, but we lack for nothing, Jan provides everything." [20]

But, amid these harsh, "confined" circumstances, he kept up his courage. He planned one book after another, about the theories of Buffon and Jefferson, the use of brass among the Greeks, the origins in morality and nature of the revolutionary spirit in the second half of the eighteenth century, and much more. His friend De Witt Clinton, governor of New York, obtained a special commission for him in 1817 to translate the old archives of the colony of New Netherlands from the years 1625 to 1664. (It was the time of an awakening national consciousness, when men wanted to learn about their own past.) The documents were sent to him from Albany by freight, and he worked at the translation with the greatest energy and devotion. "This year I shall have prepared two thousand folio pages," he wrote to Vreede in 1819. "It is indeed a treasure for Nat. Hist.—history and politics—but it is costing me my sight." His eyes began to fail, but his strength of purpose drove him on. In five years' time he completed the twenty-four enormous volumes of the *Albany Records*, which were stored in the archives at Albany but never published. Unfortunately, Van der Kemp's enthusiasm was greater than his accuracy or his expertness, and the judgment of later historians upon this gigantic work was not too favorable. It was, they said, careless, often wrong, and without understanding of the special characteristics of the seventeenth century.

In the end disaster struck that pile of paper; in the great fire in the capitol at Albany in 1911, it was all burned, down to the last sheet. This ultimate futility seems somehow characteristic of Van der Kemp's lifework. There is, in his life, when all is said and done, superficiality and sketchiness, much fire and little warmth, much glitter and little light.[21]

This is what bothered Adams about him, as becomes evident from the correspondence between them. The letters that they exchanged cover a period of almost forty years; their flow is interrupted only by the two visits that Van der Kemp, in 1813 and 1820, paid to Adams in Quincy, high points in his lonely life. Clearly there was between these two men a great mutual respect, an understanding of each other that may almost be called close friendship. This is proved by their letters. They discussed everything—politics, philosophy, and religion, but also more personal experiences and sorrows. Yet there was also an element of friction in their unusual relationship. Adams, who was obviously the dominant partner, was not always nice to Van der Kemp but sometimes dealt rather roughly with him. Van der Kemp was as eager and subservient as possible; only rarely did he venture a little joke or dare to contradict the gruff old Puritan. He was almost Byzantine in his meekness.

He told Adams of his utopian plans, but the often cynical Adams made fun of them. When Van der Kemp informed him that he wished to write a big history of the revolutionary events of the eighteenth century, Adams replied: "Lord! Lord! What a Coat you have cut out? It would require a hundred Taylors for twenty years to make it up. I would not undertake to make a Button hole in it, during the whole Remainder of my life." He wanted to protect Van der Kemp against himself, he told him in another letter, for he was too zealous. If Van der Kemp was possessed "by any

Demon, whether ghost or Hero, Sage, Saint, heathen Deity, Head Ache, or Devil, fallen Angel or Apostate Spirit," Adams advised him to read a book about those possessed by the Devil in the New Testament. His own cure, which he called "quackery," was that Van der Kemp should read and work less. They would have to live another hundred years to understand each other. After all, Van der Kemp's learning was a hundred times greater than his own, and his understanding ten times so. Ironically, teasingly, sometimes a little viciously, then affectionately again, Adams danced around his Dutch correspondent off in northern New York. And Van der Kemp responded with noble and profound seriousness.

But the furious old man in Quincy lost his temper when Van der Kemp proposed to write a book about Adams's negotiations in Europe. He questioned Van der Kemp's knowledge of the facts, which were scattered everywhere. He did not want memoirs, as Van der Kemp suggested. The Dutchman ought to write a letter to the bones of Washington: "Venerable adorable Bones, please do rise and write an History of your Battles, Sieges and Campaigns."

A plan of Van der Kemp to write a discourse on the Creation drove Adams to near frenzy: "In the name of Humanity!!! a solemn appeal!!! Do not tease torment dupe or divert the world with any new Cosmogonies or Theogonies." This time it was Van der Kemp who took the business lightly. He addressed Adams as "Holy Father," asked his forgiveness, and promised to sin no more. Adams replied with congratulations on his work to translate the old Dutch documents. That was a "providential Rescue from your metaphysical and delirious Project of writing Cosmogonies and Metempsychosies of Worlds." [22]

It is tempting to continue quoting from these marvelous letters, especially those by Adams, for he was easily the better writer. But it is Van der Kemp with whom we are concerned for the moment, and there is one other aspect of his life that we must examine, his political development in America. For even in this impetuous radical we have another example of the turning of the tide, the calming down of even the most fervid Patriot into a conservative. Was this evolution the result of the change of the spirit of the times from revolution to restoration? Or was it the personal development, shared with so many other men, from youth to age, passion to sobriety? Or must we say that this radicalism was, even in a man like Van der Kemp, no more than a flash in the pan, excitement that shrank from truly radical change?

In the democracy of the New World even the most fervid European reformers were revealed to themselves. This was not what they had intended. At first, Van der Kemp, observing the party differences between the Federalists and Anti-Federalists, thought that as a newcomer in the New World, he should stay neutral. But if he took sides, he would belong with the progressives: "It is probable that if I had been a citizen I would have been an *anti* ever since 1775." He became excited when he heard the news in 1795 of the revolution in the Netherlands. "Holland is all liberated. The tyrannical Stadholder has fled with all his adherents, and complete freedom has been established." Then, very typically, he continued: "Property is sacred for the property-owners, and there is no cause for complaint." From this starting point he soon landed in the other party, the conservatives. In the summer of 1800 he expressed fear that the party of Jefferson would win: "We have been protected from French Intrigues and brotherhood for about ten years now—God forbid that they should finally succeed."[23]

Like Adams and Luzac, Van der Kemp was a strong advocate of the "mixed constitution," which was the only assurance of freedom in a federal republic. Like so many of his contemporaries, he found a classical example for his admired state form in the Achaean republic; he wrote a sketch of its government under his old Patriotic pen name Junius Brutus with a characteristic motto from Horace: *Mutato nomine de te fabula narratur* (This tale is told about you under another name). In the introduction to this work, which was never printed, he complains about the loss of Batavian freedom. The situation is worse than it ever was under the government of the stadholder, and he fiercely attacks the French notion of pure democracy. The so-called friends of the people undermine freedom, like Pericles. They equate oligarchy with aristocracy. A "well-balanced Constitution" is necessary, in which a strong leader and a wise elite exist to keep democracy within bounds. "My principal Purpose is to expose the shortcomings of a Republican Government in a single assembly," he wrote to Luzac.[24]

Disenchanted with all revolutions, he was able in 1813 to greet whole-heartedly the restoration of the House of Orange in the Netherlands. He rejoiced at its return. Of William I, the son of Prince William V who became king of the Netherlands, he wrote: "Such a noble, great Leader, so selfless in his action, will bring more benefit to the Country and your fellow citizens than all the Patriots of 1787." And he gave an "Oration in Memory of the Glorious Rescue of the Dutch from French Tyranny" in the Presbyterian church in Utica. The Dutch minister in Washington sent a copy of this oration to the Netherlands, where it was printed and published. It is one long paean, eighty pages long, to God, the Netherlands, and Orange. Everything was turned about: Now it was the Netherlands which was a shining example for America—"May the Dutch people serve us as a mirror and example." [25]

The scale had come down on the other side. Now it was America that was threatened, not by tyranny and oligarchy, but by licentiousness and the so-called freedom of the people. "Here everything remains in confusion—a redoutable foreign enemy [in 1815, when he was writing, the war with England had just been concluded], division within—a civil war in the offing—no money—no credit—without confidence at home or abroad, with Fanatics who drive like Fools and laugh at the cliffs down which they rush." He was afraid that the United States was breaking up. Admittedly, America was growing rapidly. It was like a "full-blooded, muscular young man, full of life, rich, his own master and dissolute." But it was threatened by too much freedom, for which the new immigrants in particular were not ready; they were, our Nativist tells us, the scum of Europe. Van der Kemp lived to experience the breakthrough to greater democracy that became a fact with the victory of Jackson in 1828, and he despaired for the future of his new homeland. [26]

He was active to the last, interested in what went on about him and ready with judgment. In his personal life everything became more tranquil. His children went away, his wife who had gone through so much with him died in 1828, and in that same year his loyal friend Mappa died too. Adams had died in 1826, but Van der Kemp still exchanged letters with his son John Quincy, who was now president of the United States. In his last year of life he conceived a plan to write a book about the Bible, "a few general remarks." But he died of a sudden attack of cholera in September 1829. His grave may still be found in the cemetery at Barneveld.

The best is left for last. It is not necessary to say much more about John Adams, who has played the most decisive role in this book. His name is firmly fixed in the annals of his country. There has even come about in our own time a reevaluation strongly favorable to him, probably because he was so full of life, so defiantly himself in an age of solemnity and conventionality. No other American of his time has written letters that let us hear so clearly the living voice of their writer.

When he returned from Europe in 1788 he was soon called to high office again. For eight years as vice-president under Washington, he suffered: "My country in its wisdom kept for me the most insignificant job that the inventiveness of man has ever conceived." He was elected president in his turn in 1797 and governed for four years with much vigor but little understanding of the growing force of democracy. After 1801 he lived in retirement at Quincy, in the fine house that still stands. He kept up an extensive correspondence and wrote some reminiscences in the *Boston Patriot*. He was ninety-one years old when he died on 4 July 1826, exactly fifty years after the Declaration of Independence. His last thoughts were for his old friend and opponent, Jefferson: "Jefferson still survives." But the great accident, Providence, as so many believed, had decided that Jefferson die that same morning, several hours earlier.

Many times in his last years, Adams went back in thought to his time in the Netherlands. His satisfaction with what he had done grew larger and larger. That time, he wrote, was the most important of his life, and what he achieved there belonged to the few great things of which he continued to be proud. He was ashamed when he thought how much the Netherlands had meant for America and how little gratitude the Americans had shown. But he confessed that he could not easily find a meaning in all the history that he had lived through and helped to make. Why, complained this disillusioned eighteenth-century man, had progress been so repeatedly dashed by mad kings, pernicious nobles, and raging, blind, ignorant sans-culottes? (We recognize his favored triple division.) Could anything good for mankind be achieved without the spilling of blood? And, he asked, what do we mean by "the good"? He and Van der Kemp should talk a little about what was really useful to mankind. Hadn't he recently discovered a cure for corns? he asked his friend.

At another time he wrote: "Griefs upon Griefs! Disappointments upon Disappointments. All is Vanity! What then? This is a gay, merry world notwithstanding."[27] With that paradox of history and life, we close our tale.

Notes

The full name of author and the complete title, with bibliographical data, are given in the bibliography. The alphabetical sequence of authors' family names follows the Dutch pattern: only the main word in the name is considered. "Van" and "de," corresponding to "of" and "the," are inseparable parts of the name, but are disregarded in alphabetization. Thus the name in note 1 below is listed under "Gelder, van."

The abbreviation "Kn." indicates the number of a pamphlet in Knuttel's *Catalogus*.

PROLOGUE

1. Van Gelder, *Kunstgeschiedenis*, 379.
2. Niemeyer, "Aspects," 14.
3. Niemeyer, "Cities and Scenery," 34.
4. Gumbert, *Lichtenberg*, 23–24.
5. Hammerdörfer, *Holländische Denkwürdigkeiten*, 5.
6. John to Abigail Adams, 4 Sept. 1780, *Adams Family Correspondence*, 3:410; 9 Oct. 1781, ibid., 4:224. [Hereafter letters *from* John Adams will usually be indicated merely by the name of the recipient.]
7. Watson, *Tour*, 29, 39, 65; compare Watson, *Men and Times*; to Abigail Adams, 15 Sept. 1780, *Adams Family Correspondence*, 3:414; 18 Dec. 1780, ibid., 4:35.
8. Harris, *Diaries and Correspondence*, 2:98; Benjamin Franklin to Charles G. F. Dumas, 1 Aug. 1781, *Diplomatic Correspondence*, 3:234.
9. Colenbrander, *Patriottentijd*, 1:85–86; Sir Joseph Yorke to Lord Suffolk, ibid., 1:375.
10. Ibid., 1:69; Geyl, *Patriottenbeweging*, throughout.
11. *Werkgroep 18e eeuw.*, no. 22; Geyl, *Geschiedenis*, 5:1209–10.
12. Kossmann, "Crisis," 159; Herder, "Journal," 64–65; Harris, *Introduction*, 108–9; to President of Congress, 16 May 1781, Adams, *Works*, 7:418–19.
13. Watson, *Tour*, 165–66; Hardenbroek, *Gedenkschriften*, 2:110.
14. Dumas Letterbook, 4 Aug. 1778, 10 July 1781.
15. Thorbecke, *Historische Schetsen*, quoted in De Wit, *Nederlandse Revolutie*, 281; Pearson, *Diaries*, 507–8; compare Truman, *Off the Record*, 370, 378, 384. For general background of the problem, see Boxer, *Empire*, ch. 10, and De Vries, *Achteruitgang*.
16. Styl, *Opkomst en Bloei*, quoted in Geyl, *Geschiedenis*, 5:1205–6.
17. Abigail Adams, *Letters*, 344.
18. Voltaire, *Oeuvres*, 4:190; Mirabeau, *Aux Bataves*, 3; "Mémoire pour servir d'instruction du citoyen François Noël," Colenbrander, *Gedenkstukken*, 2:9. The verses from Voltaire read in the original French:

> Notre esprit est conforme aux lieux que l'on a vu naître,
> A *Rome* on est esclave, à *Londres* citoyen.
> La grandeur d'un *Batave* est de vivre sans Maître.

19. Paulus, *Verklaring*, 1: "Opdragt," 3:242–53.

20. Hogendorp, *Brieven*, 1:197; Hardenbroek, *Gedenkschriften*, 1:231, 2:41.

21. To President of Congress, 14 Jan. 1782, Adams, *Works*, 7:507. See also 7:329, 381, 515.

22. Thomas Jefferson to John Jay, 6 Aug. 1787, in Jefferson, *Papers*, 9:695–96; John Adams to Robert R. Livingston, 19 Feb. 1782, in Adams, *Works*, 7:513. See also De Wit, *Strijd*, 16–18.

23. Adams, *Boston Patriot*, 312; to Norton Quincy, 29 Aug. 1782, *Adams Family Correspondence*, 4:367.

24. Hartog, *Patriotten en Oranje*, 95–96; Colenbrander, *Patriottentijd*, 1:101 (n. 1); Harris, *Diaries*, 93, 97.

25. Hardenbroek, *Gedenkschriften*, 2:68, 103, 150–51, 163, 398–99.

26. Hardenbroek, *Gedenkschriften*, 2:401–2; Harris, *Diaries*, 145–48.

27. Colenbrander, *Patriottentijd*, 1:103–5; Hardenbroek, *Gedenkschriften*, 1:508, 2:673; Nijhoff, *Brunswijk*.

28. Sir Joseph Yorke to William Eden, 28–29 Sept. 1778, Clinton Papers.

29. William Carmichael to Committee of Secret Correspondence, 2 Nov. 1776, *Revolutionary Diplomatic Correspondence*, 2:184–89.

30. Smit, "The Netherlands and Europe," 13–36. See also Carter, "The Dutch as Neutrals," 818–34; Stinchcombe, "John Adams," 69–84.

31. Kluit, *Den laatsten Engelschen Oorlog*, 145.

CHAPTER I

1. Thulemeyer, *Dépêches*, 153.

2. Archief Van Bleiswijk, A, no. 1, 1773–76.

3. Ibid.; see also Archief Fagel, no. 1038; *Archives de la Maison d'Orange*, 1:422–24; Thulemeyer, *Dépêches*, 159.

4. Colenbrander, *Patriottentijd*, 1:49 (n. 2); Nijhoff, *Brunswijk*, 142 (n. 2).

5. Van der Capellen tot den Pol, *Aan het Volk*; De Wit, *Strijd*, 38; De Wit, *Revolutie*, 27–28.

6. Romein and Romein, *Erflaters*, 3:134–69; Palmer, *Age*, 1:329–31.

7. De Bosch Kemper, *Staatkundige Geschiedenis*, 214; Fruin, *Staatsinstellingen*, 336; Colenbrander, *Patriottentijd*, 1:117–18; Van der Meulen, "Een en ander," 195–224; De Beaufort, "Oranje en de Democratie," 2:11; Robbins, *Commonwealthman*.

8. De Jong Hzn., *Van der Capellen*, 190, 215–19, and throughout.

9. Van der Kemp, *Historie der Admissie*, 79; Kluit, *Souvereiniteit*, vols. 4 and 5; Suringar, *Biographische Aantekeningen*, 64; Van der Capellen tot den Pol, *Brieven* [ed. Beaufort], pp. viii, n. 1, ix, n. 1.

10. Van der Capellen to Ruckersfelder, 20 Feb. 1784, Van der Capellen tot den Pol, *Brieven* [ed. Sillem], 75; Van der Capellen tot den Pol to Robert J. van der Capellen van de Marsch, 17 Jan. 1782, Van der Capellen, *Brieven* [ed. Beaufort], 268–69; Van der Capellen tot den Pol to M. Tydeman, 8 Feb. 1768, Van der Capellen, *Brieven* [ed. Sillem], 26–34; De Jong Hzn., *Van der Capellen*, 210. An interesting comparable case of religious irresolution in America in the same period is that of Thomas Tudor Tucker, whose strikingly similar letters are quoted in May, *Enlightenment*, 147–48.

11. Van der Capellen tot den Pol to M. Tydeman, 1 Feb. 1776, in Van der Capellen, *Brieven* [ed. Sillem], 4–6; Van der Capellen to M. Tydeman, 8 Feb. 1768, ibid., 28; De Jong Hzn., *Van der Capellen*, 218; Van der Capellen tot den Pol to Pieter Paulus, no date, in Van der Capellen, *Brieven* [ed. Beaufort], 41; Jefferson, *Life and Writings*, 729–

30. On this metaphor, see also Adair, *Fame and the Founding Fathers*, 196; the metaphor also occurs in Heinrich Heine's *Reisebilder*, where he claims to have derived it from Voltaire. Heine, *Sämtliche Werke*, 2:221.

12. Van der Capellen tot den Pol, *Advis*; Trumbull and Livingston, *Brieven*; Van der Capellen tot den Pol, *Brieven* [ed. Beaufort], 5–9, 67–72, 77–78, 81–94, 111–17, 213–16, 246–58. See also Livingston, *Independent Reflector*; Van der Capellen tot den Pol to Valck, 23 April 1782, Van der Capellen, *Brieven* [ed. Beaufort], 287–88; Archief Fagel, no. 1463.

13. Erkelens to Van der Capellen tot den Pol, 22 July 1777, ibid., 7 Dec. 1778, 21 Jan. 1779, Archief Van der Capellen tot den Pol; Hardenberg, "Kolonel Dircks," 157–200, especially 174–76; Dumas to Van der Capellen tot den Pol, Van der Capellen, *Brieven* [ed. Beaufort], 118; Dumas to Franklin, 24 June 1779, Dumas Letterbook; Dumas to Commission of Foreign Affairs, 21 June 1779, ibid., and Van der Capellen, *Brieven* [ed. Beaufort], 157–59; Van der Capellen to Sayre, 16 Nov. 1779, ibid., 159–61; Van der Capellen to Valck, 8 Aug. 1782, ibid., 323.

14. Van der Kemp, *Autobiography*, 67–70, with facsimile; Van Winter, *Aandeel*, 1:35–36; Van der Capellen tot den Pol to Erkelens, 7 Dec. 1778, Van der Capellen, *Brieven* [ed. Beaufort], 81; Van der Capellen tot den Pol to Franklin, 28 April 1778, ibid., 64.

15. De Jong Hzn., *Brunswijk*, 282–83; Van der Capellen tot den Pol to Richard Price, 1 July 1777, Van der Capellen, *Brieven* [ed. Beaufort], 105.

16. Van der Capellen tot den Pol to Van der Capellen van de Marsch, 15 Aug. 1782, ibid., 328; to Valck, 12 March 1783, ibid., 565.

CHAPTER 2

1. Collection H. Nieuwenhuisen, no. 31, placard added to a letter by Van Landsberge, Dutch envoy at Cologne, 24 Oct. 1775; Archief Fagel, no. 5159, 14 May 1776; Brunswick to William V, 4 Jan. 1776, *Archives de la Maison d'Orange*, 1:430–31; Dumas to Carmichael, 11–21 March 1777, 15 April 1777, to Committee of Secret Correspondence, 1 May 1777, 14 June 1777, Dumas Letterbook; Welch, *Mirabeau*, 67–68; B. Sowden to Franklin, 7 June 1777, Franklin, *Calendar*, 6:53.

2. Hardenberg, "Kolonel Dircks," 157–200. See also Homan, "Dircks and the American Revolution," 72–79.

3. West Indische Compagnie to States General, 21 July 1775, *Archives de la Maison d'Orange*, 1:375–77; William V to Fagel, 26 July 1775, ibid., 377–78; Thulemeyer, *Dépêches*, 134–35, 138–39, 161, 166–69; Yorke to Suffolk, 15 Nov. 1774, *Documents of the American Revolution*, 8:234–35; C. Colden to Lord Dartmouth, 2 Nov. 1774, ibid., 224; Lord Stormont to Lord Weymouth, 12 Feb. 1777, in Stevens, *Facsimiles*, 14:1433; Jameson, "St. Eustatius," 638–708; Van Alstyne, "Great Britain," 311–46. See also Phillips Callbeck to Lord Dartmouth, 5 Jan. 1776, *Documents of the American Revolution*, 12:40.

4. For the events on St. Eustatius, see Archief West Indische Compagnie, nos. 630 (1773–76), 631 (1776–78), 632 (1778), 633 (1778–80), 634 (1780–84), and 639 (Deductie en Memorie van Joh. de Graaff). On De Graaff, see Harris, *Introduction*, 104–7.

5. Sandwich, *Private Papers*, 1:103.

6. Jameson, "St. Eustatius," 690–91.

7. Archief Fagel, no. 5159, 30 April 1776.

8. *Archives de la Maison d'Orange*, 1:456–61, 464, 467; Nijhoff, *Brunswijk*, 150–52.

9. Archief Van Bleiswijk, A, no. 25¹; *Resolutiën Staten van Holland*, 6 Aug. 1779.

10. Hartog, *Bovenwindse Eilanden*, 177–84, 572.

11. George, *Caricature*, 1:162–63; Rodney to Sir John Vaughan, 14 June 1780, Vaughan

Papers; Rodney to Ph. Stevens, 4, 6 Feb. 1781, Sydney Papers.

12. To Livingston, 21 Feb. 1782, Adams, *Works*, 7:523; Jameson, "St. Eustatius," 706–7; Rodney to Earl of Sandwich, 7 Feb. 1781, Sandwich, *Private Papers*, 4:51.

CHAPTER 3

1. Bemis, *Diplomacy*, 125–26; Renaut, *Provinces-Unies*, vol. 5; Morice, "Contributions," 17–28; *Verslagen . . . Archieven*, 16, pt. i, pp. 481–84.

2. To Mercy Warren, 30 July 1807, *Revolutionary Diplomatic Correspondence*, 1:604; Falconet, *Examen*.

3. Franklin to Dumas, 25 July 1768, Franklin, *Papers*, 15:172–80; ibid., 18:61; Dumas to Franklin, after 28 Jan. 1774, ibid., 21:34–37; Smith, *Relation historique*; Dumas to Franklin, 7 May 1775, Dumas Papers; Vattel, *Droit des gens*; see also Carter, "Dutch as neutrals," 818–34, especially 826–27.

4. Dumas to Franklin, 30 June 1775, Franklin Papers; Franklin to Dumas, 9 Dec. 1775, Franklin, *Works*, 8:87–92.

5. Dumas to Franklin, 30 April 1776, *Revolutionary Diplomatic Correspondence*, 2:86–89; Dumas Letterbook, 30 April 1776.

6. Yorke to Lord Suffolk, Aug. 1778, Archief Fagel, no. 1436; Harris, *Introduction*, 254–55; Jones, *Memoirs*, 1:222; Deane to Committee of Secret Correspondence, 18 Aug. 1776, *Revolutionary Diplomatic Correspondence*, 2:124; A. Lee to S. Adams, 22 May 1779, Deane, *Papers*, 3:462–65; Van der Capellen tot den Pol to Livingston, n.d. [1779], Van der Capellen, *Brieven* [ed. Beaufort], 114; J. Adams to Livingston, 16 May 1782, *Works*, 7:589.

7. Dumas to Franklin, 11 March 1777, 25 March 1778, 17 Dec. 1776 (Horace, *Odes*, Book I, III); 21 March 1777, Oct. 1778, 15 Jan. 1779, 14 June 1777, 21 March 1777, 13 Jan. 1778, Dumas Letterbook; Dumas to Adams, 1 Nov. 1780, Adams, *Works*, 7:323.

8. Dumas Letterbook, introduction.

9. Dumas Letterbook, 15 March 1779, 11 Aug. 1780, 22 Aug., 23 Sept. 1777.

10. Ibid., 30 Jan. 1778, 4, 24, 25, 26, 31 July, 18 Aug. 1780; Franklin to Dumas, 2 Oct. 1780, *Revolutionary Diplomatic Correspondence*, 4:72–73; Livingston to Dumas, 28 Nov. 1781, ibid., 5:30–31.

11. Dumas Papers, 16 Dec. 1780; Franklin to Dumas, 18 Jan. 1781, *Revolutionary Diplomatic Correspondence*, 4:140.

12. Dumas Letterbook, 30 May 1777.

13. Ibid., 14 Aug. 1776.

CHAPTER 4

1. Dumas Letterbook, 30 April 1776 (also in *Revolutionary Diplomatic Correspondence*, 2:85–89), 14 May 1778 (also in *Revolutionary Diplomatic Correspondence*, 4:90–92, but the passage about the French offer is missing there), 28 July 1776.

2. Hardenbroek, *Gedenkschriften*, 2:75; Dumas Letterbook, 14 Feb. 1777.

3. Ibid., 20 March, 6 May 1777, Deane to Dumas, 7 June 1777 (also in *Revolutionary Diplomatic Correspondence*, 2:331–33; the quotation from Shakespeare is from *Julius Caesar*, act 1, scene 2), 24 June 1777.

4. Ibid., 14 Aug. 1777; Colenbrander, *Patriottentijd*, 1:106.

5. Dumas Letterbook, 12, 16, 18, 19 Dec. 1777, 10 Feb. 1778, 30 Dec. 1777.

6. Ibid., 30 Dec. 1777, 13, 23 Jan. 1778.

7. Ibid., 24 March 1778; De Bérenger to Vergennes, 22 March 1778, vol. 533, Correspondance Politique, Hollande, Archives Etrangères.

8. Dumas Letterbook, 27 March, 6 April 1778, 10 April 1778 (also in *Revolutionary Diplomatic Correspondence*, 2:543–45). See also Lee, *Arthur Lee*, 1:138–42.

9. Bosschaert to Van Bleiswijk, 19 March 1778, *Archives de la Maison d'Orange*, 1:506–7; Dumas Letterbook, 3, 6, 23, 28 April 1778.

10. Ibid., 7–13 May 1778; Thulemeyer, *Dépêches*, 191; Dumas Letterbook, 14–15 May 1778.

11. Nijhoff, *Brunswijk*, 294–96; William V to Van Welderen, 30 May 1778, *Archives de la Maison d'Orange*, 1:522–24.

12. Dumas Letterbook, 22 May, 23–30 June, 3 July 1778.

13. *Archives de la Maison d'Orange*, 1:528.

14. Brugmans, *Opkomst en Bloei*, 3.

15. Hardenbroek, *Gedenkschriften*, 2:51–52, 55.

16. *Nieuwe Nederlandsche Jaarboeken*, 1781. On De Neufville, see Van Winter, *Aandeel*, 1:32–34.

17. Dumas Letterbook, 2, 3, 11 Sept. 1778, partly printed in Van Wijk, *De Republiek*, 186–89. Dumas returned to the subject in letters of 4 Nov. 1778, 16 Feb., 23 April, 13 July 1779, 15, 21 March 1780; see also Van Wijk, *De Republiek*, and Van Winter, "Betrekkingen," 68–82, reprinted in Van Winter, *Verkenning*, 344–56.

18. "Consideratie op zeekeren Voorslag aangaande het prepareren van een Commercie Tractaat," Familie-archief Van Slingelandt, De Vrij Temminck, no. 508, 20 Aug. 1778.

19. Dumas Letterbook, 6–8, 30 Oct. 1778; *Secreete Resolutiën Holland, 1781*, 27 Oct. 1781, pp. 430–42.

20. William V to Van Bleiswijk, 25 Oct., to Van Welderen, 27–28 Oct. 1778, *Archives de la Maison d'Orange*, 1:565–66, 568–70.

CHAPTER 5

1. Colenbrander, *Patriottentijd*, 1:135–70; Bartstra, *Vlootherstel*, chs. 6 and 7.

2. Morison, *Jones*; Adams, *Diary*, 1:370–71; Reynst to William V, 7 Nov. 1779, Archief Van Bleiswijk, A, no. 2.

3. Van Wijk, *De Republiek*, 1:190–91; Dumas Letterbook, 20 Sept. 1779; *Archives de la Maison d'Orange*, 1:117.

4. Van Winter, "Betrekkingen," 68–82; "Stukken rakende het geval van Paul Jones en de gevolgen van dien, 1779–1780," Archief Fagel, no. 1437; Jones to Bancroft, 17 Dec. 1779, Van Wijk, *De Republiek*, 191–93.

5. Dumas Letterbook, 21, 31 Oct. 1779; Archief Van Bleiswijk, A, no. 2.

6. Dumas Letterbook, 13 Jan. 1778, 6 Nov. 1779; Morison, *Jones*, 261.

7. Ibid., 257; Dumas Letterbook, 12 Oct. 1779; G. Grand to Franklin, 11 Oct. 1779, Franklin, *Calendar*, 16:31. The portrait of Jones is in *Atlas van Stolk*, no. 4299; the print *Loon na Werk* is in Muller, *Nederlandsche Geschiedenis in Platen*, no. 4365.

8. Van der Capellen tot den Pol to Jones, 13 Oct., Jones to Van der Capellen tot den Pol, 19 Oct. 1779, Van der Capellen, *Brieven* [ed. Beaufort], 123–50; ibid., 151–54.

9. Jones to La Vauguyon, 4 Nov. 1779, *Revolutionary Diplomatic Correspondence*, 3:398–99; De Neufville to Franklin, 7, 9, 25 Oct. 1779, Franklin, *Calendar*, vol. 16.

10. Captain C. H. Mulder to Admiralty, 5 Nov. 1779, Archief Van Bleiswijk, A, no. 2.

11. Extract resolution, States General, missive of William V, 26 Nov., 21 Dec. 1779, Archief Fagel; William V to Van Welderen, 9 Nov. 1779, Archief Fagel, no. 1434; Hardenbroek, *Gedenkschriften*, 1:538.

12. Jones to Franklin, 13 Dec., to La Vauguyon, 13 Dec. 1779, *Revolutionary Diplomatic Correspondence*, 3:424–26.

13. Yorke to Stormont, 14 Dec. 1779, quoted in Edler, *Dutch Republic*, 66–67; Jones to Bancroft, 17 Dec. 1779, in Van Wijk, *De Republiek*, 191–93; William V to Van Welderen, 23 Nov., 30 Dec. 1779, Archief van Bleiswijk, A, no. 2; Dumas Letterbook, 22 Dec. 1779.

14. Ibid., 1 Feb. 1780; Franklin to Dumas, 27 Jan. 1780, *Revolutionary Diplomatic Correspondence*, 3:172; A. Lee to J. J. Pringle, 3 Aug. 1779, ibid., 1:535.

15. Franklin to Dumas, 27 March 1779, ibid., 3:577–78.

16. Dumas Letterbook, 2 March, 25 April 1780.

17. Ibid., beginning of April 1780.

18. Ibid., 5, 7 April 1780; Franklin to Dumas, 23 April 1780, *Revolutionary Diplomatic Correspondence*, 3:625–26; Dumas Letterbook, 9, 20 Oct. 1780.

CHAPTER 6

1. Adams to Jefferson, 13 Nov. 1815, Adams, *Works*, 10:174; to B. Waterhouse, 20 Oct. 1805, Adams, *Statesman and Friend*, 31.

2. Shaw, *Character of Adams*, 11; Adams, *Diary*, 1:7–8.

3. To Van der Kemp, 5 July 1814, 23 Feb., 3 April 1815, Adams–Van der Kemp Correspondence; Adams, *Diary*, 2:362–63.

4. To Waterhouse, 16 Aug. 1812, Adams, *Statesman and Friend*, 61.

5. To Van der Kemp, 20 May 1813, Adams–Van der Kemp Correspondence.

6. Haraszti, *Adams*; Howe, *Political Thought*.

7. Jefferson to J. Priestley, 21 March 1801, Jefferson, *Life and Writings*, 562–63; Adams to Van der Kemp, 8 Jan. 1806, Adams–Van der Kemp Correspondence.

8. To Van der Kemp, 9 March 1806, 20 Feb. 1811, 15 July 1812, 10 April 1817, ibid.

9. To Van der Kemp, 20 Feb. 1811, 28 Oct. 1812, ibid.

10. Jones to Dumas, 8 Sept. 1780, *Revolutionary Diplomatic Correspondence*, 4:48–49.

11. Adams, *Works*, 2:488–89; Gilbert, *Beginnings*, 48–52, and throughout. See also the new criticism of Gilbert in Hutson, "Early American Diplomacy," 40–68; Stinchcombe, "Adams," 69–84; Hutson, *Adams and Diplomacy*, especially chapter 7.

12. Jefferson to W. Short, 23 Jan. 1804, quoted in Gilbert, *Beginnings*, 72.

13. To Van der Kemp, 30 Nov. 1810, 4 April 1811, 10 Oct. 1820, Adams–Van der Kemp Correspondence.

14. Adams, *Boston Patriot*, 100–101.

15. Franklin to Arthur Lee, 11 March 1777, *Revolutionary Diplomatic Correspondence*, 2:298; Adams to Livingston, 11 Feb. 1782, ibid., 5:196; Foley, "Triumph," throughout.

16. Adams to President of Congress, 4 Aug. 1779, *Revolutionary Diplomatic Correspondence*, 7:104–5.

17. Franklin to President of Congress, 9 Aug. 1780, quoted in *Adams Family Correspondence*, 3:395; Adams, *Boston Patriot*, 102–3.

18. Waterhouse to Levi Woodbury, 20 Feb. 1835, Levi Woodbury Papers; Adams to President of Congress, 14 Aug. 1780, Adams, *Works*, 7:245.

CHAPTER 7

1. Adams, *Diary*, 2:443.

2. Adams to E. Jennings, 6 Aug. 1780, quoted in Foley, "Triumph," 52.

3. Adams, *Boston Patriot*, 104; Adams to President of Congress, 5 Sept. 1780, Adams, *Works*, 7:250.

4. Adams to J. Thaxter, 23 Sept. 1780, *Adams Family Correspondence*, 3:423–24; to Abigail Adams, 25 Sept. 1780, ibid., 3:424–25.

5. To Van der Kemp, 3 April 1815, Adams–Van der Kemp Correspondence.

6. Maier, *From Resistance to Revolution*, 217, 163–64; Riker, "Dutch and American Federalism," 495–521.

7. To Abigail Adams, 21 July 1777, *Adams Family Correspondence*, 2:286–87; to John Quincy Adams, 27 July 1777, ibid., 2:289–91.

8. To Abigail Adams, 4 Sept. 1780, ibid., 3:412–13; see also ibid., 3:409–10; to Abigail Adams, 15 Sept. 1780, ibid., 3:413–14.

9. Thaxter to Abigail Adams, 21 July 1781, ibid., 4:186–87; John Adams to Abigail Adams, 18 Dec. 1780, ibid., 4:35.

10. To Norton Quincy, 28 Aug. 1782, ibid., 4:367; to President of Congress, 4 Sept. 1782, Adams, *Works*, 3:618; Adams, *Boston Patriot*, 213.

11. To President of Congress, 16 Nov. 1780, 14 Jan. 1782, Adams, *Works*, 7:329, 507.

12. To President of Congress, 4 Sept. 1782, ibid., 7:616–26.

13. To Van der Kemp, 15 July 1812, 22 Aug. 1818, Adams–Van der Kemp Correspondence.

CHAPTER 8

1. Adams to President of Congress, 25 Sept. 1780, *Revolutionary Diplomatic Correspondence*, 4:67.

2. Adams, *Boston Patriot*, 195–250; Adams, *Works*, 7:265–312.

3. *Geschiedenis van het Geschil*; *Verzameling van de Constitutien*.

4. Van der Capellen tot den Pol to Adams, 16 Oct., 28 Nov., 24 Dec. 1780, Adams to Van der Capellen tot den Pol, 22 Oct., 20 Nov., 9 Dec. 1780, 21 Jan. 1781, Adams, *Works*, 7:317–19, 332–37, 339–41, 343–46, 355–60.

5. To Van der Kemp, 13 July 1801, Adams–Van der Kemp Correspondence; Van der Capellen tot den Pol to Adams, 6 Jan. 1782, Adams to Van der Capellen tot den Pol, 14 Jan. 1782, Adams, *Works*, 7:501–3.

6. Van der Capellen tot den Pol to Adams, 16 Oct. 1780, Van der Capellen, *Brieven* [ed. Beaufort], 200.

7. "Geslacht-Boek," Oneida, N.Y., Historical Society; Van der Kemp, *Autobiography*; Jackson, *Scholar in the Wilderness*; Onnes, *Vermaner*.

8. Van der Capellen tot den Pol to Van der Capellen van de Marsch, 12 May 1780, Van der Capellen, *Brieven* [ed. Beaufort], 177–78; Hooft to Van der Capellen tot den Pol, 2 Oct. 1782, ibid., 366.

9. *Verzameling van Stukken*.

10. To Van der Kemp, 25 Nov. 1781, 11 Dec. 1785, 31 Oct., 7 Dec. 1786, Adams–Van der Kemp Correspondence.

11. *Beredeneerde Catalogus*; Van Berckhey, *Aan zijn Hooners*, 3; Hartog, *Uit de Dagen*, 99; Hardenbroek, *Gedenkschriften*, 3:197; Kluit, *Den laatsten Engelschen Oorlog*, 68–69.

12. Van der Kemp, *Het Gedrag van Israël*.

13. Van der Kemp, *Elftal*, 239–40; by a printing error, these page numbers are used twice.

14. Kneppelhout, *Gedenkteekenen*, no. 143; the drawing by Delfos is in the Academic Historical Museum of Leiden University, see *Icones Leidenses*, no. 194.

15. To Van der Kemp, 19 Jan. 1807, Adams–Van der Kemp Correspondence.

16. Adams, *Diary*, 10 Oct. 1782, 3:18–19.

17. Dumas Letterbook, 11 March, 22 April 1777, 24 July 1778; see also Ascoli, "American Propaganda," 291–307, especially 293–94.

18. 22 Aug., 1 Sept. 1780, Adams Papers, no. 102.

19. To Livingston, 4 Sept. 1782, Adams, *Works,* 7:623.

20. 13 Aug. 1778, Archief Fagel, no. 2525.

21. 25 May 1779, Collection Van Heukelom, Z, no. 42; see also Kluit, *Fransche Courant,* 74–75; Adams to Van der Kemp, 25 April 1808, Adams–Van der Kemp Correspondence; Ascoli, "American Propaganda," 301–2.

22. Adams, *Boston Patriot,* 256–57.

23. Kluit, *Politique Hollandais,* 3–4, and throughout.

24. *Lanterne Magique,* 30–40.

25. Collection Van Heukelom, Z, no. 146; De Wit, *Ontstaan,* 44–45.

26. Suringar, *Biographische Aantekeningen,* 67–68; Adams to Livingston, 16 May 1782, Adams, *Works,* 7:589–90.

CHAPTER 9

1. Van Wijk, *De Republiek,* 6; Nassau la Leck, *Brieven,* 1:5.

2. Van der Capellen, *Brieven* [ed. Beaufort], 114, 211, 249, 284, 342; Dumas Letterbook, 22 April, 6 May, 14 June 1777, 7 Sept. 1778; Adams to President of Congress, 25 Sept. 1780, *Revolutionary Diplomatic Correspondence,* 4:67–68; Adams, *Boston Patriot,* 334.

3. Vitringa, *Gedenkschrift,* 1:100; Mandrillon, *Gedenkschriften,* 96; Wagenaar, *Vervolg,* vol. 1, throughout.

4. Van de Spiegel, *Mr. Laurens Pieter van de Spiegel,* 2:82; Kluit, *Den laatsten Engelschen Oorlog,* 49–51, 145.

5. *History of the Internal Affairs,* 21; Ellis, *History of the Late Revolution,* 39; Harris, *Introduction,* 18, 286.

6. Ibid., 67–69; Wagenaar, *Vervolg,* 1:32; Colenbrander, *Patriottentijd,* 1:114.

7. Hardenberg, "Franklin en Nederland," 213–30.

8. R. Arrenberg to Franklin, 31 March, 24 May 1777, 7 May 1778, Franklin, *Calendar,* 5:131, 6:29, 9:127. See also B. Sowden to Franklin, 7 June 1777, ibid., 6:53.

9. C. S. Peuch to Franklin, 15 Dec. 1777, Franklin, *Calendar,* 7:148. See also Le Breton to Franklin, ibid., 41:89.

10. E. de Baussay to Franklin, 23 May, 25 July 1777, ibid., 6:26½, 138.

11. W. Wildrik to Franklin, 5 Aug., 2 Dec. 1777, 22 Jan. 1778, ibid., 6:166, 7:125, 8:56.

12. L. F. van Wijnbergen to Franklin, 21 May 1779, ibid., 14:128; L. Butot to Franklin, 3 Feb., 8 March 1778, ibid., 7:91, 8:159; P. van Noemer to Franklin, 9 June 1779, ibid., 14:166.

13. Adams to President of Congress, 14 Oct. 1780, *Revolutionary Diplomatic Correspondence,* 4:97; Edelman, *Dutch-American Bibliography.*

14. De Pauw, *Wijsgeerige Bespiegelingen;* Pernety, *Brief over de Bespiegelingen;* Raynal, *Geschiedenis;* Raynal, *Staatsomwentelingen;* Robertson, *Geschiedenis.* See also Commager and Giordanetti, *Was America a Mistake?*

15. Edwards, *Naaukeurig Onderzoek;* Edwards, *Geschiedenis;* Edwards, *Verhandeling.*

16. Kalm, *Reis;* Burnaby, *Travels through the Middle Settlements in North America;* the title of the Dutch translation was *Beknopte en Zakelijke Beschrijving der Voornaamste Engelsche Volksplantingen in Noord-Amerika.* . . .

17. Harris, *Introduction,* 255; *Jaarboek voor de Israelieten in Nederland,* 3:157–96.

18. *Lettre de Mr. *** à Mr. S. B.;* the publisher was the well-known Orangist Frederik Gosse. Kn. 19122; see also Kn. 19123–26.

19. Kn. 19179, 19954 (Tucker); Kn. 19119 and 19178 (Wesley); Kn. 19119 (Smith).

20. Kn. 19178; Kn. 19114: *Le Sens Commun, addressé aux habitants de l'Amérique.*
21. *De Staatsman.*
22. Rendorp, *Memoriën,* 1:67.
23. Archief Fagel, no. 2499, 31 Aug. 1776.
24. Nassau la Leck, *Brieven,* no. 10, 52–56; Van der Kemp, *Verzameling,* pp. xvi–xvii; De Pinto, *Seconde Lettre,* 20–21.
25. Nassau la Leck, *Brieven,* no. 11, 74–80; De Pinto, in Burnaby, *Beschrijving,* 348; *De Staatsman,* vol. 1, no. 1, 481–82.
26. Raynal, *Wijsgeerige en Staatkundige Geschiedenis,* 6:264–65, 7:202–5.
27. Echeverria, *Mirage in the West,* 62–64; De Pinto, *Seconde Lettre,* 25; *De Staatsman,* vol. 1, no. 1, 17–19.
28. Crèvecoeur, *Letters,* 64; Adams to Van der Kemp, 6 March 1824, Adams–Van der Kemp Correspondence; Dumas Letterbook, 8 May 1778.
29. *Drietal van Uitmuntende Dichtstukjes,* Kn. 19,973.
30. Adams, *Boston Patriot,* 431; Wagenaar, *Vervolg,* 1:35. See also Hardenbroek, *Gedenkschriften,* 3:22–23, 95–96.
31. *De Staatsman,* vol. 6, no. 1, 403–16; Van der Kemp, *Verzameling,* XXIII–XXIV.
32. *De Vaderlander,* no. 175, 4 May 1778.
33. Adams to Franklin, 17 Aug. 1780, Adams, *Works,* 7:247.
34. Adams to Luzac, 5, 15 Sept. 1780, to Van der Capellen tot den Pol, 9 Dec. 1780, Luzac to Adams, 14 Sept. 1780, ibid., 7:248–49, 253–56, 339–40.
35. Luzac, "Het Amerikaansche Volk," 443–68; Adams to Cotton Tufts, 9 Dec. 1780, *Adams Family Correspondence,* 4:29–30.
36. Amstelophilus, *Op de Onafhankelykheid van Noord-Amerika.* Kn. 19972.

CHAPTER 10

1. Adams, *Boston Patriot,* 103–4; Adams to President of Congress, 19 Sept. 1780, Adams, *Works,* 7:258–60.
2. Letters exchanged with bankers, in ibid., 7:260–62, 313, 323–28. See also Van Winter, *Aandeel,* 1:45–49.
3. Bicker to Adams, 6 Oct. 1780, Adams to Gillon, 12 Nov. 1780, to President of Congress, 14 Dec. 1780, Adams, *Works,* 7:313, 328, 342; to Abigail Adams, 18 Dec. 1780, *Adams Family Correspondence,* 4:34–36.
4. Van Winter, *Aandeel,* 1:49–50; Adams to Neufville, 11 March 1781, Adams, *Works,* 7:376; Wagenaar, *Vervolg,* 7:52; Adams, *Boston Patriot,* 377–78.
5. Foley, "Triumph," 150–51; Van Winter, *Aandeel,* 1:53–56.
6. Hardenbroek, *Gedenkschriften,* 2:105, 144–45, 187.
7. Testimony of George Keppel, 6 Oct. 1780, in Stevens, *Facsimiles,* vol. 10, no. 923.
8. *Revolutionary Diplomatic Correspondence,* 1:578–80; Hardenbroek, *Gedenkschriften,* 1:404; Doniol, *Histoire,* 5:45–46.
9. Archief Staten-Generaal, Liassen Engeland 1780, no. 5993–94; Lord Viscount Stormont to Sir Joseph Yorke, 11 Oct. 1780, Stevens, *Facsimiles,* vol. 10, no. 948.
10. Yorke to Stormont, 17 Oct. 1780, ibid., no. 951.
11. Resolutiën Staten van Holland vóór 1795, 20, 25 Oct. 1780; Familie-Archief Van Slingelandt, De Vrij Temminck, no. 508.
12. Hardenbroek, *Gedenkschriften,* 2:242; Kn. 19394.
13. Adams to President of Congress, 16, 17 Nov. 1780, Adams, *Works,* 7:329–32.
14. Foley, "Triumph," 86; Calkoen, Kn. 19430; Van Wijk, *De Republiek,* 114–20.
15. Hardenbroek, *Gedenkschriften,* 2:284, 297, 312.

16. Adams to President of Congress, 14 Dec. 1780, Adams, *Works*, 8:341–42; to James Warren, 9 Dec. 1780, *Warren-Adams Letters*, 2:154–55; to President of Congress, 18 Dec. 1780, *Revolutionary Diplomatic Correspondence*, 4:197; to Livingston, 21 Feb. 1782, Adams, *Works*, 7:523.

17. Adams to President of Congress, 25 Dec. 1780, ibid., 7:346–47; to President of Congress, 25 Dec. 1780, *Revolutionary Diplomatic Correspondence*, 4:209.

18. Adams to President of Congress, 31 Dec. 1780, Adams, *Works*, 7:348–49.

19. Adams, *Boston Patriot*, 331–34.

20. Hardenbroek, *Gedenkschriften*, 2:335–38, 538.

21. Beauchamp to Vaughan, 29 Dec. 1780, Vaughan Papers; Adams, *Boston Patriot*, 279, 334; Hardenbroek, *Gedenkschriften*, 2:448; Abigail Adams to John Adams, 25 May 1781, *Adams Family Correspondence*, 4:129; Philip Mazzei to Jefferson, 8 April 1781, Jefferson, *Papers*, 5:375–78.

22. Hardenbroek, *Gedenkschriften*, 2:311, 351, 403.

23. Adams to Dana, 18 Jan. 1781, to Dumas, 25 Jan. 1781, Adams, *Works*, 8:353–54, 360–62; Dumas Letterbook, 28 Jan. 1781 (also in Adams, *Works*, 8:363); Hardenbroek, *Gedenkschriften*, 2:422, 478–79.

24. Van der Capellen, *Brieven* [ed. Beaufort], 10 March 1781, 222–23.

25. Van Lennep, "Rendorp," 9–33; Hardenbroek, *Gedenkschriften*, 3:546.

26. Kannegieter, "Affaire," 245–89.

CHAPTER 11

1. Adams to Dumas, 25 Jan., 2, 6 Feb. 1781, Dumas to Adams, 28 Jan. 1781, Adams, *Works*, 7:360–64, 366–67.

2. Adams to Bicker, 20 Feb., 1 March 1781, Bicker to Adams, 21 Feb. 1781, ibid., 7:369–72.

3. The memoir of 8 March in ibid., 7:373, with letters pp. 373–75; La Vauguyon to Adams, ibid., 7:378; William V to Van Bleiswijk, 12 March 1781, *Archives de la Maison d'Orange*, 2:403–4; Foley, "Triumph," 116–22; Van Wijk, *De Republiek*, 136–37, confuses the two memoirs.

4. Dumas to Adams, 17 March 1781, Adams to Dumas, 17 March 1781, Adams, *Works*, 7:379–80.

5. Adams to President of Congress, 19 March, 6 April 1781, to Dana, 22 March 1781, to Jay, 28 March 1781, ibid., 7:380–86.

6. Foley, "Triumph," 126–27; Adams to Jennings, 27 April 1781, quoted in Adams, *Diary*, 2:456; Adams to Abigail Adams, 28 April 1781, *Adams Family Correspondence*, 4:108–9.

7. Dana to Adams, 18 April 1781, Adams to Dana, 18 April 1781, Adams, *Works*, 7:391–94.

8. Foley, "Triumph," 125–26; Dumas to Adams, 14 April 1781, Adams to La Vauguyon, 16 April 1781, La Vauguyon to Adams, 17 April 1781, Adams, *Works*, 7:387–88, 390.

9. Adams to Livingston, 21 Feb. 1782, ibid., 7:528–30; Adams, *Boston Patriot*, 430–33; Waterhouse to Levi Woodbury, 20 Feb. 1835, Levi Woodbury Papers, vol. 16; La Vauguyon to Vergennes, 11, 15 May 1781, *Archives de la Maison d'Orange*, 2:468–69, 478–79.

10. Waterhouse to Woodbury, 20 Feb. 1835, Levi Woodbury Papers.

11. Kn. 19506, 19506a, 19507, English text in Adams, *Works*, 7:396–404, letter to William V, 7:505–7.

12. Adams to President of Congress, 3, 7 May 1781, ibid., 7:409–10, 412–15; Dumas Letterbook, 1–4 May 1781; *Archives de la Maison d'Orange*, 2:434–44; Archief Staten-

Generaal, 1781, no. 3615; Wagenaar, *Vervolg*, 8:40–41; *Post van den Neder-Rhijn*, 1:132, 154.

13. Livingston to Jay, 21 Oct. 1781, quoted in Dangerfield, *Livingston*, 150; Livingston to Adams, 23 Oct., 20 Nov. 1781, *Revolutionary Diplomatic Correspondence*, 4:806–9, 849–51; Dangerfield, *Livingston*, 150–51.

14. Adams to Livingston, 14, 19 Feb. 1782, Adams, *Works*, 7:510–18; to Dumas, 19 May 1781, ibid., 7:420–21; to Abigail Adams, 22 May 1781, *Adams Family Correspondence*, 4:121–22; to President of Congress, 24 May 1781, *Revolutionary Diplomatic Correspondence*, 4:431–33.

15. Dumas to President of Congress, 11, 16 May 1781, ibid., 4:394; *Le Politique Hollandais*, 1:260.

16. *Consideratieën op de Memorie*, June 1781 (Kn. 19508); see also Adams's reply, Adams, *Works*, 7:524, and for other pamphlets, Van Wijk, *De Republiek*, 138–43.

17. Adams to Dumas, 1 June 1781, to President of the States-General, Adams, *Works*, 7:423; Dumas to Adams, 6 June 1781, ibid., 7:424–25 (text in French), *Revolutionary Diplomatic Correspondence*, 4:394–95 (text in English).

18. Adams to Livingston, 21 Feb. 1782, Adams, *Works*, 7:521–30; Franklin, *Writings*, 9:62.

CHAPTER 12

1. John Quincy Adams to Henry Coleman, 25 Aug. 1826, quoted in Bemis, *John Quincy Adams*, 11; Abigail Adams to J. Q. Adams, 19 Jan. 1780, *Adams Family Correspondence*, 3:268–69.

2. J. Thaxter to J. Q. Adams, 21 Aug. 1780, ibid., 3:399–400; to Abigail Adams, 19 Sept. 1780, ibid., 3:418–19.

3. John Adams to Abigail Adams, 25 Sept. 1780, ibid., 3:424–25; to Rector Verheyk, 18 Oct., 10 Nov. 1780, to Abigail Adams, 18 Dec. 1780, Verheyk to Adams, 10 Nov. 1780, ibid., 4:10–12, 34–35.

4. Waterhouse to Adams, 13 Dec. 1780, Thaxter to Adams, 19 Dec. 1780, ibid., 4:31–32, 37–38; *Album Studiosorum*; Adams, *Diary*, 2:451–52; John Adams to Abigail Adams, 18 Dec. 1780, to John Quincy Adams, 20 Dec. 1780, *Adams Family Correspondence*, 4:34–36, 38–39.

5. John Adams to John Quincy Adams, 23 Dec. 1780, ibid., 4:47–49.

6. John Quincy Adams to Abigail Adams, 8 April 1781, to John Adams, 18 Feb., 17 May 1781, ibid., 4:81, 100–102, 116; John Adams to Van der Kemp, 20 Jan. 1799, Adams–Van der Kemp Correspondence.

7. Waterhouse to John Adams, 26 Dec. 1780, *Adams Family Correspondence*, 4:53–54; Thaxter to John Adams, 1, 23 Jan. 1781, ibid., 4:57, 69; John Quincy Adams to John Adams, 3, 18 Feb., 13 May 1781, ibid., 4:74, 82, 113–14; John Adams to John Quincy Adams, 12 Feb., 18, 20 May 1781, ibid., 4:80, 117, 144.

8. Luzac, *Socrates*, 8.

9. John Adams to John Quincy Adams, 28 Dec. 1780, *Adams Family Correspondence*, 4:55–56; John Quincy Adams to John Adams, 19 May 1781, ibid., 4:118; Waterhouse to John Adams, 21 May 1781, ibid., 4:120–21.

10. Abigail Adams to her daughter, ca. 11 Feb. 1779, ibid., 3:161–62; John Adams to Abigail Adams, 11 July 1781, ibid., 4:169–70; John Adams to John Quincy Adams, 5 Feb. 1782, ibid., 4:283; John Quincy Adams to John Adams, 21 Feb., 4 March 1782, ibid., 4:286–87.

11. Dumas Letterbook, 9, 16 May 1783.

12. John Adams to Abigail Adams, 14 May, 1 July 1782, *Adams Family Correspondence*, 4:323, 337; Abigail Adams to John Adams, 10 April, 17 June 1782, ibid., 4:306–7, 328.

CHAPTER 13

1. Vergennes to La Luzerne, 9 March 1781, quoted in Dangerfield, *Livingston*, 138; see also Bemis, *Diplomacy*, especially ch. 13; Morris, *Peacemakers*, especially chs. 8–10; Stinchcombe, *American Revolution*; and Doniol, *Histoire*, 5:45–61.

2. Abigail Adams to James Lovell, 30 June 1781, *Adams Family Correspondence*, 4:164–66.

3. Adams, *Boston Patriot*, 399; Hardenbroek, *Gedenkschriften*, 2:570–71, 620, 633.

4. Adams to President of Congress, 15, 23 June 1781, Adams, *Works*, 7:427–30.

5. Adams to Vergennes, 18 July 1781, ibid., 7:444–46; the complete exchange of letters in Paris, ibid., 7:433–52; see also Foley, "Triumph," 179–90, and Morris, *Peacemakers*, 204–9.

6. Adams, *Boston Patriot*, 133.

7. Franklin to Adams, 16 Aug. 1781, Adams, *Works*, 7:456; Adams to Franklin, 25 Aug. 1781, ibid., 7:459–61; Adams to Dana, 14 Dec. 1781, ibid., 7:493–95; Adams, *Diary*, 3:105.

8. John Adams to Abigail Adams, 2 Dec. 1781, *Adams Family Correspondence*, 4:249–51.

9. John Adams to President of Congress, 3 Aug. 1781, Adams, *Works*, 7:453–56; to Franklin, 25 Aug. 1781, ibid., 7:459–61.

10. John Adams to Abigail Adams, 9 Oct. 1781, *Adams Family Correspondence*, 4:224; to President of Congress, 15 Oct. 1781, *Revolutionary Diplomatic Correspondence*, 4:780.

11. John Adams to President of Congress, 15 Oct. 1781, Adams, *Works*, 7:471–75.

12. Adams to President of Congress, 17, 25 Oct. 1781, *Revolutionary Diplomatic Correspondence*, 4:782–83, 810–12.

13. Wagenaar, *Vervolg*, 8:46–51; *Nieuwe Nederlandsche Jaarboeken*, 1781, pp. 884, 2208–12; John Adams to President of Congress, 1 Nov. 1781, *Revolutionary Diplomatic Correspondence*, 4:813–14.

14. Washington to John Adams, 2 Oct. 1781, Adams, *Works*, 7:475; John Adams to John Jay, 26, 28 Nov. 1781, ibid., 7:484–87; to President of Congress, 4 Dec. 1781, ibid., 7:487–89; to Richard Cranch, 18 Dec. 1781, *Adams Family Correspondence*, 4:266–67.

CHAPTER 14

1. Adams to Dumas, 6 Dec. 1781, Adams, *Works*, 7:489–90.

2. Adams to President of Congress, 18 Dec. 1781, ibid., 7:497–98; to La Vauguyon, 19 Dec. 1781, ibid., 7:498–500; La Vauguyon to Adams, 30 Dec. 1781, ibid., 7:500–501. See also Foley, "Triumph," 203–8; Van der Capellen to Adams, 6 Jan. 1782, Van der Capellen, *Brieven* [ed. Beaufort], 264–65.

3. Adams to President of Congress, 14 Jan. 1782, Adams, *Works*, 7:504–8; Dumas to President of Congress, 15 Jan. 1782, *Revolutionary Diplomatic Correspondence*, 5:102–3; Adams to Van der Capellen tot den Pol, 14 Jan. 1781, Adams, *Works*, 7:502–3; Van der Capellen tot den Pol to Van der Capellen van de Marsch, 17 Jan. 1782, Van der Capellen, *Brieven* [ed. Beaufort], 164–65.

4. Hardenbroek, *Gedenkschriften*, 3:264–68, 294–97, 308.

5. Ibid., 3:312–14; Rendorp, *Memoriën*, 2:142–48.
6. *De Staatsman*, vol. 4, no. 1, p. 37; La Vauguyon to Vergennes, 15 March 1782, *Archives de la Maison d'Orange*, 3:30–31.
7. Colenbrander, *Patriottentijd*, 1:228; Geyl, *Patriottenbeweging*, 58–59; Hutson, *Adams*, 105–6.
8. Van der Capellen tot den Pol to Valck, 13 March 1782, Van der Capellen, *Brieven* [ed. Beaufort], 272–75; to P. van Spaan [?], 24 March 1782, ibid., 762–78; *Zuid-Hollandsche Courant*, 25 March 1782, Collection Dumont-Pigalle; Mandrillon, *Gedenkschriften*, 102.
9. Hardenbroek, *Gedenkschriften*, 3:469; texts of the two resolutions in *Nieuwe Nederlandsche Jaarboeken*, 1782, 268ff.; the joint text of Leiden, Haarlem, and Amsterdam, ibid., 278–85; English versions in *A Collection of State Papers Relative to the First Acknowledgment of the United States of America*; Thaxter to Abigail Adams, 23 March 1782, *Adams Family Correspondence*, 4:281–92; *De Staatsman*, vol. 5, no. 1, pp. 59–62.
10. Van de Spiegel, *Van de Spiegel*, 2:59–62.
11. Rendorp, *Memoriën*, 2:169; Wagenaar, *Vervolg*, 14:28–30, 33–35; Van Winter, *Aandeel*, 1:95–97, and ch. 4, throughout.
12. Hardenbroek, *Gedenkschriften*, 2:669; John Adams to F. Dana, 15 March 1782, Adams, *Works*, 7:543–44; to Livingston, 11 March 1782, ibid., 7:538–39; *Nieuwe Nederlandsche Jaarboeken*, 1782, pp. 396–97.
13. Adams to Livingston, 27 Feb. 1782, *Revolutionary Diplomatic Correspondence*, 5:206–7; to La Vauguyon, 1 March 1782, Adams, *Works*, 7:532–34; La Vauguyon to Adams, 4 March 1782, ibid., 7:534; Foley, "Triumph," 236–37.
14. Adams to Dumas, 13 March 1782, Adams, *Works*, 7:542; Adams to Dumas, 14 March 1782, Dumas Papers; Dumas to Adams, 16 March 1782, Adams, *Works*, 7:545–46, and no date, ibid., 540–42.
15. Van der Capellen tot den Pol to Valck, 13 March 1782, Van der Capellen, *Brieven* [ed. Beaufort], 272–75.
16. Adams to Livingston, 27 Feb. 1782, *Revolutionary Diplomatic Correspondence*, 5:206–7; Van Goens, *Brieven aan Van Goens*, 3:117; Hardenbroek, *Gedenkschriften*, 3:400; Van Berckhey, *Samenspraak*, 32. The Dutch poem by Van Berckhey reads:

Op den Americaanschen Adam

Hoe Adam zeg! wat doet ge in Holland Paradijs?
Zoekt hij een Eva uit uw eigen rib te vormen,
Wees niet te roekeloos, o Adam, zijt gij wijs,
Denk dat de Oranje vrugt niet is voor zulke wormen.
Maar wil uw Eva van verboden vrugten eeten,
Zij neme een leliebol, en gij eet dan met haar?
Zoo zult gij uw Eden in America vergeeten,
En als een balling 's lands omzwerven in gevaar:
Ga, wijl gij God en uwen Koning dorst vertoornen,
Na uw woestijnen vol van distelen en doornen.

17. Hardenbroek, *Gedenkschriften*, 3:397, 411–12.
18. Ibid., 3:416.
19. T. Digges to Adams, Adams, *Works*, 7:549; D. Hartley to Adams, 11 March 1782, ibid., 7:550; Adams to Digges, 21 March 1782, ibid., 7:551; to Franklin, ibid., 7:554–55; Morris, *Peacemakers*, 255–57.
20. Dumas to Adams, 22 March 1782, Adams, *Works*, 7:552–53; Hardenbroek, *Gedenkschriften*, 3:421–22; John Adams to Abigail Adams, 22 March 1782, *Adams Family Correspondence*, 4:300–301; to Franklin, 26 March 1782, Adams, *Works*, 7:554–55; Hardenbroek, *Gedenkschriften*, 3:423, 433–37, 439.

21. La Vauguyon to Vergennes, 29 March 1782, *Archives de la Maison d'Orange*, 3:41–43; Hardenbroek, *Gedenkschriften*, 444–45; Dumas to Adams, 28, 29, 30 March 1782, Adams, *Works*, 7:557–60.

22. Colenbrander, *Patriottentijd*, 1:229–31; Hardenbroek, *Gedenkschriften*, 3:452; Adams to Van Bleiswijk, 31 March 1782, Adams, *Works*, 7:557–60.

23. Franklin to Livingston, 12 April 1782, *Revolutionary Diplomatic Correspondence*, 5:300.

24. Adams to Franklin, 16 April 1782, Adams, *Works*, 7:569–71; Morris, *Peacemakers*, 266–67.

25. Report of Utrecht on recognition, 3 April 1782, Archief van Hardenbroek, no. 28; Hardenbroek, *Gedenkschriften*, 3:441.

CHAPTER 15

1. *Le Politique Hollandais*, 2:397; La Vauguyon to Vergennes, 2 April 1782, *Archives de la Maison d'Orange*, 3:48–49.

2. *Resoluties Staten-Generaal*, 1782, vol. 1, no. 3618; *Nieuwe Nederlandsche Jaarboeken*, 1782, pp. 459–63.

3. Dumas to Franklin, 15 April 1782, Franklin Papers; Adams to Livingston, 22, 23, 24 April 1782, Adams, *Works*, 7:571–75; Adams, *Diary*, 3:1–3.

4. Ibid., 3:14; *Nouvelles Extraordinaires*, no. 35, 26 April 1782; Van der Capellen tot den Pol, 29 Sept. 1782, *Brieven* [ed. Beaufort], 342.

5. La Vauguyon to Vergennes, 23 April 1782, *Archives de la Maison d'Orange*, 3:92; Wagenaar, *Vervolg*, 12:161–67; *Eerkroon op de Hoofden*; *Gedenkzuil*; *Eerekroon, voor de Beschermers*; *De Amerikaansche Koopman*; Adams, *Works*, 7:576–78.

6. *Dockummer Almanack; Der Friesen Vreugde; Frieslands Vreugde.*

7. *Samenspraak (in 't Rijk der Dooden)*, 22–25; Wagenaar, *Vervolg*, 1:17, 22; *Onpartydige en Vrymoedige Aanmerkingen*; *Le Politique Hollandais*, 12 March, 2, 9 April 1781, pp. 87, 116, 139–40.

8. Nijland, *Bellamy*, 1:205; Luzac, *Socrates*, 7; Van Beyma, "Brieven," 275.

9. William V to Fagel, 20 Aug. 1776, *Archives de la Maison d'Orange*, 1:449; Burnaby, *Beschrijving*, 305–6.

10. *Le Politique Hollandais*, 2:71, 118–20, 130–36; *Verzameling der Stukken*, p. xxviii; *Post van den Neder-Rhijn*, 1782, p. 582.

11. Honour, *The New Golden Land*; Honour, *European Vision*; *Algemeene Staatkundige Konstplaat*.

12. "Op den Silveren Eerepenning," Archief Sociëteit Door Vrijheid en Yver; Muller, "Tweemaal Marshallhulp," 97–107; Byvanck, *Bataafsch Verleden*.

13. *Nieuwe Nederlandsche Jaarboeken*, 1783, pp. 577–84.

14. *Alweêr een Request.*

15. John Adams to Dana, 13 May 1782, Adams, *Works*, 7:583–84; to Livingston, 16 May 1782, ibid., 7:587–88; to Abigail Adams, 14 May, 1 July 1782, *Adams Family Correspondence*, 4:323–25, 338; Adams to Van der Kemp, 29 May 1814, Adams–Van der Kemp Correspondence; John Adams to Dana, 17 Sept. 1782, Adams, *Works*, 7:632–33.

CHAPTER 16

1. Butterfield, *Butterfield in Holland*, 15; Adams, *Diary*, 3:65.

2. Dumas Letterbook, 23 Feb. 1782; Hardenbroek, *Gedenkschriften*, 3:400; Dumas to John Adams, 24 Feb. 1782, Adams, *Works*, 7:530.

3. Adams to Livingston, 27 Feb. 1782, *Revolutionary Diplomatic Correspondence*, 5:206–7; Dumas to Livingston, 4 April 1782, Dumas Letterbook (partly also in *Revolutionary Diplomatic Correspondence*, 5:292–93); Thaxter to John Adams, 6 May 1782, *Adams Family Correspondence*, 4:322; Adams to Livingston, 16 May 1782, Adams, *Works*, 7:587; John Adams to Abigail Adams, 16 June 1782, *Adams Family Correspondence*, 4:324–25.

4. Adams Papers, Inventory, 14 May, 16 Oct. 1782, 24 June 1784.

5. Adams to Livingston, 16 May, 5 July 1782, Adams, *Works*, 7:587–91, 599–600; to Lafayette, 29 Sept. 1782, ibid., 7:642; Adams, *Diary*, 3:24; Adams to Arthur Lee, 29 Aug. 1782, in Lee, *Arthur Lee*, 1:59–67.

6. E. M. A. Martini to Dutch Secretary of Foreign Affairs, 11 May 1841, Archief Buitenlandse Zaken, no. 1230.

7. Dumas Letterbook, 12 Feb., 16 May 1781; Livingston to Dumas, 28 Nov. 1781, *Revolutionary Diplomatic Correspondence*, 5:30–32; Dumas Letterbook, 5 Feb. 1782.

8. Dumas Letterbook, 4 April, 25 Oct. 1782; Adams, *Boston Patriot*, 335; Adams to Dumas, 2 May 1782, Adams, *Works*, 7:578–79; to Livingston, 16 May 1782, ibid., 7:589; Dumas to Livingston, 10 May 1782, *Revolutionary Diplomatic Correspondence*, 5:408–10; Dumas Letterbook, 4 July 1782.

9. Livingston to Dumas, 12 Sept. 1782, *Revolutionary Diplomatic Correspondence*, 5:724–25; to Adams, 15 Sept. 1782, ibid., 5:728–30.

10. Oliver, *Portraits*, 14–27.

11. La Vauguyon to Vergennes, 23 April 1782, *Archives de la Maison d'Orange*, 3:92–94; Oliver, *Portraits*, 25; John Adams to Abigail Adams, 1 July 1782, *Adams Family Correspondence*, 4:337–38; C. W. Visscher to William V, 15 July 1782, Van Bleiswijk to William V, 15 July 1782, *Archives de la Maison d'Orange*, 3:121–23; Hardenbroek, *Gedenkschriften*, 4:37, 84–85, 119; Adams, *Diary*, 3:5–13.

12. Adams to Livingston, 15 June, 22 Aug., 17 Sept. 1782, Adams, *Works*, 7:598, 614, 646–48; to Jay, 10 Aug. 1782, ibid., 7:606; Secrete Resolutiën Staten-Generaal, 1782, no. 4771; *Nieuwe Nederlandsche Jaarboeken*, 1782, pp. 1161–80; Adams, *Diary*, 3:15–17.

13. Ibid., 3:25–30.

CHAPTER 17

1. Adams, *Diary*, 3:30–37.

2. John Adams to Dumas, 28 March 1783, Lewis Cass Papers; to Jay, 2 June 1785, Adams, *Works*, 8:255–59.

3. Adams to Livingston, 18 July 1783, ibid., 8:108; to R. Morris, 28 July 1783, ibid., 8:119; Van Winter, *Aandeel*, 1:86–87.

4. Adams to Willink, 10 Jan. 1785, Adams, *Works*, 8:219; to President of Congress, 10 Jan. 1785, ibid., 8:221; to Jefferson, 12 Feb. 1788, *Adams-Jefferson Papers*, 1:224.

5. Adams, *Diary*, 3:152–54; Adams to Franklin, 24 Jan. 1784, Adams, *Works*, 8:170–71.

6. Watson, *Tour*, 71–82.

7. Fagel to Van Lynden, 7 May 1785, Collection H. Nieuwenhuisen; Dumas Letterbook, 8 June 1785; Dumas to Adams, 7, 8 June 1785, Adams, *Works*, 8:261–65; Adams to Fagel, 10 June 1785, ibid., 8:266–67; Fagel to Adams, 14 June 1785, ibid., 8:267–68.

8. Abigail Adams to Mrs. Cranch, 12 Sept. 1786, Abigail Adams, *Letters*, 345–48.

9. Adams to Fagel, 25 Jan. 1788, Adams, *Works*, 9:470–72; Fagel to Adams, 12 Feb. 1788, ibid., 8:472–73; Resolutiën Staten-Generaal, 1788, 481–83.

CHAPTER 18

1. Van de Spiegel, *Van de Spiegel*, 2:161–62.
2. *Post van den Neder-Rhijn*, 1783, pp. 1039–42; Wagenaar, *Vervolg*, 12:192.
3. Diary of Carel de Vos van Steenwijk, 55–56 (now owned by A. N. Baron de Vos van Steenwijk, Doorwerth; see his article "Een Drents Patriot"), Archief Staten-Generaal, Liassen Amerika 7130, 20 Oct. 1783.
4. Schulte Nordholt, "Bevestiging," 34–65.
5. Collection Van der Meulen, nos. 30–33.
6. Nijland, *Bellamy*, 1:285–86; Luzac, *Socrates*, 4; Bosch, *Onze Verpligting*, 8.
7. Letters of P. A. Godin, Archief Slot Zuylen, no. 920; H. Hooft to Van der Capellen tot den Pol, 3 April 1783, Van der Capellen, *Brieven* [ed. Beaufort], 563; letters of G. Vogels to N. S. van Winter van Merken in Archief Six van Hillegom; see also Höweler, "Lucretia Wilhelmina van Merken," 70–77.
8. Carel de Vos van Steenwijk, Diary, 57.
9. Van Hogendorp, *Brieven*, 1:350–51; Schulte Nordholt, "Van Hogendorp in Amerika," 117–42.
10. Van Hogendorp, *Brieven*, 1:418–20.
11. Ibid., 1:284–85; Archief Van Hogendorp, 36, no. 10-1.
12. Ibid., 36, nos. 10^d, 54^a, 54^n; Van Hogendorp, *Brieven*, 1:313–15; Jefferson, *Papers*, 7:216–18.
13. Archief Van Hogendorp, 36, no. 10.
14. Ibid., 71; Van Hogendorp, *Brieven*, 1:284.
15. Van Polanen, Letters to the Batavian Government, Archief Buitenlandse Zaken, no. 358.
16. Ibid., 7 Dec., 20 Dec. 1801.
17. Ibid., 12 May 1802.
18. Ibid., 6 April 1799.

CHAPTER 19

1. De Wit, *Strijd*, 42.
2. *The Federalist*, no. 20, p. 126; Main, *Anti-Federalists*, throughout; Schulte Nordholt, "Example," 65–77.
3. *Grondwettige Herstelling*, 1:18; *Zuid-Hollandsche Courant* (Woerden), 25 March 1782; Wagenaar, *Vervolg*, 12:160; Mandrillon, *Gedenkschriften*, 102.
4. Boeles, *Swindens*, 123–33.
5. Van de Spiegel, *Van de Spiegel*, 4:503; Schimmelpenninck, *Verhandeling*; Plemp van Duiveland, *Schimmelpenninck*, 10–11.
6. De Wit, *Nederlandse Revolutie*, 157–58.
7. Ibid., 65–66; Archief Dumont-Pigalle, GGGG.
8. De Jong Hzn., *Van der Capellen*, 187–89; Van der Kemp, *Historie der Admissie*, 197; Van der Capellen tot den Pol, *Aan het Volk*, 64, 131; Van der Capellen tot den Pol, *Brieven* [ed. Beaufort], 26 Dec. 1783, p. 723.
9. *Post van den Neder-Rhijn*, 1782, pp. 881–88, 897–904; *Grondwettige Herstelling*, 1:xv.
10. Boeles, *Swindens*, 297–302; *Nieuwe Nederlandsche Jaarboeken*, 1785, pp. 1433–34; De Wit, *Nederlandse Revolutie*, 40–41; Collection Dumont-Pigalle, X; *Nieuwe Nederlandsche Jaarboeken*, 1787, p. 1364.
11. Paape, *Onverbloemde Geschiedenis*, 55–59, 67.

12. Adams to Arthur Lee, 4 Sept. 1785, in Lee, *Arthur Lee*, 2:256–57.

13. Abigail Adams, *Letters*, 344; Adams to Jefferson, 11 Sept. 1786, Jefferson, *Papers*, 10:348–49 (also in Adams, *Works*, 8:414).

14. Palmer, "Dubious Democrat," 388–404 (reprint in Peterson, ed., *Jefferson*, 86–103); Jefferson to Edmund Randolph, 3 Aug. 1787, Jefferson, *Papers*, 11:672–73; to John Jay, 6 Aug. 1787, ibid., 11:693–700.

15. Adams to Jay, 15, 30 Nov. 1787, Adams, *Works*, 8:459–64; to Abigail Adams, 14 March 1788, quoted in Jackson, *Scholar in the Wilderness*, 56–57.

CHAPTER 20

1. Kluit, *Den laatsten Engelschen Oorlog*, 28–29; Van Goens, *Brieven aan Van Goens*, 1:91.

2. Kluit, *Rechten van den Mensch*, 355, 357.

3. Van Hogendorp, "Gelijkheid der Menschen (door Pieter Paulus) weerlegd," *Archief Van Hogendorp*, no. 71; see also Schulte Nordholt, "Van Hogendorp," 117–42; *The Federalist*, 349.

4. Van der Aa, *Biografisch Woordenboek*, 3:394–96; *Nieuw Nederlandsch Biografisch Woordenboek*, 1:759–61; Van der Pot, "De twee Dumbar's," 123–42; Dumbar, *Oude en nieuwe Constitutie*.

5. Luzac to William Short, 14 Sept. 1792, Dreer Letters, Historical Society of Philadelphia; Luzac, *Socrates*; *Advisen van Mr. Matthias Temminck*, Collection Van Heukelom, family archives, no. S; John Quincy Adams to John Adams, 3 Dec. 1794, John Quincy Adams, *Writings*, 1:246; Adams to Van der Kemp, 6 Dec. 1796, Adams–Van der Kemp Correspondence; Luzac to Washington, 30 Sept. 1797, Simon Gratz Collection, case 12, box 17; Washington to Luzac, 2 Dec. 1797, Washington, *Writings*, 26:84.

6. Bemis, *John Quincy Adams*, 50–65.

7. Rogge, *Geschiedenis*, 28–29; Jan Carel Smissaert to J. Valckenaer, 30 Oct. 1796, Colenbrander, *Gedenkstukken*, 2:507–8.

8. *Het Plan van Constitutie van 1796*, xxii–xxiii.

9. *Dagverhaal der Handelingen*, 18 Jan. 1797, 4:544.

10. 19 Nov. 1796, ibid., 3:716.

11. 23 Nov. 1796, ibid., 4:25–28, 59–64.

12. 28 Nov. 1796, ibid., 4:119–20.

13. 27 Jan. 1797, ibid., 4:661–62.

14. 21 Nov. 1796, ibid., 4:41–48.

15. 14 Feb. 1797, ibid., 4:941–42.

16. 24 Nov. 1796, ibid., 4:59; 2 June 1796, ibid., 2:43.

17. 22 April 1797, ibid., 5:727–33; 22 May 1797, ibid., 6:10–14, 18–21.

EPILOGUE

1. Van der Capellen to Valck, 12 March 1783, Van der Capellen, *Brieven* [ed. Beaufort], 564–66; to [?], 29 May 1784, ibid., 849–52.

2. Van der Pot, "Bij de Grafzuil van den Onsterffelijken Ridder Johan Derk van der Capellen tot den Pol," 4–4a.

3. Adams to President of Congress, 13 May 1784, Adams, *Works*, 8:200–201; Dumas Letterbook, 12 April 1783; *Journals of the Continental Congress*, 29:835; Dumas Letterbook, 23 April, 3 Oct., 6 Oct. 1786.

4. Archief Staten-Generaal, 7462, IV, Lias Amerika; Dumas Letterbook, 22, 25, 27, 28 Sept. 1787.

5. Dumas to Jefferson, 23 Sept. 1787, Jefferson, *Papers*, 12:168–69; to Jay, 26 Oct. 1787, Dumas Letterbook.

6. Archief Fagel, no. 1467; Adams to Jay, 15 Nov. 1787, Adams, *Works*, 8:459–61; Van Berkenrode and Brantsen to Fagel, 4 Oct. 1787, Archief Van Bleiswijk, A, no. 13.

7. Abigail Adams to John Quincy Adams, 12 Oct. 1787, in Abigail Adams, *Letters*, 395–99.

8. Jefferson, *Papers*, 12:200–201.

9. Dumas Letterbook, 22, 27 Nov. 1787; Jefferson, *Papers*, 12:359–60, 388–90; Dumas Letterbook, 27 Nov. 1787, 2 Feb., 1 March 1788.

10. Dumas Letterbook, 23 March 1788.

11. Ibid., 18, 26 July, Aug. 1788.

12. Archief Staten-Generaal, no. 7462, Lias Amerika.

13. Dumas Letterbook, 26 Sept. 1788; Archief Staten-Generaal, no. 7462, Lias Amerika; Dumas Letterbook, 9 Oct. 1788.

14. Ibid., 27 April, 20 July, 26 May 1789, 23 June, 23 July 1790, 24 May, 1 Oct. 1791, 19 Feb., 23 April, 27 May, 7 June 1792.

15. Ibid., 22 June 1793, 30 Nov. 1794.

16. Ibid., 12 April 1795; Archief Staten-Generaal, no. 7462, IV, Lias Amerika; Dumas Letterbook, 11 Dec. 1795.

17. Adams to Van der Kemp, 29 Jan., 23 April 1807, Adams–Van der Kemp Correspondence.

18. Adams to Jefferson, 9 Aug. 1816, *Adams-Jefferson Letters*, 2:485; Jefferson to Madison, 8 March 1788, Jefferson, *Papers*, 12:656; Adams to Van der Kemp, in Seymour, *Centennial Address*, 18; Van der Kemp, *Autobiography*, 110–16; Van der Kemp to Luzac, 15 July 1788, Archief Luzac.

19. "A Tour," in Seymour, *Centennial Address*, 131–32; Jackson, *Scholar*, 131–32; Jones, *Annals*, 449–66; Van Winter, *Aandeel*, 2:231, 160–72.

20. Van der Kemp to P. Vreede, 25 July, 16 Aug. 1815, Archief Vreede en Van Marle.

21. Van der Kemp, *Autobiography*, 178–81; Jackson, *Scholar*, 283–97; Van der Kemp to Vreede, 4 Nov. 1819, 21 Oct. 1821, 21 Sept. 1822, Archief Vreede en Van Marle; Fried, *Early History*, 184–86.

22. Adams to Van der Kemp, 19 Dec. 1811, 15 July 1812, 30 July 1813, 10 Dec. 1817, 7 Jan., 10 March 1818, Adams–Van der Kemp Correspondence.

23. Van der Kemp to Luzac, 15 July 1788, Archief Luzac; Van der Kemp, *Autobiography*, 125; Van der Kemp to Luzac, 1 June 1800, Archief Luzac.

24. Van der Kemp, "A Sketch of the Achaian Republic in Letters to Col. John Linclaen by Junius Brutus," Oneida Historical Society; Van der Kemp to Luzac, 1 March 1802, Archief Luzac.

25. Vreede, "De laatste levensjaren," 38–39; Van der Kemp, *Redevoering*.

26. Van der Kemp to P. Vreede, 13 Feb. 1815, 16 Aug. 1818, 4 Nov. 1819, Archief Vreede en Van Marle; Vreede, "De laatste levensjaren," 41–42.

27. Adams to Van der Kemp, 28 May 1814, 3 Jan. 1823, 12 Feb. 1821, 14 Aug. 1816, Adams–Van der Kemp Correspondence.

Bibliography

ARCHIVAL MATERIALS

Amsterdam, Gemeentearchief
  Archief Six van Hillegom
Ann Arbor, William L. Clemens
  (University of Michigan) Library
  Lewis Cass Papers
  Clinton Papers
  Sydney Papers
  Vaughan Papers
Boston, Massachusetts Historical Society
  Adams Papers
Haarlem, Rijksarchief in Noord-Holland
  Collection Van der Meulen
The Hague, Algemeen Rijksarchief
  Archief Van Bleiswijk
  Archief Buitenlandse Zaken
  Archief Van der Capellen tot den Pol
  Archief Fagel
  Archief Hardenbroek
  Archief Van Hogendorp
  Archief Van Slingelandt
  Archief Staten-Generaal
  Archief West Indische Compagnie
  Archief Vreede and Van Marle
  Collection Dumont-Pigalle
  Collection H. Nieuwenhuisen
  Charles W. F. Dumas Letterbook
  Resolutiën Staten-Generaal
  Resolutiën Staten van Holland vóór 1795
  Secrete Resolutiën Staten-Generaal
Leeuwarden, Gemeentearchief

  Archief Sociëteit Door Vrijheid en Yver
Leiden, Gemeentearchief
  Archief Luzac
  Collection Van Heukelom
Oneida, N.Y., Historical Society
  "Geslacht-Boek"
  Van der Kemp, "A Sketch of the Achaian
    Republic in Letters to Col. John Linc-
    laen by Junius Brutus"
Paris, Archives du Ministère des
  Affaires Etrangères
  Correspondance Politique, Hollande
Philadelphia, American Philosophical Soci-
  ety
  Adams–Van der Kemp Correspondence
  Franklin Papers
Philadelphia, Historical Society of Pennsyl-
  vania
  Simon Gratz Collection
  "Letters of Miscellaneous European
    Writers, Collected, Arranged and Pre-
    sented to the Historical Society of
    Pennsylvania by Ferdinand J. Dreer,
    1890"
Utrecht, Rijksarchief
  Archief Slot Zuylen
Washington, D.C., Library of Congress,
  Manuscript Division
  Charles W. F. Dumas Papers
  Levi Woodbury Papers

PUBLISHED ORIGINAL SOURCES

Newspapers

*Nouvelles Extraordinaires de Divers
  Endroits* [generally known as *Gazette
  de Leyde*]. Leiden
Le Politique Hollandais. Amsterdam

Post van den Neder-Rhijn. Utrecht
De Staatsman. Utrecht
De Vaderlander. Amsterdam
Zuid-Hollandsche Courant. The Hague

Books and Articles

[Adams, Abigail]. *Letters of Mrs. Adams, the Wife of John Adams, with an Introductory Memoir by Her Grandson Charles Francis Adams.* Boston, 1840.

[Adams, John]. *Correspondence of the Late President Adams, Originally Published in the Boston Patriot in a Series of Letters.* Boston, 1809.

————. *Diary and Autobiography.* Edited by Lyman H. Butterfield. 4 vols. Cambridge, Mass., 1961.

————. *The Works of John Adams, Second President of the United States.* Edited by Charles Francis Adams. 10 vols. Boston, 1850–56.

[————, and Benjamin Waterhouse]. *Statesman and Friend: Correspondence of John Adams with Benjamin Waterhouse, 1784–1822.* Edited by Worthington Chauncey Ford. Boston, 1927.

[————, and James Warren]. *Warren-Adams Letters.* 2 vols. Boston, 1925.

[————, and Thomas Jefferson]. *The Adams-Jefferson Letters.* Edited by Lester Jesse Cappon. Chapel Hill, 1959.

[————, et al.]. *Adams Family Correspondence.* Edited by Lyman H. Butterfield. 4 vols. Cambridge, Mass., 1963–74.

[Adams, John Quincy]. *The Writings of John Quincy Adams.* Edited by Worthington Chauncey Ford. 7 vols. New York, 1913–17.

Advisen van Mr. Matthias Temminck, Mr. Hendrik Vollenhoven, en Jacob van Halmael, ter Vergadering van Holland, uitgebragt op den 11 January 1798, over het Rapport van Dirk Hoitsma en J. Nolet in de zaak van Mr. J. Luzac. N.p., 1798.

Algemeene Staatkundige Konstplaat van 't Jaar 1780. Atlas van Stolk, no. 4329.

Alweêr een Request. N.p., n.d. [1782]. Kn. 19,976.

De Amerikaansche Koopman, Zingende de Nieuwste, Fraayste en Aangenaamste Liederen, die hedendaags gezongen werden. Amsterdam, n.d.

Amstelophilus [pseud.]. *Op den Onafhankelykheid van Noord-Amerika.* N.p., n.d. [1782]. Kn. 19,972.

Archives ou Correspondance inédite de la Maison d'Orange-Nassau. 5th series. Edited by F. J. L. Krämer. 3 vols. Leiden, 1910–17.

Berckhey, Jan le Francq van. *Aan zijn Hooners.* Leiden, 1783.

————. *Samenspraak tusschen Govert Bidlo, Romeyn de Hooge en de Politieke Kruyer in de Acheronsche Velden.* Leiden, n.d.

Beredeneerde Catalogus van eene Uitmuntende Verzameling Schilderijen door de Vermaardste Nederlandsche Meesters. N.p., 1782.

[Beyma, Coert Lambertus van]. "Brieven van C. L. van Beyma aan J. D. van der Capellen tot den Pol." *Bijdragen en Mededeelingen van het Historisch Genootschap* 15 (1894): 257–389.

Bosch, Bernardus. *Onze Verpligting om tot Nut van 't Algemeen te Werken.* Zaandam and Amsterdam, 1794.

Burnaby, Andrew. *Beknopte en Zakelijke Beschrijving der Voornaamste Engelsche Volksplantingen in Noord-Amerika, neffens Aanmerkingen over den Oorsprong en Voortgang der tegenwoordige Geschillen, en des Oorlogs, tussen Groot-Brittannie en deszelfs Kolonisten.* Amsterdam, 1776.

————. *Travels through the Middle Settlements in North America. In the Years 1759 and 1760.* Dublin, 1765. Reprint, Ithaca, N.Y., 1960.

Capellen tot den Pol, Joan Derk van der. *Aan het Volk van Nederland: Het Democratisch Manifest.* Edited by Willem Frederik Wertheim and Annie Hetty Wertheim-Gijse Weenink. Amsterdam, 1966.

————. *Advis door Jonkheer Johan Derk van der Capellen tot den Pol over het verzoek*

van zijne Majesteit den Koning van Groot-Brittanië, Raakende het leenen der
Schotsche Brigade, op den 16 December 1775, ter Staatsvergadering van Overijssel
uitgebracht. N.p., 1775.

———. *Brieven van en aan Joan Derck van der Capellen van de Pol.* Edited by Willem
Hendrik de Beaufort. Utrecht, 1879.

———. *Brieven van en aan Joan Derck van der Capellen tot den Pol. Aanhangsel.* Edited
by Jérome Alexandre Sillem. Utrecht, 1883.

Colenbrander, Herman Theodoor. *Gedenkstukken der Algemene Geschiedenis van*
Nederland van 1795–1840. 10 vols. The Hague, 1905–22.

A Collection of State Papers Relative to the First Acknowledgment of the United States of
America. The Hague, 1782.

Crèvecoeur, J. Hector St. John de. *Letters from an American Farmer.* New York, 1963.

Dagverhaal der Handelingen van de Nationale Vergadering. 9 vols. The Hague, 1796–98.

[Deane, Silas]. *The Deane Papers, 1774–1790.* 5 vols. New York, 1887–91.

Diplomatic Correspondence of the American Revolution. Edited by Jared Sparks. 12 vols.
Boston, 1829–30.

Dockumer Almanack. Franeker, 1785.

Documents of the American Revolution. 17 vols. Dublin, 1971–77.

Drietal van Uitmuntende Dichtstukjes, 1. Op het Onhangelijk Verklaaren van N.
Amerika—2. Ter gelegenheid dat Engeland aan de Republiek een Vreede aanbied—3.
Op de gelukkige herstelling van . . . Mr. Pr. van Bleiswijk, Raad-Pensionaris van
Holland. . . . N.p., n.d. [1782]. Kn. 19,973.

Dumbar, Gerhard. *De oude en nieuwe Constitutie der Vereenigde Staten van Amerika, uit*
de beste Schriften in haare Gronden ontvouwd. 3 vols. Amsterdam, 1793–96.

Edwards, Jonathan. *Naaukeurig Onderzoek over de Vrijheit van den Wil.* Utrecht, 1775.

———. *Geschiedenis van het Werk der Verlossing.* 2 vols. Utrecht, 1777.

———. *Verhandeling over de godsdienstige hartstochten.* The Hague, n.d.

Eerekroon, vóór de Beschermers van Noord-Amerika. N.p., n.d. [1782]. Kn. 19,970.

Eerkroon op de Hoofden der Doorluchtige Staatsmannen, Burgervaderen, Zeehelden en
andere Personaedjen. 2 vols. Dordrecht, 1782.

[Ellis, George]. *History of the Late Revolution in the Dutch Republic.* London, 1789.

Falconet, Etienne Maurice. *Examen de la Traduction des Livres 34, 35 et 36 de Pline.*
Amsterdam, 1772.

The Federalist. Edited by Jacob E. Cooke. Middletown, Conn., 1961.

[Franklin, Benjamin]. *The Papers of Benjamin Franklin.* Edited by Leonard W. Labaree and
others. 16 vols. to date. New Haven, 1959–.

———. *Calendar of the Papers of Benjamin Franklin in the Library of the American*
Philosophical Society. Edited by I. Minis Hay. 5 vols. Philadelphia, 1908.

———. *The Works of Benjamin Franklin.* Edited by John Bigelow. 10 vols. New York,
1887–88.

———. *The Writings of Benjamin Franklin.* Edited by Albert Henry Smyth. 10 vols. New
York, 1905–7.

Der Friesen Vreugde over het Vrij Verklaren van Amerika. N.p., n.d.

Frieslands Vreugde ter Gelegenheid dat een Vuurwerk . . . ter Eeren van de Vrije Ver-
klaaringe der Staten van Amerika is Afgestoken. Atlas van Stolk, no. 4431.

Gedenkzuil ter Gelegenheid der Vrij-Verklaring van Noord-Amerika. Amsterdam, 1782.

Geschiedenis van het Geschil tussen Groot-Brittanië en Amerika, zedert deszelfs oorsprong,
in den jaare 1754, tot op den tegenwoordig tijd. Amsterdam, 1782.

[Goens, Rijklof Michael van]. *Brieven aan R. M. van Goens.* Edited by Willem Hendrik de
Beaufort. 3 vols. The Hague, 1884.

———. *Consideratien op de Memorie aan H.H.M.M. geaddresseerd door John Adams, en geteekend Leiden, den 19 April 1781.* N.p., 1781. Kn. 19,508.

Grondwettige Herstelling van Nederlands Staatswezen. 2 vols. Amsterdam, 1784–86.

Hammerdörfer, Karl. *Holländische Denkwürdigkeiten oder ausführliche Geschichte der gegenwärtige Unruhen in den Vereinigten Niederländen.* Leipzig, 1788.

[Hardenbroek, Gijsbert Jan van]. *Gedenkschriften van Gijsbert Jan van Hardenbroek.* Edited by F. J. L. Krämer. 6 vols. Amsterdam, 1901–18.

[Harris, James, first earl of Malmesbury]. *Diaries and Correspondence of James Harris, First Earl of Malmesbury.* Edited by James Howard Harris, third earl of Malmesbury. 4 vols. London, 1844.

————. *An Introduction to the History of the Dutch Republic for the Last Ten Years, Reckoning from the Year 1777.* London, 1788.

Herder, Johann Gottfried von. "Journal meiner Reise im Jahre 1769." In *Ideen zur Kulturphilosophie,* O. and N. Braun, editors. Leipzig, 1911.

History of the Internal Affairs of the United Provinces from the Year 1780 to the Commencement of Hostilities in June 1787. London, 1787.

Hogendorp, Gijsbert Karel van. *Brieven en gedenkschriften.* Edited by F. de Brouwer van Hogendorp. 7 vols. The Hague, 1866–1903.

Icones Leidenses. Leiden, 1973.

Jaarboek voor de Israelieten in Nederland, 3 (1837).

[Jefferson, Thomas]. *The Life and Selected Writings of Thomas Jefferson.* Edited by Adrienne Koch and William H. Peden. New York, 1944.

[————]. *The Papers of Thomas Jefferson.* Edited by Julian P. Boyd. 19 vols. to date. Princeton, 1950–.

[Jones, John Paul]. *Memoirs of Rear-Admiral Paul Jones.* 2 vols. Edinburgh, 1830.

Journals of the Continental Congress. 34 vols. Washington, D.C., 1904–37.

Kalm, Pehr. *Reis door Noord-Amerika.* 2 vols. Utrecht, 1772.

[Kemp, Francis Adrian van der]. *Elftal Kerkelijke Redevoeringen.* Leiden, 1782.

[————]. *Francis Adrian van der Kemp, 1752–1829: An Autobiography.* Edited by Helen Lincklaen Fairchild. New York, 1903.

[————]. *Het Gedrag van Israël en Rehabeam ten Spiegel van Volk en Vorst—Leerrede over 1 Kon. XII: 3b–20a.* Leiden, 1782.

[————]. *Historie der Admissie in de Ridderschap van Overijssel van Jr. Johan Derk van der Capellen.* Leiden, 1783.

[————]. *Redevoering ter Gedachtenis der Roemrijke Gebeurtenis van de Verlossing der Nederlanders van Fransche Dwingelandij.* Amsterdam, 1816.

[———— (pseud. Junius Brutus)]. *Verzameling van Stukken tot Noord-Amerika betrekkelijk. . . .* Leiden, 1781.

Kluit, Adriann. *Iets over den laatsten Engelschen Oorlog met de Republiek.* Amsterdam, 1794.

[————]. *De Rechten van den Mensch in Vrankrijk; geen gewaande rechten in Nederland.* Amsterdam, 1793.

[————]. *De Souvereiniteit der Staten van Holland verdedigd tegen de hedendaagsche leer der Volksregering.* Leiden, 1788.

Lanterne Magique of Toverlantaern, Tweede en Derde Vertoning. N.p., 1783.

*Lettre de Mr. *** à Mr. S. B. Docteur en Médecine, à Kingston dans la Jamaique, du Sujet des Troubles qui agitent actuellement toute l'Amérique Septentrionale.* The Hague, 1776.

[Livingston, William]. *The Independent Reflector by William Livingston.* Edited by M. Klein. Cambridge, Mass., 1903.

[Loosjes, Adriaan]. *Ten onmiddelijken vervolge van Wagenaars Vaderlandsche Historie.* 48 vols. Amsterdam, 1790–1811.

Luzac, Jean. *Socrates als burger beschouwd.* Leiden, 1797.

Mandrillon, Joseph. *Gedenkschriften betrekkelijk tot de Omwenteling in de Vereenigde Nederlanden in 1787.* Dunkirk, 1792.

Mirabeau, Honoré Gabriel Riqueti, comte. *Aux Bataves sur le stadhoudérat.* N.p., 1788.

Nassau la Leck, Lodewijk Theodorus, graaf van. *Brieven over de Noord-Americaansche Onlusten.* 6 vols. in 1. Utrecht, 1777–79.

Nieuwe Nederlandsche Jaarboeken. Amsterdam, 1766–92.

Onpartydige en Vrymoedige Aanmerkingen, Over het bekend Advis van Jr. J. D. van der Capellen tot den Pol. Alkmaar, 1776. Kn. 19,127.

Paape, Gerrit. *De Onverbloemde Geschiedenis van het Bataafsche Patriottismus van deszelfs begin tot op den 12 Junij 1798 toe.* Delft, 1798.

Paulus, Pieter. *Verklaring der Unie van Utrecht.* 3 vols. Utrecht, 1775–76.

[Pauw, Cornelis de]. *Wijsgeerige Bespiegelingen over Amerika.* 3 vols. Deventer, 1771–72.

[Pernety, Dom Antoine Joseph]. *Brief over de Bespiegelingen van Amerika.* Utrecht, 1772.

Pinto, Isaac de. *Seconde Lettre de M. de Pinto à l'occasion des troubles des Colonies, contenant des Réflexions Politiques sur les suites de ces troubles, et sur l'Etat actuel de l'Angleterre.* The Hague, 1776.

Het Plan van Constitutie van 1796. Edited by L. de Gou. The Hague, 1975.

Pot, C. van der. "Bij de Grafzuil van de Onsterffelijken Ridder Johan Derk van der Capellen tot den Pol." In [Kemp], *Historie der Admissie.* . . . Leiden, 1783.

Pot, Cornelius Willem van der. "De twee Dumbars, 1680–1744, 1743–1802." *Overijsselse Portretten* 30 (1958): 123–42.

Raynal, Guillaume Thomas François Abbé. *Staatsomwentelingen van Amerika.* Amsterdam, 1781.

———. *Wijsgeerige en Staatkundige Geschiedenis van de Bezittingen en den Koophandel der Europeaanen, in de beide Indiën.* 10 vols. Amsterdam, 1775–83.

Rendorp, Joachim, Vrijheer van Marquette. *Memoriën dienende tot Opheldering van het Gebeurde geduurende den laatsten Engelschen Oorlog.* 2 vols. Amsterdam, 1792.

Resolutiën van de Hoogh Mogende Heeren Staten Generaal der Vereenigde Nederlandsche Provinciën. 129 vols. The Hague, 1677–1796.

The Revolutionary Diplomatic Correspondence of the United States. Edited by Francis Wharton. 6 vols. Washington, D.C., 1889.

Robertson, William S. *Geschiedenis van Amerika.* 4 vols. Amsterdam, 1778.

Rogge, Cornelis. *Geschiedenis der Staatsregeling, voor het Bataafsche Volk.* Amsterdam, 1799.

Samenspraak (in 't Rijk der Dooden) tusschen Prins Willem den I en den Generaal Montgommery. Amsterdam, 1788.

[Sandwich, John Montague, fourth earl of]. *The Private Papers of John, Earl of Sandwich, First Lord of the Admiralty, 1771–1782.* Vol. 1 (all published). London, 1923.

Schimmelpenninck, Rutger Jan. *Verhandeling over eene wel-ingerichte Volksregeering.* Leiden, 1785.

Secreete Resolutiën van de Edele Groot Mog. Heeren Staaten van Holland en West Vriesland. Beginnende met den jaare 1781 incluis. Vol. 13 (1782).

Smith, William. *Relation historique de l'expédition contre les Indiens de l'Ohio en MDCCLXIV.* Amsterdam, 1764.

[Spiegel, Laurens Pieter van de]. *Mr. Laurens Pieter van de Spiegel en zijne Tijdgenooten (1737–1800).* Edited by George Willem Vreede. 4 vols. Middelburg, 1874–77.

De Staatsman, of onpartijdige Redeneringen over de merkwaardigste Gebeurtenissen van onzen Tijd. 7 vols. Utrecht, 1779–80; Amsterdam, 1781–84.

Stevens, Benjamin Franklin. *B. F. Stevens's Facsimiles of Manuscripts in European Archives Relating to America, 1773–1783.* 25 vols. London, 1889–98.

Styl, Simon. *De Opkomst en Bloei der Verenigde Nederlanden.* 5 vols. 2nd ed. Amsterdam, 1778.

[Thulemeyer, Friedrich Wilhelm von]. *Dépêches van Thulemeyer, 1763–1788.* Edited by Robert Fruin and Herman Theodoor Colenbrander. Amsterdam, 1912.

[Trumbull, Jonathan, and William Livingston]. *Brieven van hunne Excellenties de Heeren Jonathan Trumbull en William Livingston, Schildknapen.* Amsterdam, 1779.

Vattel, Emerich de. *Le Droit des Gens, ou Principes de la Loi Naturelle, Appliquée à la Conduite et aux Affaires des Nations et des Souverains.* New ed. Amsterdam, 1775.

Verslagen omtrent 's Rijks Oude Archieven. 114 vols. pub. The Hague, 1865–.

Verzameling van de Constitutien der Vereenigde Onafhanglijke Staaten van Amerika, benevens de Acte van Onafhanglijkheid, de Artikelen van Confederatie, en de Tractaaten tusschen Zijne Allerchristelijkste Majesteit en de Vereenigde Amerikaansche Staaten. Dordrecht, 1781–82.

Verzameling van Stukken tot de Dertien Vereenigde Staaten van Noord-Amerika Betrekkelijk. Leiden, 1781.

[Voltaire, François Marie Arouet, called]. *Oeuvres de M. de Voltaire.* 9 vols. Amsterdam, 1738–56.

[Washington, George]. *The Writings of George Washington.* Edited by John C. Fitzpatrick. 39 vols. Washington, D.C., 1931–44.

[Watson, Elkanah]. *A Tour in Holland in MDCCLXXXIV by an American.* Worcester, Mass., 1790.

[————]. *Men and Times of the Revolution, or Memoirs of Elkanah Watson, Including Journals of Travels in Europe and America from 1777 to 1842.* Edited by Winslow C. Watson. New York, 1856.

SECONDARY SOURCES

Aa, Abraham Jacob van der. *Biografisch Woordenboek der Nederlanden.* 17 vols. Amsterdam, 1852–78.

Adair, Douglass. *Fame and the Founding Fathers.* New York, 1974.

Album Studiosorum Academiae Lugduno-Batavae, 1575–1875. The Hague, 1875.

Ascoli, Peter M. "American Propaganda in the French Language Press during the American Revolution." In *La Révolution américaine et l'Europe: Actes du Colloque international, 21–25 Février 1978,* pp. 291–307. Paris, 1979.

Bartstra, Jan Steffen, Jr. *Vlootherstel en Legeraugmentatie, 1770–1780.* Assen, 1952.

Beaufort, Willem Hendrik de. "Oranje en de Democratie." In *Geschiedkundige Opstellen.* 2 vols. Amsterdam, 1893.

Bemis, Samuel F. *The Diplomacy of the American Revolution.* 2nd ed. Bloomington, Indiana, 1957.

————. *John Quincy Adams and the Foundations of American Foreign Policy.* New York, 1950.

Boeles, Willem Boele Sophius. *De Patriot J. H. Swindens, Publicist te Amsterdam, daarna Hoogleeraar te Franeker: Zijn arbeid ter Volksverlichting geschetst.* Leeuwarden, 1884.

Bosch Kemper, Jeronimo de. *De staatkundige Geschiedenis van Nederland tot 1830 geschetst.* Amsterdam, 1868.

Boxer, Charles R. *The Dutch Seaborne Empire: 1600–1800.* London, 1965.

Brugmans, Hajo. *Opkomst en Bloei van Amsterdam.* Amsterdam, 1911.

Butterfield, Lyman H. *Butterfield in Holland: A Record of L. H. Butterfield's Pursuit of the Adamses Abroad in 1959.* Cambridge, Mass., 1961.

Byvanck, Willem Geertrud Cornelis. *Bataafsch Verleden (Dorus Droefheid)*. Zutphen, 1917.

Carter, Alice C. "The Dutch as Neutrals in the Seven Years War." *International and Comparative Law Quarterly* 12 (1963): 818–34.

Catalogue of Political and Personal Satires Preserved in the Department of Prints and Drawings of the British Museum. Vols. 5 and 6. Edited by Mary Dorothy George. London, 1935.

Colenbrander, Herman Theodoor. *De Patriottentijd, hoofdzakelijk naar buitenlandsche bescheiden*. 3 vols. The Hague, 1897–99.

Commager, Henry Steele, and Elmo Giordanetti. *Was America a Mistake? An Eighteenth-Century Controversy*. New York, 1967.

Dangerfield, George. *Chancellor Robert R. Livingston of New York, 1746–1813*. New York, 1960.

Doniol, Henri. *Histoire de la participation de la France à l'établissement des Etats-Unis d'Amérique*. 5 vols. Paris, 1886–92.

Echeverria, Durand. *Mirage in the West: A History of the French Image of American Society to 1815*. Princeton, 1957.

Edelman, Hendrik. *Dutch-American Bibliography, 1693–1794*. Nieuwkoop, 1974.

Edler, Friedrich. *The Dutch Republic and the American Revolution*. Baltimore, 1911.

Foley, Sister Mary Briant. "The Triumph of Militia Diplomacy: John Adams in the Netherlands, 1780–82." Ph.D. dissertation, Loyola University, Chicago, 1968.

Fried, Marc B. *The Early History of Kingston and Ulster County, N.Y.* Marbletown, N.Y., 1974.

Fruin, Robert. *Geschiedenis der Staatsinstellingen in Nederland tot de val der Republiek*. Edited by H. T. Colenbrander. The Hague, 1901.

Gelder, Hendrik Enno van. *Kunstgeschiedenis der Nederlanden*. Utrecht, 1963.

George, Mary Dorothy. *English Political Caricature: A Study of Opinion and Propaganda*. 2 vols. Oxford, 1959.

Geyl, Pieter. *Geschiedenis van de Nederlandse stam*. 6 vols. Amsterdam and Antwerp, 1961–62.

———. *De Patriottenbeweging*. Amsterdam, 1947.

Gilbert, Felix. *The Beginnings of American Foreign Policy: To the Farewell Address*. 2nd ed. New York, 1965.

Gumbert, Hans Ludwig. *Lichtenberg und Holland*. Utrecht, 1973.

Haraszti, Zoltan. *John Adams and the Prophets of Progress*. Cambridge, Mass., 1952.

Hardenberg, H. "Benjamin Franklin en Nederland." *Bijdragen voor de Geschiedenis der Nederlanden* 5 (1950): 213–30.

———. "Kolonel Dircks, Een Voorloper van Lafayette." *Verslagen en Mededelingen van de Vereniging tot Beoefening van Overijssels Regt en Geschiedenis* 76 (1961): 157–200.

Hartog, Jan. *De Patriotten en Oranje van 1747–1787*. Amsterdam, 1882.

———. *Uit de Dagen der Patriotten*. Amsterdam, n.d.

Hartog, Johannes. *De Bovenwinde Eilanden: St. Maarten—Saba—Sint Eustatius*. Aruba, 1964.

Heine, Heinrich. *Sämtliche Werke*. 4 vols. Munich, 1972.

Homan, Gerlof D. "Jacob Gerhard Dircks and the American Revolution." *Verslagen en Mededelingen van de Vereniging tot Beoefening van Overijssels Regt en Geschiedenis* 89 (1975): 72–79.

Honour, Hugh. *The European Vision of America*. Exhibition catalog, Cleveland Museum of Art, 1975.

———. *The New Golden Land: European Images of America from the Discoveries to the*

Present Time. New York, 1975.

Howe, John R., Jr. *The Changing Political Thought of John Adams.* Princeton, 1966.

Höweler, H. A. "Lucretia Wilhelmina van Merken en George Washington." *Tijdschrift voor Nederlandsche Taal- en Letterkunde* 52 (1933): 70–77.

Hutson, James S. "Early American Diplomacy: A Reappraisal." In *The American Revolution and "A Candid World,"* edited by Lawrence S. Kaplan, pp. 40–68.

———. *John Adams and the Diplomacy of the American Revolution.* Lexington, Kentucky, 1980.

Jackson, Harry F. *Scholar in the Wilderness: Francis Adrian van der Kemp.* Syracuse, 1963.

Jameson, John Franklin. "St. Eustatius in the American Revolution." *American Historical Review* 8 (1903): 683–708.

Jones, Pomroy. *Annals and Recollections of Oneida County.* Rome, N.Y., n.d.

Jong Hendrikszoon, Murk de. *Joan Derk van der Capellen: Staatkundig Levensbeeld uit de Wordingstijd van de Moderne Democratie in Nederland.* Groningen and The Hague, 1922.

Kannegieter, J. Z. "De Affaire van Berckel." *Bijdragen voor Vaderlandsche Geschiedenis en Oudheidkunde,* 6th series, no. 10 (1930): 245–89.

Kaplan, Lawrence S., ed. *The American Revolution and "A Candid World."* Kent, Ohio, c. 1977.

Kluit, Willem Pieter Sautijn. *Le Politique Hollandais.* Leiden, 1870.

———. *De Fransche Leidsche Courant.* Leiden, 1870.

Kneppelhout van Sterkenburg, Karel J. F. C. *De Gedenkteekenen in de Pieterskerk te Leiden.* Leiden, 1864.

Knuttel, Willem P. C. *Catalogus van de Pamflettenverzameling berustende in de Koninklijke Bibliotheek.* 7 vols. The Hague, 1889–1920.

Kossmann, Ernst H. "The Crisis of the Dutch State 1780–1813: Nationalism, Federalism, Unitarism." In *Britain and the Netherlands,* edited by J. S. Bromley and E. H. Kossmann. Vol. 4, *Metropolis, Dominion and Province.* The Hague, 1971.

Lee, Richard Henry. *The Life of Arthur Lee.* 2 vols. Boston, 1829.

Lennep, Frans J. E. van. "Rendorp van Marquette en de vierde Engelsche Oorlog." In *Als Vorsten: Portretten van 18e Eeuwers,* pp. 9–33. Haarlem, 1967.

Luzac, Johan, Jr. "Het Amerikaansche Volk en zijn Verwachtingen." *De Gids,* June 1864, pt. 2, pp. 443–68.

Maier, Pauline. *From Resistance to Revolution: Colonial Radicals and the Development of American Opposition to Britain, 1765–1776.* New York, 1973.

Main, Jackson Turner. *The Anti-Federalists: Critics of the Constitution, 1781–1788.* Chapel Hill, 1961.

May, Henry F. *The Enlightenment in America.* New York, 1976.

Meulen, W. W. van der. "Een en ander over Van der Capellen tot den Pol en zijn aanhang." In *Geschiedkundige Opstellen ter ere van Dr. H. C. Rogge.* Leiden, 1902.

Morice, Joseph. "The Contributions of Charles W. F. Dumas to the Cause of American Independence." *Duquesne Review* 7 (1961): 17–28.

Morison, Samuel E. *John Paul Jones: A Sailor's Biography.* Boston, 1959.

Morris, Richard B. *The Peacemakers: The Great Powers and American Independence.* New York, 1965.

Muller, Frederik, ed. *De Nederlandsche Geschiedenis in Platen: Beredeneerde Beschrijving van Nederlandsche Historie-Platen, Zinneprenten en Historische Kaarten.* 4 vols. Amsterdam, 1863–82.

Muller, N. Hendrik. "Tweemaal Marshallhulp, 1782–1947." *It Beaken: Tijdschrift van de Fryske Akademy* 19 (3 Aug. 1957): 97–107.

Niemeyer, J. W. "Cities and Scenery: The Republic Put out of Doors, 1775–1795." In *The*

Dutch Republic in the Days of John Adams. Exhibition Catalog, Philadelphia, Second Bank of the United States, 1976.

————. "Some Aspects of Dutch Eighteenth Century Art." In *Dutch Masterpieces from the Eighteenth Century: Paintings and Drawings, 1700–1800.* Exhibition Catalog, Minneapolis Institute of Arts, 1971.

Nieuw Nederlandsch Biografisch Woordenboek. 10 vols. Leiden, 1911–37.

Nijhoff, Dirk Christiaan. *De Hertog van Brunswijk.* The Hague, 1889.

Nijland, Johanna Aleide. *Leven en Werken van Jacobus Bellamy.* 2 vols. Leiden, 1917.

Oliver, Andrew. *Portraits of John and Abigail Adams.* Cambridge, Mass., 1967.

Onnes Mzn., M. *De Vermaner Fr. Adr. van der Kemp, 1752–1829.* Groningen, 1905.

Palmer, Robert R. *The Age of the Democratic Revolution.* 2 vols. Princeton, 1959–64.

————. "The Dubious Democrat: Thomas Jefferson in Bourbon France." *Political Science Quarterly* 72 (1957): 388–404. Reprinted in Merrill D. Peterson, ed., *Thomas Jefferson: A Profile,* pp. 86–103. New York, 1967.

Pearson, Drew. *Diaries, 1949–1959.* Edited by T. Abell. London, 1974.

Plemp van Duiveland, Leonard Jan. *Schimmelpenninck: Levensverhaal en Tijdsbeeld.* Rotterdam, 1972.

Renaut, Francis Paul. *Les Provinces-Unies et la Guerre d'Amérique (1775–1784).* 5 vols. Paris, 1924–32.

Riker, William H. "Dutch and American Federalism." *Journal of the History of Ideas* 18 (1957): 495–521.

Robbins, Caroline. *The Eighteenth Century Commonwealthman.* 2nd ed. New York, 1968.

Romein, Jan, and Annie Romein. *Erflaters van onze Beschaving.* 4 vols. 3rd ed. Amsterdam, 1941.

Schulte Nordholt, Jan Willem. "De bevestiging van de Amerikaanse natie en haar Hollandse getuigen." *Tijdschrift voor Geschiedenis* 76 (1963): 34–65.

————. "The Example of the Dutch Republic for American Federalism." In *Federalism: History and Significance of a Form of Government,* edited by J. C. Boogman and G. N. van der Plaat, pp. 65–77. The Hague, 1980.

————. "Gijsbert Karel van Hogendorp in Amerika, 1783–1784." *Acta Historiae Neerlandicae, Studies on the History of the Netherlands* 10 (1978): 117–42.

Seymour, John Forman. *Centennial Address Delivered at Trenton, N.Y., July 4, 1876, with Letters from Francis Adrian van der Kemp, Written in 1792, and Other Documents Relating to the First Settlement of Trenton and Central New York.* Utica, N.Y., 1877.

————. "A Tour through a Part of the Western District of New York in 1792," in Seymour, *A Centennial Address.* Pp. 48–128.

Shaw, Peter. *The Character of John Adams.* Chapel Hill, 1976.

Smit, Jacobus Wilhelmus. "The Netherlands and Europe in the Seventeenth and Eighteenth Centuries." In *Britain and the Netherlands,* edited by J. S. Bromley and E. H. Kossmann. Vol. 3. London and New York, 1968.

Stinchcombe, William C. *The American Revolution and the French Alliance.* Syracuse, N.Y., 1969.

————. "John Adams and the Model Treaty." In *The American Revolution and "A Candid World,"* edited by Lawrence S. Kaplan. Kent, Ohio, c. 1977.

Stolk, Abraham van., ed. *Atlas van Stolk: Katalogus der Historie-, Spot- en Zinneprenten betrekkelijk de Geschiedenis van Nederland.* 10 vols. Amsterdam, 1895–1931.

Suringar, Pieter H. *Biographische Aantekeningen betreffende Mr. Pieter Paulus.* Leiden, 1879.

Thorbecke, Johan Rudolf. *Historische schetsen.* The Hague, 1860.

[Truman, Harry S.] *The Private Papers of Harry S. Truman.* Edited by Robert H. Ferrell. New York, 1980.

Van Alstyne, Richard W. "Great Britain, the War for Independence and the Gathering Storm in Europe, 1775–1778." *Huntington Library Quarterly* 27 (1964): 311–46.

Vitringa, Campegius Lambertus. *Gedenkschrift van Mr. C. L. Vitringa.* Arnhem, 1857–64.

Vos van Steenwijk, A. N. Baron de. "Een Drents Patriot." *Nieuwe Drentse Volksalmanak* 92 (1975): 25–44.

Vreede, George Willem. "De laatste levensjaren van F. A. van der Kemp." In *Aantekeningen van het Verhandelde in de Sectie voor de Letterkunde en Wijsbegeerte van het Provinciaal Utrechtsch Genootschap van Kunsten en Wetenschappen.* 1862, pp. 38–39.

Vries, Johan de. *De economische achteruitgang der Republiek in de achttiende eeuw.* Amsterdam, 1959.

Welch, Oliver G. J. *Mirabeau: A Study of a Democratic Monarchist.* London, 1951.

Werkgroep 18e eeuw. Documentatieblad. No. 22. N.p., 1974. Bibliography of eighteenth-century translations into Dutch.

Wijk, F. W. van. *De Republiek en Amerika.* Leiden, 1921.

Winter, Pieter Jan van. *Het aandeel van den Amsterdamschen handel aan den opbouw van het Amerikaansche Gemeenebest.* 2 vols. The Hague, 1927–30.

————. "Onze eerste diplomatieke betrekkingen met de Verenigde Staten." *Tijdschrift voor Geschiedenis* 38 (1923): 68–82. Reprinted in P. J. van Winter, *Verkenning en Onderzoek,* pp. 344–56. Groningen, 1965.

————. *Verkenning en Onderzoek.* Groningen, 1965.

Wit, Cornelius H. E. de. *De Nederlandse Revolutie van de Achttiende Eeuw, 1780–1787.* Oirsbeek, 1974.

————. *Het Ontstaan van het Moderne Nederland, 1780–1848, en zijn Geschiedschrijving.* Oirsbeek, 1978.

————. *De Strijd tussen Aristocratie en Democratie in Nederland, 1780–1848.* Heerlen, 1965.

Index

In alphabetizing Dutch family names only the main word in the name is considered. "Van" and "de" are inseparable parts of the name but are disregarded in alphabetization.